Balin

Balinese Worlds

Fredrik Barth

The University of Chicago Press
Chicago & London

The University of Chicago Press, Chicago 60637
The University of Chicago Press, Ltd., London
© 1993 by The University of Chicago
All rights reserved. Published 1993
Printed in the United States of America

02 01 00 99 98 97   5 4 3 2

ISBN (cloth): 0–226–03833–5
ISBN (paper): 0–226–03834–3

Library of Congress Cataloging-in-Publication Data

Barth, Fredrik, 1928-
    Balinese worlds / Fredrik Barth.
        p.   cm.
    Includes bibliographical references and index.
    ISBN 0–226–03833–5. – ISBN 0–226–03834–3 (pbk.)
    1. Ethnology – Indonesia – Bali (Province)   2. Bali (Indo-
nesia: Province) – Social life and customs.   3. Religion and
culture – Indonesia – Bali (Province).   I. Title.
    GN635.I65B38   1993
306′.09598′6 – dc20   92–18043
                                                  CIP

Contents

CONTENTS

CONTENTS

Acknowledgments

My fieldwork in Bali was first and foremost made possible through the cooperation of M. Ghazi Habibullah and Made Artje, who in turn worked with me as interpreters, assistants, and companions. How we worked together is briefly set forth at the end of chapter 1. My debt to them, like my pleasure in their cooperation, is very great; I only hope that their own keen interest and enjoyment during our joint efforts rewarded them as it did me. The work was further made possible by Professor Gusti Ngurah Bagus, who sponsored Unni Wikan and myself in our research project and aided us in numerous ways.

Countless Balinese have responded with generosity and patience to my field enquiries, and but for such kindness I would of course have achieved nothing. I am particularly thankful to the villagers of Pagatepan and Prabakula for allowing me to become a participant of sorts in their communities and lives. To shield them from an undesirable exposure to outsiders in the wake of this book, I use old and forgotten names for these two villages, and pseudonyms for the persons in them.

My deepest debt of gratitude goes to three dear friends: Drs. I Gusti Putu Antara, Mr. Mohammed Anwar, B.A., and Dr. Soegianto Sastrodiwiryo; together with their families, they made our stay in Bali an extraordinary personal pleasure. Subeidah Husnan, Abdul Rahman Alawi, and Ibu Huriya Abdul Rahman likewise showed great kindness to our whole family. I am forever thankful for how such friends have enriched our lives and our work.

For various forms of help, kindness, trust, and information over the years I am indebted to so many people, who cooperated far beyond the call of duty and reasonable hospitality, that there is no way I could name them all; but for exceptional patience, insight, and trust I must thank Drs. Nyoman Suweila, Jero Mangku Sukasana, Jero Balian Nyoman Lantri, Sri Mpu Dwi Tantra, Mr. Ketut Raji, Guru Ali Akbar, Pak Mengmendere, Gusti Nyoman Kwere, Klian Ketut Mariata, and Ibu Trini Mayun.

The research was sponsored by the Indonesian Institute of the Sciences (LIPI) and the University of Udayana in Bali and was financed by the Norwegian Research Council for Science and the Humanities and by the Institute of Comparative Cultural Research. I am most grateful to these institutions for their support. The administration in Indonesia, from H. E. the Governor of Bali and the Chief of the Regency of Buleleng down to the clerks in government offices, followed up whenever their support or facilities were requested.

During the analysis of the materials, I have benefited from seminars and discussions with colleagues and students in departments of anthropology in various parts of the world, including the University of Bergen, the University of Oslo, Emory University, the City University of New York, Harvard University, the University of North Carolina at Chapel Hill, Cambridge University, the School of Oriental and African Studies and University College of the University of London, and Stockholm University. Their interest and queries have been most stimulating and fruitful. Beyond that, I am particularly grateful to colleagues who have read and commented on parts of the present text and given me useful criticisms: Bruce Knauft, who read a major part of it; Peter Brown, Carol Worthman, Cameron Hay, and Arjun Appadurai, who read parts; and two anonymous readers for the University of Chicago Press who read and commented on it all.

Our son, Kim, was party to much of the fieldwork; I thank him for how he enriched our relations with many people by touching hearts with his openness and goodness. Finally, but for my wife, Unni, none of this would ever have been. She urged me to join her in choosing to work in Bali; we have been companions throughout the work; we have shared our field notes and our thoughts; and she has coaxed me, challenged me, shown me, and inspired me to learn so much more from the people of Bali than I could ever have dreamed of on my own.

PART ONE

The Challenge of
North Bali

Preamble

This book has been slow in the making, because it simultaneously attempts two very demanding tasks. It seeks to give a synthetic account of society and culture in North Bali, embracing social organization, salient cultural ideas and knowledge, circumstances and concerns in terms of which people respond to events, and insights and experience they judge central to their lives. It also seeks to explicate concepts, perspectives, and discovery procedures that could put the anthropological analysis of complex civilizations on a better footing.

These two tasks are connected: where the mainstream of existing anthropological literature on Bali fails to give an adequate account of society and culture, it is because we still do not know how to go about describing complex civilizations. We lack some of the necessary concepts and insights, and persist in using others that do not apply. Thereby we produce a consensus between area specialists that corresponds poorly to the realities of the area. Mark Hobart, drawing on lifelong studies of Balinese culture and society and extensive fieldwork in a community in South Bali, best articulates these concerns and criticisms: "Despite — or even because of — the amount of research on Bali, it is becoming clear how little we know. The plethora of unexamined, but relevant, indigenous treatises and the degree of local variation alone suggest that generalizations are rather dubious. Much of the material has reported assertions in particular situations as facts, and facts as truth. What we have mostly is a smattering of [data] . . . taken out of context and mapped onto nebulous paradigms of Western intellectual history" (Hobart 1986b:151).

Initially I shall be using some features of this local variation as my lever to shift some established anthropological views on Bali. I will argue that local variation in a traditional civilization is not a surface disturbance, to be covered over by generalization or tidied away by a typology. It is a ubiquitous feature of great civilizations, and we should make it a major component of our description and characterization of these societies rather than a difficulty to be overcome. Variation should emerge as a necessity from our analysis. How might that be achieved?

First, we must break loose from our root metaphor of society as a system of articulated parts. The image is too simple, and it misleads: the connections we are trying to conceptualize are linkages without determinate edges, in a body without a surface for a boundary. Nor are they related to each other in a part-whole hierarchy. If not a bounded thing, then how can we conceptualize this society, or this culture, which we seek to describe? The features we use to visualize it must be predicated by the object, not our descriptive conveniences. So we should look for another model. I hold that when we can see society as characterized by a degree of conceptual and statistical order, this must reflect the results of processes — processes that arise from particular combinations of ideas, material circumstances, and interactional potentials and have patterning as their consequences. The image of processes serves us better than that of a structure or a closed system. After all, we generally recognize by now that we are speaking of a reality that is at least in significant part socially and culturally constructed. Consider how the alternative metaphors position us if we ask where the work of reality construction might be taking place. Obviously, reality construction must be a process of creating connections in people's "here" and "now," centering on themselves — not out on the edge of things where "parts" articulate, or at some distant boundary where society stops. The problem of boundedness will also have to be faced, but with the difficulties we have in pointing to boundaries, it must not serve us as the very means whereby we constitute the object of our study. Our focus should be on the processes of social and cultural construction of reality, which are always here and now.

This brings me to my second main point of leverage: individual variation, in relation to the processes whereby some degree of shared reality is established. In a civilization, there is a surfeit of cultural materials and ideational possibilities available from which to construct reality. The anthropologist has no basis for assuming that all these materials are contained in one complete, logically compelling package or structure; that begs most of the very questions we should raise and entices us to proceed as if our task were to tease out a key that would make sense of it all. On the contrary, the sense that is being made, the reality that is being created, in any community or circle must be diverse. (1) There are variations in the level of "expertise" in the population: which level could hold authority for all? (2) There is diversity of received traditions. (3) There is a varied particularism of local history, contention, and context. (4) There are all the differences between people in positioning and experience, besides that of expertise: old and young, male and female, rich and poor, powerful and vulnerable. (5) Finally, there is the pragmatics of purpose and interest: differing representations for different tasks. Which should the anthropologist privilege? Or do we adhere to a belief that, if only it is thoroughly abstracted, it all coheres in its essence?

Again, these variations are not difficulties to be overcome but inherent features of the object that we wish to describe. In their way, Balinese must face the same questions when imposing some semblance of graspable shape on their world and their life: what knowledge and insights are workable for me, here and now? But living in a civilization means having some of the skills needed to construct a life from a multiplicity of available elements. I am certainly not suggesting that a person's reality is the fruit of her or his own free creativity: it is made from the knowledge and imagery that are available. But like the anthropologist, only with greater knowledge and discrimination, a Balinese will be faced with a wide range of experts and authorities, a diversity of received traditions, etc., etc. Thus the perspective I am arguing for does not deny the presence of agreements, shared premises, shared conventions, and commitments to publicly embraced values. There are plenty of them — indeed, far too many to be put together in one cohering structure or one person's practice, and too many to be universally and equally shared. They represent ranges of options from which a Balinese can choose in the perpetual work of constructing her or his reality, i.e., interpretation of the here and now so as to be able to respond to it; and the complexity of events and options is such that she/he will probably often see several alternative constructions that can give reasonable and workable insight. In such a situation, the anthropologist even more than the individual Balinese should give up the pipe dream of coherence and concentrate on developing theory and concepts for analyzing disordered systems, where events are underdetermined by rules and where — rising now to the macrolevel of communities, regions, and society — such relatively determined connections as there are will generate processes at angles and at odds with each other, producing innumerable large and small incoherences in culture and in the body politic.

Most of our experience of social life should lead us to accept as plausible this view of disorder, multiplicity, and underdeterminedness. Why then does it seem so difficult for anthropology to embrace it and develop it as a basis for theory? One reason may be that it goes against the grain of received intellectual standards of excellence: we are always best believed and rewarded when we succeed in revealing a hidden simplicity underlying the apparently complex, as when we can perfect an encompassing logical form for the data we have selected that underwrites the myth of an ordered, coherent society/culture/reality. We must rebel against this scenario, which may be more appropriate for other objects of study than ours, and which has been drilled into us through the type of solution favored in the preset puzzles of our exams. Culture, society, and human lives — the objects we seek to understand — do not come in this puzzle format, and we should not succumb to the temptation to cast them as puzzles by selecting a limited set of data, designing a solution that makes them appear coherent — and then, outrageously, claiming this to be an example of the coherence that obtains in the whole.

These arguments and misgivings, you may say, are shared by many anthropologists and articulated in many, and more subtle, ways. Indeed. Some of them have been forcibly argued in the postmodern literature, developing points I find challenging but from which I draw rather different conclusions. Many of them are currently being combined and identified as "practice theory" (e.g., Ortner 1984, 1989), drawing on a literature to which I am clearly indebted. But to the extent that practice theory builds on a concept of "contradiction" in its revolt against consensus models of culture and society, it tends to reconstruct the tyranny it was meant to bring down. Only if coherence were viewed as a "functional prerequisite" (with all the anthropological debris that phrase entails) would "contradiction" reveal the spring, the hidden mechanism that makes the wheels of change revolve. And we are again invited to model connections in terms of logical necessity (Barth 1990), when we know perfectly well that the phenomena we are depicting are neither logically coherent nor essentially contradictory: they could well have been different, probably are different in all those places we have not observed, and may by now be different in those places we did observe. I see no way that the logical incompatibility, i.e., contradiction, of two monolithic coherences could reproduce the shifting sands of multiple interpretations and interests, much less model the empirical processes whereby people's traditions of knowledge are laboriously built.

And this provides my third point of leverage. Our focus, I argued, should be on the work of social and cultural construction of reality: those are the crucial processes that generate our object. Yet most of the anthropological interest, and most of the anthropological conceptions, focus only on how cultural knowledge within some domain or other is patterned, and how it is instantiated — not how it is generated. Though linked to a salutary attention to practice, "contradiction" likewise focuses our attention on how two pre-established organizations of cultural knowledge clash, not on how they ever came to be organized. Instead, we should focus on how cultural knowledge is produced, the processes of its "construction" read as a verb, not as a substantive.

Postmodern critiques have taught us to admit more readily to the intrinsic dissonance in social life as it actually unfolds and to the surrealist qualities of the various representations that make up cultural repertoires. I accept the validity of such observations and wish to take full account of them in my analysis. This being my position, it may strike the reader as curious that I should focus as strongly as I do, in the subsequent chapters, on the gross features of social organization and knowledge, rather than critiquing and deconstructing fictions. But that is precisely the core of my chosen argument. We need not follow postmodernism in rejecting every attempt to construct coherent theory: we need only learn to construct it differently so it is not chained to an axiom of a coherent world. Our object of study is not formless, and it does not follow from the fact that it exhibits disorder and indeterminacy that it could be any old way, and that we cannot model the processes that bring about this particular form and this degree of coherence.

I accept the postmodern critique that structural representations of dissonant conditions and disordered circumstances are perforce both fictional and distorting. It makes little anthropological sense to depict an imaginary situation where order reigns, and then show how the activities of people reproduce this order with an arguable, but considerable, degree of imperfection. But if we focus instead on process, on the work done by people in the social and cultural construction of their realities, we are modeling connections and interdependencies that generate a degree of order and shape, and such models can perfectly well be compelling, simple, and bold. The recognition that there is some kind of imperfect pattern out there becomes fruitful, it seem to me, not if we extract and perfect a simplified representation of that order in itself, but only if we construct our models on a meta-level, in an attempt to represent the processes that generate that degree of order — even where such order may be quite imperfectly manifest as pattern in the observable outcomes. Such models become believable if we can show how the observed degree of coherence is brought about and reproduced in the lives of people, through processes involving those people's own ideas and activities. Indeed, if we have to construct an initial situation, we should not choose the fiction of a perfect structure but rather the fiction of an initial amorphous lack of order, which may then be given a degree of shape through the operation of the processes we have modeled.

That would make more phylogenetic sense. But we are not there in the morning of the world: "Knowledge is always a modification of earlier knowledge" (Popper and Eccles 1984:425), and this credo is notionally valid for all of culture. So we should rather look at how people through their collective and separate activities reproduce and modify the realities of their past and present lives, elaborating features or losing them, enhancing their coherence or dismantling it. Modeling such processes promises to enhance our ability to describe the complex civilizations of human societies and understand something of their dynamics.

The following monograph retraces the steps of this argument through a slow and cumulative account that allows me to depict a broad range of features of the Bali I have seen. Thus the validity and value of the position I have here briefly formulated are on trial, and can best be judged at the end of this text.

1

A Luminous Mosaic

Bali is a luminous mosaic of Southeast Asian civilization. Though small by the standards of Java or continental Asian societies, it is both a product and a producer of a spate of ideas and imagery that draws on numerous great historical streams — Malayo-Polynesian, Megalithic, Indian, Chinese, Islamic, and Western, as well as its own local innovative genius — and it composes a complex and cosmopolitan society of highly diverse organization.

Which terms, methods, and theoretical perspectives can a social anthropologist use to observe, describe, and analyze data from Bali so as to capture some of this complexity without stereotyping and distorting its features? How can we represent the intimate lives of people and the intricacies of their relationships, understandings, and representations without misrepresenting the ontology of these phenomena by fitting them to inappropriate conceptual conventions developed in the discipline of anthropology?

Anthropological materials from Buleleng, North Bali, raise these questions with great force, not only because of the riotous richness and diversity of Bali's cultural materials, but also because of the historical position of anthropology at this moment with respect to the development of both theory and ethnography. Through the work of a series of anthropologists, some of them truly outstanding, and through the force of Balinese art and artistry, a vivid picture of Balinese culture based overwhelmingly on South Balinese materials has impressed itself on general anthropological awareness: Bali "is" village-based, steady-state, theatrically oriented, graceful and calm, collectivist. This mental picture probably provides an inescapable reference for most of my anthropological readers — as it did for Unni Wikan and myself when we took up fieldwork in North Bali. Against such

9

a backdrop, North Bali seemed at first less wondrous, certainly atypical, and perhaps marginal. Yet there is no doubt that ethnographic materials from the Karangasem region of the east or Jembrana in the western region of Bali would also appear marginal and atypical. Certain well-documented Bali Aga communities, such as Trunyan (Danandjaja 1978, 1980) or Tenganan (Korn [1933], 1960; Ramseyer 1985), likewise stand out as exceptional and have with greater or less conviction been explained as unique survivals of cultural forms less influenced by Hinduization and Majapahit Javanese court patterns. Apparently the island of Bali, small at the outset, has somehow shrunk even further for us as an ethnographic exemplar to embrace only the trapezoid formed by Klungkung, Sanur, Tabanan, and Bayung Gede (see map 1) — the last already well into the marginal zone of Bali Aga mountain culture. And even in the heartland of this trapezoid, we cannot claim to know the range of community forms and institutional variations.

Where then might be the type locality of Balinese culture as it appears in our literature — the place where the anthropologist can find the desired "whole" represented — and what might be the area of its distribution? Admittedly, an anthropologist can travel to a wide region of villages, including much of the northern regency of Buleleng, and there in the tropical luxuriance of Balinese cultural expression pick up, and pursue further, the analysis of _barong_ dances, irrigation societies, exemplary court centers, Sanskritic cosmological concepts, and other themes composing parts of that resplendent image of a pan-Balinese culture we have formed from the literature. Yet my question remains. This same literature almost invariably refers to the great local variation in Balinese culture; but it proves notoriously difficult to obtain from it a picture of the morphological range of that variation and its regional patterning. Dutch scholarship focused heavily on the cumulative compilation of a record of village-to-village variation (e.g., Korn 1932; Liefrinck [1882–89] 1934; or, generally, Bali 1960 and Bali 1969), thus evading analytical and generalizing tasks, and even the construction of more detailed typologies, by postponing them. The English-language literature of the last fifty years has increasingly taken the opposite course of focusing on intensive but narrow data and developing representations that are closely attuned to currents in contemporary anthropological theory but fail to address, among other things, the empirical facts of variation. This inevitably reinforces an image of Bali as a benign tropical islet occupied by a multitude of replicating villages with a rich, but essentially homogeneous, culture.

But what are the facts of the case? The social and cultural ambience that confronted us in Buleleng seemed persistently at odds with this image from the literature, in both variability and content. The variation within Buleleng is profound, as we shall see shortly; but even its main parameters fit uneasily on the standard image of Bali, as the following examples show.

1. Accounts from South Bali have depicted Balinese culture as complexly founded on Hinduist cult and cosmology practiced under the direction of Brahmin priests. Yet Buleleng's population (like Karangasem's and Jembrana's) includes a number of Balinese Muslims, living the life of villagers in mixed Hindu-Muslim communities and in some exclusively Muslim rural communities, as well as in towns. Other areas, not only in the mountains, are distinguished as Bali Aga or Bali Asli/Bali Mula and practice highly discrepant local cults, which are not regarded as Hindu by the Hinduists. And even among the Hindus proper, perhaps half the people of North Bali do not *ever* make use of the services of Brahmins but have only priests of their own caste and community perform rituals endorsed by local tradition. It simply will not do to link our general analysis of Balinese social organization, everyday life, and cultural consciousness to particular Brahmin-modeled features of Bali-Hindu cosmological and ritual conceptions.

2. Ecology, subsistence, land tenure, and economic organization differ profoundly between communities, many of which show not even the concentration around irrigated rice agriculture that has seemed so characteristic in accounts of Balinese village organization. We need a record of, and ways to compare, how these other productive regimes are constituted, and we need to discover what their correlates may be in other domains of community life.

3. Colonial conquest took a strikingly different path in the north and in the south. The conquest of Buleleng in 1849 was only painfully achieved, against truculent and efficient resistance, in the biggest military operation launched by the Dutch in the nineteenth century in the East Indies (see Nielsen 1925 for contemporary accounts of these events). The invasion of South Bali in 1906, on the contrary, precipitated no effective resistance but instead the dramatic abdication of the *puputans*, the ritual mass suicides of royal families and their retainers. One must question the adequacy of a single model of the "theatre state" to account equally for such different performances.

4. Buleleng centers on the thriving port town of Singaraja, whose approximately fifty thousand people comprise a colorful mixture of different ethnic groups — Chinese, Hadhrami Arab, Bugis, Javanese, etc. — as well as the predominant Balinese population of urbanites of all social classes and both the Hindu and Muslim religions. The town is the commercial center for an agricultural region with a considerable sector of cash crops

Prayers and blessing in the pura dalem: virgin girls ("angels") assisting in anointing the worshipers with sacred rice and holy water.

and various specialized secondary products, as well as a center of numerous tertiary services. The region thus composes a truly complex society, the structure of which can certainly not be represented in terms of village prototypes.

Do we perhaps in Buleleng meet a society and culture fundamentally different from that of South Bali? That is, is Buleleng in some sense "not Bali"? Without an analysis of the range of variation in the south, it is impossible to judge the degree to which Buleleng indeed falls outside. But the main objections to such a suggestion are of a different order. Regional differences are recognized and sometimes emphasized by the Balinese; but Balinese identity clearly embraces both Buleleng and other nonsouthern regions as well as the south. There is a community not only of language but also of culture history to justify this: several of the ancient and prestigious temples are located in Buleleng; various mythical events are supposed to have taken place there; and the oldest (ninth and tenth century) historical records of Balinese religion and culture come equally from the north and south. There can be little gain in eliminating these branches of a common cultural stream just because they do not fit a mold created in the anthropological literature. The principle we must follow is to frame our concepts and models so that they capture the existing world as gracefully and economically as possible, not so that they allow us to purify ideal

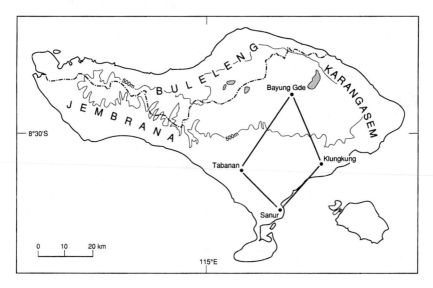

Map 1

13

types to the point where these no longer can accommodate our ethnographic specimens.

If the ultimate task we envisage is to provide an analysis of Bali as a complex society, of Balinese culture as a conglomerate and self-transforming tradition, of being Balinese in the diversity that Bali offers its two and a half million inhabitants — then how should we work toward this goal? Not, as I have indicated, by joining the ever-growing effort of Baliology (for such a field of scholarship does indeed exist) to describe the particular in every detail, nor by following the recent practice of relying heavily on materials from a single community, as have many social anthropologists working in Bali — though both these approaches have served to assemble an impressive corpus of valuable materials. I see the task, on the contrary, as being primarily a conceptual one, which would enable us to see and grasp salient features of Balinese social complexity and cultural process. This conceptual work must, in other words, be directed at solving problems that arise in the effort to describe Bali. The key lies in acknowledging variation as a distinguishing characteristic of complex society, and in using the task of describing the diversity that characterizes Bali as a *provocation* to develop the concepts and models necessary for that task. I shall focus on the diversity exhibited in parts of Buleleng, North Bali — not because it can be expected to be representative for the rest, but because it can be expected to pose the analytical challenge that is required.

As an introduction to the ethnography with which we shall be concerned, let me sketch some manifest features of spatial and temporal variation within Buleleng, so a reader unfamiliar with the area can form a first appreciation of the kinds of complexity exhibited.

Buleleng, with a population of 486,962 according to the 1980 census, lies on the steep north slope of the island, rather different from the more slack southern expanse. Rugged, though today intensively cultivated, mountains descend to a narrow alluvium, with settlements scattered from an altitude of approximately twelve hundred meters with increasing density down to sea level. Because of the lay of the land, irrigated agriculture depends on shorter and smaller drainage systems than in the south. There are also much more extensive areas of dry-land farming, of various crops at different altitudes. The main ecological zones are (1) shoreline, (2) coastal flats, (3) foothills, (4) valleys and spurs of lower slope, (5) high slope, (6) mountain and intermountain. Many communities contain land in, and all have close access to, several zones.

The population is mainly settled in zones 2, 3, and 4. The shoreline has been open to overseas contact and occupation, because of the characteristic Balinese underuse of the sea ecotype. Along the shore are thus many settlements of Bugis and Javanese origin but assimilated to Balinese identity, generally low-status, and many of them Muslim. Recently these have been swelled by an influx of Bali-Hindus from other zones, the result of general population increase and modernization.

The main ethnological areas are sketched very briefly by Grader, and we may follow his divisions (Grader [1939] 1960a). The easternmost area (see map 2) is almost without coastal flats and perennial streams. It "is linked with Bangli ethnologically (and) belongs entirely to the *Bali-aga* territory" (ibid.:189). This is today most fully true of the villages Sembiran in zone 4 and, exceptionally, Julah on the coast, from which I draw some of my field data. Other coastal villages, however, such as the minor center of Tejakula, are not locally regarded as outside the Bali-Hindu fold but show very distinctive stylistic features in flower offerings, masks, etc. Kubutambahan contains the largest temple in the area, dedicated to the cult of dry-land agricultural crops. To various degrees most of these villages have traditional political institutions, which constitute them as autonomous communities.

Sangsit is an old port town, boasting the finest example of the northern style of temple carving in its large wet-rice temple, Pura Beji. It and a group of villages in its upland form a center of cultural elaboration "where for centuries indigenous cultural life has undergone the fecund, uninterrupted influence of the presence of the court" (ibid.:189). The different communities show marked specialization and serve clienteles over wide areas of North Bali: Suwug provides trance media for consulting ancestors

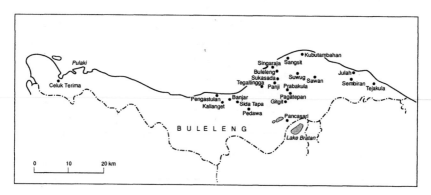

Map 2

in matters of ritual; Sawan is a center for musical and theatrical groups; Jagaraga houses a productive community of smiths; Banyuning is the center of pottery production; etc.

Further west, the valleys leading down to Singaraja are characterized by Grader as "an area with mixed forms of social organization" (ibid.). Here are the communities where I concentrated much of my fieldwork: Pagatepan, a Muslim enclave in zone 4; the neighboring Prabakula, an ancient Hindu village in zone 3; Panji, a village slightly west in zone 3, from which the kingdom of Buleleng arose; Tegallingga, still farther west, a mixed Hindu and Muslim village of more recent origin in zone 3, with extensive cotton-tree and citrus-fruit orchards; and Pancasari, a village in the high mountains settled in living memory, where extensive dry-rice agriculture has (terminally) persisted till today.

In the flats and foothills west of Singaraja are intensively cultivated wet-rice areas. West and south of this, settlements in zone 4, including Sidatapa and Pedawa (see chapter 5), "constitute a remarkable, archaic type of *desa* [community]" (ibid:191) locally classified as Bali Asli or Bali Mula, "original" Balinese. West of this again is another large alluvial area with a group of major streams for irrigation. This area is presently dominated by the long-settled, now urbanizing Sererit and the old, still densely settled village area of Banjar, the home of Bali's Romeo and Juliet (see chapter 19). Holding perhaps the finest lands in that area is the village of Pengastulan — from which I also draw some detailed data — a mixed but predominantly Hindu village dominated by a nucleus of high-caste former fief-holders claiming southern origin.

Finally, farther toward the west the land becomes drier and the coastal flats narrower again, with mostly recent and relatively mixed settlements, till one reaches the important but isolated temple of Pulaki. Here the great Siwaist priest Dang Hyang Bau Rauh, "the Holy Newcomer," is supposed to have landed in 1489 to join the recently arrived Majapahit court; and here according to myth a large, still existing population became invisible because of their deception of this holy person and his daughter.

As for the town of Singaraja itself, Grader gives a sketch map of its main wards. (Grader [1939] 1960a:192). It comprises a highly diverse town: old, integrated, and prosperous wards such as Tegal, whose central temple is the subject of Grader's essay; poorer, centrally located wards such as Kajanan; middle-class, newly prosperous wards such as Anyar; once separate upslope communities such as Bratan, which contains a nucleus of Pande smiths. During Dutch administration, from 1882 to 1942, the old town was organized along ethnic, communal lines with separate wards for communities of Arabs, Chinese, and Bugis, each having its own administrator.

By now residential separation has been reduced to a mere tendency of ethnic compatriots to cluster in neighborhoods, and the local administration gives no recognition to communal membership (although, on the national level, Chinese still have distinctive Indonesian passports). Thus today the Arabs no longer live in the "Arab" quarter; in Kampung Bugis only one house remains with the characteristic Bugis pile architecture, and most of the residents are mixed Balinese of modest means. The main Chinese temple is on the edge of the old Chinese quarter, but the Chinese families live more dispersed, and some have ancestor shrines in their compounds built in modern Balinese style, while one Chinese merchant has even been called by the god of a Balinese temple west of Singaraja to be *pemangku*, priest, of that temple.

Some brief reflections on the (fragmentary) historical evidence may likewise serve to focus our ethnographic perspective on North Bali. The most salient events seem to have taken place in the seventeenth century and are associated with the legendary hero Panji Sakti, who is identified as the founder of the kingdom of Buleleng and remains a prominent figure in contemporary consciousness. The Babad Buleleng — a traditional history of Panji Sakti and the dynasty he founded — has been admirably translated, annotated, and published (Worsley 1972) from a manuscript apparently copied in the 1920s; but the component legends live on among people unfamiliar with the manuscript and unrelated to the royal family and are associated with various localities in the *desa adat* (traditional domain) of Panji village, from which he sprang. Thus the locality by the rice fields where Panji Sakti killed the tyrant king of his village is readily identified by informants: "The trees where he sat when he pointed his (magic) kris Ki Semang at Raja Gandis used to stand here, but were cut down when the government straightened the road" (see Worsley 1972:143 for a parallel version). The place where Panji Sakti won his wealth by refloating a stranded Chinese junk is the present *pura segara* (sea temple) of Panji village, and villagers explain: "The captain gave the young Kibara, as Panji Sakti was known as a boy, the whole of the cargo of his vessel, including the statues Yulahut and Bilahut — you can still see them there in the temple, you will recognize their Chinese features" (see Worsley 1972:143–147 and notes pp. 222f. for another version of the event). The buildings of Panji Sakti's first court still stand in the village of Panji, with furniture supposedly untouched, made into the temple Pura Pejengenan Panji in accordance with his own wish. Finally, the family shrine of his predecessor Raja Gandis composes the small Pura Kaping, abandoned and with its small altars bricked up so no offerings can be made to the evil raja's ancestral spirit.

The historicity of the person of Panji Sakti as the founder of the kingdom of Buleleng has been questioned but cannot reasonably be disputed. The Babad Buleleng makes him the son of the high king of Bali in Gelgel and a servant mother from Panji; later he was driven by danger and jealousy at court to flee to his mother's native village. Whatever his origins, he seems to have proceeded by conquest from Panji to create a unified and expansive kingdom in the then politically highly divided region of Den Bukit — i.e., North Bali — sometime during the seventeenth century (de Graaf 1949). Expanding from Panji village, he founded the consecutive central places of this state structure, first in Sukasada ("the Ever-Happy Place").[1] To this new center were drawn a certain number of Brahmins as *pedanda* high priests, high-caste nobles as fiefholders, and commoner artisans and craftsmen, many from the south but also from much earlier small coastal centers in the north, such as Tejakula and Bubuhan. In effect, what we probably see is the establishment in the north of the Majapahit-modeled court and kingdom pattern already introduced two or three centuries earlier in the south. After some generations, Panji Sakti's dynasty was displaced on the throne by conquest from Karangasem, but the courtly center of Buleleng continued, and the family was briefly restored to the throne by the Dutch in 1849.

Many features that differentiate northern society from southern can plausibly be ascribed to differences in the impact of Javanese Majapahit cultural influence, state organization, and elite personnel. In the south, a fourteenth-century Majapahit incursion is generally represented as effecting a complete transformation of society. A Javanese panegyric from the time of the invasion (A.D. 1343) reports how the "vile, long-haired Balinese Princes" were destroyed, with the result that Balinese "customs are now consistent with the Javanese ones" (Ramseyer 1977:55). Following this conquest, and losses in Java against other Javanese powers, the Majapahit prince himself and his courtiers and nobles are represented to have migrated from Java to South Bali in 1478 (e.g., Forman, Mrazek, and Forman 1983:22). Today almost all the people of South Bali, with the exception of the Bali Aga, reportedly regard themselves as *wong Majapahit*, i.e., descendants of these immigrants (Geertz 1980:143).

The evidence from the north indicates a very different process, whereby a local prince, at a considerably later stage, simply sought to enhance his

---

1. Buleleng ("dryland grainfields") was the name of the downslope area north of Sukasada (cf. Worsley 1972:161, 231). It has become associated with the king's palace, and thus his whole realm in North Bali, while Singaraja has become the name of the town as a whole — despite contrary conventions found on many maps.

position and justify his imperium by introducing prestigious ideas, institutions, and pretensions from the greater and more established centers of the south. Whatever the volume of the Majapahit irruption into South Bali, it must have produced far greater discontinuity with the past, and also greater homogeneity, than Panji Sakti was capable of in the north. Nor is there any evidence for a Majapahit impact preceding him in the north: there is no suggestion that Panji Sakti, in creating his centralized kingdom in Den Bukit/Buleleng in the seventeenth century, met coordinated resistance springing from previous state structures, or that he could seek legitimacy as a restorer of a unity that had previously existed under his purported Majapahit ancestors. The village kingdoms and freeman republics that confronted him, and to varying degrees survived him, are better understood as continuations of older Balinese patterns.

What may these older Balinese patterns have been? Here we meet an embarrassment in the complete hiatus of local historical sources till we reach back to Bali's oldest historical period, dating from the ninth to eleventh centuries. A number of inscriptions on metal (*presastis*) promulgating royal edicts in Old Balinese interspersed with Sanskrit, or later in Javanese, have been found fairly widely distributed in both North and South Bali. Indeed, the earliest of them (from A.D. 881) is concerned with communications over the mountains between north and south and the need for travelers to be provided with hospices on the way (Goris 1954; Lansing 1983:26f.). These *presastis* are found spread in the north from Bubuhan in the west to Julah in the east, with a particularly rich trove of such documents from the latter village. In them, a succession of kings addresses named communities — many, among them Julah, in existence today — in documents unambiguously dated according to the traditional Balinese calendar. The impression these documents project is of a benign and omnipotent king allotting public duties to communities of his subjects governed by councils of elders. They also imply the existence of monastic centers of both Buddhist and various Hindu persuasions, of social divisions modeled on the Varna caste categories of the classical Indian scriptures, and of a complex range of specialist artists and performers of recognizably Balinese varieties (ibid.:30).

The whole question of the mode and extent of early Indian influences on Bali is aptly summarized by Lansing (1983, especially chapter 2). He argues for the view that religious and cultural influences were perhaps independent of, and certainly dominant over, colonization and trade at all times. The active agents may plausibly have been local kings or notables, shoring up their authority and aiding their (characteristic Malayo-Polynesian) drive to rank enhancement by harnessing Indian ideas of sacred kingship to their ambitions. The resulting picture of a profound fertilization of local culture in literacy, philosophy, social organization, and the arts can hardly be overemphasized (they are vividly displayed in Ramseyer 1977).

It is a striking and puzzling fact, however, that a disproportionate number of these early documents, with their implications of intimate connection with the early court centers, are associated with Bali Aga villages — i.e., communities marginal to, or outside, the sway of the later Majapahit-inspired states. In other words, the present Bali Aga villages seem to have been more integrated in the Balinese mainstream then than they are today; and North Bali seems to have been more closely integrated with the south than in the subsequent centuries before the establishment of the kingdom of Buleleng.

The hiatus of local records could be interpreted as reflecting a breakdown of the early state structure and a parochialization of the north. On the other hand, it may equally be an artifact of a change from the use of metal inscriptions to the use of the far more decomposable *lontar* palm-leaf manuscripts for writing. Traditions maintained in Julah give an intriguing hint of intervening political change. According to them, the *patih* (governors) of Julah following after the Warmadewa dynasty of the tenth century, and the high-caste elite to which these governors belonged, became increasingly proud and tyrannical. Finally the villagers, under the leadership of a holy man, overthrew their patih and abolished the institution of caste.[2] According to family records of the present secretary of the custom village (*klian desa adat*), this revolution took place seventeen generations ago. Ever since, Julah has been the casteless and seniority-governed community it is today (see below, chapters 5 and 13).

Whatever the actual events in Julah and elsewhere in the north, the overall situation indicated by these historical fragments is of a history of Indian cultural influences nearly a thousand years long *preceding* Panji Sakti's state-building in Buleleng. These influences, like those initiated by himself, probably arose in large part from the initiatives and mediation of local political and religious leaders rather than from conquest and imposition. Hence, the impact of any single source of impulses remained necessarily indecisive and its penetration variable, producing over time the diversity of communities and subjective worlds so characteristic of North

2. Identified as a disciple of Mpu Kuturan, a culture hero widely famed in Bali and also cited in the southern Bali Aga village of Tengganan as the institutor of their village organization (Korn [1933] 1960:330). Historically Mpu Kuturan seems to have been a Buddhist sage who lived in the latter half of the tenth century (Goris [1948] 1969b:97).

Bali. Indeed, since the seventeenth century this diversity has only been exacerbated by the spreading influence and challenge of Islam and the impact of a hundred years of Dutch colonial presence. A powerful force in shaping local culture during the last three hundred years has certainly been the kingdom and court of Buleleng, cast in the Majapahit mold. Geertz (1980) provides a highly provocative model of how such exemplary centers functioned in South Bali in the nineteenth century, which I will discuss later. But given the historical situation I have outlined, it should be obvious that it, or any other single model, cannot serve to frame the many forms of organization and the many strands of tradition that flourish today in North Bali. It is interesting that the Balinese, as well as Western anthropologists, tend to standardize this North Balinese cultural variation terminologically, conceptually, and organizationally by means of South Balinese schemata. But the processes whereby great traditions spread down and take root in local communities and the lives of real people, and processes whereby collective representations are shaped by the acts of such people, are far too complex to be thus shortcircuited. The exploration of these processes is indeed a major challenge and purpose of this study.

Profound changes have also been wrought during the lifetime of the present senior generation. The Japanese occupation and the subsequent years of struggle for Indonesian independence, in which the people of Buleleng participated very actively, fostered a new sense of identity and cosmopolitan participation in broad sectors of the population. The turbulence of Sukarno's charismatic leadership, ending in the violence of the 1965 coup and countercoup — likewise very extensive in Buleleng — created alignments and divisions so passionate and experiences so traumatic they cannot be fully suppressed today even by the most exquisite Balinese politeness and grace.

During these years, a modern educational system based on Bahasa Indonesia has also been constructed, which now dominates the lives of most children and youths. It radically influences the reproduction of culture, not only by imparting new bodies of knowledge but also by affecting people's fundamental orientations to knowledge (from secret and dogmatic to more pragmatic), authority (from family seniority to bureaucratic), and life cycle (from education late in life to education in preparation for life).

In agriculture, which still engages the majority of the population, a diversification that had started before independence has been accelerated. In contrast to most of the Indonesian islands, Bali never used to produce for the international spice market and so remained relatively unaffected by earlier trade and development. Agriculture was subsistence-oriented, with

rice, bananas, and coconut as main crops, as well as an extensive arboricul-
ture of local native fruits. Some production of the *robusta* variety of coffee
began in Buleleng in the nineteenth century. More recently the *indica* and
other varieties were introduced, and today the northern slope of the
mountains at altitudes above six hundred meters is extensively planted with
coffee orchards. In the 1960s clove trees were also introduced, and their
cultivation has spread rapidly in the four-to seven-hundred-meter altitude
zone, as have citrus orchards in some areas between five hundred meters
and sea level. Even more recently, vanilla in middle altitudes, and tobacco
and grapes on the coastal flats, have been introduced as cash crops. High-
yielding varieties of rice have replaced Balinese rice (generally thought
much tastier) in most areas with adequate irrigation. All this adds up to a
radical transformation into an innovative and diverse commercialized agricultural regime.

A precondition for this change has been the development of a road
network, and a result the heavy increase in modern transport activities.
Perhaps most consequential of all, these developments have been accompanied by swift population growth, increasing urbanization, and considerable growth in the rates of material consumption, generating heavy pressures on land resources. The result of all these trends is a highly modern
ambience, which strongly but variably infuses the native, traditional civilization.

How should an anthropologist — indeed one previously unacquainted with
fieldwork in Indonesia — best work to achieve useful insights into society
as large-scale and culture as complex as this brief sketch of Buleleng suggests? To accumulate field data with the desired degree of detail and intimacy from such a range of communities is, to say the least, a daunting task.
Yet I could not rely on data from one or a few locales only, as it was precisely the transferability of understandings from one situation to another
that I increasingly wished to question and test. Nor did I feel I could adopt
the templates provided by the many ethnographic accounts of South Bali,
as they failed to address the issues of variation to which I attached the
greatest importance — as I have set out in the preamble.

The challenge as I understand it is above all theoretical and concerned
with how to model an account of variation and disorder, even more than
how to merely assemble the data on variation. Indeed, it is because of the
general and theoretical nature of this challenge that I felt I could take it up
at all, considering the well-established Indonesianist expertise of many anthropologists already working with Balinese materials. Yet the theory I
seek to develop should be grounded in, and inform, the particular ethnog-

raphy: it should answer the provocation of ethnographic findings in Bule-leng. To allow my readers some chance to assess the sources and validity of these ethnographic data, I should therefore give a brief account of how they have been obtained.

The field materials on which the present work is based were collected between January 1984 and March 1989 by Unni Wikan and myself, some while we were together in the field, some on separate visits. Unni spent altogether twenty months on seven separate visits, and I made five field visits totaling fifteen months. For five months Unni, our son, and I stayed in the home of an intermediate school principal and his large family in Singaraja, and more then half my time during this period I spent working in Pagatepan. During the later, shorter field periods I revisited the com-munities I knew and added new ones, bringing me in the end to a total of about a dozen field sites.

My command of the Indonesian language was never good; as for Balinese, I developed only a limited comprehension and a certain passive vocabulary, but no speaking facility. During all my work I was thus depen-dent on assistants and interpreters. I was very fortunate in obtaining the collaboration of two outstanding helpers, M. Ghazi Habibullah and Made Artja. Indeed, it was the quality of the data I obtained in cooperation with them that led me to concentrate on this mode of data collection in the field, rather than using time and effort to enhance my language facility.

M. Ghazi assisted me in the community I have called Pagatepan and with incidental work in a few other Muslim communities. He is a native of Pagatepan and spent most of his youth in a neighboring community; when Professor Ngurah Bagus introduced me to him he was an advanced stu-dent of anthropology at Udayana University in Denpasar. Ghazi combined an intimate previous knowledge of the community with the useful distanc-ing that results from having gone to live elsewhere; and his command of anthropology and his own experience of fieldwork in Lombok gave him a keen appreciation of my purpose. He accompanied me continuously while I worked in Pagatepan; for some purposes, such as collecting parts of the census materials, he also worked independently.

Made Artja was my assistant in my work among Bali-Hindus. Without any higher education, he had nonetheless achieved an excellent command of English by attending evening classes. Combined with his maturity, ex-perience, and great love of people, this made him an outstanding collabo-rator. Made accompanied me during nearly all my work in Bali-Hindu communities, with two exceptions: a three-week period when my family and I were the guests of a family performing a major cremation, which they invited us to follow in detail; and occasional visits to Pengastulan, where I went in the company of my close friend Drs. I Gusti Putu Antara, a professor of linguistics and a native of that village.

My procedures for obtaining data were several and broad-ranging; primarily they involved participation. When in the field, I generally focused most of my attention on the current events and concerns that engaged people and about which they wished to speak among themselves, rather than imposing my own agenda of questions and themes. I used prepared question schedules only to collect certain kinds of census data, and I never used questionnaires; but I frequently formalized my initial visits with people as explicit interviews on topics in which they were knowledgeable or experienced, and at such times I would write down copious notes and verbatim passages. Most data, however, were obtained through informal conversations, and a great deal by entirely undirected participation. In situations where statements and materials seemed particularly valuable I would sometimes scribble preliminary notes, and more often retire immediately afterward to write down detailed notes and, where possible, closely paraphrased statements. My identity as an anthropologist intending to produce a book was made known to everybody with whom I interacted; but I believe that my genuine interest and attention to people as whole persons came across to most, so that a genuinely social and personal relationship became more salient to many of them as we became increasingly familiar. A sense of the value and uses of such data, and also the ethical constraints, are discussed at various points in the text, especially at pages 126–29 and 160–61.

Initially, as I worked in Pagatepan, my knowledge of Arabic and of Islam made me a welcome and respected visitor; but also among Bali-Hindus I experienced a genuine respect for knowledge and an acceptance of me in the role of a scholar. Progressively, as I returned to acquaintances among Hindus and Muslims alike, and people noticed my continued attention to them and my recollection of the small details of their lives and concerns, I felt that many relationships took on the qualities of closeness, trust, and mutual affection. Both Ghazi and Made made this all the more possible by being eminently likable and having the facility to assist rather than disturb the development of my own relations to people by being attentive and sensitive mediators.

The theoretical focus of my study developed and expanded with time, in ways that responded to the data I collected and progressively guided the further collecting. I had originally conceptualized the project as one that would focus on how the presence of Islam, with its conceptions of the Deity, humankind, history, and society, modified folk culture and conceptions among Balinese Muslims. In this analysis, I had planned to rely mainly on the literature for the necessary materials for a comparison and contrast to Bali-Hindus. But as I became increasingly aware of the extent of the variation within the vast majority population of non-Muslims in Buleleng, and developed my own sense and judgment with regard to the institutions, conceptions, and meanings among them, I chose to pursue a progressively broader and more embracing study of the region. As a result I collected materials to match those from Pagatepan from the neighboring Hindu village of Prabakula; and in due course I also collected data from another dozen diverse communities.

Though I started with a fair command of the ethnographic literature on Bali — as it was then, in 1983 — I never proceeded with the thought to use it as my guide to the culture that I was observing during my residence in the field. Too much of my field experience has been in areas where, at the time of my work, ethnographic studies and even knowledge were lacking. Inevitably, I proceeded in Bali more or less as I have done in these pioneering situations, looking to the social life that surrounded me as my only reality and authority. Besides its being a habit of life and a personal preference, I am also prepared to argue that such a stance is a methodological virtue in fieldwork, as it enhances the anthropologist's chance to transcend received theory and knowledge and to learn from the only fully valid source: people speaking and acting in a living society.

PART TWO

*Features of Social
Organization
in North Balinese
Communities*

2

Prabakula:
A Bali-Hindu Village

Most conventions of anthropology would have the fieldworker who studies an agrarian civilization place primary focus on "the local community":
the village-scale arena where most of the life of most of society's members
undoubtedly unfolds. Only by submerging oneself in such a village community can one hope to be made aware of the rules and self-evidences that
generate local lives and become attuned to the concerns and conceptions
that compose local people's realities. "To an ethnographer, sorting
through the machinery of distant ideas, the shapes of knowledge are always
ineluctably local, indivisible from their instruments and their encase-
ments" (Geertz 1983:4).

The basic insight behind this credo has great force and needs to be
honored; but its simplistic observance in the form of a community study
in North Bali would beg far more questions than it would solve. Village
organization in the region is so variable that any single village will prove
entirely inadequate as a specimen for understanding other communities.
What is more, major component traditions of knowledge in Buleleng are
organized on a scale that transcends village boundaries, and their distinctive and systematic features become nearly invisible if one's focus is nar-
rowed to a village community. In part, the ethnographer can compensate
for this threat to her or his perspective by being particularly alert to the
wider connections in which the members of a village community are enmeshed. But an added enigma must also be faced: the fact that persons,
positioned in radically differently organized local communities, are able to
merge at all into larger organizations on regional level. If local community
and circumstance are so important and formative of meanings and orientations, then how can people from widely different local backgrounds

29

Ricefields of Pagatepan, leading down toward Prabakula.

mingle without coming up against insuperable differences of conventions, concerns, and conceptions?

To deal with such issues, we need to secure a broader base than a single community study can provide — but without losing our local perspective. I shall attempt to provide this base by starting, in this and the next chapter, with an account of two adjacent communities: the village of Prabakula, a community of Bali-Hindus, and the highly anomalous village of Pagatepan, a traditional community of Balinese Muslims. Subsequently I will add further local variants of village organization, leading to a general comparative and theoretical discussion of variation in chapter 6. But first, my "tale of two cities."

Prabakula is an ancient Bali-Hindu village with a total population of 2,871 persons according to the 1982 census. The neighboring village of Pagatepan, more than two hundred years old, is a Muslim village of 3,714 persons. A series of rice terraces connects the two, descending from the large village center of Pagatepan toward the prosperous village nucleus and additional smaller hamlets of Prabakula. Prabakula lies in a domain richly endowed with Hindu temples and shrines. The village lands of Pa-

30

gatepan, on the contrary, have no such temples but contain one main and several subsidiary mosques. The villagers of Prabakula see themselves as committed to practice an elaborate cult of gods and ancestors and actualize a rich and evocative tradition of concepts and images, which their neighbors in Pagatepan passionately reject. Likewise, in the organization of their village communities — though some features are very similar — much is so different that they seem to constitute different worlds. Let me begin with Prabakula.

HISTORY AND COMPOSITION

Prabakula is recognized among knowledgeable persons as a very ancient community, and this is also noted in Liefrinck's survey from the 1880s (Liefrinck 1934). Along with Panji and Tanawan, it is claimed to be among the oldest still extant villages of North Bali. Prabakula's various origin myths are not tied together into one narrative history so much as connected with the founding of various temples, thus providing origin accounts one behind the other, so to speak; but several informants have given me a sequential account of the four successive village temples *(pura desa)*, of which the last and present temple is reputedly seven hundred years old. Even before the first village temple, the Siwa temple Silagatre was built in the then forest where eighteen hundred years ago the villagers' ancestors saw the God Betara Gutoh dancing; and another Siwa temple, the Gunungsari, is supposed to be older still. The population derives from the thirty-three followers of the king, or perhaps sage *(dukoh)*, who led them to the region and later meditated with such effect that he spontaneously dematerialized and thus achieved Nirwana directly.

Over the centuries, immigrants have also joined the community, and their descendants now make up about half the population of the village. These constitute the *sampingan* (followers), while the descendants of the original settlers are *marip* (dominant, leading). Both groups are recognized as full citizens *(krama desa)* of the village, but they constitute distinct formal moieties and usually meet in separate assemblies. Intermarriage between the two groups is unrestricted, and membership follows the male line.

Another basic division of the population is that of caste. It is also patrilineal, and today there are no formal restrictions on intermarriage, though the marriage of a high-caste girl to a commoner boy will normally be resisted by her family. About 20 percent of the village are high-caste with the honorific title Gusti, variously claimed to signify Satria or Wesia status (i.e., membership in the warrior or the merchant/managerial levels respectively of the traditional Indian caste system). The remaining 80 percent are commoners, mainly of the descent category Pasek Gelgel, the majority group in the north. All the Gustis are of the marip moiety.

According to Bali-Hindu cosmology, all of Bali belongs to the gods, and so all human habitation is located on land that is primarily the sacred domain of one or another God or aspect of Godhead. The human residents of such a sacred territory are therefore subject to a binding set of injunctions associated with the God of the domain. This will not be a universal sacred law as in the Muslim conception, but a specific, unchangeable desa adat (custom law) and *awig-awig* (rules and conventions) valid for a specific territory. Successive civil governments have often ignored these facts and established administrative divisions on other bases, overlaying the sacred geography. In the case of Prabakula, the government village *(dusun)* with its village headman *(perbekel)* coincides with a socially significant village area but embraces only part of the traditional sacred domain, which has been divided into several villages for demographic and political reasons. Internally the government village is further subdivided into three *banjar* divisions, whereas by custom it is composed of four *(banjar adat)*. The desa adat seems to have been rigidly maintained over centuries, and adherence to the custom law is seen as a sacred, collective duty. The modern village of Prabakula is thus part of a double set of territorial divisions and embedded with other neighboring villages in a larger ritual community; it is also enmeshed in a network of intermarriages with these and other communities. Only with upstream Pagatepan do no such connections obtain. People in Prabakula say that Pagatepan was established by royal edict in an unclaimed area outside their desa adat territory, and to that extent it has not affected them. But its settlement upstream caused their loss of the special invulnerability to enemy weapons they had till then enjoyed.

THE COMMUNITY

The definitions and identities of community and person among Bali-Hindus are saliently cast in terms of religious cult, so a review of social organization becomes as much an exposition of temples, congregations, and rituals as an account of secular property and task groups. Among most Balinese, the social and moral unity of the village domain is represented conceptually by a triad of temples. A temple *(pura)* in Bali is normally an enclosed area containing a series of miniature stone thrones, onto which the gods descend when called down correctly, at the correct times, by the congregation's devotions. In North Bali, the Sun-God Throne *(padma-sana)* is indispensable in the mountain-and-eastward corner of the temple square; in the grander temples it is supported by a stepped pyramid base. There are also sacred storehouses (*gedong*), which contain relics and serve as resting places for the deities during temple festivals. Many temples also contain *meru*, high towers with multiple, pagoda-like roofs. Most of the time, the temple is unoccupied by both men and gods, but the various spirits from below (*buta-kala*) may hover there at all times.

A key triad of such temples is generally subsumed under the expression *kahyangan tiga* (lit.: "the three places for God to stay"). In South Bali, this concept refers to the three temples of *pura puseh* (the navel/village origin temple), *pura bale agung* (the great council temple), and *pura dalem* (the "chthonian" temple, generally known as the death temple for its association with the unpurified dead souls) (cf. Geertz 1980:52f.). In North Bali, the term *kahyangan tiga* refers to a somewhat different set of three: pura desa (village temple), pura dalem (death temple), and pura segara (sea temple). Prabakula shares its distant pura segara in Singaraja with all the villages of a larger region. The other two temples, on the other hand, define the community and are shared only with one village, recently separated from Prabakula. Associated with the pura desa are myths of successive rebuildings, with name changes for the community and even acknowledged, but diffusely remembered, changes in religious belief or interpretation (*tattwa, alirang*) over the ages. Thus the king who led the thirty-three village founders built the Pura Ariwita, succeeded by the Pura Prabakula, then the Pura Widwasari or Darbasari, and finally the present pura, by now several times rebuilt after earthquakes. The pura desa of North Balinese villages contains both the origin or "navel" shrines and the *bale* (council hall), which in South Balinese villages are located in distinct temples. In Prabakula, however, only the "upper" moiety of the *krama desa marip* meet in assembly in the pura desa (at the time of the full moon); the *krama desa sampingan*, on the other hand, meet in the pura dalem at the time of the three-quarter ascending moon.

But the village domain in its territorial aspect is most clearly symbolized in another set of temples: the *pura dukoh* ("head") high in the southwest, in the forest belonging now to another village; the *pura kladian* and *pura cekeh* ("left arm" and "right arm") to the southeast and northwest in middle altitudes, and the *pura waneayu* ("tail") in the lowest part of the village domain. These four temples are generally joined with the pura desa (as the "body") in a group of five and expressed as a unity in ritual: of any pig offered in connection with village cult or rice cult, the head should be presented to the pura dukoh, left and right legs to pura kladian and pura cekeh, tail to pura waneayu, and stomach to pura desa.

Each and every of these temples (and also the four banjar adat) has a pemangku (priest); the more important ones also have a *klian* (secretary) and a *bendesa* (calendrical expert). While the two latter officers are elective, the pemangku may be designated by patrilineal succession, elected by the congregation, or chosen by God through a possessed temple medium. Ideally these criteria should coincide. When they do not, election supersedes descent, and the God's own choice provides the ultimate legitimacy. Some temples are associated with dedicated land *(tanah laba)* to provide for some of the costs of maintenance and collective rites; the rest is shared by the congregation under the direction of the klian or, if no such officer is found, the pemangku himself.

Each of these congregations thus forms a self-governing body, directed by the group in assembly and ultimately by the God. The same is, in principle, also true of the village as such; but in its case, there is also the secular administration led by the perbekel, an official of the state administration, elected by popular ballot.

HOUSEHOLDS

If the simple fact of territorial organization in Prabakula has involved us in some of the premises of Bali-Hindu cosmology, this is all the more true when one approaches the topics of marriage, kinship, and descent. The basic unit of village society in Prabakula is the household based on a married couple and comprising a nuclear family, with irregular additions. The average household size is 4.5 persons. Households in Prabakula do not always form visually separate units and may occupy several houses, irregularly clustered; these do not make up larger compounds or houseyards like those often found in South Bali, and they are usually not enclosed by any compound wall, as they would be in the south.

Marriages may be arranged by negotiation between the families, by elopement of the parties, or by bride capture. Thus marriages are not normally manipulated by larger kin groups to form alliances, nor is cohabitation very rigorously controlled. Nonetheless marriage is deeply constitutive of the person's social status. According to the philosophical principle of *ardha nareswari/ardha nare-iswara*, woman and man are each incomplete and complementary. Thus the married couple, not the individual, composes the smallest complete social unit. This principle underlies the radical differentiation and complementarity of man and woman in the ritual sphere: neither can substitute for the other, and both roles are needed for the performance of necessary ritual. It also underlies social life and membership rights in the community. Thus it is only with marriage that persons become voting citizens, krama desa, of the village. They retain this position until their last child marries, when they are retired to become senior citizens without duties; or if one spouse dies, the other is retired immediately, since the survivor is ritually and socially incomplete and cannot take a responsible part in public life.

KINSHIP AND DESCENT

Balinese folk ideas of physical conception are bilateral, and paternity is regarded as arising from physical procreation. But according to Bali-Hinduism, the spiritual component of the person is implanted by reincarnation, symbolized by the *lingga*, the God Siwa's phallus, and so is associated with the paternal line. Every soul is immortal and indeed partakes of Godhead as its manifestation or incarnation; after death the soul is reborn in due course with a fate prominently determined by its acts in its previous lives in accord with the principle of *karma pala*, the fruits of karma. But in contrast to the explicit philosophy of karma, North Balinese Hindus firmly believe that every soul is reincarnated as a human being, indifferently male or female, in its own family line. Descent is thus basically conceived as a spiritual relation of identity and is ascribed patrilineally. But looking upward through the generations, women as well as men are conceptualized as ancestors; and the origin temple *(kawitan)* of a descent group is frequently called its *pura ibu*, "mother temple." Women thus become in effect assimilated to their husband's descent group, and this is ritually affirmed through their being cremated by that group, i.e., by their own children or son's children. Likewise, in the work of worship, husband-and-wife together form the elementary unit that carries the responsibilities of performing cremation, praying and providing offerings to the husband's ancestors, and maintaining the shrines of the husband's line. But the living woman retains her descent identity and continues to be an active participant in the worship of her own ancestors and her own descent group, though not a "paying member" of it; and to this worship she will normally bring her husband, and certainly her minor children. The actual congregation that assembles for ancestor worship is thus saliently bilateral and affinal, a fact that reaffirms the person's perception of kinship as basically bilateral and inclusive. We thus find in Prabakula a deep and complex embeddedness of the person in an active bilateral network; but this coexists with a primary division of the population into patrilineal descent groups and an economic commitment of households to only one hierarchy of descent temples.

This hierarchy is normally composed of three or more levels of segmentation. (1) In every house there should be a shrine, if ever so simple, for offerings to the husband's patrilineal ancestors. If there is not, its members will be dependent on the shrine of the husband's natal house for its minor ritual observances. Persons with particularly close and active relations to their deceased ancestors will in addition have an ancestor shrine on a large shelf over their bed. (2) Next, most families will have patrilineal relatives in the community who jointly compose a local descent group. Unless very insignificant in numbers and influence, these will in Prabakula maintain a joint descent group temple (*mranjan* for high-caste; for commoners, it may be just an altar, *sanggah*, or if enclosed by a masonry wall, it will be called a *pura dadia*). There are five descent groups of high-caste Gustis in Prabakula, each with its mranjan temple, and numerous larger and smaller descent group temples of the commoners. Within each temple, there are a number of individual shrines belonging to different gods and ancestors, to which particular family lines and persons may be associated; but these shrines do not in any systematic way reflect the descent segmentation of the group, nor are genealogies maintained that could serve as charters for such segmentation. (3) On the highest level, all descent lines are grouped under the Siwa temples Gunungsari, Selagatre, and Darmajati. Known as the Siwa Tiga, the "Three Siwas," they represent the unity of origin of the community of Prabakula; they also serve as the origin temples of their constituent descent groups, who form three *sekaha Siwa*, Siwa associations or congregations.

The idea of the origin place and temple (kawitan) of a descent line is important and complex. Analogous to the concept of apical ancestor in lineage systems, it is perhaps best explained as a representation of the fount of the Godhead that is incarnate in the souls of the members of the descent group — in Bali-Hindu idiom naturally fusing spirit with place. The all-Bali "Mother Temple" of Besakih serves as the mythological origin temple for all, while on the level of the smallest unit, most house temples will have a *sanggah kemulan* shrine that symbolizes the descent line's origin. Most Bali-Hindus also have an identified shrine somewhere in Bali that is regarded as the true origin point of their line and from which they fetch holy water for some of the great life crisis rituals. For the families of the sampingan moiety in Prabakula this will naturally be elsewhere, but they have all been assigned one or another of the Three Siwas to serve as the local representation of their origin temple. Members of the marip moiety, on the other hand, regard one of the Siwa temples as their true origin temple, and some lines have separate family shrines within it.

We thus find in Prabakula a descent organization quite unlike anything I have seen described for Bali (Boon 1977; Duff-Cooper 1984; Geertz and Geertz 1975; Hobart 1979; Howe 1984; Lansing 1983) or indeed any-

One of the three ancient Siwa temples.

where else. It is a patrilineal organization comprising two unequal, aga-
mous moieties (marip and sampingan), the higher of which is subdivided
into two unequal castes (gusti and *jaba*). These distinctions are cross-cut
by a division into three descent-and-origin cult associations (sekaha Siwa).
Each of these bodies is composed of a set of descent groups (*purusa* or
dadia), each usually with its additional, distinct ancestor cult temple. Most
of these descent lines are also erratically subdivided into descent lines associated with component shrines within the temples, down to the level of
households. On this level, the fundamental complementarity that is defined between man and woman constitutes the couple as an indivisible unit
in the ancestor cult of the husband's line. Looking upward through the
generations, women are assimilated as ancestors to the descent group of
their husbands and children, whereas in their own life they retain their
identity as members of their natal descent group.

   The main relevance of descent in Prabakula is to a wide range of spiritual matters (see chapter 12) and to the performance of life cycle rituals
and ancestor cult, which together have such complexity and economic import that they represent a major domain of activity indeed. Through

37

succession to land (discussed below), the descent organization articulates with production and household economy; while on the highest level of moieties it articulates with village administration in providing the basis for formal village assemblies.

RELIGIOUS PRECEPTS FOR PERSONHOOD AND SOCIAL RELATIONS

We do not find in Prabakula any separate, formal organization for the systematic teaching of religious and moral precepts. In much of Bali, as in Buleleng province, there are families of Brahmana priests (pedanda) to which Bali-Hindu families of other castes are linked as disciples (sisia) — though the relation is usually limited to merely receiving holy water, and not sacred education, from one's priest. But in Prabakula no Brahmana are found and no links to pedandas are maintained. The reproduction of sacred knowledge in Prabakula is thus embedded in other relationships, and the religious discourse that defines social relations and formulates moral obligations takes place in a great diversity of contexts.

The statuses most prominently involved in this are pemangku priests and their ritual assistants (bendesa), and a diversity of balian: astrologers, healers, and advisors of various kinds. In their capacity as teachers, these may all be referred to as guru. Others who transmit knowledge but do not teach are temple possession mediums (sutri), balians who function only as possession mediums, and specialized producers of offerings tukang banten). But laypeople also involve themselves, often very deeply, in religious discourse and thought, especially during their mature years, and a considerable body of esoteric and religious knowledge is maintained in the congregation at large. Particularly striking are the detailed knowledge and manual skills of women in producing the diverse and elaborate offerings that form a prominent part of worship. These, and the corresponding philosophical knowledge of men, are mainly reproduced as a folk tradition through practice within household, family, and congregation.

Life crisis ceremonies provide formal occasions when a great deal of this knowledge is mobilized and objectified. The ceremonies, clearly of great importance to people, articulate and sanctify a particular definition of persons, social relations, and the construction of the community. It is indeed striking that the elaborate life crisis ceremonies practiced among Bali-Hindus have been left unexploited by anthropologists in their attempts to analyze the person definitions that are sustained among Balinese (Geertz [1966] 1973a; Howe 1984; Duff-Cooper 1985; Boon 1990): they seem to contain elaborate ritual statements that define and empower the person.

The moments of a person's life modeled by these life crisis ceremonies with particular salience are entry (at three months), adolescence, and death. The idioms used are elaborate concrete symbols (many in the form of offerings) and collective rites. Their focus is a double one: on the moral qualities of the persons concerned, and on their social relations, embedded in a definition of their circle of most significant others. An analysis of these very elaborate rites, and the additional, quite substantial ones at one year and at marriage, would require a separate and very extensive monograph; at this point I shall merely try to indicate their main formal social organizational entailments.

At the three-month rites *(tiga bulanan)*, the infant — till now conceived as still divine — is for the first time allowed to be placed on the ground, i.e., made into a profane human being; as such it is reintroduced to its ancestors and given a name. This is done in the context of the kin group.

At adolescence, tooth filing *(metatah)* is performed as part of an elaborate death-and-rebirth rite. The points of the canines are (symbolically) removed to eliminate the physical traces of animality and purge the youth of the animal vices: lust, anger, greed, insubordination, drunkenness, and envy. On arising after rebirth, the now responsible adult human is instructed to ask "Who are my parents?" and is led to them and reintroduced. A large circle of kin and friends participate in this sumptuous ceremony.

Mortuary rites, by far the most elaborate, serve to reunite, through a series of stages, the person with Godhead. The salient conception is that the living descendants have the responsibility to perform the rituals necessary to purify the souls of the deceased and thus release them to move toward God and ultimately merge with him. (This does not contradict the issue of reincarnation: "Does the Sun disappear from the heaven when you open the shutters and let it into your room?") This duty is matched by the dead ancestor's power to aid (or damage) descendants in this life.

Briefly, in Prabakula postmortuary rites initially involve burial for commoners, who must wait some years for exhumation and cremation, whereas high-caste persons and pemangku priests must be kept above ground, mummified, or cremated directly. The culminating cremation rites may be performed collectively for deceased members of a descent group and their wives. Cremation is paid for by the dead persons' heirs. It involves agnates, bilateral kin, and affines as mourners, who wear a white headband during a phase of the proceedings. It is performed through the collective work of the *krama banjar adat*, the citizens of the custom-law ward. There follow also a number of postcremation rites, attended by family only.

The immediate spiritual and social consequence of these rites, and of the continuing ancestor worship, is the incorporation of the deceased as continuing members of the community and spiritual guides and protectors to their descendants. Good fortune and prosperity are the results of their blessing, while many of life's misfortunes may be caused by their anger or their withdrawal of support because of your misdemeanors. They also remain part of your active social world: through spirit mediums you may call them to you for long, elaborate meetings and consultations; and during certain annual celebrations (Kuningan), and the life crises of family members, they rejoin their families for visits that extend over days and nights. It is thus necessary to recognize that the community of Prabakula embraces both the living and their ancestors as active members for a wide range of purposes; the ancestors are not only a source of moral sanctions, but also participants in terms of their knowledge and their agency. Spontaneous, socially decisive actions are understood to be initiated by this invisible sector of the family as well as by its living members.

The other important link with the ancestors is through succession to land. Land in Prabakula normally passes to males in male line only, while daughters who remain unmarried will be allocated a (smaller) share of the patrimony. Alternatively, in the absence of male heirs a (preferably related) son-in-law may be settled uxorilocally and adopted into the group, allowing succession to this couple and the couple's children.

But there are also important material implications of the fact that cremations are extremely expensive and must precede the permanent division of the dead person's estate. In the normal course of events, when a senior landowning man dies and is buried, his heirs will make a temporary division of usufruct of his fields, which may also, with some difficulty, be adjusted to changing needs. Costs of the ultimate cremation, which should be proportionate to the wealth, are so substantial that the rite has, somewhat inappropriately, been compared to a potlatch (Hooykaas 1964a:235). Geertz (1980, esp. 98–102, 116–20, 231–35), who focuses on the royal cremations but cites the relevant literature, calls into question the extent to which it is regularly performed among commoners. In Prabakula, as in most Bali-Hindu communities in the north, there is no doubt that performing it is the overwhelming rule, even in families without landed property, and that it may be done on three levels: small, medium, and great. "Small" is appropriate for households without land; "medium" corresponds to a level of expenditure equivalent to approximately half the value of the land inherited from the dead person; while "great" requires a very sumptuous ritual indeed. The scale required will frequently be specified by the spirit of the deceased through a possession medium. This was the case in the cremation in which we participated most fully, in another community, which was specified as "medium" but involved a sum equivalent to thirty thousand dollars in 1987.

These pressures generate two major sets of consequences. On the one hand, heirs are encouraged to postpone exhumation and cremation of the deceased as long as possible, to be allowed the temporary use of his full landed estate. Counterpressures to proceed with the cremation are conceptualized as the ancestor's own impatience, signaled by increasing illness, bad luck, or strife within the family, and/or the deceased's own verbal demand through trance-possessed family members or professional mediums. Delays of up to thirty or forty years are common, at which time accumulated children and junior collaterals of the descent group who have died in the meanwhile will be cremated simultaneously. (The above-mentioned cremation, for which we have complete records, involved ten adults and thirty-five children). Prabakula does not allow, as do some communities, nonrelated dependents or impoverished families to take advantage of the festivities by having their deceased cremated also. A direct consequence of these rules is that descent groups who own land postpone internal segmentation, staying together as linked households with shared interests in an estate for an additional generation after the death of the joint ancestor.

The other consequence of these institutions is a drastic rate of turnover in the circulation of land — where on the order of half of every estate in almost every generation is sold to cover the costs of cremation — and also a tendency toward redistribution of land within the community, since the more wealthy families tend to dissipate proportionally more land on these occasions. There is a concern to avoid land sales to nonresidents, which ensures a predominantly internal redistribution of the land in the village. Since the scale of cremation is conceptually linked to a fraction of the landed estate, not to a specific sum of money, the price obtained in sale need not be ruthlessly maximized on a larger market. As a result, smallholders with modest savings in the village will have recurring opportunities to purchase plots of village land — which, incidentally, will not be part of the estate inherited from their father and so do not enter into the pool that will be reduced at his cremation but remain intact until their own, many years after their death. Thus an active and relatively moderately priced market for land is created, facilitating the circulation and redistribution of land within the community.

FORMAL ASSOCIATIONS

The banjar adat (custom-law ward) normally defines the body of persons who cooperate in the cremation ceremonies of its members. It is indeed often spoken of as a formal association *(sekaha)* for this purpose. The template of the formal association, based either on voluntary membership or some allocational membership criterion, is a widely used organizational form in Bali. We shall explore its implications in the organization of irrigation and agricultural cooperation in chapter 4. But there are also a number of other sekaha with more limited importance and scope in Prabakula, which organize primarily artistic activities and include several *gamelan* orchestras, a troupe of *legong* dancers for the temples, etc. It is a point of community pride that the village should be self-sufficient in such matters and not have to bring in performers and groups from the outside. Artistic forms that citizens do not pursue, like barong dances, are not welcomed as part of temple and village festivals.

All the major temples of Prabakula have their *odalan* annual festivals, timed according to the ancient Bali-Hindu lunar-solar calendar, not the post-Majapahit Java-Hindu "permutational" calendar that predominates in the south. The culminating festival of the year in Prabakula is that of their pura desa. Special ad hoc formal committees are formed for this purpose each year, and all the village citizens (krama desa) are made to join in the dances at that time. It is a general feature of all these sekaha that membership status is egalitarian: high-caste and commoners sit on the same level, may touch each other reciprocally, and are deferred to in proportion to their competence in the particular task of the association, not in terms of their rank.

PROBLEMATICS

What I have presented so far of the social organization of Prabakula still falls far short as an introduction to the community. I have left out the whole topic of production (but will say something about its organization in chapter 4); I have not touched on the way Prabakula functions as a polity (a part of which will be told in chapter 9); I have given small fragments only of the intricate and very human religious life and cosmology the villagers construct in the Bali-Hindu tradition (though some of this will be indicated in chapter 12). It is, in brief, an incomplete and skeletal account of some of the formalia of village organization.

Yet it is necessary to have these facts in place to have a first view of the village. In the following chapters, however, I shall not be primarily concerned to flesh it out, no matter how engaging the design of these organizations, and the forms of life they entail, might be. The main problematics toward which I aim is otherwise, and it is dominated by an anthropological enigma, which can be formulated briefly as follows. Whatever organizations, institutions, and conceptions I could describe from Prabakula would constitute only one fortuitously selected "ethnography," depicting one set of machineries among many that different groups and different circles in Bali reproduce, embrace, and live by. Beyond the rather Sisyphean task of wanting to describe this variety, I should like to place myself in a position where I could say something insightful about how this diversity comes about and is maintained. For one thing, do the other village organizations presuppose and create other people? Or does the variation make no difference? With our concept of "culture," anthropologists have tended to celebrate the remarkable fitness of a community's institutions and organizations to each other, to the local and material circumstances, and to the consciousness and personality of those who live by them.

If I had chosen to reside in Prabakula all my time in Bali, or twice that again, I might have been in a position to produce just such an account, in sensitive and compelling detail. Yet this greatly enhanced ethnography might well have served to seduce my readers into that complacent set of fictions in which anthropologists habitually dwell, built on a totalizing "culture," a finely wrought "holism," and a one-dimensional "relativity" of a world of humankind divided into "localities."

And such an account of Prabakula, true as it might be in its particulars, would not engage the painful, puzzling truth that all these facts could well have been different, would probably be different ten years hence or ten years ago, and are different in every other community on the bountiful northern slope of Bali.

To drive this important realization firmly home, let me therefore pass on to the neighboring village of Pagatepan, so as to sample the variation about which I speak.

3

Pagatepan: A Muslim Balinese Village

I next present a true anomaly, a traditional Balinese village community composed of practicing, orthodox Muslims. Pagatepan is a community of 3,714 inhabitants according to the 1980 census, cultivating an area of approximately eleven hundred hectares ranging from 450 to 1,220 meters in altitude; at first glance, it is just another high-slope village among many in the upper zone of cultivation on the north slope of Bali.

The villagers, however, rightly see themselves as exceptional: members of the only true faith, surrounded by a vast sea of Hindus. No doubt for this reason they tend to adopt an isolationist, traditionalist, and often bellicose attitude to the surrounding society. While their speech is Balinese, of a relatively high or polite variant, their customs are in a number of ways distinctive, and they marry overwhelmingly within their community. No Hindu shrine of any kind is allowed inside village premises. Indeed, about five hundred Hindus do reside within the village area of Pagatepan; but they are tenants and laborers who have drifted in as expanding coffee and clove cultivation in the higher forest zone has created opportunities for employment. Together with some poor Muslim houses they make up a separate ward, or banjar, of 618 inhabitants, composed of unstable and scattered residences and exerting minimal influence on the village as a whole.

The main wards of Pagatepan are exclusively Muslim: the East-of-road (Timur Jalan) and West-of-road (Barat Jalan) wards of a nucleated village settlement with populations of 740 and 795 respectively, and a dispersed settlement area forming a further administrative ward of 1,561 inhabitants.

An initial question naturally concerns the genetic relations of the village

44

culture of Pagatepan. The traditional history of the kingdom of Bule-leng — the Babad Buleleng — links the origins of the village to the exploits of the founder of the kingdom, Panji Sakti, in his conquest of Brangbangan in East Java. "The ruler of Solo heard of the victory of Sri Panji Sakti. The two were joined in warm friendship. Sri Panji Sakti was presented with an elephant as his mount. . . . For the elephant, which was like Airawanasti, a stable (*petak*) was built to the north of the town (of Singaraja). That is why that particular *patani* is called Petak. Of the three Javanese whom the ruler of Solo furnished to look after the elephant, two dwelt in a *patani* in the north of Petak. That is why it is called Patani Jawa. The other one dwelt in Lingga, close to the beach at Toya Mala, because he came from Prabu-lingga on the island of Java. . . . So it was told of old. After a long time, when the Javanese dwelling in Patani Jawa had grown considerably in number, they were split in two by order of the king and went to settle in the forest of Pagatepan. . . . They are the forefathers of the *tindik* (guardi-ans) of the mountains" (Worsley 1972:18–19).

The villagers' own pedigrees recognize an additional strand of origin in Bugis (Sulawesian) settlers who have subsequently joined the elephant-keepers' descendants in Pagatepan. Though Javanese (patrilineal) origins are regarded as the more prestigious, the two components have effectively consolidated into a single community. No family traces any specific prac-tice or custom to external origins, and no traditions of non-Balinese speech have been retained. The characteristic male headdress, still largely worn by Pagatepan men, is regarded as distinctive to Muslims, not as a sign of a local or ethnic category. Whatever the changing historical con-tacts of this community have been over the centuries, their own perception and that of their neighbors sees them as locals, and indeed in many re-spects more conservative locals than the residents of surrounding Hindu villages. This cultural conservatism reflects their relative isolation, the re-sult of their own truculent enmity and frequent violent skirmishes with neighboring villages, their suspicion of colonial (Christian) and present provincial (Hindu) administration, and a notoriety for thievery and vio-lence. Their isolationist attitudes are illustrated by village reaction when Pagatepan in 1976 was to be linked by a short feeder road to a major traffic artery: influential voices among them warned that this otherwise desirable development should be rejected, as it entailed the construction of a small bridge that would reduce the village's ability to fend off hostile attacks.

In summary, I read this rather diverse evidence to indicate that it is reasonable to view Pagatepan in the context of variations in traditional Balinese village structure, and that we would be less justified in interpreting it as an intrusive and culturally alien ethnic enclave in the North Balinese countryside.

MARRIAGE AND KINSHIP

Are recognizable, all-Bali features of formal social organization shared by Pagatepan and Prabakula? The basic building block of the Pagatepan community is the household, characteristically based on a single married couple but allowing both for solitary residence and extended family arrangements. The prevalence of a nuclear or elementary family pattern is indicated by the census materials: despite a population structure with about 50 percent of the population under fifteen years of age, the average household size in the three main wards of Pagatepan is 4.5 persons per household — indeed the same as in Prabakula. Pagatepan similarly lacks the houseyard organization characteristic of South Bali but rare in the north. Each household forms an independent and spatially distinct unit, wherever space and wealth permit in the form of a detached house with a small front garden. The nucleated settlement has a layout based on a ring road (only partly realized because of the steepness of the terrain) and a north-south lane separating the two wards; within each ward is a simple grid of roughly east-west and north-south lanes and paths. The dispersed wards, on the other hand, have widely scattered homesteads. On the western edge of the nucleated settlement are the village mosque (above) and the village office and meeting house (below).

Marriage is the basic relationship that establishes the prerequisites for the formation of a new household. Couples show a clear preference for neolocal residence and establish a new household quickly unless they are heavily dependent on a joint economic activity with their parents or can obtain a significantly better standard of housing by temporary joint residence, or if the husband is much absent on labor migration. If the marriage is not neolocal, it is almost invariably patri-virilocal. Cohabitation is strictly regulated by the legal framework for marriage as provided by the Muslim law of Shariah in its Shafi interpretation. The essential requirement is a written document, drawn up by an officiator, specifying the names of the groom, the bride, and the bride's representative and stipulating the dowry from groom to bride (Arabic: *mahar;* Balinese: *meskawi/mas kawin*). This should be a piece of land, though of late it has occasionally been a sum of money. Custom recognizes two modes of procedure for marriage: arrangement *(ngeh* or *maideh)* or elopement/abduction *(merangkat)*; the customs surrounding these two forms are sketched below. Marriages are expected to be stable but can be dissolved in agreement with Islamic law. Of 226 married persons in a sample census, 27 had experienced a divorce. Polygyny is not infrequent: of the hundred male heads of households enumerated in a detailed census, ten were living in plural unions. Widowed or divorced persons tend to remarry swiftly unless they have some strong personal reason not to, or where the person has reached an advanced age and joins a married child in residence.

Bars to marriage are based on the Shariah; those arising out of kinship are mainly lineal relationship, first-order collateral relationship, and the ban on unlawful conjunction of closely related women as co-wives. Marriage choices have been very heavily endogamous among villagers who remain resident in Pagatepan; but with increasing mobility this may be declining slightly. Girls from Pagatepan are not allowed to marry Hindus, whereas Hindu girls are occasionally married by merangkat, in which case they convert to Islam in connection with the marriage. While I was in Pagatepan, one such converted woman was widowed, and her family wished for her to return to their (Hindu) village. The response in Pagatepan was to find her a suitable spouse in the village of Pagatepan, lodge her in the headman's house for the duration of her *iddah* period (the forty days of postbereavement impurity when remarriage is banned by Islam), and marry her off on the forty-first day. Ex-Hindu wives make up less than 1 percent of female spouses in Pagatepan, other out-of-village wives about 3 percent.

Birth places the person in a kinship system that is basically bilateral in its terminology and in most aspects of its application. This is most clearly seen in how the criterion of bifurcation is entirely ignored throughout the terminology, i.e., father's and mother's sides are not distinguished in the terms for uncle (*maman*), aunt (*bibi*), grandfather (*kaki*), grandmother (*dadong*), and their reciprocals. Indeed these reciprocals in Pagatepan also entirely disregard collaterality and sex and so are reduced to the purely generational terms *panak* (child, sibling's child) and *cucu* (child's child).

A notable feature of most variants of Balinese kinship terminologies is their emphasis on relative age in ego's generation: in Pagatepan *beli* (elder brother, elder male cousin) and *mbok/mo(k)* (elder sister, elder female cousin) versus *adi* (younger sibling, younger cousin). Many North Balinese Hindus also employ the criterion of relative age to men in the parents' generation (*wa* is senior uncle, *maman* is junior uncle, but *bibi* is aunt). This is not done in Pagatepan, however, which in this respect is structurally if not terminologically more like South Bali (Geertz and Geertz 1975:170). Pagatepan differs from the south, on the other hand, and is like the rest of the north in distinguishing father *(bapak)* and mother *(mimi)* from the uncle and aunt terms. People in Pagatepan also prefer the option of using the terms *misan* (cousin) and *mindon* (second cousin) instead of classificatory sibling terms in reference to cousins; in this they seem also to differ from practice in South Bali (ibid.:172 n. 2) and again give greater emphasis to the integrity of the nuclear family.

Family allegiance in village conflicts is likewise bilateral and expected to embrace misan, so that one is, for example, excused from practicing normal civilities toward the murderer of one's cousin and is expected to support cousins in disputes without regard to the merits of the case.

The rules of inheritance, on the other hand, in following Shafi law to the letter, favor males and agnatic heirs over females and persons linked through females but do not, as in Prabakula, eliminate the latter entirely: widows are reserved a share, daughters inherit half the share of sons, and female heirs are in some circumstances favored before distant agnatic collaterals. The agnatic line is thus significantly less favored than among the Bali-Hindus; there is a greater fragmentation of shares in inheritance; and the estate is divided immediately on the death of a person, so there will be no undivided estates to hold minimal descent groups together.

Nonetheless there is a certain recognition of patrilineal groupings, since family histories and family origins are conceptualized in terms of the male line. Genealogies are not kept and are usually not known beyond two deceased generations; but people will speak of "good family" if one or several illustrious persons are known among the deceased agnatic relatives. Most mature individuals also have an idea of a family origin and history: from the Javanese elephant-keeper, and a descendant of his who established the family in Pagatepan; or, for example, from a member of the retinue of King Yusuf of Boni in Sulawesi, who settled with his king in the Kampung Bugis in Singaraja, and one of whose descendants in turn settled in Pagatepan. But despite such ideas, no descent groups and segments emerge, as they do so clearly in the undivided estates and the ancestor-worshiping congregations of Prabakula.

Likewise, nothing in the various local theories of conception can give force to a patrilineal descent ideology. The Islamic legal and religious position as taught in Pagatepan goes so far as to deny any legal importance to physical paternity. Thus in a discussion of illegitimacy, one of the leading religious teachers expounded to me how a child born less than six months after the parents were married is *panat binjat*, out-of-wedlock. There is nothing a father can do to legitimize such a child. While there is some disagreement among the Ulama, the religious teachers, on this question, the generally accepted construct stresses that from the genitor comes only a little bit of water, whereas from the mother comes the whole body of the child, so the out-of-wedlock child must be related to its mother and inherits from her but is no relation to the genitor and cannot inherit from him. Indeed, an out-of-wedlock girl can theoretically be married to her own genitor. Religious teachers in Pagatepan cite a tradition that tells of the Prophet Musa walking with his teacher the Prophet Haidar. They see an illegitimate child on the road, and Prophet Haidar kills the child. The Prophet Musa is shocked, but Prophet Haidar explains: "There is nothing wrong with the child, so it will go to Paradise now. But if it reaches the age of reason, as an illegitimate it is outside Islam, so it will surely be damned. Better to send it to Paradise now!" In this view marriage is not merely an authorization and approbation of procreation and a legitimization of paternity — it is the prerequisite that creates the relationships of paternity and agnation, which thus arise from marriage only and are legal and spiritual, not physical, in origin.

As the religious teacher commented, this is the Islamic view, not Balinese folk belief; "look how the Balinese [Hindus] regularly cohabit, even give birth, before getting married!" Indeed, folk models of conception in North Bali, which the villagers of Pagatepan also share, seem to be entirely bilateral. All parts of the child — its bones, blood, face — are considered to arise from the mixture of both father's and mother's substances, though the more generous person of the two tends to give more of his or her substance to the child and thus influences its looks and character somewhat more strongly.

TEACHERS AND PUPILS

Where persons in Prabakula are locked into a number of different, overlapping ritual collectives through descent and locality, an entirely different concept organizes the spiritual life of people in Pagatepan. One could argue for a certain formal analogue between the Bali-Hindu village temples and the single village mosque/congregation of Pagatepan; but its philosophical bases are different, in that the local mosque is seen only as the local embodiment of the *umma*, the universal Muslim congregation. Thus a person from Pagatepan who moves elsewhere sheds his link to the local mosque. The only enduring link is that between teacher and pupil, and this is a relationship of spiritual filiation, modeled on physical filiation but ideologically overshadowing it. Every child is enrolled with a religious teacher, a guru, to be taught the basics of religion so he/she can in due course reach majority and become a full-fledged adult Muslim and member of the congregation.[3] This training establishes an irrepudiable relationship to the guru whereby the person becomes his disciple *(murid)* for life. Pagatepan people speak of the triple submission to one's father, to one's guru, and to God. No matter how high one may rise in secular status or in religious scholarship, one always owes one's guru submissive respect, expressing the spiritual parenthood of the guru toward his murid. Whenever murid meets guru, he/she should kiss both sides of the teacher's hand: the back of the hand as an expression of respect, and the inside to receive *barkat*, blessing, from him. This power to grant blessing arises from the guru's position as successor to the Prophet in his capacity as religious teacher and guide.

The guru-murid relationship is ideally, and commonly, one of enduring reciprocity through life. After reaching his/her majority, the *murid* attends the guru's lessons for adult groups and uses him as a personal and spiritual advisor. Child pupils are expected to perform chores, such as fetching drinking water and collecting firewood, for the guru. In adult life such services are transformed and perpetuated, serving both as a delayed reciprocity for the spiritual benefits one received in childhood and youth and as a partial recompense for the teaching which one's own children now are receiving from the guru.

The murid's prestations should comprise three main components: respect and acknowledgment, gifts, and labor services. These are all voluntary but morally compelling; the extent to which they are given varies considerably. Respect entails a broad range of expressions, from greeting and honoring the guru appropriately in public to the reaffirmation implied in regular visiting and personal consultation. Gifts, *siddiqah* (from Arabic *sa-daqah* = alms), may be small or large but should add up to a continuous flow. "When harvesting the rice crop, you give rice; when the coffee is picked, you give a sack of coffee. If after finishing studies with the guru you move up and live in the forest, then on Friday when you come to the mosque, you must think: I want to bring wood for my guru. That is siddiqah!" If you happen to enter the same bus as your guru, you pay his fare; when Guru Ali Akbar was fined by the authorities for practicing Shariah in defiance of modern Indonesian law, the village headman who accompanied him promptly paid his fine; giving a daughter in marriage to the guru, or land to him for his sustenance, is likewise siddiqah.

---

3. *Guru* is the general and widest term for teacher, also generally used for the imam of the mosque and for any singularly formative teacher, mentor, or paragon. *Ustadz*, teacher/master, may also be used for this status, as well as for teachers in government schools.

Third, a guru may call on his murids to provide labor for such tasks as the cultivation of his fields and construction or repair of his house.[4] This comes under the somewhat wider label of *nulungin*, unpaid labor. Nulungin also comprises the (reciprocal) work one does for neighbors and friends at the time of bereavement ("Because they know: we all die once") and labor services to all the religious officials/elite of Pagatepan. But it is the labor for one's own *Guru* that constitutes the prototype nulungin service. It may entail all phases of work in agriculture except harvesting: plowing if one has the tools and animals for traction, planting, weeding, etc. At the time of harvest, on the other hand, North Balinese conventions enjoin obligation and generosity in the other direction: *from* the landowner who receives life's bounty *to* the poor and propertyless who give labor and deserve a bountiful share.

During nulungin work, the laborers are given food and coffee, which are brought and served beside the field by a deputed woman, normally not the guru's wife. With increasing monetization of the local economy, gurus now sometimes offer their laborers day wages — at a low basic wage, about half of what a person without influence must pay to raise labor. Murids, on their part, often refuse this payment when it is offered. "But then the guru should be wise, and give them the equivalent in rice instead of money."

Even in response to an individual request to a murid for labor, there is no formal sanction if the murid fails to comply. "You may go to the guru and excuse yourself, explaining that your child is sick, or that you have this or that commitment. Or perhaps you just do not turn up. Then, the guru will not say anything — but other villagers will criticize you; and when you see the guru, you will feel ashamed." The guru, on his side, is likewise morally constrained to give his blessing, barkat, to his murids. "But perhaps you judge that the pupil has not yet done his lesson and so is not deserving of barkat — then you can withhold it, until the lesson has been done."

There is a tendency for filial succession in the guru-murid relationship, so the father brings his children to his own guru, and the son of the guru succeeds to his father's circle of murids. But one is also free to attend religious classes with other teachers than one's guru, to enroll one's children

---

4. A guru who had moved from Pagatepan to another community and was engaged in constructing a *madrasah* (Muslim school) there reflected on this Pagatepan custom: "Here, you must first get together the materials; then hire a carpenter and a mason. But in Pagatepan, it is the other way around: *first* you hire a carpenter. Then, when people see there is a carpenter ready to build the madrasah, they are respectful of the guru and will *bring* the wood and necessary materials, and assist in the work!"

with the teacher of one's choice, and to establish a primary relation to a teacher other than the son at the death of one's guru. There can thus be major shifts in the effective followings of different religious teachers, reflecting their relative scholarship, charisma, and popularity.

There are presently eleven active guru teachers (one of whom is a woman) in the community, with somewhat various followings and efficacy. The most forceful of them draw large classes, separately of children, men, and women. Since the middle 1970s, however, there has also been a government elementary school in Pagatepan, which most children attend and to which the gurus' teaching times and routines have had to adjust. The less charismatic gurus complain about the changing times: "Now parents come only *once* to see the guru with their children (to enroll them), and after that they never come again. And the children lie to their parents: they say they go to the guru, but go elsewhere. Parents no longer control their children, and many do not care."

The content of the Gurus' teaching is reading and reciting the Koran, in Arabic and translation, and the Hadith (traditions), in translation; and the pedagogical principle is repetition. Repetition strengthens the faith and makes the religious precepts grow inside the person, becoming embodied like internal organs. Morals and Islam, the guru will explain, are not to be understood and judged; they should be accepted and internalized and rest on the guru's authority. True submission to God is not just (knowledge of) Islam, but *mumin* — a union of Islam and *iman*, faith, and therefore also harmony/unity of the community.

COMMUNITY AND CONGREGATION

On the highest level of organization, Pagatepan achieves a unity that is perhaps the exception in Balinese village organization but is held up as a desired ideal: a united congregation, worshiping in one common mosque and forming a single temporal community. On the one hand, they are constituted as a single body for religious purposes; on the secular side, they are likewise one in that the unit of administration, the government village with its headmanship, coincides with the unit of custom law, the desa adat.

The central mosque around which this unity is based, the Jami' Sofinatus Salam, lies on the western edge of the Barat ward of Pagatepan's central village. It is located on *wakaf* (dedicated land) and in part sustained by eleven small plots of irrigated rice land, which have similarly been donated as wakaf and total approximately 1.5 hectares. Other small unattended mosques, graveyards, etc., comprise an additional two hectares of dry land. There is also a *kramat*, a blessed site, where according to traditional accounts a Muslim teacher and holy person hid and was saved from a pursuing Hindu army.

The mosque is a well-maintained building of unknown antiquity capable of accommodating the whole male population of Pagatepan. Its raised floor may not be trodden upon by women or nonbelievers: an attempt by a senior Indonesian administrative official, a Hindu, to visit the building was prevented by collective force and precipitated a minor riot. It contains the usual structures and facilities of a mosque, as well as the characteristic Indonesian *bedug* drum, which is used in place of the *muezzin* to call to prayer (though now loudspeakers and a recorded *azan* also signal prayer times). It also contains a *bencret*, a sundial, relied on if other timepieces fail.

The chief official of the mosque is the *imam*, usually entitled guru and also sometimes described as *penghulu* (scholar or wise man). He is assisted by a *bilal* who is responsible for signaling the times of prayers (though he generally lets young boys play the drum), sweeps the mosque and keeps it clean, and replaces the imam at prayer and sermons should he be prevented from performing. The Pagatepan mosque has two such vice-imams. The other major officer is the *bendehara*, among Hindus primarily a calendrical and ritual expert but here in Pagatepan the treasurer of the mosque and the wakaf. He receives all gifts (called wakaf whether in money, land, or naturalia), converts them and the produce of wakaf land rents into money, and keeps the accounts, which are posted annually in the mosque premises.

The active congregation is composed of all males who have reached *akil baleg*, the age of reason. They recognize the duty to attend the Friday noon sermon and prayer in the main mosque, as well as the prayers at the major calendrical festivals. The weekly scene on Fridays has considerable formality. There are early arrivals who wish to perform two extra and meritorious prayers beforehand, during which time the main body of the congregation progressively arrives. All are dressed in their best clothes, greet friends and neighbors ceremoniously, perform their ablutions, and line up, with serious and somber faces. Many people have regular places; the more wealthy or pious bring prayer mats. The imam arrives at the right moment, leads the prayers, and gives the sermon; the final prayer ends in a climaxing *zikhr*.[5] Sometimes the imam also makes public announcements to the Friday congregation, or he allows other village seniors to make a

5. "*La illah ilallah*" rhythmically repeated in chorus ninety-nine times, with a slight lateral rocking of the head, in slowly increasing tempo up to a final burst, and then breaking with the exclamation "*Allah ho akbar!*"

Mosque and village street of Pagatepan.

public address on a topic of general concern. At the end, the congregation disperses abruptly and swiftly but then recomposes itself into small, inter-visiting, kinship and friendship groups around coffee in private houses, exchanging commentaries and gossip.

The assembled congregation never acts as a deliberating or decision-making body but sees itself as being governed by a committee, the Majlis Ulama or conclave of religious scholars. I shall return below to its compo-sition and mode of operation. As for its functions, this is the body that selects the imam, adjudicates conflicts according to the Shariah, and artic-ulates village policies. People in Pagatepan see the Majlis Ulama as their leadership and government, the source of authoritative and legitimate col-lective decisions.

Civil government, on the other hand, is vested in the *kepala desa*, village headman, generally known as perbekel (though the official title of this po-sition has been changed several times in recent years). The headman is elected for an eight-year term by the villagers. He is a salaried public offi-cial, as is his vice-perbekel, who is chosen by the perbekel and assists him in accounting, census-keeping, etc. For each of the four village wards, the banjars, there is also a *klian banjar*, leader of the ward, who coordinates village voluntary work and security. On the banjar level the villagers also recognize the characteristically pan-Balinese institution of the assembly or village meeting *(bale banjar* or *powm)*, though in Pagatepan such assemblies seem no longer to be called. As a physical structure, the bale or assembly hall is merely a roofed platform connected with the perbekel's office; and the meetings that take place there today are informational and instruc-tional only, initiated by various visiting extension officers of public depart-ments (health, agriculture, education), to which selected villagers are es-pecially summoned.

The banjar is also the unit in terms of which local security is organized. There is no policeman posted in Pagatepan; and rural security of property and crops is, as in most Balinese villages, in the hands of a communally organized vigilante force of younger men, called *hanship* or *karang teruna*. The effectiveness of this organization depends on the firmness and effec-tiveness of civil government in the village, however, and therefore varies with time and locality. During my period of fieldwork, the organization was in abeyance in the two wards of the nuclear village settlement, because its leader had himself committed crop theft. The inefficiency of security measures is bewailed by concerned villagers in Pagatepan and is sometimes nostalgically contrasted with conditions before, when the village practiced its own, autochtonous system of rotating duties as sentries *(ronda)* and watchmen *(midiyan)*.

The perbekel's office is the link that connects the village with all higher levels of government and is the key organ of village administration from the point of view of the state. But within the village and in conformity with village custom — which for many purposes is recognized in Bali as having the force of law — the perbekel is subordinate to the Majlis Ulama and should always act in accordance with its directives and wishes. In this sense, Pagatepan shows the same discongruity between the "government village" *(desa dinas)* and the "village of custom" (desa adat) found so frequently elsewhere in Bali, although their territorial boundaries coincide.

LAND

Pagatepan is an agrarian community, and land is the essential means of nearly all forms of production. Variations in the elevation and the accessibility to irrigation of the land within the village territory produce a basic zoning of this resource. Proceeding from lower areas toward higher, the zones are, according to village records, roughly these: irrigated rice land, 10 hectares; lower mountain zone of predominantly clove cultivation, 325 hectares; higher mountain zone of predominantly coffee cultivation, 525 hectares; steep and high forest, 130 hectares; house sites, various, unclassified, 102 hectares.

The patterns of land ownership and formal tenure vary remarkably between different communities in Bali (Korn 1932); but those of Pagatepan and Prabakula do not happen to be so very discrepant. In Pagatepan practically all land is owned as individual private property, regulated by Muslim law. There is also a history of legislation and regulation of land ownership, but this body of rules is not particularly relevant to tenure and transactions in Pagatepan. The Japanese administration attempted a comprehensive mapping and recording of all land rights in 1943, and these records are still extant in the regency administration; but villagers in Pagatepan have no deeds to their property derived from these records. In principle, all owners should today have a certificate of ownership. But to obtain one is an elaborate and costly procedure, and very few owners obtain them. The district office can also issue certificates of sale, but sales may take place without such documentation.

Land is unevenly distributed in the population, and most households are propertyless. The village census describes 147 households as landowning farmers, 631 as sharecroppers, 70 as farm hands, and 20 as shopowners. A generation ago the wealthiest villagers owned as much as forty hectares of land; today the largest properties are below ten hectares. Title to land circulates through dowry, inheritance, sale, and mortgage. Access to land for production is also conveyed by lease and sharecropping contracts, and such lands as the larger owners retain their control of may be cultivated by hired hands, day labor, or the nulungin voluntary labor mentioned above.

Inheritance follows Shariah. Together with the systematic endowment of brides with a certain amount of real property as mas kawin at their marriage, this directs a flow of about one-third of all land to women. The management of a woman's land in production, however, is generally vested in her husband.

Land can also be freely bought and sold, with the constraint that sale is not supposed to be to persons resident outside the district. However, sale by a Muslim to a Hindu is severely disapproved, and the Shariah's option of first rights of purchase to owners of adjacent plots is acknowledged. Since most sales are negotiated in secret, and neighbors will probably not in any case have the money to match the bids provided by other buyers, these limitations are in effect rather illusory, and they can further be evaded by mortgaging arrangements. One villager summarized attitudes regarding sale of land as follows: "To sell land so as to buy other, more conveniently located, land is unobjectionable. To sell land so as to make other investments, for example in a *bemo* transport vehicle, is unwise. To sell it and use the money to no purpose is bad; it is also against religion."

There is a widely voiced concern at present that villagers are selling much land to Hindus, thereby eroding the very bases for the persistence of Pagatepan as an autonomous Muslim enclave. Since 1977 administration records show a net loss of approximately five hectares per year from Muslim to Hindu owners. This record is probably fairly complete for transactions involving Hindus, since certificates of legally valid purchase are necessary for them to have any hopes of exercising proprietary rights to Pagatepan lands. Nonetheless, these lands are clearly regarded by them as high-risk property, as indicated by high figures on circulation *between* Hindus of what is still only a small total area in their possession. The net loss of village lands to outsider Hindu owners (Hindus inside Pagatepan are too poor to buy) is thus well below 1 percent of the total land area per annum. This is less dramatic than what the villagers suspect and fear; but it reverses the historical trend to which they are accustomed whereby they were the ones who encroached on Hindu lands and expanded their village area, both in the 1930s and 1940s and most recently during the unrest in 1965.

The rate of circulation by sale within the village between Muslims, on the other hand, is probably greater than recorded, since such purchasers are not so dependent on official documents to have their titles validated.

However, with prices in the middle 1980s running at the rate of three to six hundred thousand rupees per hectare, few villagers among them can afford to accumulate land very quickly. The rates of circulation are thus clearly reduced from those that traditionally sustained the pattern of distribution. They are also significantly lower than those generated by Bali-Hindu practices in Prabakula.

The alternative ways of gaining access to land for cultivation, on the other hand, seem not to have changed significantly and are also similar to those practiced in Prabakula. Where sufficient land is not owned by the farmer and his spouse, plots are sought on sharecropping terms, generally referred to as *nyakap*. The normal division of seasonal crops is 1 : 1, with harvest assistance from outside labor paid for jointly by owner and sharecropper. Coffee groves, on the other hand, are generally given on a 3 : 1 contract *(ngam-patin)*; the sharecropper tends, weeds, and guards and is assisted in the harvesting by labor paid out of the produce, i.e., one-quarter by the sharecropper and three-quarters by the owner, who also provides food and snacks during harvesting. Alternatively, unharvested crops may be sold to middleman buyers, who arrange for harvest by hired work groups.

Housesites, on the other hand, can be obtained without payment if one has no such property, even within the nucleated village. Vacant houses are also lent to kinspeople, friends, or the needy without recompense.

IRRIGATION

Whereas land as a production factor is thus held and managed individually and atomistically, the provision of water is organized on an entirely different pattern. As elsewhere in Bali, irrigation is in the hands of the collective *subak*, the irrigation association. The rules and regulations of the subak are governed by village custom, and records and accounts are kept by an elected *klian subak*, head of the irrigation association.

Only a minor part of Pagatepan lands are irrigated, but the terraced and irrigated *sawah* for intensive rice agriculture provides the villagers with their staple food and, with modern seeds and management, yields continuously at the rate of two to three crops per year. Irrigation water is also used to support intensive cultivation of orchard fruits, vegetables, vanilla, and other crops.

Access to irrigation water is also regulated between villages. The smaller stream along the western border of Pagatepan land is used by other, lower villages. The larger stream to the east is shared with one neighboring Hindu village. Traditionally the waters were divided with a large wooden dam gate with sluice notches *(tambuku)*, which gave sixty-five parts to Pagatepan and thirty-five to their neighbours. In the 1970s a modern dam was built by the government, and since 1977 Pagatepan has received its water via a modern, lined channel from this dam. In the village it divides into four branches, from east to west the Blalu drawing 22 *taktak* measures of water, Balimuntung with 22¾ taktak, Desa with 37¾ taktak, and Kajirkaw with 27 taktak. Of the desa (village) branch, 25 taktak are *yeh banyon*, water for village domestic consumption. There are also some limited fields watered from local springs. From the four main branches, small side canals *(pumacahan)* lead off to groups of fields. Each of these is listed in the klian subak's record of water rights, e.g., 8½ taktak in one side channel, followed by a list of proprietors and their respective shares of this flow: Abdur Rasid 1½ taktak, Abdullah 1 taktak, etc.

I shall return in the next chapter to the comparison of irrigation associations and agricultural production as organized in Pagatepan and Prabakula and in other North Balinese villages. But what we have seen so far can be summarized as showing pervasive and significant differences in the organization of ownership, tenure, management, and circulation of land between the two communities. Differences in custom law (e.g., of inheritance) and the indirect effects of other differences of custom that dictate other concerns and necessities (e.g., the practice of expensive cremations) generate very contrastive contexts for agricultural activity, despite similar technology, external administration, market regime and ecologic constraints.

VOLUNTARY ASSOCIATIONS

In common with other Balinese villages, Pagatepan has a certain number of voluntary associations. These focus on musical performances: *burdah*, *hadrah*, and *sambroh*, of which only the former two are traditional.

Burdah is a drum orchestra of twenty-four members with an elected leader. Membership depends on four qualifications: being an adult male; demonstrating the capacity to read Barzanji's Arabic poem "Qassidah Burdah"; providing the burdah instrument, a large drum with a thick oxhide skin; and having the appropriate uniform, black batik sarong and appropriate headgear. The performers also sing, with two lead voices and a chorus. The style is supposed to have spread from the Bugis of Sulawesi; the lyrics are in Arabic. Performances focus on Malud, the Prophet's birthday, but also take place at marriages and other *slametan* feasts and may be called to combat illness.

Hadrah is likewise a percussion orchestra, composed of medium-sized kettledrums of cowhide *(gidur)* and pig's-hide tambourines *(rabane)*. It has presently a membership of about sixty persons, all males. At Malud, the whole orchestra plays together; otherwise only part of the group performs, called by private persons for various feasts, especially weddings, but not for sickness. Lyrics are in Arabic and Bahasa Indonesia. The exceptional use of pig's hide and the association with joyous occasions are explained by the story of its origin: "Once when the Prophet went to the forest he met a wild boar and prepared to kill it. But the boar could speak and pleaded: 'Do not kill me, I am nursing my small piglets!' The Prophet felt pity for her, and let her go — so she ran jubilantly off beating a joyous rhythm with her hoofs, which the Prophet liked and repeated on his drum. This was the origin of hadrah, and since all the Prophet did is well thought of in Pagatepan, hadrah is very popular here."

Sambroh, on the other hand, is a recent innovation, introduced some years ago by a schoolteacher. It is a girls' group of twelve members with mixed percussion instruments, who sing and perform coordinated drill or dance in the fashion of Indonesian Muslim performances seen in Singaraja and on television. Since the songs are in Arabic, or in Indonesian with very explicit Islamic values, and since the girls' uniforms are in accordance with Islam (long sleeves, and skirts below the knees), conservative resistance to this activity has died away. Leadership, as in all voluntary organizations, is by election within the membership and thus allows one of the schoolgirl band members to assume a formal leadership role.

An important voluntary association is formed ad hoc every year: the committee organizing the celebration of Malud, the Prophet's birthday. For this occasion Pagatepan mounts a spectacular show, for which it is justly famous among Muslims.

In the field of education and welfare work, the Maulana social foundation is an active force in the village, both soliciting contributions and dispensing benefits. It runs an elementary school with a progressive Muslim curriculum and arranges fosterage and subsidies for orphans in the village. Its local secretary is one of the prominent village leaders, who tries to extend and diversify the foundation's activities as a general village uplift organization and make it an effective platform for a reformist and modernizing movement.

Finally, any temporary common interest group that wishes to articulate a view or develop an activity likewise tends to constitute itself as a formal voluntary association with chairperson, secretary, and subcommittee leaders and an organizational plan for tasks and decision pathways. This is done in the best bureaucratic fashion, whether their concern is badminton, the enhancement of community influence for younger educated persons, or any other shared interest.

With this background it is of particular interest to return to the central, overwhelmingly most significant body in village organization: the Majlis Ulama, constantly referred to by all, from the imam down to the most marginal day laborer and youth. During the first part of my fieldwork I struggled long and vainly to ascertain its membership and its place and times of meeting. Indeed, despite its undeniable reality and power, it turns out to be an abstraction rather than a delimited group. Unique among institutionalized bodies in Pagatepan, it has neither a bounded membership nor an agreed time and place of existence. It simply constitutes an undefined circle of leading scholars with whom the imam consults, and I have no evidence that there has ever been an actual meeting of a group who would have said of themselves: we are the complete Majlis Ulama in session. There are clearly persons whom the imam could never afford not to consult in any major decision — maximally a short list of four or five influential gurus — and there is also a wide field of perhaps twenty or more persons whose voices he, and others of the core, would heed if they were vociferous enough. But a major force in the decision will always be the compelling logic of an argument, no matter who articulates it, if it is developed on the premises of the Koran and Shafi law, and secondarily the Hadith and precedent; and no show of hands could contradict that, only a winning counterargument. Thus this shadowy body of the Majlis Ulama is in a sense present whenever Muslim scholars in the village exchange views on the application of Islam to village affairs; and thus the opinion of the Majlis Ulama carries the full weight of authority, no matter how obliquely it may emerge.

COMPARATIVE ISSUES

Lying one above the other on the bountiful northern slope of Bali, Pagatepan and Prabakula thus seem in many ways so different that one could think they belonged to different continents or at least to historically completely distinct peoples. Their formal theology, their political institutions, and most aspects of the rules and the imagery they employ in constructing their social groups are fundamentally contrastive. Yet in certain ways that are already visible, the secular lives their respective religious idioms embellish show greater similarity; and a closer scrutiny of some of their concepts-in-use will tend to blur the contrasts further. Lest the differences between them be thought merely to reflect the difference between a Muslim Balinese minority and the majority Bali-Hindu culture of the remaining countryside, we need to make our comparative analysis on the basis of additional information on variation between other villages in the area as well; and these materials will be presented in chapter 5. But first, we need to explore in somewhat greater detail the basic organization for production these two neighboring villages, and indeed all other agricultural villages in Bali, seem to have in common: the irrigation association.

4

Irrigation Associations and the Organization of Production

Is there a danger that I may have given undue attention to imagery, ritual, and belief in drawing such contrasting portraits of the adjacent communities of Prabakula and Pagatepan? If we approach them rather from the perspective of peasant production, the differences appear to recede. Both communities are composed of family households, of similar size and largely based on a married couple as the household nucleus. The great majority of households support themselves by agriculture, some with a supplement derived from salaries or trade, and a few from land rents and other incomes only. The main principles on which the agricultural production is organized appear similar. Land is privately owned, with the exception of some limited areas of dedicated land. Households that do not possess enough land of their own try to obtain fields on tenancy or share-cropping contracts from families with more land than they can work; if they fail in this, they seek work as day laborers. The contracts governing such relations are quite similar in the two communities. And perhaps most striking: water for irrigation is obtained in both communities through membership in an organization distinctive of Bali, the subak, or cooperative irrigation association. These subaks are also important institutions for the organization of mutual cooperation, a feature of social life that receives strong ideological emphasis among Balinese and has figured prominently in anthropological accounts. There are differences in the distribution of land and succession to land, as I have noted; yet these may seem secondary and could perhaps reflect local circumstance more than deep cultural difference. In other words, the true extent of the contrast between Prabakula and Pagatepan might still appear undecided, depending on which features of village organization one chooses to stress.

The issue is important to my argument, as I wish to demonstrate that communities in the region do exhibit significant variation and that such underdetermination of form is a pervasive feature of social organization and cultural expression in the region. To address the issue, we need to look more closely at how production is indeed organized through the subak in these two communities. I shall try to demonstrate that to equate subaks of different villages as being "the same" institution would be to misrepresent them for important purposes. The economic and social realities they generate differ profoundly, and it is impermissibly simplistic to see them as one just because they carry the same label in Balinese. But this demonstration requires some detailed ethnography of our two chosen villages and of subak organization generally; we need to see how great the differences in practice and function are, and how they are predicated by apparently slight differences in formal rules.

THE SUBAK OF PAGATEPAN

I have outlined briefly the layout and technical devices employed on the irrigated land of Pagatepan. Let me now review the rights and obligations of membership in the subak in that village. It is the members themselves who are collectively responsible for the administration and maintenance of the system. Any obstruction, leak, or irregularity should be immediately reported to the klian subak, the elected leader of the association, who coordinates their collective efforts. In contrast to the irrigation associations of Prabakula, as we shall see, these responsibilities are divided in rough proportion to the area of land each member irrigates, not per capita. Moreover, they can be met in two different ways. Pagatepan custom dictates these specifics:

(a) It is the user of water, not the owner of land, who is member of the subak. Thus sharecroppers, not the owner, hold the membership and are answerable for the whole of membership responsibility. Thus also the mosque lands (wakaf) will automatically be represented in the irrigation association by the sharecropping holders of these plots.

(b) For every taktak of water, one share or person of subak labor should be provided when called by the klian subak. Farmers who share one taktak answer collectively for one share, by any arrangement they make among themselves.

(c) Responsibilities may be discharged in the form of *subak panggayeh* or *subak pangampo*. By the former, one meets one's obligations in the form of labor. Currently about fifty persons choose to perform this labor. Alternatively, by the latter one chooses to pay instead of to work, at the rate of

64

Hired labor transplanting rice in terraces of Pagatepan.

one hundred kilos of rice per harvest per taktak. This payment is not used to hire labor in place of the paying member but instead is divided among the laboring members in proportion to their shares. A logbook of attendance is kept to ensure that all fulfill their duties or compensate for unperformed labor at the end of each season. The klian subak can impose fines on members for irregularities.

(d) There is a system of bonuses or dispensations, *pelaba*, for certain village officials: the imam, the village headman, the four headmen of the banjar quarters, and the klian subak are excused from half of their labor or payment. This dispensation only holds good for lands they themselves cultivate, not for land of theirs that is sharecropped.

(e) An assembly (powm) of all subak members *(krama)* constitutes the ultimate authority of the group; it elects the klian subak and deliberates and decides on major matters of conflict or joint concern. A powm of subak panggayeh also plans and celebrates the traditional festive occasions of the subak, particularly the *slametan kapitat* in March when the dam is declared full after the rainy season.

(f) As for crops and cultivation, a farmer is left entirely free to plant and irrigate as he may wish, within the constraints of the season and his share of water. Since water is relatively plentiful and reliable, farmers can determine their crops and times of planting pretty much at will; and the plots in Pagatepan's subak at any one time show a wide diversity of growth and maturation.

THE SUBAKS OF PRABAKULA

The lands of Prabakula have been irrigated by five distinct subak. The Subak Gde, the "Big Irrigation Association," covers 145 hectares; the others range from 28 hectares down to 9 hectares. Subak Gde and two of the others obtain all their water from the Gitgit dam; local sources supply the other two. The Gitgit dam was rebuilt and expanded by the administration in colonial times and again in 1973, to provide water to nineteen *subaks* and irrigate 523 hectares in ten villages; this is by far the largest system in North Bali. With increasing pressure on water resources due to consumption in the urban area of Singaraja, supplies from the Gitgit dam have become critical, and a new water administration was introduced in 1986. My description will refer to the more traditional pattern that obtained during my first survey of the area, before this date. Each subak had then its regulated fraction of the flow of water from the dam, which was directed to a separate temporary reservoir to be used at the discretion of the individual subak.

For comparison with the data from Pagatepan, let us inspect the same data for Subak Runuh Kubu in Prabakula. This subak has the distinction of winning first prize for productivity in Buleleng in 1984, in the annual competitive scoring organized by the provincial Ministry of Agriculture. It irrigates twenty-eight hectares of land and had, in 1985, fifty-six members, so it is of roughly comparable size to that of Pagatepan. It irrigates the lower, northwestern part of Prabakula's village area and obtains its water from the Gitgit dam.

Membership in the subak is assigned to the cultivators in its drainage, whether owner-cultivators, sharecroppers, or contract tenants. The klian subak himself owns fifty-two *ara* within the subak's territory and share-crops another forty-five ara (an ara is approximately one hundred square meters). Members live scattered in several hamlets, and a few are resident in neighboring communities outside Prabakula.

Membership entails an inseparable bundle of duties, commitments, and benefits (for comparison, see the similarly lettered subpoints on Pagatepan, above):

(a) In cases of tenancy, all labor involved in current operations falls on the tenant, whereas the landowner is responsible for work that aims at improvements and investments.

(b) All labor on the irrigation system is collective, members performing equally regardless of the amount of land they cultivate.

(c) Absconders are fined; those legitimately unable to work because of sickness or other unavoidable absences must give notice and send a substitute or make up for it later in extra duty. Theft of water is controlled by subak members and not reported to the police, and fines for theft are imposed according to subak custom, at the rate of five hundred rupees (then approximately fifty cents) per taktak of water.

For all subak work, members are called by the klian subak, either simultaneously or in rotation: to clean the reservoirs and ditches, repair the installations, repair the *subak* temple and the private house of the klian subak, inspect and police the system, and prepare and perform the subak rituals. In return, each member receives water for the land he cultivates, as regulated by the klian.

(d) One extra *taktak* of water is, however, granted as pelaba to the klian for his services.

(e) The assembled subak members elect the klian subak, who is also the pemangku of the *pura subak* and subsidiary temples of the subak system. In consultation with astrologers he sets cultivation schedules and directs all rituals. The rites required of members are quite elaborate and are seen as an inherent part of the "work" of the subak, not mere frills. The rites focus

67

on rice cultivation. The opening of each cultivating season is marked by a *mapag toya* (welcoming the water) ritual by the whole village, led by the pemangku of the pura desa. The klians of the five subaks will come together and agree on a time suitable for the crops, and what is the closest auspicious date; then they will request the village pemangku to officiate at the rites on that date in the *pura bedegul*, the water temple near the top of the drainage. Thus the collective involvement of the whole community in the agricultural cycle and the fertility of their rice is expressed. Other rites which mark the stages of labor and crop maturation, are the tasks of each separate subak collective, or the individual cultivator.

The particulars of these rites vary even between subaks within Prabakula, and the terms used are complex; the main rhythm is as follows. (1) For the welcoming of the water, a suckling pig is offered at the reservoir site (with appropriate cuts presented at each of the five village temples) (2) The beginning of plowing is determined by the calendrical expert and marked by a ritual beside the seedling rice bed, in which old Chinese coins, a symbol of prosperity, are offered. (3) After one moon, at transplantation, a small offering is made by each field. From now until the rice blossoms (as also after the harvest), ducks can be freely grazed on the submerged paddies. After five or six days, fish and frogs start appearing, especially the eagerly sought *lindung*, eels believed to form spontaneously in the mud. (4) One moon after transplantation, the fields are blessed with holy water from the pura subak in a collective rite led by the klian, who is always also pemangku of this temple. (5) Thirty-five days after transplantation, i.e., one month by the Javanese-Hindu calendar, a rite for the developing rice is given at the pura subak mimicking the name-giving rite for human infants. (6) When the grains start forming, a big offering of suckling pigs, celebrated with *penjor* bamboo fliers, is given. (7) Later, but while the rice is still green, a sheaf of rice is cut, tied up, and decorated with flowers to form the *nini* — the representation of Dewi Sri, the Goddess of Rice — and placed on a bamboo platform shrine where the water enters the plot. Before harvest the nini is ceremonially carried to the granary and stored separately there, its grains being mixed into the seed grains for next year. (8) About two months after transplantation, irrigation is stopped, fish in the paddies are harvested, and the rice is allowed to dry for two to four weeks. (9) After harvest, a thanksgiving feast of the subak is held, where all cultivators offer (absentee owners providing half of their tenants' offerings) twenty kilos of rice each to the subak fund.

While these rites differ somewhat from those reported by Liefrinck ([1886–87] 1969, based on materials from the 1870s) from other parts of North Bali, and by Geertz (1980: 80f.) from Tabanan in the south, their similarities in terms of elaborateness, participation, and presence of idioms paralleling human life cycle rites are more significant.

(f) The members of Subak Runuh Kubu are severely constrained with respect to decisions of cropping and land use. A first rice crop is started by all on the same auspicious day in January for harvest in April. The dry season, with reduced and somewhat unpredictable water, in between May and August is left to the individual farmer's choice; generally beans, peanuts, or maize is grown, but whoever wishes may risk attempting an extra rice crop. Then from September to December a second main rice crop is cultivated by all. In the process of management of this production, members are not allowed to sell, or even give, any part of their share of water to another member; unclaimed water is allocated by the klian subak. The labor of cultivation is also to a considerable extent cooperative: plowing, transplanting rice seedlings, and the major weeding are done collectively by work gangs, which all members are constrained to join. The summer dry-season crop, however, is cultivated by the separate farmers' own labor. With regard to harvesting all rice crops, on the other hand, it is the world that has rights as against the crop owner: "poor people" have the right to serve as harvest labor in return for one-twelfth of the gross crop they harvest. Transport of the grain to the grain bin, finally, is an individual task.

STRUCTURE AND FUNCTION OF
SUBAK ORGANIZATIONS

The recent literature on Balinese subak organization (see Boon 1977:35–40 and 107–12 for a wide survey of perspectives and contributions till then; Geertz 1972, 1980; Lansing 1983:57–74; Lansing 1987, 1991) has placed increasing emphasis on identifying broad functional and regional features. In analyses showing unacknowledged parallels to Rappaport's (1967) seminal analysis of the ritual regulation of production in New Guinea, it has been argued that this elaborate merging of agronomy, water management, and ritual serves two functions. On the one hand, water release over a whole drainage area is staggered through the ritual scheduling of water temple feasts at different altitudes in the drainage (Geertz 1972; Lansing 1983). Second, the ritual cycling of these feasts in any one locality may serve as a mode of storage of information and organizational capacity, as well as a store of produce, with a view to fluctuations between plenty and scarcity (Boon 1977:109f.). Finally, in Lansing's (1991) intriguing analysis and computer simulation of management functions in a whole drainage in Gianyar in South Bali, the role of priests and water temples in programming production and irrigation is comprehensively demonstrated.

Important as these arguments are, however, their relevance to the North Balinese situation may be limited. On the one hand, drainage systems in the north are much shorter and steeper, allowing little scope for water distribution through staggered scheduling of irrigation. Some more general observations made by these and previous investigators (Grader [1939] 1960b:267ff.; Liefrinck [1886–87] 1969) have perhaps more general utility. Most striking is the separation of irrigation associations — in their membership, task organization, and leadership — from other groups and authority systems within the village. The relations of local subaks to central authorities, on the other hand, are less clear. The larger dams and waterworks were clearly constructed and controlled by the political center through a hierarchy of irrigation officers (sedahan). Thus the king of Buleleng represented himself as the owner of the water (Liefrinck [1886–87] 1969:44 and fn. 14) and collected a tax on crops on the basis of this claim. The same tax continues under present government institutions, and the klian subak, indeed, has his main recompense for what are very extensive duties and responsibilities in the form of 4 percent of this government tax. But Balinese kings were notorious (cf. Nielsen 1925) for collecting taxes and levies on each and every enterprise or activity, in attempts to shore up their very shaky political economies; and the relations of government to the main activities of irrigation were then probably even more external than they are now. All the North Balinese evidence thus supports Geertz (1980:69) in his assessment that subaks were constituted as self-directed corporations of peasant users, and that "Oriental despotism" would provide an entirely inappropriate model for the relationship between irrigation and statehood in Bali. It is thus high time to finally lay the ghost of Bali as a case of "hydraulic society" (Wittfogel 1957). Instead, the picture now emerging from Lansing's work shows that some centralized and coordinating functions were indeed executed by water priests and temples. "It is sobering, in retrospect, to consider the apparent ease with which the history of Balinese irrigation was rewritten into a story of feudal kingdoms. Water temples, the Goddess of the Lake, the tika calendar . . . were very nearly submerged beneath a manufactured history of subaks, sedahans, and reconstituted kings" (Lansing 1991:127).

The extent to which some degree of coordinating function was also exercised by priests and water temples in the north remains to be discovered. It is interesting that Lansing's simulation models show the importance of coordinated fallow to reduce losses from pest damage, not just for irrigation efficiency — of potential relevance to management even in the short drainage systems of the north.

Our present task, however, is otherwise. We need to return to our starting point in the discovery of distinct differences in the charters for subaks in our two neighboring villages in Buleleng. What may that tell us about uniformity and variation in the organization of production in different village communities? To obtain a useful answer, we need to specify more precisely the economic and social characteristics of these subak corporations, and their varying modes of operation.

In his celebrated comparison of traditional irrigation in Bali and Morocco, Geertz gives a vivid description of a number of the general features of the subak as an "if not wholly unique, certainly unusual" social form (Geertz 1972:27) and characterizes it as "a technically specialized, cooperatively owned public utility, not a collective farm" (ibid.:29). In a more recent restatement, he argues that "the subak never acted (and this seems to be one of the few flat statements one can venture about Bali) as a productive organization in the proper sense" (Geertz 1980:74). Whereas the subak as it is organized in Pagatepan can be comfortably fitted into this characterization, Subak Runuh Kubu comes very close to contradicting it; and a modification of the type description to embrace variants such as Subak Runuh Kubu would render it nearly vacuous.

It is essential for a perceptive discussion of the issues that we be able to distinguish clearly between the formal appearances of subak organizations and their actual modes of operation. For this we need to go beyond a schematic analysis of a Balinese cultural ideal of "the" subak; we should look into the detailed functioning of subaks and the experience and informed practice of North Balinese subak members. For this, we need an analytic language in which to describe the functionally speaking key features of these corporations, the range of their functional variation, and their internal diversity of interests and voices — not a set of evocative images of what the subak "is" and "is not." As is quite clear from my preceding descriptions, Subak Runuh Kubu and the other four subaks in Prabakula are organizational loci within which material value is created in the village. Even in Pagatepan, where the productive saliency of the subak is more limited, it is indispensable and looms large in the cultivation of staple foods. But how can we best analyze subak organizations with respect to how they function in these productive endeavors?

A useful beginning may be found in Coleman's distinction between benefit rights and usage rights in the joint resources of a corporation (Coleman 1986:267ff.) The cultivators who are members of a subak corporation invariably have benefit rights to the net return of their shares, in respect to the required fraction of the water with which to irrigate the crop on the land they cultivate, and the (net) product of the land (to be divided between owner and tenant, where this distinction applies).

Usage rights, on the other hand, are variably allocated in different su-baks. To a variable extent these differences are written into the subak con-stitution (as *adat* or awig-awig) or depend on collective decisions. Such subak decisions are made in plenary meetings of members; but the extent to which each member can make his influence felt in these meetings de-pends on a number of factors, to which I shall return. The klian subak tends to have much influence, and we may conclude from the comparative materials from Pagatepan and Prabakula that this influence does not de-pend significantly on his role as priest; the purely secular klian of Pagate-pan's subak is a very effective leader. Both klians indeed make use of a distinctly low-key leadership style devoid of the normal expressions of of-fice and rank and emphasizing his position as just one among the other farmers. Each has an executive style that is characteristically patient, per-suasive, and encouraging through his own example. But since the interests of all members depend on his performing essential services of coordina-tion and enforcing fairness in the distribution of tasks and benefits, and his recompense for this is modest, members have a wish to secure his consci-entious services — and goodwill — by granting him considerable control of corporation policy. In terms of the concepts of "voice" and "exit," he has a strong voice as a practiced expert and chosen leader of the group, and a threat of exit on his part is extremely powerful. Other members, on the other hand, are each only one among anything from one score to several hundred voices, and their exit is no threat: they may sell their plot as they wish; other buyers will step in and pick up their duties. The klian subak is also, naturally, far more committed to maximizing the success of the subak, whereas other members are more tempted to be negligent in performing their humdrum duties and opportunistic in determining the labor and re-sources they wish to invest in this particular enterprise. The pressures of the subak corporate decisions are thus in general toward maximizing pro-duction by increasing other input factors besides land, toward a conscien-tious policy of maintenance and capitalization, and toward competitive ef-fort to outdo rival subaks and win prizes — i.e., toward agricultural involution (Geertz 1963). Many participating farmers, on the other hand, will have quite other priorities.

A broader comparison of subaks in the region shows that they differ considerably in the constraints they place on the uses to which the irriga-tion water can be put, and the conditions that must be fulfilled to obtain these rights. Such differences enter deeply into the extent and organization of collective activities. Their range of variation may be summarized as fol-lows:

To obtain a share in the water the subak produces, members of some subaks must always respond personally whenever called upon to contribute labor to the corporation; other subaks leave members free to send substitutes; in others again, they have the option of either labor or payment to the corporation fund (e.g., Pagatepan). Labor duties may be divided per capita, creating a collective in terms of membership, or in proportion to the cultivated area that receives irrigation, emphasizing the factor costs in the partnership. The division of duties between land owner and tenant may be fully regulated or left to the parties concerned.

Members must also contribute certain amounts of capital to the maintenance of irrigation works. Hobart (1978a:77ff.) notes perceptively the conflicts of interests this matter gives rise to, as between wealthier members who favor capital investments in better, permanent installations, and the poorer members who prefer to avoid such expenses by constant vigilance and repairs on fragile and cheaper installations. Subaks in North Bali differ markedly in that some are labor-intensive, some are capital-intensive, and some allow individual choice in the balance of labor and capital contributed by members.

With respect to cultivation, collective regulations may be limited to secular work or embrace the wider range of expensive and time-consuming ritual tasks as well. The choice of crops to be cultivated may range from being fully determined by collective decisions to being fully individual; time of planting and scheduling of phases of work similarly ranges from collective to optional. The labor of cultivation ranges from overwhelmingly collective to overwhelmingly individual, except for harvesting, which is always collective and regulated by widely shared conventions for securing harvest labor employment of outsiders and customary rates of return on labour.

Aggregating these variations in rules and policies, we see that a very broad range of functional characteristics is represented by different subaks. Furthermore, these are differences of which village cultivators are well aware, and by the way they adjust to them, further modification of parameters will result. A number of variations emerge:

1. A cultivator who feels too constrained by joint subak decisions regarding which crop he can cultivate on his plot can in some of these systems withdraw his land from the subak. This gives him freedom of choice in what to cultivate among a range of less water-dependent alternatives: citrus fruits, other tree crops, vanilla, etc. Various negotiated arrangements can then be made to purchase the particular volume of irrigation water needed for such crops from the subak corporation direct by way of *slangg* (from the Dutch for "hosepipe"). His withdrawal, in turn, leaves the remaining membership more united in their particular policy.

2. Where subak labor is divided per capita rather than by area irrigated, supplementary tenancy contracts tend to be arranged by individual cultivators so that small holdings can be supplemented and each cultivator's field area can be brought up to relatively standard size. In these subaks, therefore, the actual commitments of the members tend to become roughly equal, reinforcing the collective structure of the particular subak.

3. Where subak customs or prevailing subak policies are at odds with the interest of a member — e.g., on the issue of having to perform collective labor duties personally rather than by proxy or by paying money; or in the balance struck between labor-intensive and capital-intensive practice — the landowner can sell his plot in one place and buy lands in the drainage area of another subak more compatible to his management preference. Indeed, land sales and purchases in North Bali are significantly affected by such issues, and the level of agreement within each particular subak is thereby somewhat enhanced.

In his analysis of modern Western corporation structure, Coleman points to a basic existential tension between the two main kinds of actors in any social system: natural persons and corporate actors. "The dilemma is a serious one: if a corporate actor is too extensively restrained by the wills of the natural person from whom its resources originally came, then it cannot exercise its power toward the outside; if it is insufficiently constrained by these persons, it can use its resources against them, exercising its powers to subvert their purposes" (Coleman 1986:8). This dilemma — between separate, individual interests and the embeddedness of individuals in social groups, public roles, and "society" writ large — can deteriorate into battle for a modicum of autonomy when a person's own interests seem under the threat of being totally enveloped by group control. Such a battle — as I have already hinted and shall try to demonstrate later — is a familiar spectre in Balinese social organiation and experience. Here, I am merely concerned to show how diversely the different particular subaks are located on the fundamental variable of individual/collective control. Thus the Pagatepan subak emerges as an intricate, instrumental technology and organization for the limited purpose of bringing water to the member farmers' fields in a manner that is sensitive to real factor costs, optimizing the individual farmer's scope for cost-effective agricultural production. In the Subak Runuh Kubu of neighboring Prabakula, the subak exercises extensive management control, demands and organizes collective field labor as well as irrigation system maintenance, and requires a full ritual participation, which is highly time- and resource-consuming. It thus becomes a very imposing corporate organization for production and worship, with a set of communally directed tasks so complex and ramifying that it comes very close to completely submerging the distinctiveness and interests of the component members of the corporation. Other subaks in North Bali that I know range themselves widely between these two extremes; some of them will be briefly noted in the next chapter.

Thus the two villages we have compared are actually highly contrastive in their organization of production in irrigated agriculture, as they are in other features of their social organization — a contrast masked if we assume that the Balinese institution of the subak predicates a particular manner of functioning. If instead we choose to exoticize less, and look closely into the particular facts of how any specific irrigation association is constituted and operates, we are able to form a more realistic understanding of the subak as a highly adaptable and functionally variable organization — with a distinctive Balinese stamp but without the uniformity a purely cultural analysis might lead us to imagine.

5

Further Variations in Village Organization

Prabakula and Pagatepan exhibit a series of striking contrasts and similarities in social organiation, thereby posing a challenge that can only be answered by some broader kind of comparative analysis. An inspection of covariation in the institutional forms of these two communities might seem to promise insight into the interconnections and interdependencies that obtain between domains of activity and principles of organization in Balinese village life. But it would be an inept methodology to choose to see these two communities in isolation from the wider region of which they are a part. We should realize from the data provided by previous generations of Dutch scholars in their *Adatrechtbundels* (collections of custom law; see especially Korn 1932 and Liefrinck [1882–89] 1934) that a wide range of formal variation is represented in the region. We should furthermore design our analysis so it does not focus simplisticly on the village level only, blinding us to wider systems and social processes. Finally, and most important, we need to adopt a critical analytic perspective on just what these features of custom law and village level formal institutions mean; we need to develop an adequate understanding of their place in the context of action and meaning of which they are a part: the living civilization we wish to understand.

In the present chapter I shall take the next step in such a comparative analysis by exploring a wider range of variation through brief descriptions of five further communities, demonstrating the place which the principle of seniority can have in village organization; the varying role of descent; the forms of coexistence between Bali-Hindus and Muslims; and the importance with which divine possession can be vested as a source of authority within a community.

JULAH

Julah, a village on the northeast coast of Bali (see also Lansing 1983:115–27), belongs typologically in the category generally known as Bali Aga, though most recognized Bali Aga villages are located in the mountains. It shows a pattern of village government based systematically on seniority, unique in its particulars but designed from ideas that are also present, and applied in various degrees, in other communities.

Julah has roughly the same number of people as Prabakula or Pagatepan and is bisected by a north-south lane into the East and West banjars. These are cross-cut by the public coastal road through the middle of the village, producing a village plan basically like that of Pagatepan. Its centrally important temple, the pura desa, is placed uphill to the south, adjacent to the village lane; there is also a pura dalem (death temple) in the lower part of the West banjar. Julah has no pura segara, but it has a seaside holy well, the Smur Suci; in the porous volcanic soil of Julah the dependable perennial sources of sweet water are by the beach. There is also a sacred seaside spring to the east of the village. These sources of sweet water represent a significant cosmological reversal of the ubiquitous Balinese emphasis on crater lakes and headwaters as the purest and most sacred water sources. The Smur Suci contains four wells placed in square formation ("like the footprint of a buffalo"), one where households draw their holy water for rituals, one for men to wash from, one for women, and one from which to water the animals.

Julah has a core population of 315 houses of krama desa, citizens of the village; the rest are "strangers" who play no role in the internal traditional administration of the village. Full citizenship depends on local descent and on being married. If the child of a krama desa person marries a stranger, the stranger spouse can be assimilated through appropriate rituals, and the couple achieves krama desa status.

As far as village government is concerned, we have seen in Pagatepan a structure where the central power lies with a small nucleus of religious scholars, the Majlis Ulama, and the elected perbekel acts as liaison between the village and the external administration. In Prabakula, on the other hand, the elected perbekel of the government system can be stronger because he has a considerable greater field of maneuver, relating as he does to two krama desa assemblies as well as to a decentered set of associations (temple congregations, clubs, irrigation associations, and banjars), each with customary charters, assemblies, and elected officials.

Julah shows a third pattern. Internal power lies with a village assembly based entirely on seniority. The principle of *nareswari*, the unity of hus-

77

band and wife, is supreme; persons can have no participatory status until they marry. At this point they join the village assembly with lowest rank, being allotted the last ordinal number in one of the two balanced *sibak*, moieties. The two sibak are named "West" and "East" but this refers to their formal seating in the assembly, not to residence in the West and East banjars. Each of the two divisions is headed by three officials, who also serve as priests in the village temples and are the most senior members of their respective moieties. The highest position in the village is the *kubayan dharma* of the West moiety; second is the *kubayan bima* of the East moiety. Each kubayan is assisted by two *bau*, of second and third rank in their respective divisions. "Ever since we rebelled against our kings and patihs we have been ruled by our kubayan."

At the monthly gatherings of the village assembly in the pura desa at full moon, the krama desa are seated in rank order on separate platforms (*balai*) for men (on the west side of the temple court) and women (on the east side). Within each gender group, the moieties (of the West and East division respectively) face each other in two rows with the kubayans on the south-and-mountainward end and the most recently married on the seaward end. The six most recently married couples in each division are known as *pemuit*, and their duties are to cook, make the offerings, and clean the temple one month each in turn.

The kubayan reigns as long as he and his spouse are alive and healthy. At his death or the death of his spouse, or when he must use a stick to be able to walk about, he and his spouse are replaced by the new couple in the division according to seniority, and all members down the line move up one number. To take care of liaison with external authorities, officials such as perbekel and klian desa adat are elected, from the middle range of seniority and with due regard to education and ability.

This system of village government goes with a basic social organization that denies caste or birth rank and gives minimal recognition to wider descent relations. Domestic worship emphasizes household unity and village egality. "When you marry, you first must build your cooking place [*dapur*]. The philosophy is: first you must work hard, and feed yourself. Second, you build your shrine [sanggah kemulan]: having eaten, you must offer thanks. Third, you build your house for dwelling: only then can you rest." Each household's shrine has the form of a small wooden storehouse, approximately two meters by one, placed on waist-high stilts and with a low roof. One of its walls can be swung open; within are various paraphernalia, including the Chinese coins (*salan*) widely used to represent the blessings of material prosperity, basketry objects, and pottery bowls and incense burners. This household shrine is used regularly for calendrical and family rituals throughout life; at the death of either of the spouses it is demolished. There are thus no enduring shrines or temples for family lines or sublineages. Each of the thirty-two descent groups of Julah, however, maintains one shared *sanggah dadia* in perpetuity, but this is constructed in the same characteristic manner as the household shrines, architecturally quite unlike the household and lineage shrines generally used in North Bali.

With the central importance of the unit established at marriage, it is not surprising that the married couple's integrity should be emphasized also in other ways. Thus every couple must perform at marriage a purification ceremony called *mewinten* — a term used elsewhere in Bali primarily for the consecration of a priest or a puppeteer — to qualify them to take up their village duties and ritual offices. The consecration involves a series of feasts the couple must host, sacrificing a total of eight pigs, one buffalo, and one sheep in the course of the rite's six phases, which may be given serially over two days or as the candidate household can afford. If a man remarries or takes a second wife, a new consecration of this new couple must be performed.

The villagers of Julah state that they perform *ngaben*, cremation, immediately upon the death of any person who has been thus purified. However, in this ngaben the dead body is in fact not cremated but buried in an unmarked flat grave, which is never revisited for any ritual or ceremonial purpose. The dead person's clothes, mattress, and blanket, on the other hand, are ritually burned at the "cremation," and great care must be taken that all clothes are included in the destruction. Should a single item of clothing be forgotten, the dead person will visit the bereaved family in dreams or as an apparition within three days, demanding that the mistake be corrected. In such cases, the clothes in question will be located and kept till the next cremation occurs in the village, when the erring family will go and supplicate the newly deceased spirit to take these clothes away with it to their dead relative.

The village lands of Julah are unirrigated, though agriculture in the rainy season is collectively coordinated in associations called subak like irrigation associations. All land has until recently been collectively owned and divided equally among the krama desa (cf. Liefrinck [1882–89] 1934:346). Its circulation followed the progression of seniority, the plot of best quality being held by the kubayan dharma until his term of office ended, when his successor would take over, and so on down the line. This land tenure system was discontinued in the 1970s by command of the district administration, against strong resistance by the village community.

Goris ([1935] 1960a:90ff.), relying in part on Liefrinck's village survey data (Liefrinck [1882–89] 1934) and his own extensive knowledge of historical inscriptions and documents, gives an overview of the titles used for village officials in Balinese mountain villages. There is little reason to be skeptical of his view that a village organization based on paired officials and a bipartite division of the population, such as we find in Julah, in Bali preceded the institution of one central village headman, and that the village titles *kebayan* and *bau* are more ancient than titles such as *pasek, bendesa*, and *klian*. In this sense, there is no doubt that the village organization of Julah exhibits an archaic form. The relative prevalence of such dualism in organization, and of the more archaic titles, in mountain areas and in Buleleng and Karangasem as compared to South Bali can also be plausibly explained by the less thorough penetration of these areas by Majapahit Javanese influences.

However, interpreting a typological series in terms of an evolutionary sequence often obscures far more than it explains. We are, after all, dealing not with historical materials but with the institutions of a contemporary village. In no sense can Julah be depicted as a survival merely cut off from the progress of time. The village lies fully accessible, open to the coast and bisected by the main road along Bali's north shore. Where today buses and trucks thunder by, other and slower traffic has passed for centuries; and the members of Julah village have participated freely and fully in modern education, enterprise, and administration for more than hundred years. An imputation of extreme isolation would be entirely false and misleading. Why then these particular institutional forms, and what are their implications? Identifying them as archaic explains essentially nothing.

What is more, framing the description in such evolutionary, quasihistorical terms may also fail to convey the most interesting aspect of the case: the radical institutional differences involved. In Julah we see a community with an elaborate ritual life that turns out to be focused entirely and exclusively on one deity, the Batara Gunung Agung–the God of Bali's highest mountain, widely revered in Bali and generally identified as Mahadewa, the supreme manifestation of Siwa. The people of Julah indeed represent themselves as confirmed Siwaists and explain their conflict with their ancient kings and patihs in terms of the anti-Siwa paganism of these old kings; but according to them this Batara Gunung Agung/Siwa has his throne and center of force *(pelinggih)* in Julah's pura desa, not in the nationally central shrines of Besakih on the slopes of Gunung Agung. Moreover, they are uniquely committed to him alone and are not allowed by him to worship any other God or to perform worship of him in any other temple — not even in Besakih. They recently came into reluctant conflict over this with their then district officer *(camat)*, who attempted to press them to join certain rites in an adjacent subregional temple.

Nor does this concentration on Batara Gunung Agung allow the normal Balinese worship of deified ancestors, thus precluding the manifestation of agnatic descent groups in cult. With communal land tenure of all fields in the village, this has left very little scope for the application of descent concepts beyond the relationship of filiation. But to doubly ensure that no politically corporate descent segments develop, the rule is followed that a man's son upon marriage will be assigned to the opposite moiety to that of his father; and every group of brothers will be likewise split between the moieties. Thus their cult prevents them both from joining the widely overlapping and integrating congregations that form around Bali's many regional temples and from constituting smaller cult units around family shrines.

Furthermore, their custom dictates that in their worship of Siwa they should use no *mantras* (i.e., Sanskritic prayers and formulas) at all, but merely concentrate in wordless absorption. This makes them effectively impregnable to the Sanskritic scholarship of Brahmins. Other differences of ritual emphasized by the citizens of Julah — e.g., their use of heterodox flowers to embody the sacred colors of red, green, and white in offerings — may seem less radical to a Western audience but certainly serve them as powerful diacritica for their own distinctive identity.[6]

Though people in Julah stress the uniqueness of their village rather than any similarity to others they are regarded as Bali Aga, and have often been thought to represent survivals of early, even pre-Hindu, cultural forms. What I am suggesting is that even a quite cursory inspection of the ideas that determine everyday practice in the community of Julah can prove more illuminating, even for historical purposes, than the most well-informed scholarly speculations directed at the task of fitting contemporary overt institutions into an evolutionary schema. It allows us to discern in Julah a local tradition of exceptional character, linked to the major historical currents of Indian influence in a distinctive fashion predicated by certain connected features of organization and dogma. These are perspectives to which I shall return later (chapter 13). In the present context, however, we may take the analysis one small step further by a comparison with the corresponding features of the neighboring community of Sembiran.

SEMBIRAN

Sembiran is located high up the spectacularly steep mountainside south of Julah. The two communities may be historically connected. Though Sem-

---

6. Identified in native botanical terms as *putcuk*, *don intaran*, and *manori puti* respectively.

biran is named as a village along with Julah as early as the tenth century in presastis that are revered as sacred heirlooms in the two communities, informants in Julah claim Sembiran to be a breakaway segment of their own village. In support of this claim, they interpret the etymology of its name: Sembiran means "those who split away"; an older name of the community, Paulah, means "(split away) from Julah." A reason for its relocation in the mountains is given in the prevalence of piracy along the coast; indeed, the coastal location of Julah was abandoned for a period in favor of a hill location inland for the same reason. Sembiran, however, is also reported to be the site of megalithic remains (Lansing 1983:120) and so is presumably an ancient settlement site.

Be this as it may, the two communities are at least close neighbors and regard themselves as connected and highly distinct from the run of newer Balinese villages. Sembiran classifies itself, and is widely named, as a Bali Aga village and is certainly both geographically and socially the more isolated of the two. Yet in regard to significant cultural features, Sembiran seems somewhat more like other Balinese villages than does Julah.

Its outstanding differences from Julah are the following. Sembiran is a closed community; it does not allow any immigration and so does not stand in need of a distinction between krama desa and other, noncore villagers. An exception was made for Bali Aga refugees from the Kintamani area after the volcanic disaster in 1963: they have been allowed to settle on village land, but only in separate hamlets away from the main village, on the extreme southern boundaries of the territory.

The village proper is divided into three government banjars. The traditional structure represented by the desa adat organization is, however, one of eight banjars, and these have both a different structure and a far greater importance than the wards of Julah, or those of Prabakula or Pagatepan. Each forms a patrilineally recruited unit; in cases where spouses come from different banjars, residence is virilocal and children inherit their father's banjar membership. Actual physical residence, however, is not entirely compulsory. You may reside outside your banjar if necessary and retain your membership unchanged, the outstanding example being the two persons appointed to highest priestly functions in the village temples, who must move to the highest southern fringe of the settlement with no house above them. Most important, the banjar was the joint landholding unit until approximately twenty years ago, when land was transformed to private property by administrative decree. Till then, usufruct to fields was periodically reallotted on an equal basis to male banjar members, women receiving a share if they were adult but unmarried.

The governing body of the banjar is an assembly of all its adult male members, whether married or not. Its function is to coordinate all ritual and secular work (except that arising from membership in either of the two subak irrigation associations of the village). Each banjar also contains one or several descent group shrines (*pura dadia*) of its resident lineages.

The major temples, pura desa and pura dalem, however, are shared village institutions, and the village is governed by an assembly based on seniority. The structure of this assembly is not clear from the available materials. Lansing gives an account rather similar to that I have given of Julah, but with other titles for some offices and positions (Lansing 1983:116, 120f.); Goris mentions a third set of titles (Goris [1935] 1960a:91). My own data are based only on a brief visit, and they differ from these again but agree with Lansing's general characterization that there is less emphasis on the dual division than in Julah (Lansing 1983:121). My data also indicate the importance of trance media in the selection of priests: the God, through a trance medium possessed by him, chooses his own priest. The role of trance possession in Julah, on the other hand, is much more limited, allowing the God to express his acceptance or dissatisfaction with particular ceremonies and offerings only. The priests of Sembiran, moreover, employ Sanskritic mantras as an essential element of their cult performances.

Lansing's account confirms the prevalence of dadia descent group temples in Sembiran but suggests a composition of dadia cult groups in which agnates are outnumbered by sampingan "additional" members who may even attain the position of seniority in the group, though they cannot serve as priest or secretary. Correspondingly, a person will frequently be a member of several dadia groups simultaneously, exemplified by a young man's sampingan membership in his mother's and his wife's dadias, as well as membership in his father's dadia (ibid.:123). Lansing regards this as a "curious hybrid" (ibid.), but I think his view represents a slight misinterpretation of the application of the nareswari principle of unity of spouses in ancestral worship, widely practiced in North Bali (see chapter 3). The salient difference from Julah is found in the complete dominance of the nareswari principle in the constitution of Julah's household temples, in contrast to the development of durable, collective ancestor shrines for patrilineal descent groups in Sembiran, no doubt corresponding to the collective land rights formerly held by such descent-based groups there.

Thus in the clearly more isolated and socially encapsulated community of Sembiran we find a social organization less exceptionally based on seniority and spouse unity than in Julah. Ritually and secularly important groups are also built on agnatic descent, and the instituted form of trance possession is one that allows divine intervention in the selection of leaders and officials, a general pattern shared by many other North Balilnese villages. It is striking that these features are associated with the possession of joint land rights by patrilineally recruited segments of the community, and the use of Sanskritic liturgy in village ritual, but with greater rather than less physical isolation from the mainstream of the wider society.

TEGALLINGGA

Between Pagatepan and Prabakula we saw a complete dichotomization of Bali-Hinduism and Islam, with essentially no enduring social relations between members of the two communities.

In the absence of significant human links and joint forums, the ideological opposition between the two religious congregations remains categorical and capable of breaking out as stark enmity on any provocation. Thus the nearest neighboring Bali-Hindu hamlet to the west of Pagatepan, formerly closely identified with the Indonesian Communist party, was gutted by vigilantes from Pagatepan at the time of the 1965 attempted coup by the Communists; while a Bali-Hindu hamlet in the northeast corner of Pagatepan was totally eliminated at that time, its survivors dispersing to other communities and its lands taken over by residents of Pagatepan. We have noted also the absence of all Hindu temples from Pagatepan territory, and there was a prompt reaction when villagers from Prabakula recently attempted to construct a small headwaters shrine where their irrigation stream originates: the shrine was smashed. The occasional romantic elopement of a Hindu girl with a boy from Pagatepan likewise fails to create bonds, since the girl's name and religion are immediately changed and her family relations severed.

In the village of Tegallingga, about ten kilometers westward from Pagatepan in the lower range of the same altitude zone, an entirely different relationship obtains between members of the two creeds. Let us first establish the Hindu community. Tegallingga seems to have been settled less than three hundred years ago within the domain of the custom village of Salat, by commoner families of several descent groups: Pasek Gelgel, Tagah Kuri, and Alang Kajang. Each such group keeps its separate *pura padarman*, origin temple, in the village. Indeed, a new "origin temple," the Pura Pulasari, was recently established according to a pattern that throws interesting light on the nature of descent and segmentation. The Pasek Gelgel population of Tegallingga has long been subdivided among seven dadia temples — i.e., descent group temples — with a joint pura padarman, and they recognized ultimate origins in the great Pasek temple in Gelgel, to which they occasionally send participants in the major rites. Several bilaterally interrelated Pasek families were, however, pursued by diverse persistent sicknesses for which there seemed no clear explanation. Finally a balian medium made the diagnosis that their shared use of the pura padarman with the other Pasek Gelgel was the cause of their misery: their very participation in these cult acts was making them sick. A separate origin temple for the seventeen stricken families was then constructed, and spiritual harmony was restored.

In other words, descent groups are obligated to constitute congregations in the cult of their ancestors in order to secure the health and prosperity of the living. But at the same time, sickness may be a sign that ancestors require changes from status quo; thus it may provide the authority to rearrange descent group congregations, here in the form of a retroactive descent myth making the stricken persons now into a separate group. What we see is thus not merely a cult of dead ancestors as collective representations of descent groups and their segments. Rather, the conception allows ancestral spirits and their descendants to form a bond of unity that is affirmed in worship; and the composition of the congregation reflects the alignment of ancestors and descendants in an active social solidarity, and so must be responsive to social divisions that the ancestors require of their living descendants. I judge this interpretation of the significance of descent group temples and cults to have wide validity in North Bali.

On the village level, the Hindu community of Tegallingga is constituted around the three temples, kahyangan tiga (in its North Balinese sense: pura desa, pura dalem, and pura segara), a *pura ulu* at the foot of the mountains where the headwaters of the irrigation system are, and a *pura taman* for village festivals. Temple activities are directed by an elected *kepala adat* (headman of custom), while the practical arrangements for the ceremonies are made by a likewise elected *parisad* official. Each temple, on the other hand, has its pemangku priest, selected by the gods themselves through trance mediums, but frequently in family lines. These pemangkus make prayers, offerings, and above all holy water, but they do not direct the festivals.

In contrast to those of Prabakula, Tegallingga Hindus seem to see themselves merely as a local congregation in a wider region; ultimate religious authority is placed outside the community. Thus they are very pleased to have four members from the village represented on the Department of Religion's regional board of Hindu religious experts. These four seniors are held to have authority over and above the pemangkus. To serve as the most senior of them, they have indeed selected an old man who regards himself as a stranger to Tegallingga: he has spent his life among them but is of different stock, his father's father having come from the Bali

Aga village of Tengganan. Above this board again, Tegallingga Hindus name Sri Mpu Dwi Tantra in Singaraja as their highest religious authority. Sri Mpu is one of the very small number (reportedly fourteen in all of Bali) of hereditary high priests of non-Brahmin, commoner stock. When they desire the ritual services of other than their own pemangkus, the villagers turn to him, not to Brahmin priests. This course is in fact becoming increasingly fashionable in sophisticated circles among commoners in North Bali, but it is claimed in Tegallingga to be a traditional arrangement. In all these various respects, Tegallingga is linked to a wider region, and to contemporary currents, in ways very different from Prabakula.

Moreover, Tegallingga is composed also of a considerable fraction of Muslims, at present about 400 families, as compared to 650 families of Hindus. Residentially interspersed with the Hindu population, they contrast with them in most of their formal features of social organization but differ also from the organization described in Pagatepan. Like the residents of Pagatepan, they lack descent groups and, of course, any form of ancestor worship. They have a central mosque with an imam; but apart from the teachers of the elementary Koran school they have only two guru teachers, one of whom is an immigrant called in from Pagatepan in a somewhat futile attempt to enhance their own orthodoxy. The Muslims form no separate assembly, other than for sporadic announcements in connection with the Friday sermon in the mosque, and constitute no Majlis Ulama. Their sons have no tradition of seeking religious training by travel outside the community, and there are no lifelong spiritual links between local gurus and their pupils. While previously each religious community in Tegallingga had its own perbekel (village headman), for the last twenty years they have had an agreed arrangement of alternating Muslim and Hindu perbekels, with the vice-perbekel of the other community. Banjar (hamlet) organization is joint, with monthly banjar meetings attended by a mixed assemble of Hindu and Muslim men. The membership of subaks (irrigation associations), of which there are three, is also mixed. Secular duties in the subak are performed jointly, whereas the religious part of the duties — on the part of the Muslims, relatively simple slametan (celebrations) at the opening of the season and after harvest — are performed separately "but *for* the whole" by members of the two faiths. Though statistically endogamous, the two groups also intermarry, both ways. As the leading Muslim Guru said regretfully: "Yes, for a Muslim woman to marry a Hindu is the greatest sin, *murtad*, [apostasy, because of the authority of the man over his wife and children], according to Islam. But this is our weakness: too much intimacy with the Hindus. So there can be no great difference in mentality, to prevent intermarriage." Apparently the relations have always been good, even in periods of breakdown of legal order. Thus no communal conflicts surfaced during the unrest in 1965, although other debts were settled than the political ones: one informant told me gleefully how while killing Communists they had also killed the most notorious thieves in the village, so now they are very little troubled by theft!

The Muslim sector of the population has been traditionally associated with trade and crafts, in contrast to the agricultural orientation of the Hindu villagers. A number of Muslim families trace their pedigrees to the village of Pengastulan (see below) on the coastal flats twenty kilometers further west; there is also a now abandoned Muslim graveyard in the closest neighboring village of Tukadmunga on the coastal plain, which they see as evidence that parts of the group may have come from there. There is agreement that they arrived as poor people, working as peddlers, laborers, and craftsmen. In particular they have been associated with a local cotton industry, a specialty of the village reported already in Liefrinck's "desa monographs" ([1882–89] 1934). Apparently the area is particularly suited for cotton-trees *(kapuk: Eriodendron anfructuosum)*, from which the stuffing for mattresses is extracted. Such work was low-status, unsuitable for landowning Hindus, and was taken up by in-moving Muslims. With an expanding market, however, prices and profits have been improving and have laid the basis for increasing prosperity among the Muslims.

Around 1970 a group of four Muslims also pioneered citrus fruit cultivation, combined with modern agricultural equipment and systematic marketing in East Java. Progressively the Muslims have bought land, so they now own more than half of the village area.

PENGASTULAN

In this older mixed village from which many of the Muslim families of Tegallingga derive we find the two faiths likewise living together, but with considerably greater separation and social distance. Pengastulan is divided into four banjars, of which one is Muslim with a population of 981 and three are Hindu with a total population of 2,444, according to the most recent census. The Muslim banjar has its separate officials, though it is under the Hindu perbekel of the village as a whole. There is no banjar meetinghouse, as there is in the Hindu wards, but the mosque on Friday serves as a place for public announcements.

The Muslim population largely considers itself descended from Bugis (Sulawesi) ancestors, though the particulars are unknown and all known ancestors lived as Balinese, mostly within Pengastulan over the three or four generations that are remembered. There has been minimal intermarriage with Hindus and little marriage out of the village, but considerable migration has taken place to other villages in the area, particularly to the neighboring, swiftly growing recent town of Siririt.

The *adat subak*, i.e., the custom law of the irrigation association of Pengastulan, is interpreted to be very strict in its requirement that all members must bring the *maturang adat* ("the means of custom," i.e., offerings) to Pengastulan's central temple, the Pura Gde. Consequently Muslims cannot be members of the subak, and this effectively prevents them from owning land in the low, comprehensively irrigated village lands. Where they do own certain limited plots, these must be sublet to Hindu tenants who will participate in the rituals; otherwise, some Muslims own land in neighboring communities with less strict custom law. But very few of them are cultivators; mostly they are traders, and perhaps a third of them are fishermen. Whatever wealth a few of them have built up has been through special enterprises. Most successful at present is a large-scale middleman in fish fry and immature shrimp, which are caught extensively along North Balinese beaches and shipped live to be raised in Javanese fish ponds.

Pengastulan's Muslims have no Majlis Ulama but may seek individual advice from a few prominent gurus, and they cherish the tradition of having once, two generations ago, had a famous religious scholar and teacher in the person of Hajji Ghazali. Recruitment for advanced religious studies is, however, quite limited, and only a few young men attend more than elementary Koran school. Whereas some pupils keep alive a lifelong link to their guru, most Muslims do not, or have never had such a relation.

The Hindu majority, on the other hand, has a complex social organization and sustains an active and elaborate ritual life. Most are of commoner descent, many Pasek Gelgel. The core of the village, on the other hand, is made up of Wesias with the honorific title Gusti, who are also the owners of nearly all the village lands. With a population of about two hundred, they are Arya Tagah Kuri by descent, conscious of their twice-born status, and consider themselves Wong Majapahit, people of Majapahit and Java, in contrast to the Sudra population, which they characterize as the descendants of Bali Asli, original Balinese. The local Tagah Kuri ancestor is reported to have lived fifteen generations ago in the neighboring ancient village of Bubunan. From there he was called by Raja Panji Sakti to become *punggawa*, district chief, of the area from Banjar to west of Grokgak and given the previously uncultivated Pengastulan as a fief. The family has retained courtly and elite connections ever since and also shows a number of distinctive customs: most conspicuously, they live in a large, extended family compound with a central death pavilion and other domestic arrangements "like in the south." The commoners are mostly cultivators, and about one hundred families are predominantly or entirely fishermen. These later perform special annual sea rituals of *ngambe paseh* in the pura segara; and there is also a special harbor temple, the Pura Pabean, dedicated to Betara Dewa Ayu Subander, "God Goddess Pretty of the Harbor."

The Great Temple, Pura Gde of Pengastulan, serves as a regional temple for several villages in the area, though these villages are indeed older than it. The temple is a complex of pura desa, pura segara, and a number of dadia shrines and other shrines. Head pemangkuship of the temple belongs with a Sudra descent group that traces its ultimate origins to Tabanan in South Bali and is supposed to have arrived in the north together with the Arya Tagah Kuri. The temple also has a second priestly official, called balian, an office filled from a particular priestly family residing in the neighboring village. The local origin temple *(pura panti)* of the Wesia nobles is known as the Pura Badung, from that family's southern origin point. The pemangkus of this family temple and other family shrines, including separate shrines within the village death temple (pura dalem) are themselves members of the family. The whole group is affiliated ritually to a house of Brahmins in Singaraja.

Though pemangkuship is thus vested in family lines, the particular choice of person is made by the gods themselves through *suri* trance mediums. Mediumship likewise runs in family lines of Sudra commoners, since high-caste persons cannot be possessed by even deified spirits and gods of lower caste without becoming drastically polluted. The major temples used to have tanah laba, dedicated lands, like some temples in Prabakula and analogous to the wakaf of Pagatepan; but such lands have now been sold to pay for temple maintenance. Traditionally Pengastulan also had its separate religious board, the Kampulan Parasulingeh, under the leadership of the perbekel and with all the village pemangkus, as well as the bendesa (ritual secretary), as its members.

SIDA TAPA

To complete this provisional view of variety on the village level, we may end up in one of a group of Bali Asli villages in the hills southeast of Pengastulan, themselves rather diverse. Sida Tapa is a village of 3,675 inhabitants, divided into three banjars. The population is casteless, though of diverse origins; some of them, judging from the descent group names, are descended from higher-caste groups. The village is open for immigration by persons who buy land but will not allow absentee land purchases. Land is private property, inherited by sons and unmarried daughters, while the youngest son inherits the parent's house. Residence is ideally in elementary family households.

Villagers who own any part of the limited irrigated land are members of a subak, together with others in the neighboring village. But the subak coordinates only the secular work of irrigation and maintenance; all rituals for the crops are done by each family separately in their own houses. Most agriculture is on roughly terraced dry land, cultivating a diversity of tree crops, root crops, and also some dry rice; and it is on these dry crops that collective ritual has its focus in seasonal first fruits ceremonies.

The village has a distinctive set of collective temples: pura desa (village temple), pura puseh (navel/origin temple), *pura munduk*, and *pura rambu-tunggan*. The pura puseh provides holy water for the rites of purification, *mlasti*, of the other temples. But the most important sacred site is the *kahyangan*, "the place where God stops," where all the major village ceremonies take place. In Sida Tapa this is not a set of three temples, and not enclosed by a masonry wall, but just an open, cleared space at the edge of the village, very different from anything found in other villages I have seen.

Even more distinctive is the set of religious officials. Temples are under the leadership of priests/priestesses called balian, who serve above all as trance mediums for the gods themselves. Bateson ([1937] 1970:112 fn.) notes the presence of a similar priestess in the mountain village of Bayung Gede near Kintamani: "She is the chief officiant at almost all ceremonies, sprinkling, praying, purifying and so forth; and at almost all ceremonies she goes into trance, possessed either by deities or the souls of the dead, according to the nature of the ceremony. She is almost the only channel through which the spirit world communicates with the village."

Each major temple in Sida Tapa has three such balians: the *balian gde* (great balian), the *balian penyanding* (vice-balian), and the *balian pangesekan lis*, who purifies the congregation by sprinkling it with the holy water. In making the offerings in the temple, the balian is assisted by a popularly elected pemangku. But it is the balians themselves, not the pemangkus, who are chosen by the gods. These choices are supposedly made without reference to descent or age, directly through the *presuri* trance mediums; and the choice falls consistently on unmarried or widowed women.

Another conspicuous difference from Bali-Hindus, with great implications for cosmological conceptions, is the absence of any pura dalem (death temple) and of any rites of cremation or notional transformation rites of any kind for the dead body that would indicate a conception of Nirwana. The dead person is merely carried in a small tower to the grave and buried. After a long period, there is a memorial rite; but this involves bringing a symbolic handful of earth from the grave to the house of the family, to provide for the presence of the dead at the memorial feast, and then the return of this earth to the grave after completion of the feast. Houses and descent groups have alters or shrines *(sanggah)* to their ancestors; but there seems to be no need for a ritual to transform these predecessors at any point from dangerous ghosts into purified spirits.

6

The Problem
of Variation

The handful of communities and organizational forms sketched in chapters 2 through 5 has exemplified some of the diversity of arenas in which persons variously situated in North Balinese society must move. The communities I have described differ greatly in the formal rules of how they are constituted and in the ways in which key shared institutions — such as the subak — function, as well as in the sacred symbols and other imagery in terms of which social statuses and groups are represented. These differences profoundly shape the lives of the people who live in the respective communities; but the particular significance of customs and positions for the people so affected is not transparent from a scrutiny of these institutional forms in themselves. What is more, we cannot naively take the institutional agenda at face value: other and more covert or implicit considerations may also be shaping the sequences of acts and the intended outcomes. These can only be discovered by knowing the range of people's multiple, simultaneous concerns (Wikan 1990, esp. chaps. 3 and 4). Thus I would argue that neither our appreciation of the functions and consequences of acts, nor our understanding of the overt collective purposes of institutions, is sufficient to establish what is really going on: a careful inquiry into various participants' interpretations and practice is necessary to establish the world in which they move. In other words, I wish to raise as an underlying problematic of this whole analysis the question of just what the connection is between the formal institutional features and the practice that eventuates, and also between the overt forms of behavior and the reality people construct and inhabit.

This means asking questions about the *relevance* of different kinds of anthropological data: just what is it they establish, and what do they *not* tell. Such skepticism is not always facilitated, even by the best of anthropological methodologies. Let a simple example serve to illustrate. Quite shortly after arriving in Pagatepan, I was made to revise my understanding of the entailments of teknonymy. Following Geertz's compelling account of the muting of individuality in the Balinese conception of personhood, I had accepted the interpretation that teknonymy formed a logical element in such a conception, since it is a naming custom that seems to reduce the saliency of the individual's biography (Geertz and Geertz 1964; Geertz [1966] 1973a). I was therefore startled to discover that the persons making use of the device saw it in an entirely different light: "The parents are so proud, for their first-born is their greatest achievement so far. So to flatter them, we like to call them by their baby's name." While a portion of Geertz's insight may hold — that it is perhaps more difficult to retain a clear sense of the singular biographies of public figures or superficial acquaintances in a population where such name changes are a regular feature of most life courses — the argument that the practice of teknonymy is a reflex of a cultural conception of personhood that attempts to mute individuality (ibid.:375ff., 389ff., 398f.) is not sustained. I find, on the contrary, again and again that these conventions actively convey an orientation between villagers in Pagatepan that celebrates individual achievement, emphasizes unique and valued personal biography, and communicates attunement to the particular emotions and subjectivity of others.

At this point, however, it is the general argument that I want to pursue. I wish to warn against abstracting "culture" away from its ontologically necessary embeddedness in behavior and interaction, so as to contemplate undisturbedly what is "culturally played up, symbolically emphasized" (ibid.:390). We need, on the contrary, to attend most carefully to the everyday life of particular Balinese, to pick up the cues provided by their variously contextualized usage, so as to distinguish our misreadings from our better interpretations — thereby to build progressively a more workable facsimile of the realities they variously construct and inhabit.

It would be consonant with much recent and contemporary anthropology to rely heavily on data of the kinds provided in the preceding chapters to arrive at a generalized picture of basic cultural conceptions — here, to extract from the descriptions of village social organization a constellation of ideas about duality, seniority, descent, origin, and gender and compose a model of person identity and memberships from these formal elements. The cultural materials required for such an operation are richly and easily accessible, in the sense that an anthropologist can establish relations to a set of "informants" who, if they are willing to give any information at all, will readily codify them and present rules and institutions in relatively systematic fashion. Moreover, such a construction lends itself easily to logical and comparative analysis, leading directly either to a typology of forms and a mapping of structural similarity and diversity, if one has comparative interests, or to an increasingly rich contextualization through "thick description" of associated institutional complexes, if one's bent goes toward the representation of cultural "wholes."

It is possible, of course, to produce valid insights and generalizations from such materials. For example, we might note that the forms of dual organization exemplified in these villages are characterized by an isomorphy and balance between their dual divisions, rather than by functional reciprocity. Even the groups in such a profoundly dual organization as that of Julah are not exogamous, nor do they perform any reciprocal ritual services. On the other hand, there are usually elements of hierarchization that contradict the formal equality of the two divisions. Thus the kubayan bima leader of the East division of Julah ranks after the kubayan dharma of the West division. Likewise, the assembly of the nonautochtones in Prabakula meets in the death temple during the ascendant moon, whereas the autochtones meet in the village temple at the full moon, paralleling arrangements noted by Goris ([1935] 1960a:93) for some of the mountain villages around Lake Batur. Such renderings of dualism can then readily be compared to those reported from other parts of Indonesia (de Josselin de Jong 1952; Barnes 1974; and particularly the intriguing parallel in the Moluccas, where dual divisions of autochthones and immigrants are opposed, as in Prabakula, Valeri 1989:118).

Or we might seek to develop an analysis of the cultural construction of formal authority. In some places seniority reigns supreme in all domains, as in the numbered hierarchy of married couples in Julah; or it may be modified by a Buddhist-like conception of the proper phases of a person's life, so that the senior generation is retired from responsibility in secular matters on the marriage of their children, as in many North Balinese banjar organizations. In other areas major compromises with other criteria are developed, such as caste, lineal descent, or election (as in Pengastulan or Prabakula), the meritocracy of command of sacred knowledge (as in Pagatepan), or selection by the gods (as in the selection of priests to many village temples, and most spectacularly in Sida Tapa). In descent organization we likewise find various accommodations of the principle of patriliny to the recognition of women and matrilateral ties, leading to effective kindreds (as in Pagatepan) or to various institutionalizations focusing on husband-wife unity (rather than the brother-sister unity found in some other East Asian seaboard societies).

But, interesting as such reflections on these cultural materials might be,

I cannot see how they would come to grips with the questions of what these institutions, and the praxes they generate, mean to the conceptions and lives of the people themselves. Would it, for example, make any sense to claim that the constructions of people's experienced identities in these communities vary as fundamentally as do their village constitutions? My purpose in this study is to enhance our anthropological understanding of the civilization of Bali as a way of life; I wish to characterize the consciousness in which Balinese participate and grasp the meanings they construct, and to lay bare the complex social relationships they sustain and the experiences generated for them by a life led in this way. This entails an analysis of what anthropologists are accustomed to calling Balinese culture and Balinese society; but already in such a representation of my object I sense a subtle reification and a shift in focus. My chosen object is reality as perceived and lived by Balinese, and the complexities of their relations with each other — not "society" and "culture" per se. "Culture" and "society" come about through the practice of Balinese lives; and we must not use our constructs of these in turn as a kind of explanation of those very events, activities, and relations of which they are our representation. There is a place for the construction of models, but I have long argued that they need to be models of process and causation if they are to serve explanatory purposes (Barth 1966); and it is important to be aware that it is the analyst's choice of perspective that determines the direction in which causality points in these matters. The various representations, meanings, and identities that appear as "Balinese culture" may perhaps be more fruitfully regarded as the precipitate of the experience of taking part in Balinese life, rather than its cause; and the shape of Balinese society is surely the product of interaction between Balinese, as much as its blueprint. To grasp what Balinese life is about we may need to take the world for granted and observe the processes by which Balinese endow it with meaning, rather than try to generate the world *from* those meanings.

But while it is my ambition to discover what is entailed in seeing and acting on the world in Balinese terms, I also want to go beyond this and ask how such ideas, identities, and acts are interconnected and reproduced. In other words, once we know something of their import, we also need to inquire into their generation and their consequences. My reservations concern whether the processes that produce (i.e., reproduce and change) the patterns that can be observed in Balinese life are best retrieved by the standard anthropological usage of the concepts of society and culture, which so fundamentally confound percept and precept. Moreover, if a focus on the form of society and culture stands in danger of limiting and reifying our object, then, given the great diversity of organizational pat-

Bali-Hindu wedding ceremony.

terns, cultural expressions, and dogmatic structures we have glimpsed in the preceding chapters, we are faced with a further danger. A methodology of classifying and comparing these forms would quickly bog down in quite elaborate typologies and constructions — or it would have to seek escape from that, but also from contact with the realities of Balinese lives, by excessive abstraction and generalization. I need a methodology that simultaneously allows me to penetrate to the locally embraced, experiential levels of meaning *and* facilitates the analysis of formal diversity.

The central foci of this study thus comprise the complex patterns of Balinese society, the diversity of lives that it molds, *and* the meanings and identities that are generated within it. This requires us to show how the interpretations of events made by people from their diverse vantage points are aggregated so they converge on shared meanings — i.e., an ethnographically ascertained degree of common reality. In other words, I am not attempting to construct a conceptual structure supposedly encoded in a culture (though it is certainly a useful step to identify pervasive features of Balinese traditional conceptions), nor the formal organization of groups and statuses (though we do need to know the institutional constraints that

Balinese Muslim wedding ceremony.

impinge on communities and persons). Rather, I need to focus on the situations and practices that emerge in interaction between people and on the precipitate of interpreted experience that results. Analytically speaking, *this* must be the locus where every cultural tradition is reproduced. I belabor these dualities of conception and action, intention and experience, large-scale and local or individual, because I expect them to be significantly connected, but to be so in ways that are complex, not simply productive of isomorphy and harmony. I insist that the empirical processes that connect them cannot be ignored in an anthropological analysis without severe loss of naturalism, whereas their careful modeling will provide essential insights into the operation of Bali as a complex society and civilization.

A critical step, then, must be to discover the meanings, for the actors themselves, of their institutions and concepts – i.e., the interpretations by which they variously construct their worlds. But this understanding should not come as the spare conclusions of elaborate analyses (as so often in contemporary anthropological exercises), but as far as possible as primary data, on which we can base an analysis of something else. And this "something else," I propose, will be the connections and processes involved in the reproduction of North Balinese institutions and ideas — i.e., a model of that which delivers the continuing premises for the events of Balinese lives.

In practice, the functionalism of Malinowski, with its close observation of the connectedness of acts, interests, concepts, and interpretations in a local population, has for most anthropologists provided the main method whereby we in the field gain a sense of the meanings embraced by people. Following his example, the anthropologist tries to combine a growing knowledge of local institutions and conventions with a deepening personal acquaintance with individuals — their temperaments, relationships, assets, interests, and ideals — as a basis to identify what their acts are about. The resulting nexus of cultural rules and particulars of property relations, social relations, biographies, and local history is illustrated, for example, in the explicit and exemplary detail of Leach's materials on the village of Pul Eliya in Sri Lanka (Leach 1961), a community in a civilizational context very comparable to the Balinese villages we are discussing. But a core of such data presumably provides the primary context for every anthropologist's imputation of purpose, meaning, or significance to the acts of real people in real situations; only by means of it can the anthropologist hope to transcend received theories and the outsider's view of the exotic and puzzling and partake in the common sense of the actors' own world.

However, the sheer mass of such particulars, and the need to systematize and schematize, prevent us from remaining on this empirical level and force us to construct models and generalizations. Our theories of society, or culture, or interaction, necessarily inform such models and generalizations. To the extent that we allow them to enter into the production of our data, of course, it becomes impossible to use our findings to transcend these theories: any critique of them must then depend on other findings, differently generated. The issue I wish to make explicit is this: at what point in our collection of data should we allow our particular theoretical positions to take over and dominate the methodology by which we generate our data, in this case our understanding of the import and meaning of events and patterns in the interactions we observe? I am not raising this as a general epistemological question only — though as such it is also well worth addressing. Rather, I direct it specifically to the task at hand: how can I avoid locating the actor's intent and experience in some particular level of cultural representation, thereby obscuring the possible gap of discrepancy between it and the experienced meaning that I wish to identify?

The methodological point may be best illustrated with reference to materials outside of Bali, and I therefore return to the study by Leach (1961), which has raised issues of a similar nature to the ones I am now trying to face. I refer to an unresolved enigma in the work of Leach and his associates in their analyses of social structure among the villages of the Dry Zone of Sri Lanka.

Leach, as noted, based his model of village social structure on a meticulously careful analysis of the data on the 146 inhabitants of the village of Pul Eliya and their landholdings, cooperating groups, and kinship and marriage networks, with major parts of the data covering a time depth of sixty-five years. His general problematic was to identify the main features of social form, and the underlying determinants of these forms, essentially in a theoretical polemic. The then prevalent British structural-functional view was that the structure of society was to be found in the structure of its enduring groups and the jural rules of recruitment deriving from kinship relations on which such groups are based (ibid.:5–12). Leach's main conclusion from his study of Pul Eliya was that more significant determinants of enduring organization were found in the (partly man-made) stable topography of village lands – i.e., that technical and economic constraints are prior to the constraints of morality and law (ibid.:9). In the process, he also identified the main social organizational features of the community, basing his account precisely on the comprehensive contextualization I have emphasized. We are thereby provided with an analysis of the meaning of the native concepts whereby the actors themselves identify and organize their social groups, particularly the concepts rendered by Leach as subcaste *(variga)*, compound group (*gedara*, i.e., shareholders in a minuscule territorial "estate"), and family or faction *(pavula)*.

Robinson (1969), reviewing the small but distinguished handful of Kandyan Singhalese village studies that followed in the wake of Leach's influential monograph, uncovers a troubling enigma. Through comparably meticulous contextualization and analysis, highly divergent models of these salient social groupings have been produced, labeled by the same native concepts and represented as "the social structure" of culturally, socially, and economically closely related communities. Thus the words *variga*, *gedara*, and *pavula* are reported to be used in these other communities to refer to groups of very different construction from those Leach had described in Pul Eliya. In Robinson's words: "Are we then prepared to state that in the same cultural area and social system there can exist: some *variga* which are bilateral endogamous groups and others which are matrilineal exogamous groups; some *gedara* whose 'basis' is property and others without even a fiction of *gedara* property; some *pavula* which are factional groups based on cores of affines, and others which, if they exist at all, are small non-factional compound groups?" (ibid.:420).

As far as I know, Robinson's question has remained unanswered, presumably because there was no way whereby the discrepancies could be resolved from available materials — although the main justification for Leach's publication of such massively detailed data was precisely to enable a "reader to exercise his skepticism where and how he will" (Leach 1961:12).

It is a short way indeed from Robinson's enigma to the kinds of materials I have been presenting in the preceding chapters. In our discussion of "the North Balinese subak" we were confronted in Pagatepan with a subak that operated as a communally run public utility to provide private farms with irrigation water, whereas the subaks of neighboring Prabakula are collectives responsible for most aspects of the mystical and agronomical enterprise of producing rice from the land. The concept of sekaha in Julah refers to pervasive dual divisions in the political and religious structure of the community, while the sekaha of Prabakula are voluntary clubs for the pursuit of artistic activities such as gamelan orchestras and dancing troupes or, in another sense of the term, congregations worshiping at each of the three Siwa temples. Villagers in Sida Tapa point to an open space at the periphery of their village as their kahyangan, whereas the term is known in the literature on South Bali as the concept for the focal set of three massive temples (specifically defined as such by their encircling masonry walls) conceptually constituent of village communities, and elsewhere in North Bali it refers to another set of masonry-enclosed structures. The balian of Pura Gde in Pengastulan is a hereditary male priest, whereas a balian in most places is a private consulting trance medium; the term many also refer to a midwife, a calendrical expert, a Muslim divine acting ex officio as wizard (in Pagatepan), or (in Sida Tapa) a possessed female priestess. Some villages are exceptional in not performing the postmortuary rite of ngaben, cremation (e.g., Muslim Pegatepan, but also until recently the Bali Aga village of Sembiran); while the vast majority do, as the essential rite that releases the soul and purifies it for ancestor worship. But the object of cremation is variously, and dogmatically, a fresh or mummified corpse (high-caste persons and pemangku priests); or many-year-old exhumed bones, or a handful of soil from old graves (most Pasek villages); or a sandalwood representation of the dead person, or a lontar name-tag, leaving the bones undisturbed (Pedawa); or the dead person's clothes, burned at the time of the dead person's burial in an unmarked grave (Julah).

This morass could be almost endlessly extended, and it embraces (concepts for) social groups, key customs, and whole exegetical schemata. The data appear to reiterate the pattern of Robinson's enigma. For the purpose of our broad comparative analysis and synthesis of North Balinese society and traditions, it seems essential to resolve it and find a methodology that protects against it. Perhaps we can learn a lesson from this comparison: where may those analyses of social structure in Sri Lankan villages have gone wrong?

I would expect the lesson from the Singhalese Dry Zone to be somehow theoretical and methodological. There is no indication in the ethnographic materials reported of any failure of local and social contextualization in the sense of inadequate attention to village groups and institutions, the distribution of property and kinship relations between village members, etc. But presumably some unquestioned and misplaced assumptions have been allowed to invade the systematization of the otherwise well contextualized observations that the authors employ for their data. I sense two such assumptions:

(1) Leach's original analysis — in conformity with most anthropological writing — seems to assume a one-to-one relation between native concepts and salient social groups within the community. In his theoretical framework, this relates to his emphasis that social structure belongs to the realm of ideas, what people say rather than what they do. This has proved a most productive and insightful perspective. Yet it must be misplaced if it leads to a tacit assumption that the particular words *variga*, *gedara*, and *pavula*, because they are used by villagers to refer to groups in the community, are rightly identified as sociological concepts signifying types of social groupings, with the added assumption that villagers will regard patterns of recruitment and composition as the salient and distinctive features of such groups. Perhaps the terms, though they can be used to refer to certain social objects, embrace a very differently constituted semantic field from our terms "subcaste", "compound group," etc. — even while these remain quite adequate concepts by which to characterize those village groups in Pul Eliya for some typological purposes. Only thus could we explain that other villagers, apparently speaking the same language, could use the same terms to designate groups that are, in terms of their sociological characteristics, in our view quite different.

(2) A related or additional tacit assumption seems to have been that native terms will provide the correct categories for sociological comparison. This also is a widely shared view, entailed by the form of words in Leach's analysis and articulated as a methodological premise by Robinson. At issue is a poorly explicated problem in comparative method in anthropology. Any systematic comparison entails, of course, the establishment of equivalences — i.e., the construction of overarching categories within which institution A of village x and institution B of village y can be mean-

ingfully identified as "variants" of "the same." We are not particularly clear on our criteria for such identifications. Robinson's enigma arises only if native words referring to institutions and groups are assumed to be infallible identification tags for such comparative equivalences.

Once these assumptions are read into the interpretation, systematization, and generalization of data, then, no matter how well contextualized the data may otherwise be, these assumptions become nearly invisible and lead — at best! — to enigmas and more commonly to undiscovered and unacknowledged confusion in what are presented as data. We are hardly in a position to provide a substantive answer to Robinson's enigma; but her perceptive though inconclusive discussion should prod us to sharpen our discovery procedures, particularly through a more searching critique of our own ontological premises.

At issue are really our fundamental anthropological assumptions about the nature of society and culture and about the basal or generative processes in their reproduction. I see these processes take place in a world of considerable disorder and within a broad field of variation between people and groups where knowledge and particular concerns are differentially distributed, and most events of interaction are predicated by limited and partisan perspectives among the actors and agencies involved. The weight of an anthropology that has fashioned too many of its concepts to the mold of an ideal model of simple, stable, and homogeneous small unit societies may teach us to locate our terms and descriptions of system falsely. By performing our analysis in conformity with received anthropological language and conventions, we are in danger of unwittingly perpetuating inappropriate tacit assumptions regarding the nature of society. Suspecting this, our best course will not be prematurely to embrace a new set of axioms and another paradigm. Rather, I urge that we proceed, if we can, more tentatively and descriptively. We need to formulate simply, with the humility of suspended judgment, some provisional viewpoints on how complex societies, and the lives within them, may be shaped, so that the implications of these viewpoints can be explored and confronted with observed events. Thereby we enter them among the open questions in our discovery procedures and expose them to falsification or modification.

Elizabeth Colson's reflections on her thirty-five years of observation among the (relatively speaking simple and homogeneous) Gwembe Tonga articulate a number of challenging suggestions. "We have found people revising their memories as they tailor their ideas about the appropriate ordering of their society to their experience of the compromises of their daily lives. Moreover, their expectations of other people and themselves have changed drastically. . . . [W]hat brought about such changes, what are their consequences, and how are they seen by the different sets of people who make up society[?] ... When we looked at societies or cultures as unitary phenomena, we could not ask such questions, especially if we emphasized values as controlling behavior and limiting experience in some drastic fashion. We now know we are not dealing with stable systems. ... Values once thought to be fundamental for guiding the way particular people dealt with each other and their environment have turned out to be situational and time linked, rather than eternal verities that can be used to predict behavior over time, under all circumstances" (Colson 1984:6–7).

The acknowledgment of the empirical occurrence of change is of course not new, though its speed and comprehensiveness may startle. What differs in Colson's statement are (1) the observation that people's guidelines for how their society should be are tailored from their experience of their daily lives as much as vice versa — a view I have already expressed above and shall seek to retain through my subsequent analysis; (2) the recognition that the different positioning of persons is a significant aspect of these processes — an insight I shall try to pursue; and above all (3) the discovery that change can occur as swiftly and deeply in what we were taught to think of as basic features of society as in what was considered to be more ephemeral.

This last observation undermines the premises on which most representations of change have been based. Thus, in the manner of Firth's (1954) early and admirable attempts to acknowledge change and analyze it in terms of "structure" and "organization," we have been led to construct representations combining some unchanging, deep parameters with interstitial areas of greater free play. This may distort the facts too much. Our response to Colson's observation should not be an intensified search for other, more truly enduring parameters to replace our previous concept of "values." Rather, we should recognize that *all* our observations and descriptions must be constructed so they can represent systems in flux.

This is not to assert that any change, and every condition of the world, are possible: we can retain the notion of system even as we acknowledge a considerable degree of disorder and the ubiquity of flux. But where our objects of study are in flux, it becomes particularly critical how we conceive and specify the relevant continuities that make any two events or proposed systems of events into "cases" or "variants" of "the same" objects to us. I have argued elsewhere, and tried to illustrate by analogy and example, that any description of change, as also any comparison, becomes meaningless unless we are able to specify correctly the *continuities* between the systems we are identifying or comparing (Barth 1967; Barth 1981:11ff.). Different specifications of such continuities lead us to construct entirely different models of the dynamics of reproduction and change, so our models of processes must incorporate valid assumptions of what it is that connects the forms which we compare.

But again, we should never confound continuity with the sense of changelessness. If we reflect for a moment on North Bali over the most recent life span of people, where do we find sufficient enduring factors to provide us with a compelling framework of continuity? Certainly not on a macrolevel of Society, where, for example, gross political institutions come and go: the Dutch colonial regime and its hierarchy of Dutch and local officials; the years of Japanese rule; the struggle for independence and the Sukarno revolutionary regime; the failed Communist coup and the years of military rule; the present variant of party organization and balloting. Nor can I see geography, ecology, or material production as compellingly enduring: improved and expanded coffee cultivation and the introduction of cloves and other crops may not have caused water to start running uphill, but they have certainly raised the relative value of uphill lands and production drastically; while improved dams and new seeds and fertilizers have recently made it possible to raise up to three crops of rice per year where only one grew before.

My descriptions of North Bali so far have mostly focused on villages as what I might now term my "objects-in-flux." Most village units have indeed endured, with the constitution of their temples, desa adat, and subaks largely unchanged; but the variations I have uncovered *between* these villages, and as I hope I have shown also between their subaks, are such as to raise major analytical enigmas, comparable to those discussed for Sri Lankan villages. However — and this is where we can break out of the tacit assumptions that generated Robinson's enigma — the fact that certain features of formal village constitutions have endured does not mean that these features need have any singular significance in underpinning the meanings, the interpreted reality, of people's lives. We should not assume ipso facto, as have most anthropologists in their construction of social structure, that formal groups and statuses, because they endure, comprise the most salient components of persons in the sense of being the most important identities they conceive and embrace, and in terms of which they act. As I have stressed, these formal features of organization have undeniable importance in defining and structuring the *arenas* in which people act. But they do not predicate *how* people will act and what their actions will be about, what their experienced meanings will be.

I suggest that we have now finally arrived at a point where we can obtain a handle on the discrepancy or gap between cultural representations and the experienced meaning of actions. It is mainly a question of changing one's perspective on events, not of observing a very different range of events. We need to recognize that persons, even as they act within the framework of formal institutions, bring *concerns* (Wikan 1990:80ff.) to most occasions and activities and that they will interpret events and options in terms of such concerns. Where the externalist view will always focus narrowly on tasks that are institutionally explicit, and construct an understanding of the place of the activities in a schema of collective or social functions, the participants in most situations will primarily understand and interpret events in terms of the difference these events make to their concerns and how the outcomes will affect their life trajectories.

If we choose to depict people's lives within a paradigm based on principles of recruitment and the formal composition of groups and gatherings, in the tradition of the structural-functionalists and many of their successors today, we shall surely remain within the externalist perspective and are limited to seing people enacting their statuses. If we try to pursue the cultural nexus of ideas on which these organizations and other institutions of village life are based, in the tradition of thick description, we shall still remain insensitive to any discrepancy and construct an externalist account of meanings derived from an impersonal logic of collective representations. If, however, we strain to discover the concerns of people, and recognize the capacities and relations they bring to bear in their pursuit of these concerns, then we may be successful in seing both cultural representations in action and something of the intentions and interpretations of actors.

It is by attending systematically to people's own intentions and interpretations, accessible only if one adopts the perspective of their concerns and their knowledge of the constraints under which they act, that one can start unraveling the meanings *they* confer on events, and thereby the experience they are harvesting. This will be my purpose as I now return to the description of the two communities of Pagatepan and Prabakula, embedding the activities of persons in the nexus of their concerns, circumstances, and social relationships.

PART THREE

Realities and Practical
Concerns of Village Living

7

Leadership, Faction, and Violence in Pagatepan

In an early tour de force attempting to generalize over the variety of South Balinese village organizations then known to him, Clifford Geertz (1959) has made the only comparative analysis of Balinese villages found in the newer literature. To get a grasp on the variety, he tries to do his typology on a meta-level: "What is constant in Balinese village structure is the set of components out of which it is constructed, not the structure itself" (ibid.:991). These constancies are conceptualized as "planes" of social organization, each with its distinctive principles of group affiliation. Thus, according to Geertz (ibid.:992ff.), every Balinese is categorized according to her or his (1) obligation to worship in a given temple; (2) residential membership in a hamlet (banjar), with duties to participate at appropriate stages of life in community work and decision-making; (3) subak membership arising from ownership of land in a particular watershed; (4) commonality of ascribed status from birth membership in a "caste"; (5) consanguineal and affinal kinship ties; (6) membership in voluntary associations; and (7) legal subordination to a particular government official, the perbekel.

Fitting the variety of organization depicted in the preceding chapters to such a scheme might be a feasible, though tortuous, exercise. In the case of Pagatepan, for example, we could go down the list and point to (1) their obligation to worship on Fridays in the central mosque; (2) their banjar divisions, though these have fewer implications then in most Bali-Hindu villages; (3) their subak, though membership here depends on usufruct and not ownership of land; (4) their ideological denial of caste, but de facto identification with the Sudra population, which is also the universal caste status of many Hindu local communities in North Bali; (5) their organization with respect to kinship ties; (6) the presence of a certain number of voluntary associations among them; and (7) their subordination to a single perbekel. In addition, the Muslims of Pagatepan are significantly segmented on an eighth plane, in enduring relations of spiritual filiation to their guru religious teachers. This indeed may be represented as paralleling the ritual relation that obtains between many Bali Hindus and their hereditary house *(gria)* of Brahmin priests (pedanda).

The other villages described, from Julah to Pengastulan, would stretch the interpretation of these seven or eight planes in other directions and perhaps introduce further candidates for addition. Indeed, the operation of generalizing each plane to encompass the diversity of rules and groupings found in different villages may already in Geertz's attempt to embrace South Balinese villages have passed the point where they become relatively vacuous. I can only assent to Robinson's warning of how her Sri Lankan enigma ought *not* to be solved: "The ways of social action 'connoted' by these terms will be understood only when the common themes underlying the variants of social structure are identified. In this connection, I should like to emphasize that further analysis on this topic should not be attempted through the process of widening the relevant definitions, thereby rendering them essentially meaningless" (Robinson 1969:420).

Geertz's model, however, may have an additional claim to validity, which is closely tied to a particular, substantive assertion widely embraced or tacitly implied in anthropological accounts of Bali. The underlying principle of social structure has been represented as one where the "various social functions . . . are . . . each provided with a separate autonomous social apparatus" (Geertz and Geertz 1975:30). If so, the different planes can be seen as mirroring the Balinese conceptual schema for separating these functions; and the emphasis would be on the fact of their division and autonomy, rather than the particular morphology of the institutions found on each plane. Such a model embodies the quality frequently ascribed to the Balinese village: a consensual and sectorialized mode of operation where each collectivity and each organ of the local society goes about its business calmly and correctly, without assertive leadership and command, in an intricately ordered but independent way — rather like the way each separate limb and part of a Balinese dancer seems to be moving autonomously, as if dancing a dance of its own (Bateson and Mead 1942:16ff.) On the widest interpretive canvas, this connects with Geertz's persistent and evocative depiction of Bali as a society where persons interact as "stereotyped contemporaries, abstract and anonymous fellowmen" (Geertz [1966] 1973a:389).

If this picture is correct, it must have pervasive and profound implications, not least for the way in which an anthropological analysis of Balinese materials should be pursued. If social functions are separated according to some cultural scheme, and each is organized by an autonomous social apparatus and enacted by persons whose concern is to perform roles to the greatest possible perfection and without consideration of any aspect of individuality, then social life falls apart in a series of tableaux, connected only by an emic theory of functions and a culturally shared aesthetics of performance. Significance and meaning could only be retrieved by the anthropologist in such a world by tracing the logic of these cultural rules; and any attempt to contextualize acts in terms of persons and interests would be irrelevant.

We may test the validity of such a conception by seeing the extent to which it lends order to the events that unfold in an actual community. I will start with the community of Pagatepan and chronicle first the recent history of its leadership. A description of the political field should allow us to assess the degree of functional autonomy of planes. Leadership, by Geertz's account, will be refracted in relations of superiority and precedence, not power and instrumentality (Geertz 1980:121ff.). Succession could be expected to occasion rivalry, but to be consistent with his representation this would take the form of a rivalry of status, to be resolved by formal criteria, and not a pragmatics of cross-sectoral mobilization of interests and factions.

Pagatepan seems to present a very different aspect. My data on leadership careers, and the fragments of village history they convey, show that functionally diverse fields of village activity fuse in a single, connected arena for politics, and that turbulent and pragmatic modes of operation are characteristic of social relations and factional dynamics. As I shall recount, the people who enter this arena are represented by their fellow villagers as moved by highly personal, individual interests; they confront each other in a highly personalized politics and try to mobilize the support of followers by diverse and pragmatic means. Let us first explore the more ambiguous evidence, in respect to succession to imamship, and then the struggles for the office of village headman, the perbekel.

The office of imam is without doubt the pivotal and dominant position in the village of Pagatepan. As the highest authority on Islam, which demands submission to the will of God in secular life as well as sacred matters, and as the leader, convener, and articulator of Majlis Ulama opinion, the imam stands for the kind of order this devout Muslim community embraces.

The line of remembered imams in Pagatepan leads back from the present incumbent through Hajji Jayadi, Hajji Maxfuz, and Hajji Dahlan. The present imam claimed to have held office for many years in 1984. His predecessor, Imam Jayadi, served more briefly. The period of Hajji Maxfuz is widely recognized as a golden age of considerable duration. He died in 1964 but may have ceased functioning as imam some years before his death. Hajji Dahlan was imam in the youth of the present octogenarians, i.e., in the 1910s and 1920s. The sequence of succession and approximate duration of dominance of each is thus clear, though the exact chronology proved difficult to establish decisively.

The one all-important criterion in the selection of imam should be his command of Islam. It is through this superior knowledge that he can lead the village by reaching the right decision on all matters through applying the Shariah correctly. One shrewd old villager pointed out explicitly: "This is essential; for the imam, and the Ulama which he leads, have the function above all to judge by correct Islamic law, to express a *correct opinion*. To force people to comply is not important; what is essential is for the imam to see that the Ulama decision *is not wrong*. Only thus can God's blessing be secured."

A subsidiary, ideally derivative, requirement is that the imam should be able to maintain the respect of all people for religion and his knowledge of it. This is reflected very clearly in the imam's self-representation: in the highly competitive milieu of the Ulama and the other gurus he must show his (superior) command of the scriptures, his infallibility in their application, his intellectual and charismatic force in expounding and explaining the text.

The mode of selection, as noted, is by consensus in the Majlis Ulama, the conclave of leading religious scholars. Naturally, there may be differences of opinion among them and differences between insider and outsider opinion on who is the most outstanding religious scholar. It is allowable to champion the wisdom of one's own guru, or of another religious teacher of excellence, but inappropriate to make invidious comparisons with the incumbent imam. Indeed, respect for religion and for the office of imam are inseparable, and this serves to suppress all but the most oblique criticism of the imam; such criticism must be voiced in very vague and general terms, or be directed to small details of expression and performance, and be broached in intimate and informal circles only. But the villagers' ears are subtly attuned to innuendo and swift to notice and transmit criticism, though also swift to sanction the critic. Informal village conversation is indeed continually but discreetly loaded with such judgments. The leading gurus bewail the resulting divisiveness among them and how *pitnah*, slander, keeps them from cooperating in raising the level of religious instruction in the community.

Imam of Pagatepan, praying by a fresh grave.

An incumbent imam is wise if he gives visible recognition to potential rivals by allotting them various supportive tasks: as vice-imam (bilal), leader of the Thursday prayer in the mosque, occasional guest speaker at the Friday sermon, etc. The present imam follows a sensitive practice in this respect, as apparently his predecessors did. Indeed, presumably as a result of such delegated and secondary public activities on the part of other religious figures than the imam proper, there is considerable public confusion as to just what has been the line of succession to imamship in the past. Thus several old men claimed incorrectly to have once held the position themselves, others that their fathers had, in attempts to aggrandize themselves before me and before junior members of the community. However, at times the rivalries have been sharp and overt, and linked to party politics. Thus, in the late 1950s, the rift between factions associated with the two parties of Masyumi ("the union of Indonesian Muslims") and NU ("Action for the Ulama") caused the then leader of the losing Masyumi faction and main pretender in line to succeed Imam Maxfuz finally to leave the village and move elsewhere.

By conventional etiquette in Pagatepan, as in all of Bali, persons of higher status and power are shown very marked respect: they are greeted submissively and treated obsequiously; if seated, then others moving past them crouch with right arm extended downward so as not to loom above them, etc. This is true in relation to both religious and civil luminaries; but "in terms of respect, the imam is infinitely above the perbekel. The perbekel deals with material things, and with government; the imam deals with things from God." Consequently one owes the imam the extreme of respect, and this was particularly observed before, in contrast to now. "If you saw the imam come down the lane, you took a side lane so as not to meet him, out of respect. If you sat talking like we do now, and we saw him pass by the door, we would be very ashamed [*malu, ngidalam*]." Why "ashamed"? "Because his knowledge was so great. Because of *minder* [from the Dutch: inferiority complex]."

The present imam receives less dramatic acknowledgment but is treated with great formality and reserve, whereas his own style is lively and expressive, indeed highly loquacious, gesticulatory, and humorous when the occasion is not formal. Now quite sedentary, he traveled and studied extensively in his younger days. His first love, however, may be his garden and its cultivation rather than his scholarship. Through friends in Java he has obtained and introduced a series of new crops to North Bali, most prominently the cultivation of vanilla in the early 1970s, for which he propagandized at his Friday sermons; he also claims to have been the first in his area to take up the cultivation of cloves, now a major crop in Buleleng.

The ideal image of an imam is represented by people's memories and characterizations of Hajji Maxfuz. At the age of twelve Maxfuz went to Mecca and studied with the Shafi scholar Omar Sumbaah. He stayed in Mecca for eighteen years, the last three years of which he himself lectured and taught in the Masjid-i-Haram in Mecca. In the words of several villagers:

"His predecessor, Hajji Dahlan, was famous in my childhood, because he could give the complete Arabic texts and then translate them to Balinese. His school was always full: he taught on the platform under his rice-barn [sakman, 'the pillar house'], which is a cool and dry place to study, both day and night. There would be up to sixty or eighty pupils crowded together there. But after Maxfuz Guru came home, *he* was able not only to translate, but to *teach* Arabic, really properly. Imam Dahlan was good; but Hajji Maxfuz was excellent, really superior."

"yet he was gentle as well as brilliant. In the old days, gurus often beat children mercilessly. Guru Maxfuz never did."

"He always taught. If he saw or heard someone in the street doing wrong, he would immediately stop, and teach and explain and instruct him!"

"Imam Maxfuz was a very influential man. One word from him, and everybody listened. But he never became rich — he was rich only in sons! He had altogether forty children, by four wives."

So far, our exercise of inspecting the field of leadership and village politics may appear still inconclusive. We have seen a very strong normative emphasis on particular, ideal criteria for the selection of imams, a formalistic emphasis on correct decision rather than effective action, and a pervasive ceremonial acknowledgment of rank in the respect behavior of villagers toward their imam. When his authority extends so widely into nearly all aspects of daily life, this may reflect the ideology of Islam more than a fusion of formally autonomous functional planes. On the other hand, there is an undeniable ambience of community criticism of performance, and of divisions and alignments, that suggests a more pragmatic politics of faction and power underlying the formal appearances.

This latter view is strongly supported by a corresponding account of perbekelship in Pagatepan. It is indicated by the mode of selection and the criteria used; but most clearly it is shown in the mode of execution of the role and in the biographies of successive perbekels.

The perbekel, village headman, of colonial times was appointed from above by the administration. Since independence the post has been elective. However, the sponsorship of the administration is still regarded by villagers as being of great importance: their view is that a clear endorsement from the camat (district officer) is sufficient to secure a candidate a majority of votes. The administration's problem, on the other hand, has been that they have difficulties identifying any person in the community who could unite village opinion and provide trustworthy leadership and liaison. Villagers recognize the same problem.

"For good leadership, there are three important qualifications: knowledge, wealth, and physical strength/bravery. There is no one in the village with an outstanding combination of even two of these today. Though XX has knowledge and some degree of wealth, he is now far too old. Besides, today religious knowledge is no longer enough — you must also have practical knowledge, which he lacks. The only rich man is YY — though really it is his wife who has the good business mind. And the only strong man is ZZ, but he lacks the other qualities."

The remembered perbekels of Pagatepan are these (pseudonyms are used to allow candid reporting):

1.	Hajji Safwatullah	Colonial period
2.	Hajji Saleh	
3.	Muxtar	1949
4.	Basik	Sukarno period
5.	Hajji Musa	
6.	Basik	
7.	(Serma Untung of the Indonesian Army)	1965
8.	Fatehul	
9.	(Pelda M. Noor of the Indonesian Army)	Soeharto period
10.	Harunan	
11.	Basik	

Perbekel Safwatullah is reported to have occupied the office for thirty-five years and to have combined the three components of good leadership: he had a considerable level of religious knowledge in his own right; he knew the Shariah; and he was a member of the Ulama. At least by the time of his death, he was also a very wealthy man, owning thirty-six hectares of land. During his time in office, and thanks to his strength and bravery, he also extended Pagatepan's territory toward the north, in the irrigated zone, without payment and at the expense of the Hindu village of Prabakula. What is more, he shared this land with others rather than seizing it all for himself. Yet "though he was influential as perbekel, it was then like now: many small leaders, and no uniting person."

"Saleh was a *very* strong perbekel: an iron hand, good but *too* strong, and never listened to the opinion of any other man." Others are more detailed and more critical; today he has a number of denouncers, and his few supporters are concentrated among his closest kinsfolk and affines.

"Saleh was a poor man but worked his way up in the service [lit.: "as a spy"] of the colonial power. He served the Dutch for a while in Ambon. . . . Then he was involved in the elopement raid [merangkat] for a girl from Tanawan — they were surprised and had to fight; he killed a man and so spent three years in jail. Under the Japanese he came up again and became perbekel. . . . When I was only a poor small boy, herding our family's ducks, he used to come and simply help himself from the flock. He once even took a calf from us. He handed my brother over to the Japanese; they sent him to forced labor camp, and he never returned. . . . When the Dutch returned, they kept Saleh on. . . . He was physically so strong that he thought no one could beat him — so he became too self-assured and proud."

"He was invincible [*taguh*, magically invulnerable] against Hindus — but not inside Pagatepan."

"He was a great friend of the governor of Bali, who paid for his Hajj. . . . Saleh was spoiled because he became *jago* [proud] from his privileged contact with high circles, worst of all the *bupati* [the highest official of the region]; many called Saleh his godson."

"The trouble was, he became *nanggoang kanah* [spoiled and overconfident] from always getting his will. So he refused to pay anything for his water: he claimed pelaba dispensation when he was no longer perbekel, and anyway that would only have excused him from half the payment. When he refused for the third year running, the *krama subak* stormed his house, and he was killed in the swordfight" (in 1965; for more on this incident, see below).

I have no special information on Muxtar. For Mr. Basik, whose first of three periods as perbekel followed, see below. Hajji Musa, the sixth perbekel on our list, is the son of Saleh. During the turmoil following the war of independence, many in Pagatepan held out for a strict Islamic government rather than Sukarno's pluralism; some fighters from Pagatepan even withdrew into the mountains and continued a guerrilla resistance for a time after independence. Hajji Musa, on the contrary, appears to have cooperated closely from the very beginning with certain Indonesian government officials while publicly supporting the fundamentalist Nahdatul Ulama party. He thus attained perbekelship; but in due course his position in the community became impossible, and he finally moved to a mixed Hindu-Muslim village a considerable distance away.

Mr. Basik won the next election as a member of Sukarno's Parti Nasonal Indonesia. But much unrest resulted, and after the local violence at the time of the Communist coup and army countercoup in 1965, the authorities placed Pagatepan under administration by the army officer S. Untung. After two years, Fatehul, the son-in-law of Hajji Musa, was appointed perbekel by the administration; but the old dissatisfactions, conflicts, and quarrels resumed, and the army again took control for a year and a half, in the person of the officer P. M. Noor, to reestablish law and order.

At the subsequent election, Harunan won the perbekelship. He was the senior son of a highly respected member of the Ulama and seems to have had wide village support. But within two years he died — according to villagers, from lethal sorcery (*sihir*) by outsiders who were jealous of his winning first prize in a Koran-reciting competition.

At the most recent election, in 1982 Mr. Basik won for the third time, with an edge of only eighteen votes against his main challenger, the eldest son of the late imam. This result was still controversial as late as 1986, and village politics was in constant turmoil. Gossip would have it that Mr. Basik had "won votes by giving people money and promising them favors, and some ballots for his opponent were not even counted. But once the election was over, there was no more money or promises to be had." Letters were periodically sent during 1984 to the district officer from opposition faction leaders complaining about deteriorating village security and increasing theft, poor administration and the embezzlement of public funds, moral decadence, and failing morale in the village self-help activities.

By his own account, "I wish I were not perbekel. It is my third time; the first was as long ago as 1951. I did not want to stand for the last election, but the Ulama and many other important persons implored me. I will *not* seek a further term — being perbekel in Pagatepan is an impossible task. The people who are opposed to the perbekel *want* to create chaos. It has been like that for a long time — people of Pagatepan are that way. Their emotions boil over; they speak and act without thinking of the consequences. The only way is always to answer with smoothness, gentleness, and patience. It you act crassly, it sparks off emotion and violence."

When Mr. Basik died in 1986 from the aftereffects of surgery, the authorities decided to reinstate temporary military administration rather than hold a by-election.

As far as village opinion is concerned, the perbekel is subject to the Majlis Ulama in all matters. He is the liaison to the outside world and can obtain resources for the villagers from government; but he is constantly admonished to take the opinion of the Majlis Ulama and consult with the imam and is criticized when he acts without such clearance. Seen from the inside, village politics thus constitutes a single arena, in which the Majlis Ulama is the center of power and the perbekel the executive.

But just as the Majlis Ulama proved to be a somewhat nebulous institution, more like a climate of informed opinion than a deliberating body, so also the wider arena of village politics is a diffuse field without clear place and agenda. Certain factional cores of persons can be identified who, for the moment, share positions and interests; but most persons have their particular networks of friendship, kinship, sympathies, conflicts, and enmities, which for each one of them covers less than the village as a whole. Therefore, linkages do not add up to larger factional groups, and few longer sequences of events can be identified as resulting from the systematic strategies of such groups. In the course of three consecutive days, randomly chosen from my notes, we can thus observe fragments of a number of personal conflicts and agendas. One villager goes to the perbekel for the third time, obsequiously and with forced smiles repeating his report of crop theft and inquiring what can be done. A respected guru as guest speaker at the Friday sermon berates the village for thievery and low morals; he blames the perbekel for not consulting the Ulama and advises that one should not go and report everything to the police, because that only brings shame to the village as a whole. A modernist village notable gossips with a circle of juniors: he has written repeatedly to the perbekel urging that he do something about the recent spate of thefts, without obtaining an answer, and now the perbekel blushes whenever they pass in the street. Another gathering of laborers laughs at how the perbekel no longer dares to go out at night but sits in his house waiting for others to come and bear false witness. Is this a concerted factional campaign? Hardly, when during these same three days the imam comments of the sermon that it was a partisan piece in favor of the speaker's own brother, who had been reported (by the same modernist notable!) to the police and fined for performing unauthorized marriages — and indeed let off the hook by the perbekel, who accompanied him to the police and paid his fine for him, as siddiqah — while the gossiping laborers pass on to laugh at the sermon-giving guru, pointing out that his own son is one of the thieves!

Thus the pattern of factional activity in this village arena seems more concerned to divide than to rally and is more effective in preventing collective action than in enhancing the positions of alternative leaders.

The subak irrigation association forms a separate, and different, organ of the village community in that it has its separate leadership position — the klian subak, elected by and among the subak members — and its separate book of rules in the awig-awig of subak custom. The subak actualizes the communal potential of Balinese egalitarian values by affirming collective responsibility and control and casting leadership functions in the guise of coordination only. This means that the klian subak obtains very few material benefits and no symbolic ones from his efforts, though his task is demanding both in skills and in the amount of time it consumes. He is of course an active cultivator, and he speaks and acts in ways that emphasize this. His only material benefit from the job is the dispensation from half the costs of irrigation society membership — which is a fiction, since he more than makes up for that by the extra hours he puts into supervising labor and resolving conflicts. Receiving no overt expressions of respect and rank, he must find his rewards in a subtle sense of wielding influence and in the satisfactions of a job well done. The present klian has served since 1977. His predecessor retired after more than thirty years, including his eighteen months in prison for complicity in the subak membership's lynching of Saleh. Both men are singularly social and unpretentious persons conspicuously embodying the virtues of simplicity, honesty, and hard work in a way most suitable for the consensual leader of an association of cultivators.

The subak of Pagatepan thus uniquely in the village exemplifies a mode of organization based on the formal separation and autonomy of a functional domain. The extent to which this also characterizes its de facto operation is more difficult to ascertain; but I found no strong evidence to the contrary. I think the reason is found in the particular prerequisites for leadership effectiveness, given the nature of subak tasks and personnel: the necessity to mobilize independent farmers with heavy workloads of their own to do their fair share of recurring labor for a collectivity. This seems to prove difficult also in other Balinese communities (Hobart 1978a:76), and any klian who could be identified as an active participant in factionalism would quickly run into a quagmire of noncooperation, occasioned by both suspicion and hostile intrigue. That could only precipitate the election of a new klian; and since the klian's tasks are demanding and his rewards modest, the post would appear at best an ambiguous prize to rivals, whereas the loss to each and every member of the subak is palpable if these tasks are not attended to. Even the most ardent faction leader can therefore be understood to shrink from going too far in pressuring a klian to join his partisan intrigues.

With regard to all other functional domains, the general assessment of villagers tended to be that activities were ultimately explicable only in terms of factionalism and private ambition — a point of view very difficult to falsify, for anthropologist and villagers alike. I found most striking the reflections of a former villager who had emigrated, commenting on a widely acknowledged increase in the frequency of crop thefts (see chapter 8) in Pagatepan:

"Before, when there was thievery and destruction in Pagatepan, it was always part of perbekel rivalry, encouraged by the failed candidate so as to create a crisis where the district officer would have to intervene. It was not so as to eat. But now, thieves do it for a living; theft and destruction have become customary occupations. Before, even if a mango fell on the ground, no one other than the owner would take it."

The evidence from village events and their local interpretation thus does not support a model of the social organization of Pagatepan that would divide village organization into a set of separate, autonomous planes and minimize the roles of power and striving individuals in its functions. There is clear evidence to the contrary, indicating that a robust and pragmatic contest for power merges most aspects of community life into a single, competitive arena. In this arena, imams emerge in leadership positions through a strong and competitively achieved excellence in the field of scriptural knowledge that has widely ramifying relevance in village affairs. Thereby they gain an actively sought and highly valued personal authority. But the perpetual struggle is aptly reflected in the slander that prevails among rivals, and the fact that scholarly excellence on the part of the few elicits a general reaction of "shame" among the many, motivated by the emotional experience of inferiority. In the case of the village perbekels, the ambience of turbulence, personal ambition, and conflict is even clearer. Half the terms of perbekelship in Pagatepan in the present century have terminated in violence, and in death or premature interruption of functions, because of pervasive internal unrest in the village.

Some of the newer literature on South Balinese Hindu villages shows them indeed to be far from devoid of individual and factional turbulence (e.g., Hobart 1975, 1978a, 1985c; Howe 1989; Boon 1977:72ff.; Boon 1986). Nor are these findings remarkable in wider comparative terms: factional divisions to the point of crippled leadership are only too familiar from many small, primary communities all over the world. In the context of previous analyses of Balinese society, however, such findings pose a challenge. There has been a tendency for anthropologists of several theoretical persuasions, all too easily emulated, to try to cope with Balinese expressive luxuriance and capture the distinctive features of its society and culture by constructing a description based on certain *formal* institutions alone. The patterns that compose them and the ideology and values these seem to embody are thereby elevated to the level of definitive structure, while discrepant data and everyday realities are relegated to the status of a subsidiary, "informal system." This informal system is thereby robbed of its power to act back and influence its own structural preconditions, in a manner rather reminiscent of the analyses pursued in early industrial sociology. The whole gamut of events of transaction, dominance, discord, and rivalry is thereby not necessarily denied, but its relevance to a cultural interpretation is effectively muted. Most spectacularly in Bateson's "steady state" model of Balinese village structure ([1949] 1972a), it has been possible by such foregrounding and backgrounding of materials to construct representations of great theoretical interest, which in a certain sense derive from Balinese data but no longer give an adequate account of social life as it actually unfolds in Balinese communities.

I shall return in chapter 9 to the question of how far and in what ways Pagatepan may be similar or contrastive to other Balinese communities in the actual structure of its factionalism. At this point I wish only to establish firmly that a description of Pagatepan favoring harmony models and relegating strife to an arbitrarily abstracted informal system would be most inadequate for the analysis of this community, and thus its comparative impact would be irreparably reduced. It would be powerless to explain the events of village politics, especially the pervasive inability to reach collective decisions and make cooperative village institutions function that characterizes Pagatepan village life.

On the contrary, the cultural model that villagers of Pagatepan use to interpret political acts, and through which their reality in this field is thus socially constructed, sees a covert battle of wits, and the ambiguities of its outcome, unfold as an opaque tournament of power, faction, maneuver, respect, and offense. Others participating in this tournament are recurrently characterized, in confidential conversations, as driven by ambition and practicing slander, emotionality, deceit, and covert violence. A failure on the part of the anthropologist to recognize this when interpreting the meanings that events and interactions hold for the actors concerned would limit us to the scrutiny of what, to villagers in Pagatepan, are merely the polite surfaces of behaviors only, not their real import.

This view of their own politics goes together with a general self-portrayal of people in Pagatepan as excessively emotional and idiosyncratic persons. Fellow villagers are represented as being both prone to harbor grudges and extremely sensitive to insults: it is a model of social actors that ascribes their covert schemes not to cold rationality but to "high emotion" (baingut), a predisposition to take offense easily and then strike out with passionate, socially destructive action. We see it exemplified in Perbekel Basik's remarks cited above; and I find the same conception in Bateson's perceptive interpretation of "Balinese social organization with the smooth relations of etiquette and gaiety metaphorically covering the turbulence of passion" ([1967] 1972b:150). While the expectation in Pagatepan is that such passions will shape people's covert purposes, and may at any time break through and take possession of their behavior, people's high valuation of control and polite surfaces is shown by their reaction to any such eruptions. Thus when the village tailor was late completing a shirt he had promised, and his angry customer raised his voice and used an insulting pronoun (*nani*, the low Balinese speaking-downward *you*), the tailor's wife, overhearing the exchange, became so started (*terkajut*) that her breast milk turned "hot" and her nursing baby became ill with diarrhea (see Wikan 1989a for this syndrome and other elaborations of the effects of anger).

This model of propriety and of persons is most clearly evinced in villagers' understanding of the occurrence of violence. Villagers report ten cases of intravillage killings over the last twenty years (i.e., after the unrest of 1965 had ended), of which I have a multiplicity of retrospective accounts from parties to the acts and from others. Four of these were between close relatives (uncle-nephew, or cousins), and most involved disputes over property; but when pursued they all develop into convoluted stories of accumulated grudges, misinterpretations, and then some particular insult or offense as the precipitating cause (see also the extended case presented in chapter 16).

Thus when ex-Perbekel Saleh was killed, the issue was his refusal for the third year running to pay his dues to the irrigation association; but the one who struck the fatal blow was his cousin. Saleh's relation to the klian subak at the time is described as worse than bad from accumulated mutual grudges; it followed shortly upon Sukarno's fall, and Saleh was widely identified as having been a Communist; but the particular factor that precipitated the fight was his insulting behavior toward the assembled krama subak. According to his cousin Ghazi, Saleh had been politely asked to attend the meeting even if he would not pay. He refused. Ghazi was sent during the meeting to summon him; Saleh answered by summoning *them* to *his* house. At this point the assembly was aroused and stormed toward his house. Saleh emerged from the door, sword in hand, shouting "Ngamok!" (i.e., the warning "I am amuck!"). Ghazi, in the front of the crowd, fortunately (his word!) carried his sword in his belt and drew it swiftly enough to defend himself. They fenced; he cut Saleh's foot, which caused him to leap and fall. Ghazi managed to cut the side of his head. As he leaned over to finish him, Saleh's son came at him from the back; others shouted a warning, and Ghazi managed to twist away but was wounded in the elbow though able to continue fencing with Saleh's son. In the confusion of these sword duels, and with Saleh's four wives crowded around to protect his body, there was little the throng of fifty or so irrigation society members, armed with knives and rocks, could do. A visiting Javanese holy man tried to separate them, but Ghazi was so angry he turned on him. But Ghazi's friend stayed his arm, shouted "He is a guest!" and managed to grab Ghazi's sword and throw it away. At this, Saleh's son escaped and hid. Ghazi went searching for him but later returned to beat up the dying Saleh and set fire to his house. At this point, the police arrived — within an hour after the fighting began. The two branches of the family are still, twenty years later, very cool toward each other but now at least able to greet each other in public.

Similarly, when an eighteen-year-old boy was killed recently in a fight with his mother's half-brothers, this was the result of a long sequence of grievances involving inheritance (his mother's mother brought land with her into the marriage but died long ago, and the daughter's rightful share as heir had not been passed on to the boy's mother); debt (his mother's brothers had pledged land as security for a loan from his father but has not repaid in full and yet prevented his parents from farming the plot); threats (his father had been threatened with murder when he tried to have hired hands harvest the uncle's crop on this plot); etc. But the precipitating cause was the boy's humiliation when his mother's brother thrashed him in public for having fought with a younger collateral over these grudges. The boy sharpened his knife and entered the uncle's compound; in the resulting skirmish the boy himself was killed. "We neighbors want no part in it. It is very disrespectful to fight like that in a family, especially when their common grandfather is still alive."

A special propensity to violence is regarded, by both themselves and others in the region, to be a characteristic of Pagatepan and part of their tradition. According to male villagers, seven out of ten always carry concealed knives — because they are proud of their martial traditions, because they want to be prepared to defend themselves, and so that they will be ready to ritually slaughter (halal) any animal that might be in danger of dying and thus become inedible. This martial tradition is seen as essential to the survival of the community through the centuries, surrounded as they were by enemy Hindus. Older men tell of a series of confrontations with neighboring villages — especially the village to the east, with which they have had to divide irrigation water from a common dam on the river — and various other Hindu hosts. The scenarios of these accounts are largely of a kind: a large enemy force threatens; the Majlis Ulama (represented as a body of unnamed and faceless wizards) arranges a ruse and by sacred prayers secures some magical means — a small stream swells till it looks like an ocean no one can cross, or a handful of appointed villagers marches forward shouting the declaration of faith and terrifies the Hindus by appearing to them like a whole army; then Pagatepani villagers counterattack and rout the enemy.

In more recent times, there have been minor incidents of collective truculence, of which the villagers are largely proud, as in the story they tell of an important Hindu government official who demanded to enter and inspect their mosque; this caused a riot, and he was chased from the village by an enraged mob. The last major case of collective violence was at the time of the fall of Sukarno and the events surrounding the anti-Communist riots, which are generally referred to here as elsewhere in Bali as the National Tragedy. At this time, the closest neighboring hamlet was identified as Communist and eliminated, its lands seized by Pagatepan and its population partly massacred and partly scattered. Whereas most villagers do not wish to associate themselves with these events today or speak of them, one old fighter was prepared to give his account:

"All the Hindus there were Communists, in a zone extending to the foothills. And Prabakula had a Communist Perbekel, so they were allied, and so was the village to the west of us, whereas those south and east were not Communist. I had my *padang* [sword], from my father, and my *kadutang* [thrusting spear], with its wooden sheath that turns it into a walking stick, from my *kumpi* ancestor from Blangbanang. Its steel is perpetually perfumed — the aroma does not come from the sheath. When you stand behind that spear, you become invisible; the enemy cannot see you. In one night we killed thirty-four persons — men, women, and children — in one hamlet. I stood behind my spear, invisible to those Hindus, and killed with my sword. We were *ngamok*, a state when you no longer can distinguish your own family even from the foe. The proof that we were ngamok: we killed children, not only men."

The fact of violence, of course, is only too familiar in every nation and population in moments of chaos; moreover, my evidence is not from an inquest designed to discover what really happened, merely a glimpse of how a few participants appear to conceptualize these events. The important fact for our present purposes is the cultural model of the adult male person these accounts reveal so dramatically, one in which the conventions of normally polite social behavior overlay, imperfectly and provisionally only, turbulent and violent emotions inside the person. We shall return in due course to a further exploration and elaboration of the implications of such a model for how Balinese interpret each other and thereby construct their life and their society.

8

Family, Marriage, and Making a Living in Pagatepan

It has not been my intention with the preceding chapter simply to counterpoise those rarified and externalist interpretations of cultural expressions, which color much of the anthropological representations of Balinese consciousness in our literature, with a story of factionalism and violence in the village of Pagatepan. No doubt it may be useful for the reader to be jolted into recognizing that the world villagers inhabit is composed of other plans and scenarios besides those of their rituals. But my point is the very general one, that both the acts and the cultural imagery of villagers require contextualization in their world, if the meanings they carry for Balinese persons are to be retrieved. Furthermore, our struggle for greater realism requires not only that we penetrate the quiet surface of politeness — which the people of Pagatepan, like other Balinese, try to and largely manage to maintain — to see the covert purposes that motivate acts and the occasional eruption of violence. We also need to take up a much wider, and more humdrum, range of themes. In the present chapter I shall therefore attempt to embed the lives of villagers in Pagatepan in that set of elementary physical concerns they share with other North Balinese villagers, and indeed every other peasant population and most of the rest of mankind. Measured in waking hours and units of sweat and effort, there can be no doubt that work and poverty are the dominant facts of their lives; while among their social relationships, the most important and complex are surely for them, as for us, those to kinsfolk and spouses.

FAMILY LIFE

Observing the daily round of life of villagers in Pagatepan, it is immediately evident that kin and affines have a prominent place in each person's circle of interaction. Groups of socializing villagers form on other bases too, such as common age, gender, or neighborhood: there are flocks of young boys, small groups of men who are regulars at noontime in a *warung* snack shop, and clusters of women doing the laundry together at the local washing-place by the village ditch. But intimate socialization is above all focused on homes, within a family circle of grandparents, parents, children, and intervisiting kindred and affines. The norms of behavior in this close circle are explicit and cherished: close family, kin, and affines are people you are tied to and can rely on; they should be warm and supportive, concerned for your welfare, generous and loyal. These are, roughly, the normative sentiments of kinship in most societies; I would not be prepared to argue that they are more compelling or more explicit here than elsewhere in the world. But it is important to remember that the primary community counts no fewer than thirty-seven hundred persons — thus we are not faced with a tribal community pervasively structured by kinship. Most persons, though lifelong members of the same primary community, are *not* within this intimate circle: kinspeople can be counterposed to the majority of fellow villagers. The special intimacy of kin finds expression, beyond the cheerfulness and smiling friendliness that is so marked a feature of all etiquette in Bali, in a greater degree of identification, proximity, and company. It strongly influences the patterns of visiting: on Friday after the noon prayers and sermon, men habitually drop in on one or several of their married sisters, and relatives drop in on each other at all times through the week exchanging news and gossip.

But life has greater complexity than can be represented by such general norms. Becoming more familiar with the community, the anthropologist discovers that there are also close kin who do not visit each other, and that people are aware of strands in the relations of close kin that are not so positively valued. Closeness and loyalty also entail control, interference, and disapproval; generational difference provides the basis for dominance as well as respect. People in Pagatepan are extremely reluctant to be explicit on their subjective feelings on such issues; indeed, they embrace a common Balinese ideology of respect, compliance, and "positive thinking" (Wikan 1990, and below). They are also enjoined to be polite in their account of others, particularly when speaking to outsiders. But they sometimes do not succeed in repressing their bitternesses and hostilities toward some particular kinspeople to the extent of wiping such feelings from their

127

consciousness; and they are not always above gossip and slander, or making shrewd observations on what is really going on in the intimate lives of their neighbors. There is also, obviously, a complex but intimate connection between the two: their understanding of their own experiences and strands in their own relations are both illuminated and reflected by the gossip and observations they find plausible and insightful as commentaries on the relations of others.

My concern in the present phase of the text is to explore what kin and marital relations in Pagatepan are "really about" — i.e., the quality and content of relationships as practiced and experienced by participants; and neither depicting the impact of bitterness in a few intimate relations, nor reporting a body of village slander, will provide us with adequate data for such an exploration. But neither will an equal number of informant's statements about norms give these insights. Both need to be evaluated against each other, as well as supplemented by a considerable body of other data. As I have argued (and see also Wikan 1990 for a compelling argument for such a view) the anthropologist can only approximate such insights by building up broad and highly contextualized materials on the life situation of a number of *particular* individuals, thus better to understand these very complex and multifaceted relations and judge them with sensitivity and insight to arrive at a basis for making valid statements, even of quite general and approximate kinds. This means building up a mental dossier of facts, circumstances, interpretations, and revelations for a number of persons with whom one has entered into social relations of some degree of intimacy. On the moral issue of practicing anthropology in such a way, I might observe that it does not in principle involve anything different and more reprehensible than what one does in relations of friendship within one's own society; however, it needs to be pursued with a certain amount of charity, and in proportion to the sympathy one feels for the person. The difference is more on the practical side: one's unintended insensitivity to the implications of facts and statements in a foreign culture; the amount of circumstantial context that one needs, as an outsider, to accumulate before aspects of the person's real situation are appreciated; the limited time available for the task, which means one must go about it intensively rather than leisurely. But these practical hurdles must be overcome, for in my view, without a considerable body of such contextualized knowledge of real persons coping with the issues that arise in their lives, not even a moderately meaningful "cultural" interpretation of the life world of others can be achieved, and one's representation of another culture and society becomes thoroughly distorting and false.

A second major problem is documenting or supporting the account one gives, once one has arrived at a picture. Here the very multiplicity that strengthens the anthropologist's insights militates against the presentation: there is simply no way to give a review or summary of the bases on which the different elements of one's construct are built — especially not if this is to be done piecemeal as documentation for the presentation of each of these elements. The reader must be asked to suspend judgment until a body of data of a considerable variety of kinds can be presented. It is also necessary that the reader cooperate in building up a composite picture of the set of concerns and interpretations that make up the interpretive context of the anthropologist's account, and supposedly of the whole population whose ideas, acts, and interpretations are reported on. This is, hopefully, a cumulative matter through the whole monograph. I am not able to sort it out systematically so it can be done topic by topic, domain by domain.

Documentation also raises the moral issue of confidentiality. I see no way that the identity of this particular village could be effectively disguised if even the most elementary facts about it are given. This means that any comprehensive description of persons will also make them identifiable to anyone with local knowledge, even if they are anonymized. Obviously I know little that the rest of the village does not already know, and that little I do not tell. But a written, compressed account of circumstances that are in principle already known may yet be both subjectively offensive and objectively damaging; moreover, being in part composed of the constructions placed by fellow villagers on certain intimate or fateful events, it can also be very mischievous. For most of the individual case materials I have, there is no middle ground between being so simplified as to be banal and being sufficiently contextualized as to be identifiable. For these reasons, I am forced to large extent to give my conclusions, generalizations, and interpretations arising from my case materials without exhibiting these materials as primary documentation. To indicate something of the nature of these data and how they were collected, however, I give in chapter 17 an abbreviated account of my notes on one extended case of elopement that unfolded during my presence in Pagatepan. A complex real-life story that involved many persons in gossip, condemnation, avoidance, and conflict, it is yet a story handled by the main protagonists with such realism and integrity that it commands respect, and thus in my eyes should not even be in need of the formal anonymization I give it.

It is no coincidence that these questions come up with particular force in connection with an exploration of kinship and marriage, though they are of course relevant to nearly all materials on village life. But close kinship relations, and the relations of spouses, have such fundamental importance to most people's existence in Pagatepan, and are so wrought with crossing obligations and multiple significances and interpretations, that they come to involve the core of people's identities and most of the outstanding events, achievements, and defeats of their life performances. It would be naive to ask why they are so troublesome here — surely, wherever we have the information, we find that close kin and marital relations are troublesome, formative, and fateful to people in all human societies. But the configuration of feelings, conventions, and practices that characterize close family relationships is affected both by local culture and local circumstances. Balinese neighbors make the villagers of Pagatepan out to be more cantankerous, divided, and violent, but also more clannish, than themselves; and they will tell how close relatives among them are divided by strife. To an outsider from another culture, on the other hand, what appears most characteristic of their intimate family relations is rather the force of the conventional facades, often accompanied by the will to practice some degree of relationship in the face of conflict or despite deep animosities. We are thus confronted with a series of paradoxes: a general recognition that the relations of close kinsfolk are often poor; strong social pressures that public appearances should be maintained; the expectation that kinsfolk will in fact support each other against nonkin; a tendency to identify close kinsfolk, and make them responsible for each others' actions, even when they are known to have a poor relationship. The fact that many of these generalizations might be accepted as valid also for close kinship relations in many other societies does not appear to enhance a Western anthropologist's capacity to analyze the syndrome.

Certain local conventions and values should be recognized. People in Pagatepan share the general Balinese condemnation of anger, rebelliousness, and "high emotion," though they control such reactions less completely than do most Balinese; they also exercise persistent social pressures toward conformity, politeness, and expressions of friendliness. They feel themselves to be under heavy constraints of public opinion. The combination of ascriptive, enforced intimacy and profound interdependence within the family can easily aggravate these pressures and controls. With the very strong ideological emphasis on respect and authority in the relationship between seniors and juniors in the family, and particularly between parents and children, such pressures are thus easily experienced as stifling. Pervasive shortage or poverty exacerbates the situation and leads to jealousies and resentments. Thus many siblings who have been very close during childhood drift apart during adolescence or later and become almost completely estranged, often nurturing bitterness over a particular injustice, act, or quarrel and avoiding social contact.

Most deeply ambivalent, because most irresolvable, are one's relations to lineal relatives and spouses, in which conflicts easily produce deep clashes of loyalties. Marriages, of course, can be dissolved; but they form the basis for the household unit, which is crucial to a person's economic and social activity, so any breakup has its considerable costs; and ascendants, on their part, really cannot be replaced. It is indicative that the Maulana social foundation (see chapter 15) lists as its main function besides children's education the provision and payment of foster parents for orphans in the village, not normally a public concern in communities organized on a kinship basis.

To exemplify the personal and social legacy of conflicts in these core relationships, let me illustrate the constellations in the family background of one young man with whom I became closely acquainted, as they emerged through a series of encounters and confidences. Shortly after their marriage, his father had started mistreating his mother; after she had given birth to the boy, the mother's father intervened and took his daughter back, dissolving her marriage. The old man was twice widowed and living at the time with his third wife. She became jealous of her returned stepdaughter and the infant boy, having herself lost six of her seven children to infant mortality, an all too frequent fate in the village. After a while, the baby started crying excessively and exhibited marks and bruises. The grandfather suspected a form of witchcraft (*leak*) and, as a competent magician, tried to fight the occult forces (this indeed was also necessary later in the boy's life). This time it was discovered that it was the stepgrandmother (herself a magician) who was tormenting and physically attacking the child. Whether true or not, this was and still is the view of the family, and the old man divorced his wife, who has since remained single — at first supporting herself by occasional labor in a small shack in the coffee garden zone, later keeping a shop in the main village. The boy's mother, on her part, also remained single and devoted the rest of her life to keeping house for her father and raising her one boy. The boy thus grew up having no contact with his father and ambiguous relations to all his father's kin, including suppressed enmity with a group of slightly younger half-brothers, and bearing deep resentment to the old woman who had been his stepgrandmother. Yet all these relations persist in a face-to-face community that demands an appearance of politeness and civility between all the persons concerned.

Most regularly painful, perhaps, are the relationships of fathers and adolescent or adult sons. It is not intended as a metaphor when Father, Guru, and God are named in Pagatepan as those whom a child should respect and obey: the ideal of submission to paternal authority is as absolute as that of submission to God. Yet it is a familiar fact in the community that boys and young men will chafe at such submission, and that sooner or later their father's control of them fails, more or less comprehensively. Some pass through this phase and manage to redesign a relationship of symbolic respect but enhanced de facto equality and comradeship; in other cases the growing awareness of economic and political dependence forces the son into a reluctant deference and servitude; finally, some sons "quarrel" with their fathers and never again become reconciled. Only these last cases are regarded as tragic in Pagatepan. About men who do poorly in life, one is sometimes told in great confidence and solemnity that "he quarreled with his father and they became estranged — so his father withheld his barkat [blessing]; and therefore the son is never able to succeed in anything he does in life."

Though most such background on every villager's personal history is fairly ubiquitously known by agemates and seniors, there is no genre for giving it a coherent representation, either in biography or transformed into ballad or chronicle. But apart from everything that is hidden in the hearts of the principals, most episodes in a person's life are also objectified by others in discursive form, as anecdotes or as asides and reminders associated with current news and gossip. Behavior within the village is constantly observed and widely commented upon in the guise of news or amusing anecdote — with subtle innuendo that becomes even more guarded if the speaker means to convey criticism, judgment, or condemnation. Villagers observe wryly how swiftly all news passes from one end of their village to the other, and they have no illusions that constructions placed upon events will be charitable.

MARRIAGE

The social entailments of close consanguinity are thus in Pagatepan represented as prescriptive, practiced as elective, and commonly judged as petty or tragic. Love and matrimony, on the other hand, are treated as high romance and drama and recognized as providing the essential foundations of most lives. Young and old alike speak of marriage not as an alliance between families or groups but a union of two persons. The community is concerned only because sin must be avoided and reproduction controlled. With the passions that fire young people, this is sometimes critical. There has been an extended conflict between one of the most influential gurus of Pagatepan and the Indonesian authorities on this count. Present Indonesian law stipulates a rather cumbersome procedure for legal marriage, with documents, fees, and delays in the bureaucracy. The guru in question, on the other hand, performs marriages that follow the (minimal) stipulations of the Shariah and can be completed at very short notice. Persons wishing to reduce his position in the village report him to the authorities for performing such orthodox but illegal marriages, and he has repeatedly been summoned, admonished, and even fined by the police and courts. When he persists, it is not only with the fundamentalist argument that he acknowledges only God's law; it is also for the widely accepted pragmatic reason that once two people wish to marry, they will surely sin unless they are wed quickly.

Falling in love seems to take the typical form of innocent, romantic passion. Courting is normally discreet and constrained, extending rarely beyond whispered conversations through a half-opened window, in the small hours of the night, between the girl inside and the boy outside. When I wondered how a man married to an ex-Hindu woman ever met his wife, from the now nonexistent neighboring Hindu hamlet, the answer was self-evident: the two communities used the same spring for collecting drinking water, and so he might have seen her there occasionally. One glance may be enough to fall in love.

But more ominous forces lie close under the surface. People in Pagatepan fear, and practice, a large variety of love magic, *guna-guna*. A sudden irresistible infatuation may not be true love but only the result of such magic; and whereas some forms of magic can have results of infinite duration, others are confessedly short-term. There is magic for maidens and magic for boys, for one-night seduction and for life, and for breaking up marriages. Though *dukun* (Muslim) and balian (Hindu) wizards claim both sexes as their customers, boys seem to be in the majority, and many young girls seem to live in terror of being enchanted and entrapped. When ill-matched couples marry — pretty girls and ugly or lazy men, for example — then magic is suspected. There is ambiguity about whether guna-guna is white or black magic, an important distinction to the local practitioners; confessed specialists in such magic insist that it is white magic, since it causes love and good feelings between people, not bad feelings and death. Yet its consequences are construed sometimes to be tragic, as in the case of a pretty and educated urban girl of our acquaintance who was supposedly magically induced to fall in love with an unreliable, idle, already once-divorced boy and found herself, when the infatuation disappeared, stranded with a baby and an inattentive husband in a poor hovel in a backward village.

Yet it would be wrong to represent romantic infatuation as the only criterion of marital choice. Though the young may be prone to such passions and the old also susceptible, people who wish to marry regard other considerations as highly relevant and are subject to considerable pressures from the family to choose or not choose certain partners. Families generally favor relatives; responsible youths are aware of a number of factors that should be considered: morality, reputation, and dedication to religion; emotional suitability; mystical suitability, indicated by astrology and especially the letters and "weights" of their respective personal names; whether the two are *jodog*, fated to marry because it is the will of God; whether they are "balanced" with respect to background, physical size, intelligence, and beauty; whether the future spouse's family has a good reputation.

How much is the choice of spouse made by the persons themselves? The years before (first) marriage are certainly spent with pressures and proddings from parents and others; but in the case of boys there is no evidence that these have notable inducive effect, though they may be more successful in dissuading some boys from realizing a particular union. In the case of girls, the situation is not quite the same. Parents become actively involved not only to prevent unsuitable marriages but also to secure good ones. There has been a tradition of fathers giving their daughters in marriage to aspiring gurus as siddiqah, "free gifts," without any consideration of the girl's own wishes; and daughters are expected to be more obedient and compliant to their parents' wish than sons. On the other hand, there is a general reluctance among fathers to give their daughters in marriage at all: it entails a loss of labor and attention, it costs much money, and there seem to be emotional barriers to overcome. Indeed the father is expected not to be present at his daughter's marriage even where he has consented to it, because of shame and sorrow. And girls are acknowledged to have their own strong will and desires.

Two formal roads are open to the couple: marriage by agreement between the families (maideh), or marriage by elopement (merangkat). The former easily bogs down in minor disagreements or affronts on the part of one or another of the family members involved. Young couples are sometimes reputed to have created scandalous incidents (e.g., being surprised embracing), to force their family's compliance and swift action. The other course, merangkat, ranges from a fully expected and accepted act of elopement to simplify the whole procedure, through elopement to overcome or in defiance of a parent's recalcitrance, to more precipitous acts, even true abduction to overcome a girl's own reluctance and force her compliance. Whereas merangkat in all its shades retains an aspect of the romantic and heroic, maideh is regarded by all as the more correct and responsible way to proceed. Of 161 marriages comprised in a detailed count, 62 percent were reported by the spouses themselves to have been elopements, and 38 percent to be maideh, the latter probably somewhat overreported because

Eloped Muslim couple, waiting for marriage rites.

it is the more prestigious form. People will usually say that merangkat is an uncivilized and old-fashioned custom now hardly ever practiced – but all the marriages that actually took place during my presence in the village were such.

Whichever form is chosen, the customs and conventions surrounding marriage in this Muslim population are quite elaborate, more so than for any other life event except death. Let me outline the main elements of the more typical merangkat, noting only how a maideh marriage will differ

135

from this. Normally there will be a secret arrangement between girl and boy as to the place and time for elopement: at a time when people are not about, or at a place from which they can make an easy escape, she will be waiting with her clothes packed. The abducting party should be composed of at least three persons; it is best that they should include members of the boy's family to show that he has support for the scheme, and that a girl or a woman should be among them to reassure the bride. Once the boy and girl have escaped, one of the party, the *mujati*, goes to the girl's home and shouts the message that the girl has been abducted — and then escapes swiftly; otherwise he will be beaten by the girl's indignant relatives. There is no question of ravishing the girl or consummating a marriage. She should be taken to a trusted senior couple, best of all the boy's grandparents, where she is protected and hidden, while the boy hides in another place. Thereupon a senior relative or patron delegated by the boy approaches the girl's father to seek some sort of settlement and also mobilize the Ulama (religious scholars) to obtain community support and arrange for the marriage. In a well-designed and properly supported merangkat, the couple will also be able to mobilize a delegation of women, representing the girl, to visit the Ulama and apologize for her "impolite" behavior. A member of the Ulama who works at the district's Office of Religious Matters presently receives most of these appeals and delegations, as the necessary papers for a legal marriage are best handled through him.

In the case of a maideh, naturally, negotiations *(ngideh)* between the girl's father and the boy's father precede all other activities and contacts. The problem in such negotiations, however, is that refusal, and other differences or issues, are easily taken as insults by the other party, so the course toward agreement (ngeh) is both hesitant and wrought with dangers. The major step is *nyangkap*, when agreement about the bridewealth (mahar, mas kawin) is formally reached.

In the case of merangkat, the girl remains in hiding while the formal papers are hurriedly gotten together. If her father accepts, or at least is willing to name a *wakil* (representative), then all is well. If not, the legal marriage *(nikah)*, proceeds without his consent and the community elders themselves appoint a wakil for the ceremony. A handful of senior male members of the community are invited to attend as witnesses, and the imam performs the marriage. He assures himself of the documentation of the bridewealth and gives the groom advice regarding his duties as a married man. The papers are then signed by the groom and the wakil, and the witnesses are served the wedding meal: rice and meat (or eggs). Only a little of each person's portion is eaten; the rest is wrapped by him in banana leaves and taken home as barkat, blessing. The same meal is also eaten by the couple; according to custom they should be sitting facing each other on a bed *(mepatadak)*, preferably with a relative's young baby between them to ensure their lifelong fertility.

The marital union *(kawin)* follows the nikah. Next morning relatives, friends, and neighbors will come and congratulate the couple, bringing gifts of uncooked rice. Some days after the nikah comes *ngunya*, "begging pardon" in a ceremonial visit to the house of the new wife's kinsfolk. By a custom claimed by Pagatepanis to be unique for their village, three kinds of sweets must be prepared for this visit, each with a spiritual and sexual significance: *Pasung* are slightly flattened, leaf-wrapped cones of white and sweetened brown rice meal. These are explained to have the spiritual meaning of making the heart always sweet. Materially they represent the union of white semen and sweet brown women's secretions, making the first coitus sweet. *Bantal* are large, pencil-shaped sweets wrapped in yellow coconut leaf sprouts with a tassel on the end, tightly lashed with purple string. Their spiritual reference is to the indissoluble character of the marriage. Their material reference is to the woman and the string of her sarong, which can now be untied and opened for enjoyment. *Cerorot* are long, firm cones of white pudding contained in a spiral of yellow coconut leaf. To eat them you pull down the open, wide end of the spiral and press out the mush. Their spiritual meaning is that the husband should always be fully satisfied with this one wife; their material significance is to represent the penis in its first, successful ejaculation.

Equipped with these unambiguous symbols, a group led by the husband's elder female relatives goes from house to house and gives some of each kind of sweets to the mistress of each house, with the words "this is siddiqah" (a free gift of goodwill), to which the answer is "we receive your siddiqah." People are observant of who is included in this round of visits and will be insulted if they feel they should have been included but were not. In the case of maideh marriages, the cakes are distributed when the bridewealth has been settled, before the nikah. The visit to the bride's family after the marriage is then not called ngunya, because there is nothing to apologize for, but instead *ziarat*, a visit of respect or pilgrimage.

The preceding synopsis is intended to function as a kind of descriptive deconstruction, to make plausible an account of marriage in Pagatepan that depicts it as a union of two persons acting on their own, albeit with social support, not as the agents, much less objects, of larger groups. The documentation is relevant to an anthropological audience, since the picture I present runs counter to many professional descriptions of "marriage systems." There is a tendency to depict such systems as tightly organized exchanges between groups and to focus on the canonical principle on which they are constituted. Where such systems are not fully realized in a statistical sense, they should at least be clearly abstracted in a conceptual sense for any analysis to be regarded as complete. There is the added empirical generalization that the more marriages entail collective political relations and/or the transfer of wealth and property, the more are the groom's and bride's opportunities for individual choice controlled or at least channeled by tight conceptual and transactional structures.

In Pagatepan there is no doubt that every marriage has ramifying political consequences, since village factions and alignments are strongly affected by consanguinity and affinity. It also has implications for property through bridewealth and inheritance. Yet it would not seem that significant structures can be found in the case of the merangkat majority of marriages, which mediate between the romantic attractions and impulses of young people and the systems of relationships and alliances that arise from marriage. No person, groups, or interests can be identified that effectively influence the desires and efforts of boys, and girls are influenced only questionably and marginally. Nor does there seem to be any constraining conceptual structure imposed on this reality; and the instituted authorities of the community in fact function mainly in *support* of the whims of young people where these are in defiance of their parents. This will be richly illustrated in the case materials contained in chapter 16.

There are thus very wide limits of convention set for this exercise of individual choice. The most compelling is that marriage should be within Islam, which for sociometric reasons till now has essentially meant within this isolated Muslim enclave of Pagatepan. Yet even this can be overruled by the private passions of the young man who suddenly falls in love with a Hindu girl. His friends will then show their bravery by rushing to his aid in abducting the girl, while the Ulama will show their Muslim zeal by abetting him and converting the lovestruck girl to Islam by a swift ceremony. Only the marriage of a girl from Pagatepan to a Hindu man is categorically not allowed and, according to the villagers, effectively prevented, though such cross-religious marriages do take place occasionally in other circles in North Bali.

The result of these conventions and forces in the field of marriage is the perpetual introduction of disorder into the village alignments based on kinship, and therefore an unpredictable fluidity in the pattern of village factions. Compared to Bali-Hindu villages, we find an enhancement of factors also found among them and a loosening of the intervening structures that give a somewhat higher degree of continuity and order to their kinship alignments (see also Boon 1977: 119ff.; and below). Thus the ideas

138

and praxis governing marriage in Pagatepan contribute significantly to the organizational volatility of this community.

PROPERTY, WORK, AND POVERTY

Households in Pagatepan generally find that their income falls far short of their felt needs, despite a very low standard of consumption. Many complain that life is a constant battle to keep stark hunger and need at bay; what is more, they see few hopes and opportunities and have difficulties finding gainful work. The extent of poverty is somewhat concealed by the villagers' perpetual struggle to appear graceful, happy, clean, and well dressed; but with the undeveloped state of public facilities and a very low purchasing power, there is no denying that poverty is indeed the condition of most households. For an agricultural community pressing on its land resources, in an island environment generally agricultural and overpopulated, this condition may not seem surprising. Yet these features of Pagatepan village economy cannot be a result of population density alone, since a similar condition seems to have prevailed at the beginning of the century, when the population was perhaps a fourth of what it is now and the total area under its control was larger than at present. In the epigrammatic style of one of the oldest members of the community: "People in those days were stupid and lazy. Here is rain and water, here is land. There were such good opportunities — yet most people were so poor, they had to mix taro and cassava-meal in their rice!" An account of the economy of the village must thus face the task of identifying structural features that reproduce this poverty, not merely documenting land shortage.

The immediate symptoms can be summarized under three headings: the lack of diversification in the economy, i.e., an overwhelming dependence on agriculture among the resident households; the absence of any economic enterprise larger than the single-household unit; and a distribution of property such that four out of five households who support themselves by cultivation are landless. This situation becomes almost universally frustrating in that it implies a typical development cycle in which domestic units start out propertyless (since even those with landowning parents will normally not yet have inherited) and opportunities for employment for young people are very restricted.

One may indeed wonder how a landless household of cultivators can be viable. Women are not allowed to participate in agricultural labor in Pagatepan, in contrast to the customs of Bali Hindus. Sharecropping contracts give labor a poor share of the product: from one-half to one-quarter of the crop minus the costs of harvest and transport (about one-eighth). If the land one sharecrops does not require all one's labor, income can be supplemented with occasional day labor (at rates in 1985–86 equivalent to US$0.50–1.00 for a six-hour day) and by harvest labor. The hitch, however, is that both the market for sharecropping contracts and the labor market are such that few opportunities for work arise, and most cultivators are seriously underemployed. Two ameliorating strategies suggest themselves: minimizing living costs, and supplementing farm income by other activities.

Living costs can best be reduced by moving out of the nucleated settlement of Pagatepan and living "in the forest." This means that clothes, soap, and domestic equipment can be minimized without manifest shame, and opportunities for collecting and foraging to supplement food and fuel are enhanced. But it is hardly an adaption that enhances a young person's self-esteem or marriage prospects. Tolerable to a long-married man who obtains a large land area on tenancy contract, and a final resort for middle-aged, resigned persons, it is nearly intolerable for an underemployed and impatient young person or couple: better then to be in the nuclear village and try to bluff or impress agemates and others. Thoughtful senior people criticize youth for their irresponsibility and spendthriftiness, the excessive importance they place on modern consumer goods — wristwatches, shirts — and their quest for false status and prestige.

But life stories indicate that the alternative strategy of moving to the dispersed farming area or the coffe forest zone, except to farm land that is one's own property, is an abdication to poverty and cannot lead to any form of accumulation and change. The persons who have worked their way into property and increased wealth have all done so through other activities that supplement agriculture, best pursued from the village center.

These, however, show a narrow range of options: the performance of a few local services, employment on government wage, and trading. In 1984 and 1985, the self-employed service activities were limited to tailoring and sewing, haircutting, minor watch and motor repair, midwifery, native doctor and magician, and religious teacher. The last three of these will be discussed below. The first three are the source of the main income to only two households and of a small supplement to a handful more. Government wages provide supplementary temporary road-building employment for some young and middle-aged poor men; whereas five persons obtain government salaries in highly valued positions as civil servants. For most persons, however, the only sector of importance has been trade. For the most desperate, cutting wood in the highest forest zone, carrying it to the roadside, and either selling it to middlemen or taking it to market for direct sale provides a means of survival. Eleven bemos (small pickup trucks rebuilt for passenger and goods traffic) were owned by villagers in 1984 but gave only break-even incomes because of low fares and considerable competition. Some young boys in Pagatepan also earned money as assistants on these bemos. Local retailing gave income to twenty persons according to the village census, mainly women, who buy supplies in Singaraja perhaps once a week and keep a small stall or shop in Pagatepan. Some trading of similarly modest scale going the other way is attempted by both men and women: buying vegetables, fruits, eggs, and banana leaves (used for wrapping) and taking them in the mornings for sale, largely retail, in Singaraja.

The only trading activity that is more than a stopgap survival aid is the buying of agricultural produce and livestock in bulk for delivery to market in Singaraja. For this, capital is needed. Perhaps a score of the wealthier households have such capital and engage presently in wholesale buying; some of them seem only to hold their own, while four or five are clearly expanding. Life stories in the oldest generation show a few persons to have worked their way into wealth by this means. Some obtained their working capital as loans from relatives, others as advances from their Chinese merchant connections to whom they delivered. The two important products have been coffee and cattle. Of these, cattle seem to have given the greatest profits to those with the knack. Middlemen auxiliaries are employed to wander through a large area and make bids, then pass the offers and later the stock on to the buyer for a small bonus, while the buyer stables the cattle, arranges for transport, and delivers them to butchers or exporters in the towns. Several villagers pointed to the reputation of Pagatepan for violence, and also for clannishness, as an important prerequisite for these successes. Collecting the livestock and delivering the payments were necessarily lonely tasks, and large, transportable amounts of value were involved. In former and more lawless times, the reputation of the men of Pagatepan for being brave and always armed, and the assumption that they would wreak relentless vengeance if one of their fellow villagers were robbed or cheated, gave their enterprises in this risky field enhanced security.

The histories of these successful persons and enterprises reveal some essential features of the economic system. First, the main profits were placed in land: the successful businessman had no need to increase his working capital beyond a certain point, so the excess was siphoned off and used to accumulate property, up to forty hectares of land in several successful life stories. This land has subsequently constituted a fund the owner could rely on in his old age; the most long-lived of them, now reportedly ninety-eight years old, has only one hectare left of his forty-hectare fortune. The most successful men have also tended to have more wives, and more children to divide the estate. I know of no person who has inherited more than four hectares from his parents. Second, land thus circulates swiftly, and landed estates tend to be subdivided or consumed by the end of the life of the person who created the estate. Third, the uses of wealth are limited and do not create economic enterprises that change the economy so that new opportunities for employment are created for others. Nor is capital even put into irrigation development; it is simpler to buy already irrigated land than to organize labor and construct irrigation schemes. Such developments of irrigation as have taken place have been communal and led by village headmen or by government. Private income thus mainly goes to consumption: better food and clothing, better housing, expanded family size. Part of it is converted to religious merit in the form of wakaf contributions (religious donations), in one case a major building project to construct a high tower for the village mosque; or it goes to the performance of Haj, a goal for many, realized by a progressively diminishing few. What is religiously meritorious and what is secularly prestige-giving show a broad area of overlap. Large-scale feasts at circumcision and marriage of one's own children and at the death of ascendants give *pala* (religious merit, see below chapter 11) *if* they are done with the honest intention of honoring God; but in any case they give prestige *(gengsi)* in the community. Traditionally, there were two major slametans given occasionally by personal option, in association with the circumcision or marriage of a child. *Megainan* required the slaughter of at least one cow and the invitation of at least two hundred guests. The last occasion when it took place was a circumcision approximately twenty-five years ago. Even more sumptuous was *ngatog desa*, which was announced in the mosque, implying the invitation of the whole village population. A minimum of four cattle had to be slaughtered, and the whole village was treated to a feast of cooked rice and meat. The last ngatog desa is reported to have been given at the first marriage of Hajji Habibullah, now approximately eighty years old. Thus a traditional pattern seems to have obtained in which accumulated wealth was converted to social prestige by standard feasts approximating feasts-of-merit, of two grades. The implication of this, like the implication of the present use of surplus for private consumption, for the village economy as a whole has been simply the destruction of wealth, preventing its use as capital.

Whether this pattern of allocation reflects a positive choice or the absence of investment opportunities, the result is an unexpansive economy.

The growth that *has* taken place during the last forty years has had the form of increased irrigated area and new crops. The latter, indeed, represents an impressive record of innovation and initiative: a new variety of coffee *(robusta)*, high-yielding rice with everything it involves, the planting of extensive clove orchards, and the introduction of vanilla, as well as experimentation with new kinds and varieties of fruit trees. But none of this has led to a structural change in the basic organization of labor and enterprise; and population pressure combined with modernizing consumption pressure has clearly outstripped the growth in production, resulting in persisting or increased poverty.

The resulting fears and frustrations are evocatively embodied in the traditional imagery of magical mice, *brorong/belorong*. These mice are white, in contrast to the darkness of *bikul*, normal mice. They are obtained from black magicians at great expense but will make their owner rich swiftly without work. The brorong steals from the wealth of others: it can enter a locked cupboard and carry away, by small increments, the money kept there; it enters the villager's grain bin and takes away his store, grain by grain; it finds money, no matter how carefully hidden, and carries it away. But the person who has used brorong becomes at death a *jerangkong*, evil-smelling ghost: not just for four or forty days until it moves out and becomes a forest spirit, as do the ghost of gamblers, prostitutes, thieves, and the like; no, the owner of a brorong must remain a jerangkong for a very long time, for having committed a most despicable sin.

More common than suspicions of using brorong are belief and gossip that persons who seem to be gaining in wealth are profiting from regular theft, i.e., from being *tukang tadah*, a dealer in stolen goods. Stories circulate about fellow villagers who drive along the mountain road at night, filling up their bemo vehicle with the wood that poor people have placed by the roadside in readiness for morning transport. These persons likewise trade in stolen crops, particularly coffee, that have been harvested by thieves, asking no questions in return for very low purchase prices, thus enhancing their profits.

According to villagers, crop theft is done mainly by small gangs of boys or quite young men; they are not led by senior men, though they may be encouraged and abetted by them. To simplify the harvesting of coffee and other tree crops, thieves will sometimes cut down the trees. The gangs are violent and seek to frighten owners into staying away. On the other hand, strong and agile men can discourage them by guarding their crop. "If you do not shoot at them, they will generally not molest you, rather move on elsewhere. After all, they are mostly boys, and from our own village." Most coffee farmers estimated that they had losses from theft of one to two hundred kilos of coffee in the 1983–84 season. Even the imam is not safe against them. He reports being much bothered by thieves, as well as by wanton destruction: persons enter his orchards and "sometimes just tear up my seedlings to destroy, not to plant them for themselves. Maybe they do it because they had a bad relation to me, or simply because they are afraid that one man will become rich. It is so bad that many farmers are discouraged and no longer cultivate, because it is all destroyed or stolen anyway." In the words of another villager: "Gangs of them, around five or so, go out together at night armed with rocks. One serves as lookout, the rest of them harvest. If they climb a durian-tree and the owner comes and surprises them, they pelt him with rocks so he must flee. They have strong young men as leaders, but also smaller boys take part. Think what effect it has on their morals and their upbringing! Because many are involved, we generally know who they are. But what can we do, without proof and fearful of their revenge? Often they cut down the trees, for example the coffee, to harvest it more quickly. Indeed, the thieves are of two kinds, those who simply do it for profit, and those who *want* to destroy."

The imam's introduction of *panili*, vanilla, to the area in the early 1970s is now told in the form of a cautionary tale: "I obtained plants from Java, grew them, and made my first harvest [the plant grows for three years, gives two crops and dies]. For one kilo of dried seed, I got eighty thousand rupees that first year; and the price is still about fifty thousand rupees [about US$50]. I spoke about it in the mosque, explained how all of Pagatepan could become rich from the seedlings I would distribute. But farmers from neighboring villages were eager to buy plants, and many were stupid and sold the seedlings directly, without letting them give a crop. Others started stealing cuttings. Now panili is a special plant, it is impossible to understand and illogical, but if you *steal* the plant or the cutting, it will not grow and even the mother plant will suffer. . . . There was so much stealing that now none of the panili in Pagatepan grows well any more, and we are just as poor as we ever were!"

Though this prevalence of theft and destruction is generally presented as a modern and worsening crisis, it is not limited to Pagatepan and not unique to the present. To varying degrees other villages in the region, both Muslim and Hindu, are troubled by it. The insecurity that led to military administration of Pagatepan in the sixties took the form of extensive theft and destruction; and the military officers that replaced the local perbekels, more free to pursue ruthless means, are reported to have ordered public floggings and the shaving of the heads of young culprits. Even further back, theft and struggles arising from theft appear as elements in village stories: some old men are whispered to have been very active thieves in their youths. The syndrome thus seems to arise out of basic features of village organization; and I would suggest that it is clearly connected with the structural features of production and circulation militating against investment and expansion in the economy.

9

Factionalism in Prabakula

I have sought in the preceding two chapters to penetrate the surfaces of politeness, rules, and formal institutions in Pagatepan and ask how the patterns of events in this community are shaped by decisions and acts designed by villagers for the "real" world of political, economic, and personal struggles in which they see themselves embroiled. I argue that this attempt is necessary to avoid giving a flawed and misinterpreted account of these events and their meanings. An interpretation of the symbols and concepts that articulate a people's thoughts cannot rely on a hermeutics of their occurrence in formal contexts only (Wikan 1990:chap. 2). Their significance and meanings to actors, i.e., what they convey to persons *within* a lifeway and a culture, must depend heavily on the events they are used to interpret and the intentions they are used to serve, and the *way* they are used for these purposes. An anthropological account is of limited interest if it only addresses a select sector and level of cultural manifestations — rules, rites, texts, or people's statements of abstract principles — and not the broad flow of events that can be discovered to take place in those communities and those people's lives.

We therefore need to work closely with those flows of events, and their construal by participants, so as to be able to trace the connections between many levels of phenomena and arrive at an appreciation of the social life that is generated and the precipitate of interpreted experience that results. This will be illustrated by an analysis of some further materials from Hindu Prabakula, showing how concerns reminiscent of those revealed in Pagatepan are pursued in the very different idiom of Hinduist cult in Prabakula. I wish to show that any attempt to interpret the reality the villagers inhabit by concentrating our attention on the forms of their cultural codes alone, without benefit of insight into the subjectivities of the particular actors involved, can lead to a very externalist and incomplete construction being placed on the events of their lives, quite wide of the mark from the interpreted reality in which the actors themselves participate.

An account of a particular series of political and ritual events that unfolded in Prabakula during my field visits there may serve this purpose. At the time of my second visit, certain things had started happening that were significantly affecting the political field in the village.

In August 1985 one of the regular calendrical rites of the Pura Mranjan Agung (lit.: Temple [of the] Ancestor-shrine-of-twice-born-caste [the] Great) was held. This temple contains the ancestral shrines of one of the five Gusti (i.e., high-caste) branches of the village, indeed a family from which according to village lore used to come the deputy, of the king of Buleleng during the rule of the Karangasem kings before the Dutch victory of 1849. This deputy was known as the Jero Gde Prabakula, or more generally the patih.

A regular feature of this rite in the Mranjan Agung is the fetching and carrying, in solemn procession, of certain sacred objects from the nearby *pura pejengenan*. These objects are reported to be very filled with *sakti*, power, so much so that if unauthorized persons try to carry them, even one that looks quite small, four men are just barely able to lift it. Most of the objects are lances, knives (*kris*), and other weapons of war, along with sets of gamelan and gong musical instruments, which recently had been moved to the pura desa. The term *pejengenan* suggests association with a reigning princely court; thus the first court of the founder of Buleleng, Raja Panji Sakti, in his home village of Panji, today constitutes a pura pejengenan. The buildings comprising this pura in Prabakula are storage buildings, with grounds and architectural remains indicating a formal layout, ceremonial gates, etc. In other words, there is indeed material evidence for continuity with a previously existing structure of rank and power, a subcourt of some kind.

A number of myths, known to varying extent by a few senior persons, embody such traditions connected with the origins of the village and the building of its main temples by a king/sage (dukoh) of ancient times. Starting with the Pura Gunungsari, the first of Prabakula's exceptional set of three Siwa temples, he proceeded in the manner of a culture hero to move from location to location and create institutions, and then miraculously he dematerialized and achieved Nirwana. As I had been told them, these myths were associated with temples and the origin/history of the community as a whole, not with particular groups and lines of descent within it.

At the culmination of this particular ceremony in 1985, however, one of the village trance mediums (*presutri*) who had been called to attend the occasion — a poor man in his forties, of Sudra family — was possessed by the God, who then spoke to the congregation. It is a normal feature of many rites that one or a sequence of spirits/gods communicates through such trance mediums to the congregation and at least gives evidence that the offerings have been accepted and the worship received. In this case, however, the message was far more elaborate and specific. The God revealed the whole history of the ancient kingdoms that had created and ruled the village and from whom had issued the distinguished line of Gusti descendants composing the congregation of the ancestor temple. The God thereupon proceeded to admonish that *all* the family — about twenty couples of permanent residents in the village, and also the many emigrated members, when they visit — must regularly gather for ceremonies at the temple from now on. Why? Because they were once a great family and must be united again.

It is important that this was not merely a spontaneous trance possession such as also frequently occurs: the presutri in question is one of the authorized mediums of the village temples. In Prabakula these are from either of two particular families, and they have been called by the gods and sanctified by the village. The sign that one has been called is generally a chronic disturbance of some sort, or the God may suddenly announce his choice, while possessing another trance medium, in the context of a ritual. This particular presutri had shown characteristic symptoms as a young man of being seriously disturbed: he could never stay at home and concentrate on anything; instead he would wander about and be constantly out-of-place, even at night — characteristic symptoms of *bingung* (serious confusion, being out of balance). His parents consulted a series of balians, native healers, and they all interpreted his condition as a sign that he must become a presutri, or else he would always remain like this. So as a young man he dedicated himself and promised in the village temple that he would serve as a presutri if he became well.

The village, i.e., the krama desa adat, then made the appropriate ritual in the pura desa: the offering (at their expense) of *banten panganinganing* or *banten panyapsap* to purify his body. Its key component is blessed holy water from the six temples: the pura desa, the pura dalem, and the four boundary-marking temples at the top, east, west, and lower boundaries of the village area. Subsequently, when wanted at a ceremony, the presutri is first summoned by the pemangku and congregation bringing a *canang pamandak/canang pangulam* offering and then fetched by a procession bearing regular offerings once the ceremony is under way.

Trance is stimulated by music and incense. Subjectively, the medium in question reports, it feels as if a material presence is coming, surrounding him and descending on him. The hair on his head, neck, and body stands on end; his body becomes very heavy and it feels as if his chest were opening up wide — and then he loses consciousness. If someone tries to pierce him with a knife while he is in a trance, he feels nothing and the point of the kris cannot penetrate him. He has no recollection of the what the God says while possessing his body. When the God leaves, he gradually regains consciousness, the weight lifts, and he feels very light-headed. While possessing him, the God speaks in intelligible language, for all of the congregation to hear; but only the pemangku can address questions to the God.

News of the revelations spread quickly through the village to people outside the descent group congregation. It confirmed, but elaborated on, traditional knowledge and myth; and the old village calendrical expert, who was a puppeteer in his younger life and is the respected repository of village traditional history, was very pleased with this independent and authoritative confirmation of the rightness of the oral traditions he himself had been transmitting.

To a certain Gusti Kapal, however, it held special significance. For several years he had been engaged in a search for the family's kawitan (origin/origin-shrine). He had traveled widely and enquired of knowledgeable persons in Bali, but no one could give him useful information. Other branches of the family claimed origins from Tabanan in South Bali as Arya Kabukabu, a minor Wesia line. Everyone, it seems, could sense from his appearance and his presence that his origins were not *kasar*, common or vulgar; but he obtained no specific information elsewhere. Now, that was clearly demonstrated to be because the family's kawitan is right here, in their family shrine in Pura Gunungsari, and that they are Satria Dalem from the original founding king, specifically Sirarya Damar.

Gusti Kapal had only recently been reemerging to his rightful position of influence. For years he had been sick, both in body and in spirit. His life had been in disarray, his search for his kawitan inconclusive. Then a message reached him: a middle-aged woman in Pancasari village, previously a resident of Prabakula, one night had a dream that she received a letter from God, who instructed her to take the letter to Gusti Kapal. She went to an old man in Pancasari and consulted him; he took the message to Prabakula: that Gusti Kapal should become pemangku of the family shrine in Pura Gunungsari, the first Siwa temple. This temple has its regular pemangku for the congregation at large, of Sudra caste, and it would be improper for a Gusti to hold this position as he should not make offerings and obeisance even to the deified spirits of persons of commoner caste. But the temple also contains a separate shrine for the Gusti family, and the pemangkuship of this shrine had for some time been vacant due to the death of the previous pemangku. The elder men of the family congregated and decided they would heed God's message and make Gusti Kapal pemangku of this shrine. He had also allowed his household shrine to fall into disrepair, but about six months before the recent ceremony with its epochal revelation, he had renovated and repaired it. Now, just like his household temple, his life also had passed from disarray to order.

The special significance of God's admonition that the whole family must join in worship at the Pura Mranjan Agung, where Gusti Kapal is *not* ritually in charge, arises from the secular political history of Prabakula. A prosperous and progressive community, it acquired during the early Sukarno years an influential circle of Communist villagers, led by a Gusti relative of Gusti Kapal who became perbekel. Whereas the previous Perbekel, also of his Gusti family, had combined an open and progressive attitude with respect for tradition and local Hindu teachings, the Communist Perbekel increasingly used his position to force the villagers to abandon all traditions and modernize. Gusti Kapal tells how, when the time of major calendrical ceremonies came up, he and his wife would be stopped at the gate of the pura desa by young Communists who had been placed there to break up the worship. Gusti Kapal, a hero-veteran of the war of independence, had answered coolly: "Yes, you can stop me from entering. But if you do, I will surely kill you for it." So they were allowed to pass, but they were constantly harassed and prevented in their practice of family and temple ritual.

The perbekel and several other leading Communists, reportedly altogether fifteen villagers, were killed in the 1965 unrest; but the family had become split by his persistent intriguing, in which he had utilized every division and destroyed all family authority, and a majority of them remained alienated. They did not honor God, so they became poorer and poorer — even to this day. Thus the whole family's prestige and influence had been destroyed, and Gusti Kapal had himself for years been indifferent. Then one day, people of a neighboring village turned to him to settle a long-standing conflict between priest and congregation: a few words from him, and it was resolved. He realized he had sakti, force, like Panji Sakti, as his *bakat*, natural skill from inheritance. Now he wishes to let bygones be bygones and unite the family in the proper worship of their holy ancestors.

In this he received the active support of the leading village pemangku, who is priest of the pura desa and also caretaker of the pura dalem and a number of other important temples in the community. As such the priest is also the custodian of the sacred gamelan instruments and makes them available to the Gustis for their mranjan rites. He was himself present at the ceremony and trance events in question and confirmed to me Gusti Kapal's account of the revelations — though he also dryly observed that the news was hardly new: everyone must be aware there had been kingdoms here before Panji Sakti. Thus Panji Sakti's main royal temple in Sukasada is named to reflect just that fact: Pura Anyar, the New Temple.

But the pemangku's own career had also been almost as checkered as that of Gusti Kapal. The priestly title has been in his family a long time, and his father held it. When his father died in 1935, his eldest brother took over. Then during the Japanese occupation, people were taken for forced labor, whether farmer or pemangku. His brother was taken, when he finally came back, he only reluctantly took up his duties again. Perhaps he was too strong-minded ["hard-hearted"]; anyway, one village faction, especially three particular persons, became jealous. Apparently they thought the profits from priesthood were greater than they really are. When the brother heard about their criticism, he became offended and stopped functioning. The present pemangku, at that time, preferred to live on his small plot of land elsewhere, having retired from working as a carpenter in hotel construction in the south.

So in 1968 the other faction took over — and they were of the Communist Gustis, or front men for them. But the gods did not want them, and they were sick while they held the positions and afterwards; one promptly died when he took up pemangkuship. The pura desa, and the pura dalem even more swiftly, passed to a succession of persons without sacred authorization, backed by·the same faction. Finally, when they were all sick, another faction offered him village land to sharecrop if he would come home, and then asked him to take up the pemangkuship, which should pass on by inheritance: ever since they have prospered.

When I visited the village next year the process of Gusti restoration continued, though there had been no new trance revelations. "That means the knowledge we received then was enough; now the family must keep [embrace, practice] that knowledge." The only small sensation was Gusti Kapal's discovery, when digging in a corner of his compound beside the household altar, of a natural spring of holy water. The present Perbekel, of a third faction, steered a pragmatic modernist course and avoided any partisan involvement, while Gusti Kapal was an exceptionally active participant in all family and community cult and performed his ritual duties with dispatch.

By the next year, however, new developments were under way. On April 1987, at a full moon ceremony in Pura Gunungsari, where Gusti Kapal had become the pemangku of the family shrine, a recently widowed relative of Gusti Kapal was the only presutri to be possessed. The God was asked the whereabouts of more of the family heirlooms, which had been dispersed during the years of confusion. The answer was "So you want it back? It is here!" and, turning to one of the persons present: "Why do you keep hiding it? You must give it back to him!" And next day, the person so addressed turned up and handed Gusti Kapal a beautiful, long kris blade, which had been missing since almost six months before the unrest of 1965. Previously, parts of the sacred *angklung* gamelan had also been returned to him. It is bad luck for persons to keep such things unauthorized; the person who had been hiding the angklung had become increasingly sick and finally died, and the heirs rid themselves of the danger by returning it. The one who had taken the kris, on the other hand, admitted to having tried to sell it as an antique to a collector in Pancasari (where the woman who received the message about Gusti Kapal's pemangkuship lives, and where Gusti Kapal goes once a week to collect the market tax — a minor administrative perk of the type allotted to veterans of the war of independence). The antique collector in question had offered one million rupees for it — but then became afraid of its power and withdrew his offer. Gusti Kapal hopes that the God will next provide them with presastis, the ancient documents of metal that serve as charters and sources of mystical power. No such documents are known — but they surely must once have existed, and therefore the God will retrieve them for his descendants. The God, at this point, is also supposed to have recommended that all the sacrae might better be kept in Gusti Kapal's house than constantly be carried back and forth to the pura pejengenan or pura desa. The pemangku of the pura desa, on the other hand, will not confirm this, as he had left the temple before the possession took place. Moreover, he claims that this presutri trance medium has not yet been purified by the village in solemn rites, so her trance possession has a less authoritative character than that which led to the first revelations.

Two weeks later followed the Kuningan festival, an annual festival (according to the Javanese-Balinese *uku* calendar of 210 days) that receives the souls of the dead to their annual ten days of revisit among the living. Gusti Kapal was delighted with the volume of participation in the family's pura ibu, mother temple, dedicated to family ancestors. Not only did most family members join in the ceremonies, but a number of sampingan also attended — nonagnates attached to the group by affinal ties or because they were traditional followers of the patih. Gusti Kapal is not pemangku of this shrine, but he took prominent part in the organization of the rites and emphasizes its very special character. A very simple and beautiful structure set among coconut and other stately trees at the edge of the village, it contains, besides a small *pasamuan* meeting pavilion and the *papati* temple guardian altar, only two shrines: a *rontlu* of three altars under a common roof ("for Brahma, Wisnu, and Siwa") and the focal shrine, in the mountain-and-eastward corner, for Batara Nyang Lingsir. The family claims that for the original inauguration of this shrine both a Siwaist and a Buddhist priest were required, and that the pura, uniquely, is equivalent to Besakih, the Mother Temple of all of Bali: the *pitara*, purified souls of cremated ancestors, go directly from here to Heaven and do not need to pass via Besakih as must everyone else.

Other informants whisper a more gloomy story: that the Gustis' pura ibu is really a case of "Nungsung Dewa Pitri," "the Sacred Burden of the Dead Soul." Long ago, a person of that Gusti family must have murdered another person with a knife. To do penance for such a crime, the murderer and his family must erect a temple on the spot, and the murderer's soul becomes linked as servant to that temple for ever after. Unless this is done, it is very dangerous: the family will be pursued by bad luck, internal strife, and accidents. The Gustis' pura ibu is *that* kind of temple — but since they hold such high rank, it is never mentioned, and the pura is never referred to by so stigmatizing a term.

In the wake of the progressive restoration and unification of a major segment of the Gusti family as a conservative force, the wider factional alliance around them thus seems in the process of dissolving. Sudras now exacerbate this with gossip about the gustis' pretentiousness, their arrogance in seeming to think they own the village. At the krama desa meetings of Prabakula there is no formal seniority or privileged seating arrangement; all members should be equal. But in fact the Gustis always sit centrally, while the Jabar/Sudra majority is pressed out to the periphery, and the Gustis always dominate the proceedings.

The idioms in terms of which the factional ambitions and alignments of Prabakula are cast are thus strikingly different from those employed in Pagatepan. Yet, at a somewhat higher level of generality, the similarities that emerge may be equally striking. Nor does the pattern seem to be unfamiliar in other Bali-Hindu communities, as already noted. Indeed, after an extended complaint about slander and the difficulties of mobilizing community cooperation in Pagatepan, a village elder there reflected how these things were problems everywhere: "If you study a Hindu village, you will learn all about quarrels like these among them too!"

Bateson ([1937] 1970) provides a somewhat enigmatic account of an episode reminiscent of the preceding story both in substance and sequence. Though he does not explain the personal and factional interests that lie behind the maneuvers, their existence can be sensed; and he com-

ments on "the general stiffness and the quarrels" (ibid.:113) that characterizes the ambience of the main village involved. An outside visitor I brought
on a visit to Prabakula made the general reflection apropos of their situation: "You see how villagers align as 'Communists' or with other political
parties. It is not because they know what it is and have ideas about national
politics. It is only because there is someone in their village that they want
to *be different from!*"

The pattern repeats itself from village to village. Thus, for example, in
the village of Panji, on visiting its pura pejengenan I immediately stumbled
on similar divisions. Consonant with the towering position of Panji Sakti,
the founder of the dynasty, these remains of his first court are surrounded
by a very powerful aura of awe and sakti. It is told how the shrine was a
place of refuge for freedom fighters during the war of independence: the
Dutch were unable to find them when they stood within the temple. Likewise, "during the 1965 unrest, some young men who were Communist-
influenced but not wicked were gathered there, praying. The soldiers
came looking for them, but marched right by. They could not see them."

But control of this sacred place is a great and divisive bone of contention. The son of its previous pemangku tried moving to Singaraja but became sick, and the balian he consulted discovered that he *must* remain
close to the shrine, as its attendant and the eighth-generation descendant
of the king: it was God's orders. But the main dynastic line claims it as *their*
shrine; whereas the senior of the Sukasada branch now serves as its pemangku. There is also division in the village itself: half of them want the
representative of the traditional line of pemangkus to live by the shrine as
its attendant; the other half would have him move up to the top of the
village as attendant to the Government's Heros' Monument that has been
erected there in memory of the freedom fighters. And finally, a neighboring balian claims that it is *he* who controls and dispenses the sakti of Panji
Sakti.

Thus the patterns of factional activity in Prabakula and other Hindu
villages seem as divisive as those we found in Pagatepan, and as linked with
personal and covert rivalry. But the Hindu context provides a special set of
factional prizes: control of sources of supernatural sakti — krises, other
heirlooms, and the shrines and temples themselves — besides the ubiquitous formal offices. These various material objects, from which power is
believed to flow, have a focusing effect on the designs of strategy. They
may also have a certain structuring effect on the way pretenders attempt to
construct followings: the power of these sources of sakti is dangerous to
anyone who unrightfully seeks the control of it; it therefore becomes essential to see that one's claims are socially validated. But below this surface

of forms, the struggles seem as multiple, open, and divisive among Hindu as among Muslim villagers.

How should such a pattern of divisive local politics best be understood? There is a strong tendency in social science to see factionalism only as a secondary, and highly disvalued, deviation from proper political activity, representing it as a kind of illegitimate and parasitic growth on other and primary political institutions.

In the Balinese context, I would suggest another view: recognizing it as a political form in its own right. To clarify its significance, we must take as our point of departure the character of Balinese village communities and Balinese social interactions. As we have seen, these are very dense social communities, with strong pressures toward consensual decisions and obligatory cooperative action. The politeness, attentiveness, and suppression of conflict and aggression that characterize social surfaces are likewise inducive to conformity. Social control by subtle and diffuse but massive group sanctions is a characteristic mode, and it induces sensitivity to, and a fear of, social ostracism. Behind this again lurks a pervasive fear of sorcery (Wikan 1987; below, chapter 15). To all this must be added also the extreme precedence given to respect and authority in Balinese etiquette, and the positive evaluation of submission. It is indeed indicative that insubordination is counted among the six deadly sins, to be expurgated at the Bali-Hindu rites of passage at adolescence, together with lustfulness, drunkenness, and similar "base and animal urges."

The result of such a combination of social pressures is one of mutual reinforcement, strengthening social controls and threatening to overwhelm and stifle the individual person. I shall return in chapter 17 to an analysis arguing that this is indeed a major component in how the individual experiences these pressures. Be that as it may, the resultant enmeshing of persons in group control precludes a political organization based on the free articulation of a diversity of opinions in pluralistic debate. It also inhibits any overt resistance to abuses of power by high-ranking persons, and indeed most processes of socially negotiated controls on the powers of persons with rank and high authority.

In such a situation, divisive factionalism has the effect of relieving somewhat the overwhelming weight of society and collective opinion by dividing it, and of strengthening the autonomy of individuals by providing collectivities prepared to marshal diffuse resistance to authorities. Thus, in a sense, institutionalized factionalism in the village is a functional analogue to the principle of separation of powers in American constitutional theory. By the introduction of a system of mutual checks and balances – in the Balinese case between shifting, divisive cabals rather than functionally differentiated state organs — the interests of the individual are defended. It does not define rights and due process or allot mutual control functions between institutions; but the same end is achieved by empowering the individual to form defensive alliances within a disorganized field. We shall return to how such a pattern of factionalism is effected in conception and motivation. At this stage, I only wish to point to the structural and functional entailments of the factional structure shared by the politics of Pagatepan and Prabakula, despite their drastically different formal organizations and idioms of political discourse.

10

A General Framework
for Analyzing the
Meaning of Acts

A closer scrutiny of social relations and activities in Pagatepan and Prabakula thus shows that we need to transcend the level of formal rules and
institutions to depict their structure and function in any realistic manner.
To describe the life that unfolds in the village we must depict the patterns
that emerge when these institutions are activated and put into practice by
people, who each have multiple simultaneous purposes and know that so
do their fellow villagers. Thus we saw in chapter 4 how subaks, though
deceptively similar in their formal construction, generate very different
functional systems of agricultural management by virtue of the variations
they set in the parameters for cooperation and individual opportunity. Ob-
versely, the very great differences in other village institutions described in
chapters 2, 3, and 5 may be put to use for rather similar purposes by villagers in their respective communities, generating a social life within these
villages whereby, for example, factional patterns become strongly conver-
gent in form and function.

In emphasizing this, I am in no way arguing that formal organization is
irrelevant to what is happening — only that formal organization is not *what*
is happening. Moreover, I argue, the significance of that which unfolds
cannot simply be read from a formal book of rules of the institution we are
observing in action; such rules provide only one partial set of criteria by
which acts are understood and interpreted. The significance we impute to
the observed events of life is always affected by the frame in which we place
them and the keys with which we read them. This goes a long way to
determine the face and the import of what people see, and thus the effects
the events will have, as anthropologists have long known and recent developments in anthropological theory have made increasingly explicit. Yet we

have not drawn the necessary theoretical consequences of this theoretically clear and simple, but practically so difficult and elusive, insight. It means that when observing human interaction we must identify correctly the keys that the parties to such interaction themselves are using, *as the events unfold*, to be able to give an account of what is going on. This is necessary because the parties to interaction are responding to each other and each other's acts in unfolding chains, where the behavior, i.e., the observable events, performed by one actor is predicated by the actor's interpretation of the events (i.e., her or his transformation of these events into interpreted "acts") that preceded it. Unless we as observers are using similar keys, we will be seeing a very different spectacle from that in which they are participating.

And there is no promise that "the right key" (I shall continue to use the image of "key" in this broad, metaphorical sense for the sum of knowledge used to interpret an event) will be the formal book of rules of formal institutions, as we have been all too ready to assume. Nor can we proceed on the convenient structural-functional assumption that there is isomorphy between an aggregate level of patterns of social organization and the ideas, concepts, and imagery used to interpret action within a population. Important and valid as both these sets of facts may be, we must be prepared to explore their connection in far greater detail and find it far more complex. We clarify the issues by, first, drawing Weber's distinction between (1) events, or behavior — the objective, perceptual things that happen — and (2) acts — human behavior as interpreted, or understood, within a cultural framework of meanings. Where can we as anthropologists best hope to break into the enchanted world of others, where events take on the meanings that are operative, and consequential, in their lives? Presumably right where those connections are being generated: by recognizing the processes involved in the transformation between "event" and "act," and by directing our analysis in both directions from the point at which an event occurs: to its preconditions, and to its consequences.

To the actor, the event of own behavior is an act by virtue of the intent that shapes it, i.e., what the actor sees herself/himself as doing, and why that is desirable and feasible: this is its "meaning" and, to a large extent, determines its form. To other parties, on the other hand, event becomes act through interpretation, through the way its purposes and entailments are understood at the time of its manifestation.

In the short or the longer retrospect, or in anticipation of encounters, people reflect on these intentions and interpretations and shape them in the forms of "plans" and "experience" respectively. Various templates, imagery, dialogues, and musings are no doubt involved in the (re)interpretation of events into experience. Some of this occurs as a social process in its own right, a discourse with sympathetic or critical others. Some of it may be internal to the person but make use of public imagery, knowledge, and stereotype. In the process, we must expect the materials to become increasingly conventionalized and shared, and thus domesticated into cultural forms, though some will be culture-in-the-making, requiring the creation of new images to accommodate new (aspects of) events as experience. In the opposite direction, analytically retracing the emergence of events from intentions and planned acts, connections lead back to the actor's ideas of instrumentality, values, goals, and identities. An actor is also well aware that her or his act, once manifested as event, will also be interpreted by others; and to that extent the actor must also cast acts as "statements," encoding them with reference to the keys she or he anticipates that others will use in interpreting them. But I cannot accept this communicative aspect as providing the only, or even primary, context for our analysis of acts: from it we cannot retrieve how acts are broadly designed to affect the world, whereas if we see the actor's intent as primary, we can yet retrieve the act's communicative dimension.

The slight privileging of intentions over interpretation in this schema

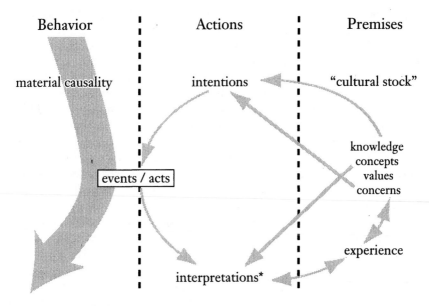

*i.e., interpretations both of what was intended *and* what was effected.

is a question of analytical strategy, not an effort to identify independent variables and final causes. The cultural materials in terms of which actors design their acts, and those they use to interpret the acts of others, are of course connected; so we are dealing with an encompassing circuit that embeds events in their cultural preconditions and consequences. The accretions of experience — molded by premises, tacit assumptions, and cultural imagery variably shared in a group — also play an essential role in reproducing and marginally changing the cultural stock of knowledge, and thereby in turn affect the purposes, plans, and intentions that actors embrace and employ to shape their behavior (Barth 1983:191–96). But this is a very complex connection; and the exploration and modeling of the whole circuit I envisage as an "anthropology of knowledge," which largely remains to be developed. There is the further important point that such cultural processes, in shaping people's acts, also profoundly channel the form and occurrence of objective events. They thus generate salient patterns in that world with which the people in a society are confronted, i.e., the tasks they will face when struggling to interpret the world. Thus "reality" has a double set of cultural roots: one through people's interpretation of events, the other through the collective effect of people's activities causing material patterns in these events.

The important point at this stage of my argument is this: with a reasonable amount of patience and genuine interest in the lives of particular individuals we encounter in another society, their intentions and interpretations can become to a large extent accessible to us as anthropologists. We achieve this attunement progressively through observation, reflection, conversation, and participation, i.e., through social and cultural immersion. There is no way we can enter inside the skin of another person, but this is an impediment inherent in the human condition, not a special difficulty of the anthropologist's task; it is as true of a person at home as of a person doing anthropological fieldwork, so it is a circumstance all communication and social participation are designed to handle. We cannot stop the moment's action and demand to have delivered to us the keys people are employing to interpret that passing moment. But there is nothing to prevent us from progressively equipping ourselves, through participation in the social intercourse connected with planning and interpreting acts, with the knowledge and insights needed to make increasingly intelligent guesses at what is going on as further events unfold. To do so, we need to build up progressively a formidable inventory of cultural and social facts and a knowledge of the particulars that position a considerable number of different actors. Thereby we can increasingly accumulate experience from events alongside the true participants: not by a hermeneutic reading in solitude of certain cultural products, but by knowing an increasing store of the premises for people's actions and interpretations, and entering into the dialogues and interactions of others whereby their experiences are shaped and shared. The point to recognize is, this learning is embedded in the social process of participation; and it is immensely simplified to the extent that the anthropologist is able to perform it in the context of practice rather than in the limbo of formal interviews and abstract theory. For it is in practice that the appropriate keys of interpretation are linked with the appropriate contexts and events to which they are applied – a linkage it is highly questionable one could reconstruct post hoc, from logic and first principles.

I am now finally prepared to return to Bali and to the opening paragraph of this chapter. We have observed a disjunction between the (diverse) formal charters of village constitution whereby finely tuned cooperative institutions are designed, and the (ubiquitous) divisive factionalism that characterizes living communities. Indeed, there seems to be an enigma in many of the behavior patterns reported from Bali, in the fusion they exhibit between communalism and instrumentality, grace and provokability, control and excess. Where do we turn for the necessary materials to interpret these behaviors, and what does our account of them become? I find that my understanding of "what is going on" in these Balinese villages is in important respects at odds with well-known and compelling accounts of Balinese society and culture found in the anthropological literature. The enigma of cooperative formal design and divisive practice that has emerged so strongly in the preceding materials is only one of these differences; but it may serve as my provocation for a general confrontation with the design and content of these other analyses. Indeed, even where the patterns I report are relatively in accord with the descriptions offered in this earlier literature, I find myself constructing somewhat variant interpretations to those generally favored, because of my model of factors and processes, which I use to generate these patterns and explain their meaning and form.

Looking back over the argument of the preceding pages, I would not suggest that the difference lies in some fortunate or superior feature of my field materials. The field materials of all anthropologists in Bali — many of them no doubt far richer than mine — are surely composed in part of insights obtained through the immersion of participant observation and careful contextualization. The difference is found in the theoretical perspective. I have developed these brief reflections on the circuit in which events and actions are embedded to articulate some theoretical and methodological ground rules for where and how we must seek our premises for interpreting behavior. My argument will be that the representations of Balinese culture and society with which I am at odds have overlooked these considerations: they are insufficiently designed in terms of those interactional processes that constitute and reproduce culture. Without this link with practice, "culture" becomes a very rarified and ultimately mystifying abstraction.

But first, I need to depict the main thrust of these other accounts and how they compare to the thesis I am developing. An insightful presentation of the whole sweep of Western interpretations of Bali has been provided by Boon (1977). For my present argument, I need note only the few authors who have been most formative of the conceptions held by contemporary anthropological readers: Jane Belo, Margaret Mead, Gregory Bateson, and Clifford Geertz. The work of Miguel Covarrubias ([1937] 1973) ethnographically perhaps the most generally adequate text, is of a different kind: his theoretical position is less explicit, but that book's thematics and general tenor are considerably closer to mine, and I find his materials to lend a certain support to my position.

Jane Belo sets the tone for the literature's image of Bali in her disarming portrayal of the general Balinese ambience as she experienced it: "The babies do not cry, the small boys do not fight, the young girls bear themselves with decorum, the old men dictate with dignity. Every one carries out his appointed task, with respect for his equals and superiors, and gentleness and consideration for his dependents" (Belo [1935] 1970:106). We are thus invited to perceive Bali as a harmonic spectacle of motivationally inaccessible, collectively evoked tradition and aestheticism. This provides the framework for Belo's interpretations, despite her occasional attention — also in the context cited — to the exceptions and to the nonconformism, deviance, and outright rebelliousness of some individuals.

The essence of Mead's ethnographically rich and detailed account seems to be summed up in the imagery of the Balinese love for *rame* (Bateson and Mead 1942:3f.), the noisily crowded festival atmosphere, where she observed that participants can "stand completely remote in spirit, yet so close in body to a crowd" and where "in the most rapt crowds, when the clowns are performing . . . one can still see face after face which contains no response to the outside world." She also sees a muting of cumulative time in their calendrical system (ibid:5f.), a suppression of personal emotions, a conformity with regulations and rules of behavior, and an industriousness designed as if only to fill spurts of time (ibid:47). Mead captures a strong sense of the ambivalence of expressions and attitudes, especially the coexistence of gaiety and freedom of theatrical caricature (ibid.:12) with pervasive respect (ibid:xiv) and fear (ibid.:47). Yet in her basic understanding, she privileges the features of "a character curiously cut off from inter-personal relationships, existing in a state of dreamy-relaxed disassociation" (ibid.: 47). The forces and processes that she identifies behind these patterns compose a psychodynamics of early childhood development that generates personalities incapable or afraid of emotional climax and thus distanced from social participation of any intensity, rather than any dynamics of society or of culture.

Bateson, in a number of more fragmentary contexts, gives a series of insightful and theoretically productive characterizations; but these point in several directions, which he has not chosen to collate and reconcile. His most coherent and influential account is tied to his construction of a "steady state society" (Bateson [1949] 1972a), closely compatible with the absence of climax emphasized in Mead's psychological model. From his identification of Balinese society as nonschismogenic, he is led to search for "the motives and values which accompany the complex and rich cultural activities" (ibid.:116). He identifies the conception that "offense is felt to be against the order and natural structure of the universe rather than against the actual person offended" (ibid.:119), a pervasive anxiety about making an error (ibid.:120), and the idea of balance arising from carefully contrived motion (ibid.:125). He then constructs a Theory of Games model essentially depicting members of Balinese village councils as individually and collectively intent on maintaining the steady state of the system by continual but nonprogressive change (ibid.:125).

Geertz ([1966] 1973a) links up most of these ideas and embeds them in a detailed synthetic account of certain formal institutions and cultural conceptions and idioms, modeling this construction in counterpoint to Schutz's concept of "consociates" (ibid.:365). His emphasis is less on ambiguities and more on what he sees as the logical entailments of each institutional apparatus. The Balinese culture he thus pictures upholds as an "obsessive ideal" that people not become involved in each other's biography and forms a cultural design of mutually reinforcing symbols that block from sight "the individuality, spontaneity, perishability, emotionality and vulnerability of others" and places fellow villagers in a "sociological middle distance" (ibid.:399). The main factors he identifies are (1) a symbolic order of person-definition that stereotypes and anonymizes others, (2) a calendrical system that immobilizes time, and (3) a pervasive playful theatricality and contrivance whereby social action is designed in terms of aesthetics rather than ethics or instrumentality (ibid.:400). The result is that "events happen like holidays. They appear, vanish, and reappear — each discrete, sufficient unto itself, a particular manifestation of the fixed order of things. Social activities are separate performances. . . . Life is . . . qualitatively ordered, like the days themselves, into a limited number of established kinds" (ibid.:403f).

Each of these characterizations of Balinese culture and society is vivid and fascinating, and each certainly represents Bali in a way so that it is deserving of Mead's statement that it is a culture "in many ways less like our own than any other which has yet been recorded" (Bateson and Mead 1942:xvi). My problem is that while some of the patterns these authors emphasize are recognizable in terms of what I have seen, they are infused with meanings and entailments that are different from those I would recognize; and the forces that are invoked to propel the Balinese to act in these ways are largely obscure or implausible to me. None of them gives a sense of Balinese consciousness that could inform the actors I have experience of, who people the stage in my analysis. The activities that give village politics its pervasive form of divisive factionalism in Pagatepan and Prabakula; the painful ambivalences of close kin relationships that mold social organization in Pagatepan; the struggles to make a living that shape village economy and class and determine life trajectories — these are understandable to me only if people's main purposes are *not* aesthetic; if they are indeed deeply and emotionally involved in their own particular lives and aware of such an engagement in themselves and their consociates; if their interest is *not* in maintaining a steady state in their community; if they are very keenly observing and linking events and social performances in long-term strategies of their own and each other's making.

The difference between the account I am developing and those in the literature referred to above is not just a question of alternative interpretations, more or less interesting renderings containing varying emphases. In terms of the argument I seek to develop, the assertions I am making must be valid, or they will have no explanatory force: I am trying to model a set of empirical components and processes, observable in the field materials, that will generate the particular range of events that take place and the aggregate forms that characterize the region and its civilization. This generative model thus strives to be at once both compelling and naturalistic. It should be compelling in that any change in any part of such a model should affect the totality of what the model generates: it is no use explaining something by means of elements only loosely connected, a change among which will make no difference. And it should be naturalistic, in the sense of being reconstructive of empirical processes (Barth 1966, 1981, 1987), in that any particular component or process that the model posits, but that cannot be empirically identified, should be excised from the model: it makes no sense trying to explain something that is there by means of something that proves not to be there.

The precision to which I can aspire in this modeling is modest, but it must be defended and improved: basically contrary assertions regarding the consciousness that informs the actors, and the purposes that propel them, cannot be tolerated. I need to convince my reader that I have identified, within broad but sufficiently specific parameters, the plans and intents of actors in the system, and the keys they employ to interpret each other's acts, because I am arguing that these will determine the whole patterning of social events and event sequences that unfold between them, which as interpreted by them form the life of these communities and the society.

Where, then, are the sources of discrepancy between my account of what goes on in the villages on which I report, and those very different accounts of Balinese culture and society that we find in Belo, Mead, Bateson, and Geertz? Are they in observed events; in the selection of events that are treated as salient; in the keys used to "read" the events and animate them with meaning and significance; or in the anthropological theories that inform our methods and our modeling?

The first and simplest explanation would be that the events I have been observing are really different from theirs: both time and place separate their observations from mine. Indeed, in their joint foreword, Bateson and Mead (1942:xiv–xv) note that whereas most of Bali is surprisingly uniform in ethos, among the Satria caste and in the culture of North Bali "may be found an emphasis upon the individual rather than upon his status, an element of social climbing and an uneasiness of tenure which contrasts strongly with the rest of Bali." Their own explanation of this difference is limited to the observation that North Bali had at the time, in the 1930s, been more exposed to external contacts and colonial Dutch influence. External influences have since, of course, only accelerated, and this would be consistent also with differences between Geertz's materials from the early 1950s and ours from thirty years later.

If so, the discrepancy is not particularly interesting: my analysis refers to another Bali or not-Bali. I have two objections to this view. First, I am dissatisfied with recent external contact as a sufficient factor to cause such profound and general change in the north, across a broad range of local institutional variation, between villages as markedly insulated as Pagatepan, Julah, or Sida Tapa and communities as open and connected with the world as Pengastulan, Panji, or Singaraja. Second, I judge both the particular events and the formal institutions and symbols on which these other accounts base their constructions to be essentially compatible with the range of patterns I have observed in North Bali. I recognize the appearance of most features that are described, but I cannot agree with the framework of interpretation in which they are placed. Thus I recognize the elaborated, well-wrought ceremonialism of interaction, and how etiquette comes to be like a kind of dance (Geertz [1966] 1973a:400), but not its motivation in a "radical aestheticism." Wikan (1987, 1990), on the contrary, gives a compelling analysis of how this grace and beauty in interpersonal interaction is complexly motivated by concerns about virtue, elaborate conceptions of health and emotions, and a pervasive fear of sorcery. In other words, with her I identify these as necessary factors in the processes that make a characteristic ceremonialism manifest in much Balinese interaction: it is not understood by characterizing it as a reified property of "a culture" or as directly motivated by an asserted "aestheticism." It is only by correctly identifying the concerns of the actors who behave in this fashion, and laying bare the cultural constructions of knowledge to which these concerns of theirs refer, that these features are adequately interpreted. Likewise, I observe the same occasional "awayness" of persons in the midst of the madding crowd as did Mead but do not identify it as a symptom of inability to relate with intensity to others; with Wikan (1990:83), I find that it reflects a safety in spectatorship generated by the same forces that explain interpersonal ceremoniousness. I see the prominence of maneuver and balancing in village councils, and their consequence in impeding progressive changes, so perceptively recognized by Bateson — but not their purpose in these effects: I need also to identify the interests that propel particular actors to pursue such factional policies, which lead to a very different construction being placed on these village politics (cf. chapters 7–9, and below chapter 19). Most fundamental, I fail to find compelling any account of South Balinese — if anything, even more creative than North Balinese in their artistic imagery expressive of evil, fear, humility, goodness, respect, people's manipulation of others, responsibility, and the Nemesis of unjust acts — that depicts them as themselves unmoved by, and so presumably without insight into, morality, climaxing emotions, long-term ambition, and attentive and perceptive interests in their consociates.

I am further struck by the indications I see that these other accounts would provide suitable materials for the analysis I am pursuing. Thus Belo's deviant case stories are contextualized and made intelligible in ways that she fails to attempt with respect to the nondeviant behavior she reports, though surely both possible and necessary for it as well (Belo [1935] 1970:85–110). Mead (Bateson and Mead 1942) gives an overwhelming impression of massive empirical evidence for her portrayals through the photographic record she and Bateson accumulated. Yet it is undeniable that those thousands of photographs depict what we, in my emphatic terminology as elaborated in this chapter, must call "events," not "acts," and even less "meanings." It is much less clear what her sources, her methods, and her successes were in obtaining the actor's *own* keys to the interpretations of these events. If she depended heavily on her main assistant, who was himself from North Bali, her greater awareness of individuality, social climbing, and uneasiness of tenure in the north can plausibly be explained as an artifact of this circumstance. In any case, an attention to the ongoing, petty and humdrum conflicts and politics of Bayung Gede would have placed all these events in a necessary metacontext of interpretation that is now lacking, and without which I mistrust the ascriptions of meaning.

Geertz's construction — quite apart from his disregard for whole persons and life situations in favor of a systematics of cultural materials — depends on a careful selection of the cultural materials he includes in his profile. His category of "person" seems arbitrary and could well have been made wider (Howe 1984); a consideration of sorcery and concepts of health and emotion, as well as social events focused around trance (cf. Connor 1984), or respect and rivalry, would fundamentally change his picture. He has acknowledged that an exploration of "witch experiences" and trance behavior would reveal structures quite incompatible with his account. Yet he chooses to set them aside as the "culture's own negation" (Geertz [1966] 1973a:406), "sub-dominant" as contrasted to the "primary" patterns, without entering into any discussion of how these priorities should be established (ibid.:407 fn. 46). A consideration of a fuller set of relevant cultural materials would clearly be necessary to construct any representation of the concepts within which Balinese experience moves. But above all I would argue for the necessity to embed concepts in practice in order to judge their meanings to the people who entertain them.

A similar critique must be made of Bateson: the narrow base of empirical considerations that he makes relevant to his "steady state society" construct proves inadequate when one attempts to transform it from an abstract model to a framework for the representation of Balinese concepts and actions; it does not embody the naturalism to make it serve as a challenge to alternative representations of Bali. As a prototype of abstract modeling, on the other hand, I find it exemplary and, like several other insights and perspectives contained in his writings, productive to the analysis of my North Balinese data.

Against these constructions one may counterpose the actor's own concepts of person and the self as necessary keys to interpreting the meanings of the acts and institutions that compose Balinese life. These North Balinese ideas of personhood have been analyzed by Wikan (1987; 1989a; 1989b; 1990). Based on field data that overlap what I am using in this study, and developing a theoretical argument compatible with, and in major respects anticipating, what I am presently pursuing, she has already developed a critique of the depersonalizing and aestheticizing interpretation that turns Balinese self-concepts into such an inaccessible enigma. By analyzing people's coping strategies in connection with crises involving health, bereavement, and the management of various close and distant social relations she shows persuasively how these concerns are conceptualized and handled, what their interactional entailments are, and how they reproduce the ambiguity and multivalency that are such characteristic features of Balinese life.

North Balinese person concepts vary in the extent to which they employ a Hindu-Buddhist philosophical vocabulary, but all appear to conceptualize a "self" that embraces both an inner consciousness and an outer social persona. Wikan (1990) refers to this as double-anchoredness: the person has at once two aspects, referred to as "face" *(mue/mukane)* and "heart" *(keneh/hati)*. "Face" is the template for appearance, performance, and act. This is very different from English-language uses of the image, which stereotype supposed Mediterranean or Chinese templates and equate the idiom of "face" with "mask." As a Balinese friend observed to us, "If we wear a mask, then it must be on our hearts, not on our faces.") The "heart" is identified as the mover, the source of impulse and passion. The function of "thought" *(pikiran)* is to mediate between heart and face, in both directions: impulse is transformed into plan and action; but also, moral principles embedded in the obligations of social performance are carried into the heart and imposed on it by one's own moral effort. Balinese are deeply and consciously involved in the management of their emotions and orientations, ubiquitously engaged in a struggle to mold both their acts and their impulses, to be dutiful and good. Let a vignette of a friend's own reflections on a small incident, as recounted by himself, serve as an illustration. At the annual boat race organized by the local authorities, his boat, captained by his employed crewman, won the race. "I was very proud. The government gave a prize: forty kilos of rice, to the winning captain. I felt it, in my heart: it was *my* boat; I was not happy. Then, when I went to congratulate the captain, he said: 'Here is the rice prize, you must take half!' I said: 'No, you won the race.' But he insisted. *Then* I could say no with good feeling: 'You should have the rice; I have rice at home; it is all for you!' But I took it, the diploma!"

It is not that there is no goodness in people's hearts too; but humankind's natural condition is morally imperfect, so one's heart will also contain pettiness and passion, in each according to her or his true character (*sifat asli*). Thus the heart is a turbulent area of the self which "must be kept, controlled, shaped to allow the socially sanctioned appearance to surface unruffled" (Wikan 1989b, 1990). The politeness, grace, composure, and obligations of conventional behavior, on the other hand, are all good, no matter what personal intentions may motivate them. "As a man said: 'Society does not need arrogance or unfriendly behaviors. Society needs gotong-royong.' Gotong-royong is the form of communal cooperation that sustains community life and ensures cooperation on numerous tasks Balinese define as collective: irrigation management, agricultural production, temple organization, life cycle ceremonies, and general give-and-take. These might suffer irretrievably were hearts to be exposed" (Wikan 1990:110).

Ideally the performance part of the person, conforming to conventional roles, could indeed — using Geertz's expression — be called "depersonalized"; but that is neither in the Balinese view a complete model of a person, since it lacks impulse and emotion, nor is it capable of accounting for the behaviors that emerge among Balinese. The North Balinese understand a great number of events and social facts to be the product of the hidden, individual features of people's hearts and the imperfections of their moral discipline. What is more, knowing that an imperfectly bridled heart, turbulent with desires, emotions, and evil, hides in every fellow human being, the Balinese orient themselves accordingly. Contrary to Geertz's understanding and description, they are exceptionally, though usually quite discreetly, alert to every slightest clue to each other's individuality. This makes good sense: only by observing closely can one hope to read the true import of acts and reactions, with the avoidance of offense and fear of sorcery reprisals as critical concerns that permeate nearly all social intercourse.

Such a model of the person is capable of providing a framework for interpreting many social facts among Balinese, though in Balinese thought it is combined with a wide range of supernatural agencies and other immaterial forces as explanations of the flow of events. It thus has much greater potential than the constructs established in the previous anthropological literature on Bali; and I shall return to Balinese elaborations on this model as well as to an account of the many other agencies and forces with which they populate the world, and how these affect their actions and their experience of self and others.

First, however, a basic ontological premise of the Belo-Mead-Bateson-Geertz constructions should be discussed. They share the basic premise of simple congruence between (a) the formal rules by which institutions are constituted, (b) the observed patterns of behavior, and (c) the purposes and priorities of the participants in the society, i.e., their consciousness. Only such an assumption of full congruence would provide the context in which one could expect to move directly between cultural institutions, overt forms of action, and the meanings and orientations embraced by actors, and use information on one to supply data for the other. Yet so simplistic an assumption is indeed entailed, for example, in Mead's description of personality from a wide range of data on custom; in Bateson's ascription of motive and purpose to individuals from his model of systemic features of a steady state society; or in Geertz's reading of stage fright, and the absence of consociation, from naming customs, calendrical systems, and patterns of ceremonial etiquette.

The effort of making the various bits of ethnographic evidence fit together in terms of so patently misplaced assumptions of homogeneity and congruence must lead to distorted interpretations and misdirected analytic efforts. To escape the distortions arising from such templates, I have already proposed elsewhere (Barth 1989:134ff.) that we construct our model of Bali explicitly in accordance with another set of assertions:

Meaning is something conferred on an object or an event by a person, not something enshrined in that object or event — that is, it arises in the act of interpretation.

Culture is distributed, and major aspects of its structure inhere precisely in its patterns of distribution in a population.

Actors are (always and essentially) positioned, and the interpretations they make will reflect this positioning and the knowledge that they command.

Finally, the outcomes of interaction are usually at variance with the intentions of the individual participants, and so we cannot judge people's interpretations and intents directly from the observable consequences of their acts.

The first of these assertions is of course familiar, especially from Weber, and is indeed articulated by Geertz in the very essay on which I have focused in my critique (Geertz [1966] 1973a:405). The second was, to my knowledge, first articulated in general terms by Schwartz (1978). The third is also part of our theoretical heritage but has been argued with increasing clarity in recent literature (e.g., Schweder and LeVine 1984; Rosaldo 1989). The fourth, with its ramifying implications especially for micro-

170

macro modeling, has long been a concern of mine (Barth 1966, 1981). In contrast to the highly idealized assumptions of homogeneity, congruence, and harmony, these assumptions seem to me well founded and naturalistic for every society of which I have firsthand knowledge, and most particularly so for the more complex ones, like that of Bali (Barth 1989).

But these assumptions have theoretical implications that have not been fully developed, or even recognized. If people by virtue of their social positioning vary in the ideas and knowledge they embrace, and yet construct their reality by conferring meaning by making interpretations based on these ideas and this knowledge, then the relevant context for all their acts will be eternally contingent. True, their acts, singly or in the aggregate, will have determinate physical consequences where they occur; but equally significantly they will have consequences in terms of the different meanings they acquire through people's interpretations, and the contexts into which they are thereby linked. These contexts and connections must be crucial for our understanding of the intention and meaning of acts. We need a framework that allows for greater complexity, and specificity, than we have been accustomed to require.

The perspective introduced in the first part of this chapter takes us part of the way toward allowing us to model some of these more complex processes. It is a major step to recognize the place of experience and knowledge in enabling people to make their interpretations of events and to construct their views of contexts, opportunities, and plans of action. Thereby we dismantle the received, totalizing view of culture. We can no longer claim that a "society's culture consists of whatever it is you need to know or believe in order to operate in a manner acceptable to its members" (Goodenough 1957:167). People know quite different things and have had very different experience. This operationalizes the important insight of positioning. Persons are not only socially differentiated in observing society from different positions; when they meet they also bring very different capacities to their encounters: they know, can do, and value different things.

But there is another, even more tacit, assumption that I have so far not sufficiently questioned: the localizing and totalizing view of culture that identifies it with a local context. Contrary to this view, we must recognize that there is no way an anthropologist can frame a unit of study and analysis in terms of such a determined locality, community, or society and yet capture the connections I have been discussing above. The context in which any act belongs is contingent and depends on the (probably various) constructions that actors and participants place on it. A major task of ethnography must be to discover and give an account of how acts are placed in these *particular* contexts, frameworks, or worlds in which people themselves embed those acts through their interpretations of them. Only by modeling our descriptions in a way that captures these connections can we secure the meanings of acts, and understand the processes whereby both lives are shaped, and ideas and knowledge are reproduced and changed.

The relevant connection does not necessarily have a form that can be depicted as a localized "community." Most culture — knowledge, values, skills, and orientations — is embedded more specifically in a particular context of related ideas, a tradition of knowledge; ideas cluster and are tied to a set of social relations, a circle; and syndromes of them are learned and largely exercised in a particular pattern of activity, a practice.

To grasp these connections, we need to use a framework that allows for more complexity and specificity. Yet in my analysis of the materials so far, I seem implicitly to have accepted the localizing perspective: I have focused on village communities as the self-evident entities of cultural variation, describing them as distinct worlds of social organization. To an extent, this is true and useful: villages do constitute obtrusive entities in the landscape, and in everyday interaction they are also primary units of reference in North Balinese awareness. They likewise provide the context into which the fieldworker must submerge herself to discover the lived significance of so many acts and relations: each is an arena for a bustling and distinctive social, economic, factional, and ritual life. But if this focus is allowed to dominate, it hides from view the complex ways in which many events in a village are linked in other systems and connected with forces that originate and unfold in other contexts of diverse scale (Barth 1978, 1992).

Indeed, a focus on village communities as primary units of description represents a holdover from the received emphasis on culture as the ideally shared and homogeneous basis for social life, and on explicit native concepts as the causes and repositories of all significant social structure. To escape from these limitations, I need to retrieve the sense of events being embedded in the wider world of a complex society and civilization, which I suggested in my opening chapter. This perspective I have so far failed to develop in the subsequent chapters analyzing village variation.

The task of describing these wider connections has generally been formulated as one of modeling the way in which lives lived in face-to-face agricultural communities also articulate with, and indeed compose parts of, a larger society, and it has been a recurrent and often perplexing problem in much anthropology. Concepts that address the task constructively have in part been developed by Redfield and his students (Redfield 1956;

Marriott 1955, 1959), and by students of peasantry working in the tradition of historical materialism (Wolf 1966; Scott 1985). Though drawing on the vast literature arising out of these two scholarly traditions, I have pursued a slightly different approach (Grønhaug 1978; Barth 1978, 1983, 1989, 1992). Its basic thrust is that we must adopt a discovery procedure whereby we can unravel whatever connections and constraints direct the interpretations people make, and thereby give shape to the lives and meanings we are trying to understand. Where might we locate such possible determinants? Returning to the schema on p. 159, I have described these determinants as a "cultural stock" of knowledge, concepts, and values. The task then is to explore the possible pattern, the degrees of internal coherence and interpersonal sharing, that might obtain within this, or parts of this, stock. Such patterning must evidence the dynamic result of processes, since the "cultural stock" of every person will be continuously modified and replenished by new experience. Thus it would seem to require a perspective that accounts for "the sociology of knowledge" (Mannheim 1954). But above all we need to inspect the empirical materials themselves and carefully develop only such concepts as the description of these materials seems to demand.

I propose that we can start by looking at the way certain connected activities in the village link up with the historical traditions or streams that have contributed to the cultural stock presently found in North Bali. One can readily identify several such, each with distinct organizational networks and discongruent knowledge and assumptions. Among the most important ones on the local scene are the great traditions of Bali-Hinduism and Islam; the vast modern current transmitted by public education, mass media, and nation-building and involving participation in the world market; the traditions of the old kingdoms and their associated ideas of rank, caste, and authority; and the tradition of knowledge which constructs its model of social relations and emotions on a sorcery-based view of agency and responsibility. Each of these is today embraced to variable degrees, or by some persons only, within the total population of Buleleng. And each such stream is itself constituted as an internal discourse, a process reflecting a distribution of knowledge, authority, and social relationships, which propels those enrolled in it. Pursuing the social links within such a stream, moreover, will regularly lead us not just outside villages but also outside the region of North Bali, embedding local persons and circles in systems of much larger, and in some cases global, scale.

To unravel the premises for action within the various communities in North Bali, I need to analyze the main ideational and organizational features of each of these traditions. This should allow us to trace the contexts

PART FOUR

Major Traditions of Knowledge

11

Islam in North Bali

Islam constitutes a clearly demarcated, historically intrusive cultural stream in the Balinese world. While sketching its main properties as a tradition of knowledge, I shall also take the first steps to develop my perspective for the analysis of the other streams found within the broader flow of the civilization of North Bali.

Islam goes a long way for its Balinese followers toward defining a whole world in which to participate; a set of concepts and representations to live by; and a universe of discourse in which to frame one's awareness, design one's social relationships and acts, and interpret oneself and one another. But Muslims in Bali do not live in a world apart: they must also considerably mix and mingle with others who are uncommitted by, and relatively ignorant of, Islam and its premises; and so Islamic institutions must accommodate to this larger society. Nor are the persons who embrace Islam equally and completely committed to practicing only its tenets: their life is also molded by other considerations and other traditions of knowledge besides Islam, as we have already seen in the materials from the village of Pagatepan. The Islamic stream thus does not correspond to the anthropologist's ideal construct of a "culture" and is not the charter for a "whole society": it comprises only a part of such constructs and is characteristically what has been called a "Great Tradition" (Redfield 1956), a structure of ideas and practices that penetrates but does not encompass the lives of its practitioners. My basic concern in this analysis will be to show the nature and extent of its distinctness and unity, and thus to identify its character as a dynamic part of the larger regional system and as a framework for processes of cultural reproduction and change. I thus seek to identify and focus on the distinctive organization of this particular tradition of knowledge and the ideas on which it builds. The wider question of how Islam in its application to life is colored by local cultural influences, and how its adherents accommodate their practices to their various other concerns and commitments, will be temporarily left aside.

Muslims in Bali are mainly concentrated in Buleleng, in the westernmost province of Jembrana, in parts of Karangasem, and in the rapidly growing capital of Denpasar. According to the most recent census, Muslims comprise 33,948 of the total 446,812 persons in Buleleng, i.e., nearly 8 percent of the population, whereas the all-Bali average of Muslims in the population is 4.8 percent. A greater proportion of the Muslims in the north is furthermore composed of older, culturally Balinese, families, in contrast to the more recent influx of Javanese/all-Indonesian officials, professionals, traders, and migrants in Denpasar. Within Buleleng Muslims are mainly found in Singaraja and in local concentrations as communities or neighborhoods in some, irregularly scattered, villages. Among these Pagatepan stands out as exceptionally strongly consolidated.

Muslims who consider themselves Balinese generally have an idea of their family origins, whether from Bali-Hindu ancestors or from settlers arriving from Java, Madura, Bugis (South Sulawesi), or Sasak (Lombok). In addition, there is in Singaraja a Muslim ethnic enclave of approximately four hundred Arabs hailing from southern Arabia, mainly the Hadhrami town of Shibam; these are the descendants of male migrants, among whom the first known arrived around 1870 and the last in the 1920s. These men married local Balinese girls, who converted to Islam at the time of their marriage, and mostly settled and died in Singaraja, though their sons and even grandsons have in some cases made return visits to Shibam and maintained contact with relatives there. Wives were never brought from Arabia, but as the local Hadhrami community grew it tended to become endogamous. The population's oral command of Arabic has deteriorated and even disappeared over the generations. But their greater Arabic literacy and command of Islamic knowledge are recognized; and a number of men among them, and several women, are widely recognized as outstanding Muslim gurus and also dukuns, traditional healers and wizards. It is plausible that the presence of this community in Singaraja has had an impact on the form and content of the local tradition of Islamic scholarship, as argued for Indonesia in general (Benda 1958; Geertz 1960:125; Noer 1973), but this was not salient in local accounts from Pagatepan and other North Balinese Muslims.

As we have seen from the story of Pagatepan, Islam in North Bali has a much longer history than these Hadhramis of Singaraja. According to a widely distributed set of myths, Islam was brought by scholars arriving from Java, who subsequently moved on to missionize Lombok and Sumbawa farther east, in a pattern paralleling stories of Bali-Hindu sages. Indeed, the great Brahmin teacher Dang Hyang Bau Rauh, who is reputed to have arrived from Java in Majapahit times and reformed Balinese Hinduism (p. 16), is sometimes himself represented as having moved on to Lombok as Tuan Guru and there instituted Islam. More commonly the Islamic proselytizers are linked with traditions of the Wali Sanga (Nine Walis) of Java or their sons. Stories circulate that one or several of them are buried in Bali; recently an inspired woman in Madura had a dream that led to the identification of such a grave on a hill by the village of Pancasari. The Kramat (Beloved/Sacred place) of Pagatepan is likewise often linked to these traditions. In other words, a fairly lively set of accounts gives the mythical story of Islam as a cultural stream into North Bali.

Java as the source of Islam in Bali is indeed most plausible. Arabs and Indian Muslims were in contact with Malacca and the North Java coast from the eleventh century; by the fourteenth century there was a constant stream of Muslims to and through the North Java ports (Tjandrasasmita 1978:144f.). This led to the emergence of what has been called the Pasisir civilization in the Javanese Muslim trading ports during the fifteenth century and to the spread of the eastern variant of this civilization from its centers in Gresik and Tuban to the islands of Madura and Lombok (Koentjaraningrat 1985:49). Local traditions and relics make it clear that the northern port villages of Bali, such as Pengastulan and Tejakula, and later also Singaraja, were in contact with this traffic in the Java Sea, even though Muslim traders never achieved the ascendancy on land in Bali that they did elsewhere.

The meeting of Islam and Hinduism in Java produced a characteristic division within the victorious Islam. On the one hand there developed a majority tradition embracing mysticism and heterodoxy on the part of certain religious thinkers, considerable syncretism on the part of the courts and judges surrounding the converted rajas, and widespread laxness and "animism" among the rest of the population — sometimes referred to as Priyayi for the higher and Abangan for the lower strata (Benda 1958:17–18; Geertz 1960:125). In other parts, an orthodox or Santri form emerged, led by Muslim scholars (Kiyayi) (Benda 1958:10–18). In Bali, on the contrary, there is little evidence for a similar florescence of mysticism and heterodoxy, and all Balinese Islam gravitates to the Santri form. Before taking up the question of how this relative orthodoxy is produced and maintained, we should briefly review the ideas that characterize its basic content.

Islam is a design for living: the imperative of submission to the will of

God so as to live by his command, as specified in considerable detail in his revelations to mankind. It also comprises a cosmology in the narrow sense: it positions man in a material and celestial sacred geography; it provides a calendar; it gives an inventory of spiritual beings and their relations and functions vis-à-vis mankind (angels, devils, and spirits of a diversity of kinds); and it also provides a model of man himself: his soul, his life course, his rewards and punishments in this world and in an afterworld. Using the male gender in phrasing this is justified, in that the sane adult male Muslim is the prototype moral human being, responsible as guardian for the children and women of his family — though they too are regarded as moral persons with a degree of moral responsibility placed upon them.

Islam has an axiomatic and pervasive relevance to human life and action: it is supposed to set out all the necessary rules for right living and the standards for morality and performance in choice and action. Its main thesis is a conception of individual responsibility for action and choice, and it explains the events that befall the person now and in the future as the will of God *and* as the consequences of the moral quality of the choices the person makes. It thus comprises a comprehensive body of knowledge for life. The structure of how this knowledge is embodied in sacred texts, and the way these texts are made immanent in the Muslim's consciousness, have profound effects on the realization of Islam as a cultural stream.

First, all the necessary premises are according to Muslim tenets enshrined once and for all in the scriptures: above all the Koran, which is regarded as the word of God; the Hadith, the traditions of the teaching of the Prophet; and various derivatives from this body of doctrine. A first premise is thus that final authority is contained in this text, notably the Koran.

But it follows from this premise that there must be institutions to actualize these scriptures in contemporary life: fathers or guardians, teachers, judges, preachers, the assembled congregation. The task of taking a comprehensive, complex sacred text written in the totally foreign language of classical Arabic and interpreting the humdrum events of daily life in terms of the authoritative formal schemata of its structure is a formidable intellectual task; few persons would venture to do so unaided. A need is inescapable for a supplementary institution: a body of particularly competent persons to teach the basics of the text and be available for lifelong guidance of the nonspecialists. Thus the very constitution of the absolute authority of the sacred text entails the constitution of a second authoritative body, a literati of Islamic scholars. Their mode of function follows from their defining structural position: teaching (the gurus), sermons and coordination of rites (the imam), and adjudication and government (the

A leading guru of Pagatepan.

Ulama). In each field the procedure requires identification and logical construction or inference from the text, which remains the ultimate authority.

It is striking that, whereas this structure does not predicate any particular level of Koranic scholarship, it seems to entail a powerful propellant for the literati to improve their command and versatility in Islamic scholarship, with a view to compete and excel among themselves. One meets this tendency again and again in Islamic communities throughout the world. We have seen in the description of Pagatepan how it asserts itself there. We may review the resulting processes from the two perspectives of current day-to-day functioning and the distribution of culture and positioning of persons it generates, and the processes of reproduction and change within the stream as a tradition of knowledge.

The cornerstone of Islam as instituted in Pagatepan is the guru-murid relationship between teacher and pupil: the lifelong, universal relationship of every person to his/her guru. The gurus of Pagatepan have traditionally separated their pupils as between men, women, and children; thus Guru Ali Akbar teaches the hour after high noon prayer to adult women, after 3:30 P.M. prayer to adult men, and after sunset prayer to children. They are not separated in terms of levels of advancement, however, and this reflects an explicit theory of pedagogy. "I have said the same things, so many times, to my elder murids. That is good: repetition strengthens the faith, it makes you internalize it so its parts become like physical organs inside of your body, just inherent parts of you. Accepting Islam is not a question of understanding. Its validity should rest on the guru's *authority*. And it should be all one consistent school of law, here in the east from Mecca it should be Shafi — not one piece from here and one piece from there!" (In this credo Ali Akbar is also in fact arguing against a more modernist alternative, also present in Pagatepan; see below.)

The obligations of pupil to teacher can not be abrogated, even if the pupil moves on to additional gurus later: "even if you yourself become a great guru, or president or king, you must continue to show respect to your original guru." But the obligations of the guru are also perpetual and entail a vocation. "If you have knowledge and you use it to teach and illuminate others, then your knowledge is a blessing to them, and you receive merit. But if you do not teach and uplift them, there is no merit to you from your knowledge, however great and true it may be."

Though obligated to learn Islam like men, women are marginal in certain ways, particularly in not having access to the mosque for public worship. But the option of literacy and scholarship is open to them; and there was one highly respected woman guru in Pagatepan during my fieldwork, with pupils of both sexes. The teachings transmitted by these gurus consist mostly of the particulars of theology and the laws and injunctions of the Shafi school. But most interesting from our general point of view is the underlying, general tenor of how concepts of person, morality, and action are projected in these teachings. The individual is basically represented as a morally responsible agent, perpetually under God's scrutiny. "On your right shoulder sits the angel Rakib, noting down your merit [pala] from every act; on your left shoulder is Atid, noting down your wrongs (*meksiat*,

Arabic; *dosa*, Indonesian). The balance of their records will determine your fate after death. Even this simple coffee in hospitality to a guest gives pala recorded by Rakib." Innocence is an excuse, and ignorance may be cited as a mitigating circumstance of bad acts — though a failure to learn is bad, it is worse to be knowingly evil.

The core paradigm of action and morality is one that ensures we each will harvest our just deserts. In daily discourse this is referred to by the term of *pala* (or *pahala*), a Sanskrit word for the results or consequences ("fruits") of acts — among Hindus, but of course not among Muslims, usually in the context of karma pala, fate resulting from acts in a previous life (Gonda 1952). How then do people in Pagatepan explain injustice and suffering in the world? They stress, first, that we must distinguish between *pala dunya* (rewards of this world), which are insignificant, and the *pala akhirat* of the next world, which is good. In the words of one villager, a Hajji but not a guru: "This world is the prison of the Muslim. It has no value in itself, and is full of forbidden acts and things. Akhirat is the Paradise of Muslims." But equally, "God alone knows what is in a person's heart, and what are his true intentions [*niat*, Arabic] or purposes with his acts. Man is deceived by appearances; but God sees all. Thus if your good acts are intended only to impress men, they will give no pala; whereas if they are to please God, they give pala. At the hour of judgment, it is pala and dosa that are counted." Barkat (blessing, good fortune, from the Arabic *baraka*) on the other hand, is of this world and given by people. Whenever things go easily and smoothly in life, that is the result of barkat, whereas of the person who never succeeds, people will start whispering that his father withheld barkat from him — an unnatural act, but probably the result of extreme provocation. The power to give barkat is held by one's parents and one's Guru, and one obtains it by showing respect, particularly in the form of gifts and services to them. Such barkat is given by allowing the child or disciple to nuzzle or breathe from the giver's open right hand. A second meaning of barkat is for the gift of food one customarily carries home, wrapped in banana leaf, from a public feast. People in Pagatepan claim this to be a quite distinctive concept (but compare the Bali-Hindu customs regarding offerings brought home from temples). Barkat thus serves to conceptualize the rewards in this world for prototypically moral acts.

Balinese Muslims do not see any serious paradox in the coexistence of moral responsibility, and rewards and punishments for one's acts, and the conceptions of an almighty God and predestination. Iman, belief or faith, explicitly has six essential parts: there is one God; Mohammed is his prophet; the Koran is his word; angels exist; there is a life after death; and there is *nasib*, predestination. Nasib is the ultimate explanation for events in this life: that it was written as the will of God, that so should be. However, nasib is invoked only as an ex post facto explanation of basically non-moral events or circumstances, usually listed as (1) whether you will be rich or poor in life — you must work, but nasib determines whether such work will be cumulatively successful; (2) the date at which you will die; and (3) whom you will marry (*jodog*, fate with regard to spouse). "But nasib does not eliminate man's choice, and his responsibility for acts. There can be no religion without logical thought. Thus the knife that cuts takes no share of responsibility: it is you who have the intention to kill. But it is God who ultimately decides whether you will be successful in killing, as he decides whether your work will be successful and bring you wealth." Or, as elaborated by the imam: "When a particular misfortune befalls you, without reason — that is nasib. If the police arrest you when you have done no wrong — that is nasib. Or like when you were in Norway, you did not know you would be coming to Pagatepan: your own intention only said you were going to Buleleng. So it is nasib that you came just here, that we were brought together."

Thus moral responsibility should permeate all aspects of life that are subject to intentional action — although sometimes, as will be discussed below, a person's acts are explained in terms of (magical) agencies other than him/herself. But the person is not entirely without means to change the balance of faults over merits even retrospectively, after death; nor is he/she entirely alone in atoning for faults. "Three kinds of acts continue to have effect also after you die, so pala keeps flowing from them: one, siddiqah [gifts in excess of regular alms given to the poor, or to one's guru]; also, two, wakaf [donations of land to the mosque] because they remind people of God also after you are dead; and, three, descendants who pray."

In their mortuary rites, people in Pagatepan also try to assist the deceased by doing *pidiyah* (from Arabic *fidiyah*, atonement). It is a repayment of the dead person's debt to God, caused by his/her failure to perform the full count of five daily prayers every day of his/her adult life. Before the burial, teams of relatives and neighbors will congregate to perform what amounts to marathon prayers to eliminate any such shortfall: aligned in two long facing rows, they pass baskets of unhusked rice between them, chanting: "I pay the pidiyah for NN!" and "I receive the pidiyah for NN!" If done a sufficient number of times, this will compensate for the fault. In the funeral of one old man, three teams of twenty men each were thus engaged for an hour and a half: a sweet and pious man, it could yet be assumed from his considerable age that he must have missed a number of prayers over the years, so extensive pidiyah rites were performed for him.

The memorial feasts, *ratipan* (from Arabic *ratif*, to remember), may likewise have a marginal effect in enhancing the dead person's chances of salvation. Given three days and seven days after the burial by the bereaved household and family, it collects a considerable number of invited guests — neighbors and family — in prayers to God and a shared meal of sweets. It is intended to have two results: to console the bereaved by turning their thoughts to God, which always soothes the believer; and to enhance the dead person's pala because he/she is posthumously causing you to remember God. Thus, though the principle of individual moral responsibility is strongly stressed, a certain degree of embeddedness of the person in a wider moral collective is allowed for, whereby the acts of one's kin and congregation may atone for the individual's own failures, and thus enhance the person's chances for rewards in the next world. The place of these Islamic constructs in understanding and interpreting the human condition, as compared to other possible cultural constructs, i.e., other streams, is a topic best treated when the other major streams in the region have also been discussed (see especially chapter 18). But the relative place of Islam as a powerful stream within Muslim communities may be seen by the force of its prohibitions (e.g., against any worship of spirits, ancestors, or other gods than the One God; the impossibility of possession by spirits of deceased persons; etc.) and above all by its positive application in structuring so many aspects of daily life, from defining central institutions such as marriage, gender roles, and inheritance, through procedures and standards of litigation and adjudication, to the premises for daily discourse in praise and gossip concerning others among Muslims.

In the reproduction of this stream, the systematic and lifelong formal teaching of its principles cannot but be of central importance. The structure of this educational apparatus should be scrutinized more closely. In Pagatepan in the middle 1980s, eleven gurus (including one woman) were engaged in the traditional pattern of teaching, with a (declining) clientele of approximately six hundred children of both sexes. In addition, the class-organized local Madrasah Ibtidaiyah Islamiah Miftahul 'Ulum, operating since 1955 with six gurus, had an enrollment of 240 children, with a lower proportion of girls in the higher classes. This represents a near-universal coverage of the child population in Pagatepan — an exceptionally intensive educational effort compared to other Muslim communities in North Bali.

But the further enhancement of Islamic knowledge among boys depends on an instituted pattern of travel and studies outside one's village of birth. In Pagatepan this too is nearly universal, and has been for many generations. Almost all boys in their early teens leave Pagatepan to attend the traditional Muslim educational institutions of *pesantrens* — residential schools run by Muslim scholars, in Java and the lesser islands (cf. Dhofier 1982). All boys from Pagatepan traditionally used to go to Lombok for such studies: its scholars were recognized as orthodox and its Tuan Guru teachers as skilled; through Balinese (Karangasem) conquest West Lombok was politically linked with Bali, and there were kinspeople settled there; and the Sasak language of its Muslim population is close to North Balinese and much easier for the body to learn than, for example, Javanese.

Generally a boy's first guru decides when he has the necessary maturity and scholarship to leave Pagatepan for further studies, and then sends him, perhaps as one of a small group, to the pesantren the guru himself attended, generally in Bengkel or Kediri in West-Central Lombok, or Pangcor in East Lombok. Costs are reduced through joint cooking and living arrangements in small hutments (*pondok*); and the boys are provided by their families with rice and some cash. Teaching in the Lombok pesantrens has been organized in a manner known as "unified": whether novices or advanced, the whole group of boys under one teacher will congregate and listen while he reads, interprets, and discusses passages from the Koran, the Hadith, and other religious texts. Teacher and pupils also congregate for the five daily prayers; otherwise the boys are left free to look after themselves with cooking, clothes-washing, collecting firewood, etc.

Students normally attend the pesantren for three to eight years. The intensity and success of the training obviously vary greatly, but the Tuan Guru's authority and prestige are very great and the standards of knowledge and textual analysis exacting and competitive. The brightest and most dedicated young men will often move on, with their guru's blessing, from one school to the next. In the early years of the present century, two young boys from Pagatepan who were later to become major scholars, Makhfuz and Jibrail, thus moved on to Jombong in East Java for further studies, and since then many boys from Pagatepan have followed their footsteps there or to other East Javanese pesantrens in Ponogoro, Banyuwangi, Muntilan, etc., often going there directly from Pagatepan. These schools, incidentally, tend to be divided into class levels and have a more systematic curriculum structure but otherwise work on the same organizational pattern as those in Lombok. A recent alternative is also the Islamic Teacher's Training Academy in Negara, West Bali, for pupils who have completed public school.

The very best of these young men have then finally wished to move on to Mecca, not only for Hajj but for advanced studies. Over the generations, a number of men from Pagatepan – at least thirty remembered persons – have spent extended periods in Mecca for studies, some settling and dying there as members of the extensive Indonesian community. The most widely acclaimed among them was Hajji Makhfuz, who even had the distinction of teaching regularly in the Masjid Haram during the last three years of his residence in Mecca, before returning to Pagatepan and becoming imam of the local mosque.

I have no reliable historical evidence of how long this pattern of cosmopolitan participation has existed in Pagatepan. Very old informants, born before the turn of the century, have claimed that the oldest scholar they remembered, a teacher born in the 1830s or 1840s, was the first ever to study in Mecca; but I am doubtful what the bases for such assertions may be. More interesting are the implications of this pattern for what it tells us of the processes involved in the reproduction of the stream of Islam, i.e., its implications in terms of a sociology or anthropology of knowledge. The famous Islamicist and administrator of the Dutch East Indies in the nineteenth century, C. Snouck Hurgronje, leaves no doubt of the importance he attached to the scholarly community in Mecca: "Here lies the heart of the religious life of the East-Indian archipelago, and the numberless arteries pump thence fresh blood in ever accelerating tempo to the entire body of the Moslem populace in Indonesia" (Snouck Hurgronje 1931:291). Snouck here, of course, is referring to the Muslim majority populations in Java, Sumatra, and some of the lesser islands; but if anything the impact of such a cosmopolitan connection would be even greater in an isolated, mountain-slope village like Pagatepan, surrounded by a vast majority of Hindus. The transfusion of vitality thus achieved to this numerically so weak, yet major, cultural stream of Islam is palpable in the modest collections of books and rudimentary teaching facilities, but spirited and vital teaching, of the leading scholars of Pagatepan.

Yet the essential basis for the reproduction of Islamic scholarship is found in the solid structure wrought by the links with the pesantrens of Lombok and East Java, rather than the direct connection with Mecca. It is thanks to extensive access to these pesantren centers that local Islam in Pagatepan can retain its broad cosmopolitan orientation, fed by a rich regional network of scholarly relationships and standards of excellence. Since the Second World War, when Saudi visas for extended residences in Mecca became difficult to obtain, North Balinese Muslims have become ever more dependent on this regional base for reproducing its scholarly elite of gurus. Other Muslim communities in North Bali do not show as great strength in their observance and organization of Islam, though the same elements are present. People tend to be more lax about prayers and fasting and less insistent in applying Islamic law to their affairs. Identity as Muslims is unequivocal; but its practice becomes less formative of collective institutions and personal lives. Thus, among the Muslims of the villages of Tegallingga and Pengastulan (see chapter 5), there is greater variation of practice and its observation is more dependent on individual volition; also, the institutional support system is weaker. This does not prevent some individuals among them from aspiring to, and participating in, the same level of practice and orthodoxy as Pagatepan; but constraints are seen as a question of the availability of teachers, the organization of training, and the level of knowledge present in the community. To enhance their own zeal, the Muslims of Tegalingga have called a teacher from Pagatepan to reside among them, and they have also organized a *madrasah ibtidaiyyah* — the more "modern" alternative to the personal guru — staffed with local teachers. The Muslims of Pengastulan have at times had prominent scholars among them; about a third of their children study with a traditional guru, while most attend a madrasah. The present leading scholar among them, Hajji Hassan Hamza, spent eleven years (including the period of the Second World War) in Mecca.

I see the implications of this participation in cosmopolitan Islam as numerous and as essential to the reproduction of the stream we are describing. Thus the fact of participation shapes a worldview by locating Muslim communities conceptually in a global sacred geography, and it launches sons of the community on career trajectories that take them widely through that geography. It is an essential feature of these processes that the persons thus moved are propelled by local standards and ideals embraced by community members; they are not pawns in the hands of a higher-level scholarly administration, but themselves creators of the options they pursue. In this way, they seek out and link into the "circle" in which they participate: its remarkable scale is a product of their individual efforts, using the structure of pesantrens available and propelled by ideals and ambitions nourished in their relations to their village Guru. We thus see a self-animating structure of numerous related parts, generating the complex and cumulative activities that reproduce Islam.

The involvement of a number of villagers in the vitalizing, perpetual discourse that takes place in this larger stream also exposes them to the flow of changing ideas current in it. Paradoxically, the effort of Pagatepan's scholarly elite to reproduce its own orthodoxy thus has a certain number of troubling, as well as satisfying, consequences from their point of view. Most distressing to these traditionalists are presently the encroachments of ideas from the Muhammadiya movement into their world.

Muhammadiya can be briefly characterized as a modernizing movement for the reform and purification of Islam from the accretions of tradition (Noer 1973; Peacock 1978). Founded in Jogjakarta, Central Java, in 1912 by Muhammad Dahlan, it drew its inspiration from certain thinkers and debates in Cairo and Mecca at the time, and also somewhat from parallel currents in British India and the subsequent Pakistan. Within Indonesia it has also periodically emerged as an important political force.

Its distinguishing theological features are found mainly on three levels: (1) certain details in the performance of daily prayers, strongly emphasized by many of its detractors; (2) elements of fundamentalism in the sources of law it recognizes: only the Koran and the Hadith — traditions of the acts and decisions of the Prophet — and not those of precedent within the tradition of Islam (fatwa), extensions by analogy, etc.; and (3) a strict ethical position on the unalterable nature of individual responsibility for one's own acts, entailing also a resistance to slametan celebrations and sacrifices in general, especially the various remedial rituals of the traditionalists.

All these issues provoke lively debate among Balinese Muslims. Traditionalists generally argue that Muhammadiya, though it provided a valuable counterthrust to Christian proselytizing during colonial times, represents an incomplete and therefore impoverished version of the message of Islam. Many people, especially among the younger and more educated, are impressed with the force of Muhammadiya ideas in what they see as the ultimate testing grounds of scholarly debate. There, Muhammadiya spokesmen tend to come out better every time because their position is more consistent and their advocates better prepared and more practiced.

Another important, though ideologically very low-profiled, influence emanates from Saudi Arabia. Still often referred to as "the Wahabis," the Saudis are remembered as the enemy during their conquest of Mecca from the Hashemites in 1924. But Saudi subventions have become available for the building of mosques and support of other Muslim institutions in Indonesia, including Bali, and this has led to an adjustment in public sympathies if not in theological positions among North Balinese Muslims. Thus the traditionalists, because of their own efforts to reproduce their orthodoxy, come under a double pressure from both modernists and fundamentalists.

Through their cosmopolitan participation, many North Balinese Muslims have become deeply exposed to these crosscurrents and had their positions and consciousness affected by the attendant debates. Confronting modernism with considerable textual knowledge and sometimes glittering debating skills, the established gurus of Pagatepan have largely managed to hold their own against these ideas, defending a bastion of faith and traditionalism and winning a reputation for being fanatik — in the idiom of

189

Bahasa Indonesia implying a quality of strength and intensity without most of the derogatory connotations of the word's European roots. The Muslim congregation of Pengastulan, on the other hand, has become deeply split over these issues, not least because their most qualified scholar brought the seeds of Muhammadiya activism with him from his long residence in Mecca itself. In the more modernist circles of Singaraja Muslims, the impact of Muhammadiya positions is even greater — perhaps also because their stand against slametan feasting is particularly attractive to the pressed and monetized households of urban citizens.

The discourse within Islam engages questions that are fundamental to the conception of the social person, particularly on the tortuous issues of morality and responsibility. The Muhammadiya position, which is increasingly winning adherence, uses the image of "closing the book" at the moment of death: nothing can subsequently change the balance of good and bad entailed in the sum of your acts through life. Traditionalists soften somewhat this piercing moral light on the individual by speaking more in terms of blessing, fate, fault, and debt rather than duty and the finality of judgment. Thus they embed the actor more deeply in a social and collective context. Human agents can in their view award mystical barkat on the basis of their moral approval of your performance and thus further — or hamper — your strivings for a good life. Certain pious acts and donations, performed in time, will eternally produce posthumous merit and make up for wickedness committed. Descendants and the community at large have a role in compensating for your sins of omission by paying up some of your debts to God. Indeed, your own children who have died before you can even reduce your sufferings in the deserts of purgatory by bringing you pots of cool water.

I would suggest that the prominence of these themes in the discourse of North Balinese Muslims should serve as a measure of Balinese sensibilities — their concerns with morality, compassion, virtue, and the place of the individual within the community — quite as much as a report on Islam at a certain time and place. Islam provides only one of the traditions of knowledge in which these concerns are articulated, and only one component in even the most committed Muslim's consciousness. The present chapter has sought to take one step only, to explore the thrust and the constraints that spring from the particular structure of that particular stream and thereby characterize its dynamics.

190

12

Bali-Hinduism as a Tradition of Knowledge

Bali-Hinduism is a vast body of lore, images, concepts, ideas, and practices; it composes a cultural stream so diverse and so infiltrated in most of the daily life of most Balinese that their whole culture has seemed to observers inseparable from it and describable only in its terms (Covarrubias [1937] 1973; Bateson and Mead 1942; Ramseyer 1977). The mere existence of a Balinese community such as Muslim Pagatepan, however, invites us to conceptualize in a different manner. We must recognize that Bali-Hinduism provides only some — rich, fascinating, and productive — ways of being Balinese and is neither all-embracing nor a necessary identity for every member of the society: it is but one among several major streams that compose Balinese civilization. The task of this chapter is to depict Bali-Hinduism as such a stream, showing the connections that obtain between its mode of reproduction and its cultural content.

An analytical challenge is posed by the complexity of the institutions and ideas of Bali-Hinduism and by the extraordinary cultural richness contained in its diversity and prolific expression. The contrast with Islam could hardly be greater. For Islam, I could provide a brief summary of its essential premises and doctrines, with the added convenience of knowing that my readers would command a basic knowledge of its features. For Bali-Hinduism, the riot of diversity and expression is such that to arrive at a grasp of its essentials would at best be the end result of a formidable cultural analysis, charting forms unfamiliar and ideas inaccessible to nearly every reader, and far away to myself. After testing these waters in the first part of this chapter, and indicating what such an account of the content and structure of Bali-Hinduism would have to embrace, I then choose a different methodology: to base my description of the tradition on the sociology, rather than the logic or systematics, of its knowledge. Thus I shall argue that its very diversity, wealth, and incoherence reveal the character of Bali-Hinduism as a tradition of knowledge and are generated from its social and conceptual structure as clearly as was the case for Islam, if one approaches it from the perspective of how it is reproduced rather than trying to depict it as a stable structure of logically interrelated ideas.

First, we should recognize a basic quality of the subjective world in which Bali-Hindus partake: it is a world of immaterial entities and forces as much as one of material objects; a world of invisible agents that surround us and even enter us; a world alive with gods and spirits and ogres and holy priests. It is hardly possible to exaggerate the extent to which the unseen penetrates the seen, the divine is a continuous and complex presence in everyday life, and material causality is only a small part of the causalities that govern our existence: magic and sorcery, ancestral pleasure and displeasure, karma pala, the relentless effects of ritual error not properly remedied, the whim and anger of spirits.

A first hurdle is trying to cast this reality in conceptions that do not irreparably distort it. The Balinese divide reality between *sekala*, the material realm we know through our senses, and *niskala*, the realm of the unmanifest (cf. Hobart 1985a:112, 117ff.). Hobart rightly points out that this distinction cross-cuts Western notions of natural and supernatural: unexpressed emotions, time (but not space), and the future resolution of presently unsolved issues are niskala together with gods, spirits, and magical influences. It is, in other words, an epistemological distinction of considerable subtlety, which encourages caution and skepticism with regard to beliefs. Yet the distinction may also be argued to provide an epistemological habitat, so to speak, for a host of supernatural constructs. Skepticism focuses more on the veracity of particular occurrences and cases, and less on the falsification of the existence of whole categories. So the unpalpable aspect of the reality we are part of can be populated with myriad gods, spirits, souls of the dead, witches, ogres, and influences, conceptualized with great particularism and vivid imagery. Such particularist taxonomies create a world where one is perpetually surrounded by the hordes of supernatural agencies and forces, toward whom one needs to relate and act in particular and suitable ways.

I believe it would be a fundamental distortion to attempt to construct or elicit a description of this immaterial realm in terms of a comprehensive and consistent taxonomy — no matter how convenient such a key would be for the anthropologist's presentation of data in this realm. By thus prejudging the nature and extent of systematics, and sharing, in a vast field of constructs and knowledge we would easily prevent ourselves from discovering precisely what we most want to find out about this whole tradition. But it is useful initially to have four important components of the cosmology in mind, which emerge from recurrent ritual acts and objectifications: (1) a pantheon of gods and demons; (2) a vast number of place spirits and spirits inhabiting trees, stones, and other material objects; (3) the souls of remembered and unremembered ancestors; and (4) Brahmin high priests (pedandas). In addition various other metaphysical objects or premises must be added that cannot readily be subsumed under these four headings. Let us briefly review these components one by one.

1. *Gods.* The village temples we met with in the description of Prabakula are, as they would be in every other Bali-Hindu village, preeminently places where gods become present (the literal meaning of *kahyangan*) by descending (and thus the concept of Betara, gods = those who descend) onto their thrones (pelinggih). These gods are primarily gods of place, territory, and community. It is characteristic, not least as an idiom of respect, that their identities are only very vaguely designated and that the specifications linked with them are such as describe mainly the code of human duties and rules (adat) their congregations should observe, not the particulars of the deity. These rather vaguely specified gods of place are, however, linked into a ladder of manifestations, constituting a hierarchy of generalization or abstraction. Thus the less important local shrines are known as *taksu*, i.e., deputies or guardians only of village gods, while these major village gods in turn are seen as local manifestations of general cosmic principles, represented above all by the Hindu trinity of Brahma, Wisnu, and Siwa. Thus the God of a village pura desa (though in another sense a generalization of the souls of village founders) is a manifestation of Brahma as creator, that of the Pura segara is Wisnu as the sustainer, and that of the pura dalem is Siwa — or more strictly, his wife — in the destructive aspect as Durga. The Betaras of the numerous Siwa temples are manifestations of an even higher level of unity and abstraction, Siwa as the lingga and thus origin, as well as sustainer and destroyer; and in the innumerable tripartite sanggah kemulan (the shrines of origin found in household shrines, as well as larger temples), Siwa is the unity of the Tiga Sakti (Three Holy Forces) represented by Brahma, Wisnu, and Iswara. In the east-and-mountainward corner of the temple is also generally a high lotus throne (padmasana) for the Sun-God, who is again a manifestation of Siwa, as is the Betara Gunung Agung of Bali's highest mountain, identical with Siwa as Mahadewa. Another representation of cosmic unity-and-diversity is found in the *nawa-sangga*, the nine gods of the lotus symbol, representing the eight cardinal directions and eight colors and Siwa as the polychrome center and unity of them all (Grader [1940] 1969: 169ff.;

Ramseyer 1977: 109). Finally, behind Siwa in his most comprehensive as-pect is Sang Hyang Widi Wasa, the abstract principle of Godhead or the uncreated cosmos, a conception given emphasis over the last decades by the movement interested in stressing conceptual monotheism of Bali-Hindu thought (Geertz [1964] 1973d:170ff.; Forge 1980:229ff.).

The image of a ladder of manifestations is indeed too orderly for these conceptions, as identities and manifestations criss-cross so that Sri Dewi, for example, the lovely Goddess of maturing rice, is variously the spouse of Sedana, the God of wealth (Grader 1969:143); or of Wisnu; or of Siwa in the destructive aspect; or of Betara Gunung Agung (Grader [1949] 1960c:166f.) — and she is manifest simultaneously in every nini (a term that also signifies "grandmother" in High Balinese) sheaf of rice on altars by the paddy field.

Moving downward along the imaginary ladder of sublime abstraction and particularistic manifestation, on the other hand, taksus may be the frightening guardians of specific temple grounds and merge into the hordes of butas and kalas, spirits of the netherworld who may be seen as demons, ogres, personifications of passions and evils, or the gross aspect of the gods. These buta-kala are perpetually present everywhere, and they require attention by worship and offerings on the ground whenever the more sublime aspects of Deity receive offerings and worship on elevated platforms and shrines. Bali-Hindus thus partake in a world governed by village gods, who on the one hand merge into a panoply comprising most of the traditional Hindu pantheon, and on the other hand are accompanied by a host of netherworldly demons and spirits. From the way they are given substance in myth and lore, and from how Bali-Hindus comment on and explain them, my understanding is that these images and conceptions are above all imbued with properties from a moral world of character and sensibility. Thus Siwa loves humankind so, he grants magic powers of witchcraft because he has not the heart to refuse; Betara Desa demands such inordinate respect (which creates his anonymity as its artifact) be-cause he represents community solidarity and protects his children as the quintessence of authority; ogres are here to test your courage and forti-tude. Used more abstractly, these images are metaphysical templates for properties of cosmos: the balance that must obtain between creation and destruction (or the world would be filled up by people and things); the miracle of growth in the rice fields; the serenity of the world in the high mountains; the spectre of evil.

As for the adat responsibilities associated with each village temple and Deity, an essential element is the date and form of the odalan, the calen-drical celebration of the particular God and temple. In most of North Bali these are fixed by the ancient Hindu-Balinese lunar-solar calendar (for 60 percent of temples around Singaraja, 100 percent in the northeast, according to Goris [1933] 1960c:118), not by the Javanese-Balinese "permutational" calendar of 210 days, which is used for all odalans in South Bali.

2. *Place spirits.* Besides this comprehensive set of territorial/village gods linked to temples and major physical features of the landscape, the whole Balinese countryside is also animated by another set of supernaturals — its rocks, trees, winds, birds, streams and lakes, indeed even many unmarked bits of ground are inhabited by multitudes of local place spirits, residing separately and severally in all these features. These spirits are the "owners" of the objects and will resent their use and destruction unless appropriately placated; they can also easily be disturbed and must be shown respect with shrines and avoidances. No house can be built without carefully investigating the locations of spirits of the ground; no tree should be felled without begging the pardon of spirits that might live in it. This aspect of the world also is modeled on morality: the reciprocities of giving succor and showing moderation, the balances of respect and gratitude to other life forms rather than the imbalances of dominance and exploitation.

3. *Ancestors.* As important as these gods and spirits of place and cosmos in Bali-Hinduism are the ancestors, who are the recipients of elaborate worship and ultimately merge with Godhead. One might say that just as deified ancestors eventually merge with the Deity, and cosmic gods are manifest in village gods that have arisen from village founders, so also do the territorial and the descent-based dimensions of divinity become ultimately merged through the conceptualization of descent in terms of kawitan, origin point and localized dadia or mranjan temple. But in their common sense conception and application, the two make up very clearly distinguishable sets: while the conceptions of village gods are linked to realm and to cosmic principles, those of ancestors are linked to kaki and kumpi, grandfather and great-grandfather. The conception is strictly patrilineal but tends to retain the awareness of male-female complementarity: grandmothers, great-grandmothers, and original ancestresses are generally mentioned and placed beside the agnatic ascendants; and the pura ibu — as temples of the mother/ancestor — figure recurrently.

Ancestor worship focuses on the ancestor shrine found in every household and on one or a short hierarchy of descent group temples, generally with a multiplicity of component shrines, some of which may be linked to segments within the group. The general belief is that the living are closely tied to deceased ancestors, who can help their descendants — or fail to help them, and even hinder them, if they do not honor their ancestors: the individual remains inextricably linked with kin, especially with deceased

195

patrilineal ascendants. This again is basically a structure of moral, social relationships.

This linkage manifests itself in the event of death in the form of death pollution (sebel), which affects the whole community of the dead but particularly his/her household and kin. The elaborate mortuary rituals aim at purifying the survivors, and then at purifying the dead, raising their souls stepwise toward deification and unification with Godhead. The particulars of these rituals vary greatly according to region and community, the wealth of the family, the status of the dead person, and the caste membership (and to some extent particular family ancestors) of the family. An essential stage in nearly all these forms is cremation, where high-caste persons and priests (pemangkus) are burned as corpses or mummies, whereas most commoners are buried and later exhumed for burning.

The idea of cremation is generally linked to a concept of Nirwana: the separation of the bodily remains into their elementary components of earth, water, air, and fire furthers, though does not ensure, the liberation of the soul from the wheel of rebirth. Until cremation has been performed, the souls of the dead are *pirata:* unclean and dangerous, living in a kind of purgatory, or in the graveyard or near the pura dalem, governed by the Betara Gede of that temple. After the purifications of cremation, on the other hand, the dead becomes a pitara: still a distinct and individual soul, but purified, and a proper object of veneration inside the household dwelling, with a shrine placed on or above the bed but — according to Goris, who expresses scholarly doctrine on this point — *not* in the household temple (Goris [1935] 1960a:84). Only after further memorial offerings, in connection with the odalan of the appropriate pura dalem, and after a pilgrimage to an all-Bali circuit of major temples (five, or seven, or thirteen) culminating in Besakih, the Mother Temple of them all, does the ancestor obtain full divinity and merge with the ancestors of the household temple; then he/she can have a sanggah shrine built.

4. *High priests.* If I have understood the theological premises correctly, these priests, known as pedanda (or prande or pendeta), are themselves to be regarded as a form of the deity, because the Supreme God Siwa incarnates himself in them during their liturgy (Goris [1948] 1969b:93), independent of their location in any temple. As manifestations of Surya/Siwa they can then produce their supremely valued *tirta prande,* (holy water from pedanda), which removes pollution in connection with life crisis rituals.

To embody such exceptional holiness, pedandas must be select in birth status, life-style, and consecration. Thus pedandas are Brahmins by birth and by marriage; some very few high priests, called *rsi* if Satria or Wesia

A high priest, in a cloud of incense, preparing holy water during a
tooth-filing ritual.

by descent and *mpu* if they are Sudra, have similar functions, but these belong to very special lines, vested with holy scriptures and holy water from ancient times. Pedandas are consecrated as priests in elaborate rites comparable to the consecration of temples (Korn [1928] 1960). With these extreme pretensions to rank and purity, their lives are heavily circumscribed by positive rites and negative taboos intended to keep them suitable vehicles for the manifestation of Siwa (Hooykaas 1966).

In a sense, the religion pedandas practice and embody is thus quite different from that of the rest of Bali-Hinduism, which is so definitively territorially anchored (Forge 1980:223, 224). Thus also, their contribution to community and life cycle rituals is highly specialized and partial. In many, if not most, North Balinese villages they are dispensed with — in which case the holy water of Siwa is produced from special Siwa temples by ordinary commoner priests, as we saw in the case of Prabakula. They also exclude themselves from the worship of village deities, as their rank and holiness are such that they cannot make obeisance to village gods. Indeed, where they appear in life crisis rituals they do so as outside accessories: placed at the side or in the back, on a raised platform, they mumble their mantra prayers and invocations, assume elaborate *mudra* hand/prayer positions (for a vivid catalogue, see De Kat Angelino 1923), ring bells, light fires and incense, and make intricate sequences of flower offerings to produce their holy water. Thus they can hardly be credited with controlling the main course of ritual, even when they are present.

On the other hand, they are regarded as essential to the consecration of every new temple (though in fact, even this is often ignored in North Bali); and every pedanda has the right and obligation to minister to a circle of descent groups of other castes tied to his house (gria). Most ubiquitous, however, has been their role as the authoritative embodiments of the Hindu-Buddhist heritage of theology, philosophy, and Sanskrit, and the active agents of its influence. We shall return shortly to a more critical account of how and to what extent this has been effected; the extent to which pedandas in this role exercise great public authority and elicit a super human reverence among most Bali-Hindus can hardly be exaggerated.

WORSHIP

Bali-Hindus direct an elaborate and picturesque worship to the divinities of category 1 above, into which the deified ancestors of category 3 merge. Probably because of their profusion and complexity, the forms of worship have never been confronted as a cultural domain in the anthropological literature on Bali-Hinduism. A brief overview may therefore be useful.

In the context of everyday life, worship is subsumed under the various categories of duty pertaining to members of collectivities (temple groups). In the abstract, however, it is known as *yadnya*, "holy duties to obtain forgiveness for oneself or for the dead relatives," according to a prominent Guru in Singaraja. In a conception that bears the stamp of Indo-Buddhist and pedanda codification in its focus on the separate individual, yadnya can be categorized in four "paths": *karma marga*, the actions of offering, praying, doing good deeds; *bakti marga*, reverential/devotional expression to God, and loving nature and mankind; *yoga marga*, seeking union with God through mental concentration; and *jenyanga marga*, studying and practicing the philosophy of religion.

Offerings *(banten)* hold a central place in the first and most ubiquitous path of worship; and "the art of the offering," in Ramseyer's felicitous phrase (Ramseyer 1977:135ff.), provides an elaborate vocabulary of symbols through which people articulate their worship of the gods. One of the most developed genres in this field is the very intricate work in cutout and plaited young yellow coconut leaves (for illustrations, see Covarrubias [1937] 1973:172–77; Ramseyer 1977:figs. 180–204; Forman, Mrazek, and Forman 1983:32; and especially Hooykaas-van Leeuwen Boomkamp 1961:43–56). These symbols also occur in a number of other contexts. Especially interesting is the construction of the *lis* sprinkler/whisk for sprinkling holy water on congregation and sanctified objects during ritual occasions. This very central ritual object — which superficially looks like a simple bundle of dry straw — is composed of a number (thirty-two in the example described by Hooykaas-van Leeuwen Boomkamp 1961:10) of coconut-leaf symbols, many of which also reappear in soul-representations for cremation rites. The lis sprinkler is referred to as Siwa's lingga (Hooykaas 1964:148ff.), indicating one of its essential symbolic referents.

Offerings are also composed of flowers, fruits, pastry, Chinese coins, and other objects and are coded according to the nature of the container, its overall height and shape, component colors, etc. Food offerings *(maturan;* see Forman, Mrazek, and Forman 1983:110 for striking photographs) enter into ritual commensality when they are retrieved from the temple as a material return from the Deity, enhanced ("like by adding vitamins"!) because the gods have partaken of their essence.

The idea readily presents itself to the field anthropologists searching for systematic insight that if only one were able to break these codes and read the communications cast in them, much could be learned about the

ancestors, gods and spirits

Representations of the dead — children in foreground, adults in the back — during
a family exhumation and cremation ritual.

conceptualization of the gods, of humankind, and of the relations between
them. The roomful of highly differentiated offerings to high gods, ancestors, and spirits of the underworld prepared for even the smallest cremation would seem to constitute a veritable library of such conceptions. Yet I
would suggest that such an idea may be seriously misconceived. That so
many persons with various specialities and various esoteric knowledge enter into the specification and production of offerings adds dimensions to
the task of their interpretation that render questionable the basic assumption that they should represent a coherent and readable text on cosmology.

Whereas all Bali-Hindu women have a considerable level of specific
skills in producing many elements of offerings, they lack the knowledge of
how they should be combined for diverse ritual occasions. Such orchestra-
tion is the task of *tukang banten* specialists — generally women of Brahmana
caste — who make a living producing vast deliveries of such offerings for
major life crisis rites. They in turn subcontract component tasks to neighborhood women, who thereby come to share some of this expertise; but
their attitude to the task seems much more akin to that of Westerners pro-

ducing elaborate Christmas decorations than one of making explicit cosmological representations. The vast majority of men, on the other hand, appear to be quite ignorant of even elementary typological classes in the field. But certain categories of balian healers, and family and temple pemangkus as well as pendandas, act as authorities in specifying the correct compositions of offerings for different occasions. They will variously provide — or hold back, as being too advanced and powerful — fragments of identification or interpretation. Do the systems these specialists use to generate complex offerings and ritual acts build on shared cosmological understandings and coincide with regard to the meanings ascribed to elements and idioms? The elaborate fieldwork required to find out has never, to my knowledge, been done; and I can see no reason why one should assume that the answer one would find would prove to be affirmative. Yet unless it is, *and* nonspecialist participants and audiences share these meanings at least in abbreviated form, the anthropologist cannot turn to these offerings and performances for a representation of "Bali-Hindu cosmology." I am reminded of a delightful scene in Padangbulia, when a very old lady kept returning to the main village pemangku's modest house (addressing him as "Little Brother," to which he suitably reciprocated with "Senior Sister") with a recipe he had given her for the composition of offerings to a minor remedial rite: "The sixteen bananas — should they be raw or cooked? And the coconut — stripped or with the grass left on, whole or split? Oh, I can't be bothered to remember — I'll do them whole!" The idea that efficacy depends on meticulously correct composition is universal (the old lady came back once more to check); nor do I doubt that specialists have more or less elaborate formulas for specifying appropriate compositions; what is at issue is the degree of sharing or consistency between specialists, and the degree to which such shared rules cohere as a tradition of knowledge representing a cosmology. The issue, as I say, has not been settled; but my own position is one of profound skepticism.

Many other arts and other specialists also enter into worship and thereby add their voices to the Bali-Hindu discourse. Every performance of *wayang kulit*, shadow puppet theatre presenting episodes from the Hindu epics of Mahabharata and Ramayana, is itself an act of worship and an act of reproduction of Bali-Hindu imagery in the audience (Lansing 1983:75ff.; for a more detailed treatment of the art, see Hobart 1987 and Zurbuchen 1987). The *dalang* puppeteer is often an impressively sophisticated scholar as well as artist; he is also an essential source of holy water for a number of ritual purposes, including every child's 105th day name-giving rites (at three months by the Javanese-Balinese calendar). Likewise, music, theater, recitation, and a variety of dance forms are performed to please the gods as acts of worship; and each genre entails its own level of practice, sophistication, and knowledge in performers and audiences.

A PERSPECTIVE ON BALI-HINDUISM

These materials actualize a fundamental methodological issue. Let us confront it here: the vast number and elaboration of genres of cultural expression that embody Bali-Hindu thought and imagery indicates the existence of an extraordinarily rich cultural stream. More disturbing, it also indicates the startlingly snowballing character of any attempt to provide a "thick description" (Geertz 1973c:6ff.) of any part of such a tradition. If conscientiously pursued, it quickly deepens and thickens to overwhelm the format of this, or any other, monograph. Nearly every paragraph in the text of the preceding pages has led me on to elaborations, contextualization, or further systematics that swiftly left me mired in multiple uncompleted descriptions. There can be little doubt that every exemplification of each of the phenomena I have named reverberates in Balinese with multiple referents, many of them embedded in elaborate structures only partially and variously known to actors and audiences.

Unless the anthropologist is prepared to sidestep the issue by arbitrarily restricting the description's "thickness" — in scope, depth, or both — in the service of literary constructions, a methodology must be found either to systematize, or somehow transcend, this vast descriptive task. Such a methodology will be required above all to provide criteria for acceptable silence on aspects of the material: procedures for simplifying the cultural miscellany without in that very process fabricating the regularities for which we would be searching in the data. Respect for the data requires that we produce a description that yet contains within it such empirical features as would allow us to transcend that description's own categories and *discover* patterns.

Let us first consider the systematizing strategy. A methodology deeply ingrained in our tradition of scholarship, which is meant to serve this purpose, is that of classifying: a procedure whereby the scientist sorts a fortuitous collection or assembly of observations until he finds a ramifying typology that "works" — i.e., produces a limited set of classes within the collection — and can then be inspected for its underlying logic. Such a procedure is indeed akin to the systematization that reflective members of a tradition themselves perform, certainly among the Balinese, and so it is all the more possible for the ethnographer to pursue, as the findings may prove to coincide with (or, more commonly or conveniently, simply be grouped in terms of) what are called "native concepts" — words or schemes members of the society employ.

But thus employed by us, we must recognize, such words are made to carry a different, and far larger and more pretentious, load than they do in the native tradition of knowledge. As the anthropologist would use them, they are no longer a context-specific way of referring to complex, familiar phenomena; they are asked to serve as a blueprint for *constituting the description* of such phenomena. The procedure thus begs the very question that I wish to pose: how are these phenomena constituted and generated, and within what frame of premises and limits is a particular representation of them valid? It assumes, on the contrary, the existence of one homogeneous "logic" that sorts chaos into a cosmos of entities and categories, between which one prominent, systematic pattern will be recognizable, and it assumes that native words hold the key to this order. Bali-Hindu philosophy, as a matter of fact, seems to teach the opposite: that everything in the visible world is under continual "Heraklitian" transformation, and that apparently very different things are often best understood as distinct manifestations of the same (Barth 1989; Hobart 1983, 1985a).

Observe, for example, Bali-Hindu ideas about the deceased. Ethnographies from Bali ubiquitously report the concepts of pirata and pitara in terms of which the procession of the deceased ancestor from unclean corpse and ghost to deity is mediated (as noted above). These stages of the ascent have a compelling logic; and standard anthropological procedure would be to structure our understanding of what it is the Balinese understand in terms of them. But to do so would entail adopting the double assumption that this particular schematism provides the adequate framework for reporting on Bali-Hindu eschatology, *and* that such a formal eschatology provides an adequate basic representation of Bali-Hindu ideas and attitudes toward the dead.

Only slight effort is sufficient to show us, in this case, that something is amiss. I was alerted to this when I naively tried to show off my knowledge of Bali-Hindu concepts in my first gathering of persons involved in the exhumation of a family's accumulated deceased members for cremation. When I referred to the imminent transformation of these dead from pirata to pitara, people lowered their voices and complimented me on my knowledge but swiftly changed the subject. In an analogous case, they responded more boldly to Wikan: "You are right, but that is not how we feel-think!" (Wikan 1991:272). Their embarrassment and avoidance reaction was not merely a matter of polite sensibility, of not calling a spade a spade: it reflects the patterns in terms of which Bali-Hindus conceive, and act in relation to, the deceased. Thus their praxis of ancestor worship disregards

Family group in the process of exhuming their deceased relatives in preparation for cremating them, at midnight in the burial grounds. The bones are washed as a first step of purification, and the skeleton laid out to ensure that no bone is left behind.

the distinction with sovereign indifference: the unpurified recently dead are regularly worshiped, in ancestor shrines as elsewhere — as has also been noted by Boon in South Bali (Boon 1977:87ff.). Moreover, the salient emotions observable during an exhumation rite bear witness to other conceptions. Participants started out with spooky fear as the graveyard was approached at midnight and the first digging began; but the attitude changed to loving care as identified dead were uncovered and their bones were cleaned and washed; and it rose to worshipful respect as the remains were carried in procession and placed on temporary shrine platforms — though in theological terms, nothing had yet been achieved and the beloved deceased were still the mere polluting, dangerous ghosts we approached with such trepidation as we entered the graveyard.

Thus, though the pirata/pitara distinction is a constitutive premise of Bali-Hindu religious knowledge, it is *not* formative of attitudes and observances in ancestor worship, and it retrieves only very partially, and thus basically in a distorting fashion, the "meaning" of the dead to the living. This example not only provides me with an occasion to make a methodological point. It is also substantially important in describing Bali-Hindu cosmology, since deceased ancestors play such a very important role in Bali-Hindu consciousness, as we have noted above and shall see in more detail shortly. But if "native categories" do not provide the required concepts whereby we can order the morass of supernaturalist detail, how can we then structure a generalizing and contextualized account?

I suggested above that our options were either to systematize, or to transcend, the vast descriptive task of giving an inventory of supernatural entities and the beliefs and observances connected with them. To attempt the second course, I propose we turn to the sociology-of-knowledge perspective adopted in the discussion of Islam: let us order our data on cultural forms not by a typology of such forms, or a congeries of native concepts, or indeed by Balinese philosophical conceptions, but by the social organization of the social action that generates them. To retrieve a basic naturalism in the way in which these cultural expressions are existentially linked, let me turn to an abbreviated account from my own notes of a ritual occasion in one community: one night in the odalan (calendrical festival) of the pura dalem (death temple) in Pengastulan village.

Streams of women, beautifully dressed, are carrying the tall, elaborate offerings toward the temple as darkness sets in. Outside the temple are the makings of a secular fair, with at least twenty booths selling food and trinkets. More than a thousand persons congregate. The women enter the temple and deposit their offerings, row upon row, on the platforms and either file out again to wait for other family members or join the growing congregation within the temple walls. When the temple is crammed with worshipers, the gates are closed (the rites will be repeated for a subsequent assembly, until all have been purified). Loudspeakers transmit sacred mass-like singing (in Sanskrit and Old Javanese varying among three levels of purity/admixture with Balinese, I am told by my companion). Colored rice (black, yellow, and white) is scattered over us by temple attendants to ward off butas. Then the girl attendants circulate sprinkling holy water on the congregation. We pray, offering a white, a red, and a yellow flower. The girl temple attendants again circulate, purifying each of us with holy water and anointing forehead and temples with sticky rice. We pray again, and chant with the loudspeakers. Then we vacate the temple to make room for the next batch, and join the crowd outside. Many stay there (some have been keeping vigil through all three nights of odalan); others disperse and go home to wait.

About midnight, the (somewhat reduced) crowd assembles again. Groups of men, each with two ceremonial parasols and a pressure lamp, wait at various crossroads for the presutri temple trance mediums. Singing from the temple meets us at a distance: solo hymns in Old Javanese, with interspersed spoken Balinese translation. The temple slowly fills up. Twelve pemangku priests and five presutri mediums (two women and three men) assemble and sit down on mats before the altars. They converse, then have a meal served from the high platform on the left, where also the heirlooms (*pejengenan*) are laid out, wrapped in white cloth. A full gamelan is playing.

After some delay they line up facing the altars; the congregation fills up, row upon row, behind them. Large quantities of incense are lighted. Sudden silence; then an opening dance by two pemangkus. Prayers and invocations are mumbled; the incense thickens; the gamelan repeatedly crescendos, like a bandleader, the klian signals the young men to shout and make clamor — but no spirits incarnate. Finally, the klian sends groups of men with umbrellas to the crossroads, to try again bringing in the spirits/gods. In the ensuing quiet, a distant muezzin's call to the 3 A. M. Muslim prayers reaches us.

Then the parasol-carriers return; there is a new buildup of prayers, incense, gamelan, and shouting. Suddenly one of the male mediums catapults forward and lies flailing wildly among the closest offerings. He is picked up and supported by the pemangkus, then tears himself free; having loosened his hairknot, he rushes up the steps to the highest shrine with hair flowing. Turning in the door of the temple at the top of the step pyramid, face contorted, he performs a stationary dance within the temple, with fingers extended like Rangda. Two pemangkus climb up to assist him; he staggers unsteadily, ever so slowly, down step by step while dancing all the way. At the foot of the steps a chair, covered with a white sheet, is quickly set up; he reaches it and is helped to sit down on it. He is Durga, the cosmic destructive principle in its bad manifestation. She is angry, but also sobbing. She says she has blessed Pengastulan in so many ways. "Why do you not listen and honor me?" She calls for the holy, cloth-wrapped kris among the pejengenan — attendants rush up to the platform and fetch it. She jabs it toward her belly, raves and sobs, hits it sharply against her thigh so the whole congregation is startled, then vents her anger directly on the pemangku of the pura dalem: "When my kris was last taken to the pura segara [the sea temple, for ritual cleansing] you were careless and its point was bent!" The Jero Mangku Dalem breaks down in hysterical, convulsive crying under this criticism; two fellow pemangkus support him and raise him up; he flees up to the platform among the other pejengenan heirlooms, sobbing all the while. Now Durga berates us all: why do you not listen to me, your Betara? I made your land good and flat — who has been tilting it? Jero Mangku Dalem again throws himself on the temple ground, sobbing hysterically.

Durga calls for holy water, to wash away the Ten Bad Substances. Two pemangkus join the Jero Mangku Dalem to help prepare it; they scurry around desperately for the ingredients while Durga continues to lord it from her chair. All the assembled pemangkus separately and in chorus repeat her words, comment on them and interpret them, and nod their heads, as do also several in the audience, assenting and explaining the background or the significance to each other. Durga suddenly complains that the holy water is certainly slow in coming! and there is snickering in the congregation. Finally it is ready, Durga is sprinkled with it, the Betara transforms into a more benign manifestation, is conciliatory and blesses Pengastulan — finally asks "permisi?" and leaves the medium. The medium is lifted off the chair, is sprinkled with arak, and washes his face and head with it.

Since the gods always appear in ascending order, and Durga is the highest in the temple, no more emanations will occur at this session. So the gamelan starts playing again, and pemangkus and their assistants pick up trays of offerings to be consumed by the gods, and the shrine heirlooms, and forming a long procession they circle the shrines (inside the temple walls) three times, while sprinkling them with holy water. Thus the whole procession dissolves into dance, each holding the object he or she has carried. So different from the art performances seen on secular occasions: here are old men and women big and small, unchoreographed and uncoordinated but serpentine in their movements and each in his/her way in time with the music, swinging and swaying.

Then two pemangkus start dancing duets, holding a succession of paired sacred objects given them by a third pemangku. These two are particularly talented, also as comic performers, each representing the object he is holding in his dance. Particularly the young men in the congregation crowd forward and provide a very attentive and appreciative audience.

Finally the congregation slowly dissolves and disperses, as the first trees start standing out against a slowly blushing morning sky. On the road back to the village we meet the first shadowy figures of women, coming to retrieve their offerings as the blessed returns, to be consumed in the houses.

The episode illustrates the interweaving of complex cultural expressions in the framework of institutions widely shared in Bali-Hindu rituals in Buleleng. Compared to the social organization of Islam, we see a striking distribution of interdependent roles on many persons: temple virgins, pemangkus, singers, musicians, mediums, congregation. But the outstanding feature is the ostensible presence, by courtesy of the mediums, of divinity as a direct and active party to interaction and discourse. The contrast to Islam could not be more significant: there God, though omnipresent, does not manifest himself in any particular signs, and his command is finite and given once and for all in the Koran; here, Godhead descends among us and addresses unique and new commands to persons and congregations. We see, in other words, a potential source for drastic and authoritative innovative change in the tradition of knowledge.

As skeptical observers, we will wish to analyze the participation of Godhead, and the associated potential for innovation, in terms of the human sociology that positions mediums and canalizes their knowledge and orientation. This does not mean to suggest that we need to question the authenticity of trance, the dissociation of their normal consciousness and personality. In the dissociated state I see them bring to bear another personality and other knowledge; yet I would expect this to be, at least largely, knowledge that has its source in the traditions of knowledge represented in the community.

First, we may note their organizational positioning: they are seconded to a temple and directed by an institutionalized priesthood through the latter's privileged monopoly to question them and interpret their statements. Trance possession may also occur spontaneously in the audience; but the voice thus heard is far less authoritative, and again subject to questioning and direction by the pemangku. Bali-Hindu institutionalization thus differs fundamentally from that of some Bali Aga communities, like Sida Tapa (chapter 5), where the priestess herself is possessed and the institutional constraints are exercised by the secretary of the temple only. Yet our very example shows the imperfections of the pemangku's control of the medium's/God's statements and acts within the Bali-Hindu framework of organization. I see no evidence that the opinions and urges of the possessed medium can be directed or constrained — only in the extreme case vetoed by disqualification, as being wrongly possessed by a deceiving and nondivine agency.

What then of the mediums themselves: what are the qualifications and competences in terms of which they act or speak? Essentially none, other than "being loved by God" and having the ability to fall into trance. A history of persistent sickness or disturbance is characteristic, leading to a diagnosis by one or several healers that the God is calling them. Even where the disposition runs in family lines, as it sometimes does (e.g., in the case of the presutri reported from Padangbulia, chapter 9), the vocation is seen as purely personal. Apart from the rites of purification/consecration, there is no preparation for the role, and no training. Frequently the duty is seen as onerous and the mediums remain reluctant or ambivalent. This is seen in the history of one of the leading presutris of Panji village, Luh ("Miss," high language for "girl") Marte, as recounted by herself and her parents. At about six years of age she became very ill. The balians her parents consulted said: "She must promise to be *pesaren*, temple attendant, in the pura desa when she grows up." So her parents made the promise, and she became well. But she was always afraid of temples and tried to hide to escape having to attend rituals. When she grew up she became sick again, and for six months she was also mentally disturbed. Now the balians said God wanted her as presutri; she procrastinated but started taking up pesaren duties in the pura desa and pura segara (village and sea temples). Once she and another pesaren were out in a boat on the sea making offerings from the pura segara, and the boat sank; the cause was later discovered to be that one of the boy pesaren was impure from death pollution. Fishermen from a neighboring village saved them; but as Luh Marte was brought to the beach, she fell into trance and spoke a great deal. As always, she herself remembers nothing of her trance behavior. She still does not wish to be presutri, arguing that she feels shy, she is too young (approximately thirty years old), and she does not want to leave her friends among the pesaren, just to be one of them. She now does these pesaren duties faithfully; but the High God of the Pura desa loves her, and toward the end of every ceremony he possesses her. Luh Marte remains unmarried: generally, women presutris who are regularly possessed by the High God do not marry, but there is no law forbidding it; she just is not interested. Similarly in other presutri biographies, I found no indication of close contact and collusion with temple priests, nor of special training or knowledge of religious or theological topics.

I shall return to the peculiar innovative factor this mediumship may represent. But presumably the main reproductive processes in the Bali-Hindu tradition are secured through the pemangku priests of village temples. Surprisingly, the recruitment of pemangkus shows a strikingly similar pattern, though the legitimacy of agnatic succession receives a certain emphasis. The picture in Padangbulia, partly given in chapter 9, has been exceptionally disturbed by national political movements, though elements of the pattern could also be retrieved from there. A simpler and more representative account can be presented from the kahyangan tiga, the three major temples, of Panji village.

Thus Gusti Mangku Desa tells us:

> My grandfather was pemangku, long ago; he was succeeded by my widowed grandmother. When she died, the grandfather of Gusti X took over. He lived very long but became weaker and mentally slower. So people became increasingly dissatisfied, wanted to find a new candidate. Many suggested my name, despite X's strong wish to succeed his grandfather. But I know very little about religion, I was tied down with a government job, and I had always been very lax about praying and worshiping — I was a naughty person. Thus I started being sick: felt weak and listless, had sudden surgings in my head like when you fall into the water, and my stomach was full of wind. Doctors gave me injections, but nothing helped. . . . The perbekel saw my condition and prepared me holy water from the pura desa: from two stones, and a flower offering. . . . Suddenly the glass tipped and spilled — but only onto the tray, not to the ground. I drank what was left and was overcome by three successive waves of blood, rushing from my head through my body. I cried out and promised: "I shall be your pemangku, if you so wish — but you must teach me!" When we looked in the glass, one of the stones had disappeared. . . .

That night, the perbekel could not sleep. And suddenly the God came before him and said: "Why are you helping him? It is not for *you* to do that — he belongs to *me*! . . ." A week later, I received a letter from the village assembly: without my knowledge they had acted, and called me to come dressed in white and yellow to the pura desa tomorrow! I was very surprised, and very unprepared. . . . But Jero Mangku Segara stood beside me, and I moved like he moved, and moved my lips when he said the mantras, but made no sound! The first year, I felt very shy, and yet people kept coming every day for holy water and so on. It felt very difficult, but Jero Mangku Segara supported me, and I read a book to learn the praying. Everything I was taught, I learned very easily, as the God was helping me. And my sickness disappeared, and after a year I felt more assured. . . . Now I have been Pemangku for eight years.

The Jero Mangku Pura Dalem of Panji is close to eighty years old, but with strong wit and vitality.

I used to be a farmer only, working the ricefield. Then the old pe-mangku, my grandfather, died, and there was a big ceremony to identify the new pemangku — and the *permas* [temple medium] pointed to me! I was flabbergasted and refused. . . . For seven years I resisted — yet they made me pemangku, in 1933. I felt healthy, there was nothing to indicate that the God was pressing me — but people said no, you are not normal, you are a little bit crazy! I could speak no mantras, had no religious knowledge. . . . Nor have I had anyone to teach me — when I make offerings and bless the Holy Water, I just speak my own good thoughts. . . . By the law of the Desa, my conse-cration ceremony should be paid by the village; but I insisted on pay-ing it myself: I wanted to be free — otherwise the village might feel it could tell me: Go there! Do this! Do that! . . . I do not wish to per-form at the big cremations; I only give holy water. About half the families here use pedandas, Brahmin high priests, anyway. But also the pendanda has come to me to obtain holy water from the pura dalem . . . Over the years, I have consulted others on difficult points, and I have discussed philosophy and questions of religion with learned persons. Now, I am happy and confident about the functions I perform. But I still do only those things I feel like doing.

As for Jero Mangku Pura Segara, there was recently a conflict following an incident involving a possible ritual breach with respect to handling one of the temple heirlooms. A member of the congregation tells:

211

Temple scene, with the pemangku in the background preparing offerings.

A majority of the congregation wished to get rid of him. They called a trance ceremony and prayed and prayed – but the God would not come. They went on and on till after midnight. Finally one of the presutris went into trance. They asked who the God wanted for his pemangku. He said: "Why do you ask? I have one!" They explained: "He is not good, we want another." The God answered: "Why? I still love him!" But they persevered. Suddenly two bright lights appeared: the eyes of a sea serpent. It grew very big, rose up out of the sea and leaned over them. The people stood up, in great fear, and wanted to flee. But Jero Mangku said no, stay here and sit down. So the whole congregation sat down, and prayed for forgiveness, and declared that they wished to keep their pemangku. This is a true account – it *really* happened that way!

Thus village priests are always ostensibly selected by the Gods themselves, no matter what pattern of other claims they may make: family line, the support of the congregation, or a wish to serve. And in the execution of their priestly functions, they also have to confront these very gods before the eyes of the congregation, as they become embodied in the trance mediums and speak their minds – sometimes in disagreement with each other. "With several presutris in trance at once, one may say one thing, one another. They disagree, just like people do. They may argue – perhaps they cannot agree and must come back to the question later, at the next big ceremony."

In her sensitive introduction to a monograph describing a temple festival (odalan) in South Bali, Belo observes ([1953] 1966:1):

Bali belongs to the gods. The inhabitants are no more than transitory tenants of the land, who cultivate it and are nourished from its yield during the short span of the body's residence upon the earth. People die, but the earth remains – the property of the gods.

The relationship, then, between the living inhabitants and the dead souls, the ancestral gods who are the true owners of the land, is a close one. As the years roll around members of an ancestral line will die, and be born again, so that in the unending cycle of reincarnation it is the ancestral line which continues to hold the apportioned lands, and the individual members merely return from time to time "to ask for rice." In a sense, it is only upon the indulgence of the gods that the living are allowed to be fed from their lands. Therefore the living take great care to show the proper respect for the gods, not to neglect to do them honor at every turn, and to be at pains to propitiate them when signs of their displeasure are manifested.

So indeed is the basic premise of Bali-Hinduism. But Belo's account fails to address the existentially critical issue of how one ascertains just what *is* the will of the gods. Islam builds its whole apparatus of elaborate teaching, scholarly training, competition, and ascription of authority on the availability of a knowable text that *is* the Will of God. Bali-Hindus, with the gods descending among them, have the eternal problem of interpreting their cacophony.

As if this were not enough, the other set of sacred authorities represented by one's deceased ascendants and deified ancestors equally engages itself in the interaction and discourse of society. The relations with one's dead ancestors remain social relations, to persons whom one can call and converse with, and who interfere on their own initiative in one's life.

Ancestors, as noted, are the objects of veneration in elaborate household and clan cult, with rites ranging from the daily devotions and offerings at the household shrine to the protracted and exceedingly expensive cremation rituals. But the dead are also parties to continued interaction. Direct contact with a deceased will normally start shortly after death, if only for a technical reason: it is necessary to ascertain, if there is any reason to harbor such fears, whether the death was a normal or a "bad" death, a *mati salah pati*. Suicide or murder (including by poison, and therefore also by most forms of sorcery) results in this latter form of death, in which case the dead must be specially purified after a period of waiting, not moved directly into the normal sequence of postmortuary rites. The best way to find this out is to ask the dead person her/himself. This one does by approaching a *balian matuunan*, a trance medium who specializes as a private practitioner in having other people's ancestors incarnate themselves in her/his body. There are numerous such practitioners scattered across Bali, and families prefer anonymously to seek out the more distant ones, who have no previous knowledge of persons and relations and are thereby precluded from dissimulating possession. To defend against other spirits insinuating themselves into the session — there is often a clamor of many voices wishing to speak — the family may first visit the pura dalem with sandalwood representations of the person(s) with whom they wish to speak, asking the Betara Gde to give the souls leave to appear and incarnate them in the sandalwood figures, which are then taken along to the balian. It is also better to go without telling collaterals and neighbors, maybe even travel at night, so others with evil intent or past acts to hide do not cause interference and magically block the communication. A large number of deceased reveal, on this first contact, that their deaths were indeed caused by sorcery.

This is usually only the first of a series of irregular, direct conversations during the life of descendants. There may be problems one wishes to discuss and advice to be had; the family may wish to mobilize support against misfortune; or such misfortune may have been caused by the deceased themselves, as a sign or compulsion for the living to seek contact or as punishments for annoyance they have caused or infringements they have committed. Sometimes the sessions seem to be essentially family reunions, introducing new spouses and new descendants to ancestors. Powerful emotions are released: perhaps most touching, I attended the first meeting of a young woman and her mother who died giving birth to her, with both parties crying profusely from love and happiness; but I have also attended more painful scenes where the emotional aftermaths of unhappy marital relations between a living and a dead spouse are reworked, or painful conflicts between now dead parents and living children are exposed. Remarkable too are the detailed reminiscences and intimate knowledge the deceased soul articulates through the medium, and the matter-of-fact way these are responded to by the descendants. Concentrated, deeply felt, and intense as these interactions are, I suspect that things are said during them that would never be said in dialogues between the living. Given this, and the linguistic and informational difficulties in properly comprehending passages of these interchanges, I do not try to document them in detail but use them as indications of the relations between living descendants and their ancestors and of the cosmological constructions they embody.

Ancestors are also called upon to resolve conflicts between the living. Thus a senior man tells how the group of his brothers and cousins finally called in their deceased uncle to settle their dispute over his estate. He had been childless and taken one of his nephews in fosterage, and it was known but resented among the collaterals that the uncle wished to favor this foster-nephew with a considerable inheritance. When asked directly, the dead soul responded immediately: "You all know that I want my *cucu* [lit.: grandchild] to have my land!" "Yes, I know, dear *we* [father's senior brother]," answered the favored nephew, now a man in his late sixties, "but this is causing strife in the family; I fear it would be better if we brothers and cousins divided equally." Only after considerable argument was he able to convince the dead uncle, finally arriving at a settlement acceptable to all parties (which has so far not been executed, however, due to acute conflicts that erupted among the heirs for other reasons; see chapter 17).

It would lead too far to pursue the substance of this and other sessions I have witnessed; and my main concern is with the general structure of the discourse and the kind of topics it treats. Briefly, the dead are treated with great respect and familiarity, and they engage actively and often decisively in the discourse of the living. These interactions are characterized by a schematic and very explicit appeal to social and moral obligations and a general discourse on values, together with expressions of suitable mutual emotion; and senior and junior roles and responsibilities are graphically modeled. But the impact of all these ancestral souls, speaking through numerous different media to diverse, intimate groupings of descendants, can hardly be to effect a unity of dogma in Bali-Hinduism; rather, it exacerbates the confusion by generating an even richer diversity in its discourse.

Are there then no sacred texts anywhere to embody Bali-Hindu doctrine, and teach it, and ensure its coherence? Yes, there are such texts, which are believed to present ideas, conceptions, and knowledge with superhuman authority, but they fail to function in a way that enhances a unity of doctrine and dogma. Whatever the coherence of their content — which is questionable, but for others to judge who command the required philological and philosophical competence — they enter into the living tradition in such a way that only adds more voices to its diversity. We are speaking of a considerable combined heritage of lontars: manuscripts written in Sanskritic script on palm-leaf materials, composed, copied and reedited over many centuries, written in various classical and more modern versions of Javanese and Balinese. Under Dutch and subsequently Republican Indonesian auspices, a central library of such lontars has been established in the Gedong Kirtya in Singaraja, comprising a vast collection of perhaps half of all the manuscripts that may be in existence. But this has effectively served to remove such manuscripts from their traditional functions in Bali-Hinduism, making them available to a very small elite of scholars only. The remaining, dispersed part of their heritage, however, continues to function in traditional fashion. Locked away in shrine houses in village temples, or privately kept by family lines of priests, balians, and others, they are approached with great ceremony as manifestations of divinity and an embodiment and direct source of sakti, sacred power, to their possessors. They are only most reluctantly and exceptionally made available to outsiders; and if they are read at all by their keepers, this is done as an act of ritual, at the appropriate occasion and with the offerings and prayer appropriate to a deity. Indeed I have had the experience of privileged access to a few such manuscripts, after appropriate purifications, prayers, and incense-burning, sometimes to find at the climactic moment of unlocking and unwrapping by the document's keeper that the document was in fact a typewritten text — in one case with an appended Bahasa Indonesia translation — as the lontar had been in the process of disintegrating and its sacred content thus been salvaged many years ago. My point is, these fascinating and important texts add significantly to the Bali-Hindu stream of tradition, but not as a literary heritage allowing reference, comparison, and a critical scholarship of establishing a shared authentic knowledge. On the contrary, they are separate, independent sources of authority to their priestly possessors, at best read for their unique and place-and-person-specific knowledge, each sacred and powerful and unchallengable in its particular validity.

Add to this the authority manifest in temple and family heirlooms, in magic kris knives and precious stones set in rings, in masks and garments and temple architecture — then perhaps an appreciation of the plurality of authoritative voices constantly speaking in the Bali-Hindu tradition can begin to emerge. Finally, the sheer *volume* of activity must be added: the more than twenty thousand, perhaps forty thousand, public temples on the island; the shrines in every Bali-Hindu houseyard and over most beds; the recurring daily round of worship, and life cycle events, and multiple calendars, thumping out their crossing rhythms and creating that vast, syncopated polyphony of ceremony that comprises Bali-Hinduism.

The contrast we see between Bali-Hinduism and Islam in Bali serves to bring out major dimensions of systemic variation. Islam's simple and hierarchic structure conforms very closely to the features emphasized by Redfield (1956) in his concept of a "great tradition": a set of sacred scriptures, a class of literati who convey its content to the masses, a sacred geography and a sacred calendar to position these activities. Thus "in a civilization, there is a great tradition of the reflective few, and there is a little tradition of the largely unreflected many. The great tradition is cultivated in schools and temples" (ibid.:70). On this pattern Islam in Bali has its Koran, its Mecca, and its pesantren. As against Redfield's conception of "the reflective few," Balinese Muslims show rather a broad participation in the lower echelon of its hierarchy; but all significant impulses pass downward in this hierarchy, as the model suggests.

Bali-Hinduism is clearly very differently structured — in a way that also throws into relief the elitist assumptions unquestioningly built into Redfield's model of cultural creativity and cultural processes. Bali-Hinduism must be acknowledged to be fundamentally embedded and decentered. Yet it would make little sense to deny it its character as a great tradition. It has successfully reproduced a Hindu heritage of theology, philosophy, literature, and arts for seven hundred years after contact with the originating Hindu centers was broken. Yet there is nowhere within it that concentrated knowledge and authority posited by Redfield's model. Whereas Indian Hinduism with considerable justification can be represented as centers and channels of communication (Marriott 1959), Bali-Hinduism exhibits such a structure neither physically nor conceptually. Events originate much more on a grass-roots level and develop in complexity and subtlety; the image of a flowerbed set in exceptionally fertile earth replaces that of centers and channels. Observe some varied examples of this decentered character of North Balinese Hinduism: in Desa Tangguwisa is a charismatic pedanda who has turned his village residence into a place of discourse on philosophical, cosmological and magical matters, expounding his own knowledge and vision to young and old who care to come. In Banjar Sekar is the house of a brilliant dalang puppeteer who carries his show to birthday celebrations and weddings around the countryside and vitalizes classical literature and imagery for village audiences. In the hills above Tegallingga lives a modest and poor watchman, reputedly more than a hundred years old. He counts himself as a stranger in the region, as he has spent his life there but is of a different stock than the villagers, being descended from a settler from the southern Bali Aga village of Tenganan, to which place he returns for its great rituals. But he regards himself as Bali-Hindu and has cultivated an interest in philosophical and moral questions. When the region was asked by the modern, centrally sponsored organization of Parisada Hindu Dharma to send a representative to a supreme conclave of Hinduist scholars, the choice fell on him for his simple goodness and wisdom. In Prabakula sits the former puppeteer Pak Mengmendere constructing a subtle synthesis of the sacred and doctrinal history of his region and village, based on the village lontars, oral traditions, and temple medium revelations available to him. And ubiquitously, in every village, are temple mediums, inspired balians, trusted and commandeered pemangkus contributing to the tradition by applying various bits of it — reproducing them and making them relevant in response to the complex particulars of everyday human life and strife.

These are not the terminal points of channels of communication; there is essentially no system above them: no schools have been available for the training of pemangkus or mediums, no libraries for their studies, no scholarly refuges for their development into an elite of the reflective few, and only a very fragmented heritage of sacred texts has been imperfectly accessible, much of it indeed treated as relics rather than books by its keepers. To the extent that these "reflective many," as I would prefer to call them, are innovative, or improvise and fill in where their knowledge fails them, or introduce new ideas direct from Godhead through their inspiration and possession, this is not a matter of parochialization, of transforming advanced and sophisticated thought into homely imagery and simplified didactics. It is, on the contrary, a supplement of creativity exercised autonomously to augment the stream of transmission and reproduction that rests squarely on these practitioners for its perpetuation.

There are two possible modifications of this extremely decentered, locally based account I have given. One is the government-sponsored Parisada Hindu Dharma, founded in 1959, which works actively to vitalize and systematize Bali-Hinduism and in the process effects a transformation of it (Geertz [1964] 1973d; Forge 1980). But what can be observed as Bali-Hinduism in Buleleng today is clearly not the product of such an organized religion, but mainly its predecessor, still lacking in the committees, texts, and systematics now weakly and rather unprofessionally being created by the self-appointed authority of the Parisada Hindu Dharma. Another force toward coordination and systematization is lost in an opaque past, when the kingdom of Buleleng commanded courtly resources and authority and apparently saw itself as the protector of the Bali-Hindu faith against an encroaching Islam. The question of the extent to which the court in Buleleng served as a center for the reproduction of Hinduism will be discussed, but not resolved, in a later chapter. But it should be recognized that whatever the answer, Bali-Hinduism reproduced itself for more than a hundred years in Buleleng after the kingdom was crushed and before the Parisada Hindu Dharma was founded, and also for many hundreds of years before the founding of Panji Sakti's court. For the generations stretching back behind living memory it has been capable of reproducing itself as a vital religious, philosophical, and artistic stream, a "great tradition" in any reasonable sense of the term, on the basis of the extraordinarily decentered institutions I have here described. The cultural product it generates bears the clear stamp of these processes. It contains a constant influx of fresh and erratic creations searching for traditional foundations; a troubled morality of principle *and* accommodation, often articulated in generalized tenets but hammered out in the very moment of application to the particular and crossing pressures of community life; incident upon incident of transcendent contact with a spiritual world made compelling to whole village congregations; unresolvable epistemological conundrums of human existence actualized and made immanent in the flow of humdrum life.

The major thrust of this vital, engaging tradition goes into constantly positioning persons and communities in a relationship to the unknowable, the ultimate realities behind appearances: niskala. Compared with most traditions of knowledge that attempt this, and certainly in contrast to Islam in Bali, what stands out is its praxis of humility and suspended judgment combined with the remarkable force and presence of cosmic powers *within* the cultural materials that communicate them. In Bali-Hinduism we see not a human tableau *en*acting a vision that represents cosmic relations: we see a tradition of knowledge that makes these forces immanent and parties to *inter*action; with its construction it compels the word to be made flesh and to dwell among us — not once only in history, as memorialized in the Christian eucharist, but regularly, as a recurring aspect of worship. Thus in this tradition of knowledge the conceptions addressed in ritual become a recalcitrant presence in the material world, a force that does not "reflect" secular social relations so much as offer stimulus and resistance to them. It has its own immanent dynamics, which compels and shapes physical caus-ality and society, as Balinese truly experience them: it generates material reality by entering deeply into the discourse and action of the community.

Participation in this spiritual experience cannot but profoundly affect Bali-Hindu consciousness and world view, in ways that have been exempli-fied above and will be exemplified further in the remaining text. A truly satisfactory analysis would have to be capable of showing how cultural form generates spiritual force. In lieu of that, we must at least recognize the elusive, grass-roots groundswell of spirituality whereby a great many members of the society participate in creating a subtly exquisite complex-ity bordering on chaos as the combined product of their multiplicity of insights, imagery, interpretations, and constructions.

13

Kings, Courts, Castes, and the Bali Aga

The traditional political institutions of Buleleng are now at low ebb but once constituted a powerful social organization with a fecund impact on cultural activities. I need to explore the legacy of social and cultural features they may have bequeathed to the Buleleng of today. Indeed, early European observers of Bali placed great emphasis on the central role of kings and nobles and were fascinated by the glittering spectacles of courtly custom that surrounded them. Boon (1977:10–35) provides apt illustrations of such materials and also indicates how thoroughly European models of kingship (and, secondarily, European impressions of India) colored those perceptions and accounts.

With a growing volume of ethnographic materials during colonial times, the tendency became, on the contrary, to depict more humble villagers as the quintessential Balinese and village communities as the cultural and even political foci of Balinese society (ibid.:35ff.) — though high-caste persons continued to be strongly favored over commoners as informants for a view of village life. More recently, with Geertz's (1980) eloquent argument for a "theatre state" interpretation of Balinese kingship, this balance has again been reversed. We are invited to understand Balinese kings and courts as exemplary models of the whole social order, "paradigmatic, not merely reflective" (ibid.:13).

Geertz is very emphatic. "The state ceremonials of classical Bali were metaphysical theatre: theatre designed to express a view of the ultimate nature of reality and, at the same time, to shape the existing conditions of life to be consistent with that reality: that is, theatre to present an ontology of the world and, by presenting it, to make it happen — make it actual" (ibid.:104). Or more specifically: "The state cult . . . was an argument,

221

made over and over in the insistent vocabulary of ritual, that worldly status has a cosmic base, that hierarchy is the governing principle of the universe" (ibid.:102). "The whole of the negara — court life, the traditions that organized it, the extractions that supported it, the privileges that accompanied it — was essentially directed toward defining what power was; and what power was was what kings were" (ibid.:124). This would make traditional Balinese political institutions the most highly perfected examples known of Southeast Asian divine kingship. It also ascribes to their great rituals an authoritative and emphatic capacity to "embody doctrine in the literal sense of 'teachings'" (ibid.:103).

If these assertions have force, then the *negaras* of Bali, the various kings and court centers that were scattered through the island, can be analyzed as yet another "cultural stream" within Balinese civilization. We need not therefore follow Geertz in his particular mode of representation, which largely depoliticizes the political institution of the negara while at the same time making it hegemonic within a unified and totalizing culture. I suggest we limit ourselves to adopting Geertz's basic insight and investigate the extent to which the negara may have embodied a distinctive corpus of knowledge and concepts and a set of institutions by which this knowledge was instantiated and reproduced. We may then look for the possible perpetuation of some of these same ideas in the contemporary context.

We can accept Geertz's view that the rites "teach" without concurring fully as to just what it was that was being taught. I believe his emphasis on the identity of power and kingship, as the essential message of the negara, is too narrowly conceived and fails to capture how radical a view of society it projected. I would rather see the whole of Bali's highly distinctive so-called caste system as the main message of the negara.

The perspective I favor allows us to supplement his analysis with data on the variable of positioning: who embraced, or were made to embrace, the teachings of the negara, and what were the limits to enrollment into this particular constellation of knowledge and premises within the population as a whole? I shall try to show that a closer attention to Bali Aga communities, which remained *outside* the active control of the court, can give us important evidence regarding precisely what was propagated *within* it. There were also great variations in the strength, or degree of penetration, of the ideas embodied by the courts. The attitudes of Balinese subjects to their rulers, even in South Bali, may have been at best ambiguous (Hobart 1986e; Boon 1977:145ff): in the proximity of the court a whole coterie seems to have participated eagerly in its opportunities and sycophancy, while at further distance a persistent concern may rather have been to contain its influence, while making occasional use of its existence. This seems to have been only more true in the north. Yet that does not mean that we need to minimize the cultural impact, i.e., the complexity and magnitude of ideas embodied and perpetuated in institutions of the negara; it merely means that we should specify more clearly who were the main carriers of this particular tradition of knowledge, and who remained peripheral or outside it. For one thing, the king of Buleleng was also the king of Muslims, who saw the royal ceremonies from the vantage point of Muslim premises, yet had to submit politically to the king's writ.

First, we must ask what the evidence indicates that the negara "taught." We need to look critically at the unstated assumptions Geertz brings to his proffered reading of this. In framing his account, he makes much of the phenomenon of the puputans, the royal parade into the fire of the attacking Dutch troops, in Badung in 1906 and in Klungkung in 1908, in the hour of defeat. "It was quite literally the death of the old order. It expired as it had lived: absorbed in pageant" (Geertz 1980:13).

What might be the basis for identifying this as pageant, as pure spectacle? That we have only seen such things ourselves as a theatrical end flourish? Yet we are capable of interpreting the ritual suicide of a Japanese samurai in rather a different light, evoking controlled violence and supreme commitment to honor. When Geertz chooses the theatre model to interpret this self-destruction of Balinese kings and retainers, I submit that the reasons have little to do with a Balinese construction, but derive from Western sensibilities: we are invited to see pageant because we cannot be made to feel fear. The Balinese court walking into death looks too graceful, walks too slowly, and carries ceremonial parasols. These gentle-looking persons do not frighten us, and so we do not pay them the respect of taking their fury, desperation, and honor seriously.

Yet surely it takes a powerful combination of passion and discipline to make oneself walk knowingly and calmly into death, no matter in what manner of style one does it. When Balinese today speak of these events, it is indeed as I understand them with hushed terror in their voice. Nor is this ritual suicide a unique historical event, connected with the death of the old order: Balinese history shows it to be a predictable and appropriate response of rulers and their closest retainers to final defeat. Where enemy soldiers do not oblige, the king and his commanders have used their own krises, or poison, as did the fleeing ruler of Buleleng and his general Jelantik after their magnificent resistance and final defeat by the Dutch in 1850, and as have other Balinese princes at other occasions in conflicts among themselves. I submit that the significance of this pattern is far from transparent and needs to be explored. A first step is to recognize that rulers were regarded as Satrias, members of a warrior caste, and that particular and exacting standards of bravery and honor are applicable to them. They laid claim to spectacularly exalted rank; and their suicide in defeat is a measure of how fully and fiercely they must have embraced those pretensions to outstanding honor and rank.

TRADITIONAL KINGSHIP IN BULELENG

The present study focuses on the northern region of Bali; and my task is thus to model specifically the teachings of the negara in Singaraja, literally the "tiger-king," and how they affected the realm of Buleleng. One of the few sources available on kingship in Buleleng is the Babad Buleleng, a courtly account of the life and works of Panji Sakti, the founder of the northern kingdom, and his successors (Worsley 1972; see also above, chapter 1). Let us seek an initial grounding in the representation of kingship contained in this native historical account. It pictures the king as a manifestation of cosmic and social orders coming together (Worsley 1972:37ff.). There is no suggestion that the king is alone in defining or possessing power, if by that we mean sakti, for sakti is known to dwell in a great number of objects besides kings and to have Divinity as its source. Even the king's regalia are represented as having sakti independently of the king, as when the future king Panji Sakti's sword spoke to him and, as an independent actor, killed his predecessor Raja Gandis for him, according to the Babad Buleleng (ibid.:24).

The context for a dogmatic Bali-Hindu construction of the relation of king and realm is given, in a broad sense, by the concepts of *bhuana agung*, macrocosmos or the great world, and *bhuana alit*, microcosmos or the little world, generally understood to be within us. It is a first premise of the good life that these should be in harmony and indeed isomorphic; and a disturbance in the one induces a corresponding disturbance in the other. This is true of all of us, but most spectacularly between king and realm. If the king transgresses the moral order, both he and his realm and subjects will suffer (ibid.:40); whereas his good character resonates as harmony in the world (ibid.:42), and his conspicuous enjoyment of the good things in life reflects/induces prosperity in the realm at large (ibid.:46).

The king should (as does Godhead in general) have a fearsome aspect — to frighten evil people and smite the enemy — but also a gentle aspect, turned toward those who are loyal to him. This resonance of the great and little worlds, however, is simply the order of cosmos and thus is Godhead; it does not in any special sense have divine kingship as its prototype. But by accepting a model linking king and realm specifically in this fashion, it seems to me that Balinese as royal subjects were trapped in a perplexity of their own construction. As Hobart points out, "kings exemplify or instantiate the Will of Divinity and the scale of their claims to embody It is limited largely by manifest failure" (Hobart 1986e:10). But in this schema of conceptions such failures, and thereby the judgments of subjects, are at best knowable only after the event. It is not that every Balinese was committed to the view that every kingly act is right and desirable; but it does seem as if it would have been gross hubris for royal subjects to evaluate and judge the appropriateness of a king's acts in this complex world where kings (properly) instantiate the Will of Divinity, and Divinity is synonymous with a morality encompassing both benign and ferocious aspects as divine manifestations, and both creation and destruction as cosmic processes.

The king, however, was not alone in representing Divinity at the court. When Panji Sakti, the founding king in the north, established his court he called a distinguished Brahmin, of the high Brahmana lineage of Kumenuh, to join him (Worsley 1972:153–55). Though not greatly emphasized in the Babad Buleleng — which after all was written as a partisan tract glorifying a particular king and his dynasty — this unity of king and priest in the court appears to have been ideologically central to ensure the proper governance of the realm. "In a sense, high priests are, however imperfectly, the intelligence of Divinity operating on earth, and kings, or princes, are Its will" (Hobart 1986e:10). We should recall the qualities these high priests represent in their functions, according to Bali-Hindu cosmology: the High God Siwa himself is incarnate in them during their liturgy, and they are his emanation. When they make the holy water during their rite, they are not asking Godhead to bless it: they *are* God and *create* the blessing of the holy water. In connection with the court, as the fulcrum of the state structure, such pedanda high priests carried the title of *bagawan purohita* (Worsley 1972:155), in which capacity they acted as judges and were repositories of law, i.e., the divine order of things — but they also acted as leaders of armies and producers of swords of extraordinary quality.

Below kings and priests in the hierarchy that made up the kingdom of Buleleng were patihs and punggawas, title holders responsible for order in assigned districts and areas. Such persons, if not of even higher birth, would carry the title of Gusti and generally be identified with the Wesia *warna*, the third and lowest category of the twice-born castes who together make up the *triwangsa* (three peoples) or *jero* (insiders). Below them again were the *paseks* and bendesas, title holders on the village level, who together with the *pande* smiths constituted the top-ranking members of the commoners or fourth caste, referred to as Sudra or jaba (lit.: "peripherals" or "outsiders"), presumably in relation to the inner sanctuary of the negara temples.

CASTE

We see, in other words, a degree of coherence among (1) a hierarchy of state titles, (2) the basic fourfold division into warnas corresponding to the varnas of the Indian Vedas, (3) the vesting of these titles and functions in patrilineal and preferably endogamous descent lines, and above all (4) the conception of the state's ontology as based on emanations of the Will and Intelligence of Godhead. The conglomerate formed by these ideas in constellation, I would suggest, composes the vexed conception of a Balinese "caste system." My central thesis in this chapter is that it was above all this conception of caste that the negara of Buleleng "taught." By this construction, the king and his courtiers represented the state not merely as divinely sanctioned, but as itself a manifestation of divinity. It did not simply identify kingship and "power," whether sakti or other Balinese conceptions (see Hobart's critique of Geertz's discussion in Hobart 1986e), as a basis for royalty's claim to rank. Rather, the negara constructed an extravagant and comprehensive model of human rank differences and hierarchy by the notion of embodying the major societal functions in descent lines who are, in terms of Bali-Hindu cosmology, themselves divine manifestations. Since every living descendant is indeed the reincarnation of divine ancestors, these different aspects of Divinity — cosmic Will and Intelligence versus humble material works — entail truly incommensurable differences in rank between their embodied descendants. Thus are generated the Rulers, Priests, Executives, and Toilers as embodied parts of the cosmic Divinity. Such ranks, on the other hand, are clearly linked to the societal, governmental *functions* of persons, not to the substance of persons as such. Thus, for example, when these same high- and low-ranking persons together perform their social function as members of a sekaha — be it a gamelan association or an irrigation society — then they are on the same level of social function, and the various ritual expressions of rank deference are in abeyance.

We should, however, refrain from verbal contortions to depict this model as based on a unitary logic or make it paradigmatic of the structure of a supposedly "whole society." I am far more faithful to the available data if I leave its incoherences and inconsistencies visible and emphasize the partiality of its penetration of the body politic in the north. Indeed, I would expect the ideas that were embodied in the negara in Buleleng to have articulated poorly, and I see them as connected above all by the fact that they were constitutive of a single, powerful political institution, capable also of compelling those who did not embrace its conceptions, such as its Muslim subjects. As a tradition of knowledge, I submit it is in this social and institutional, not in a supposed logical, unity that we should seek the coherence of the ideas that compose the model.

Compared to Indian conceptions of caste, by which they were of course deeply influenced, these Balinese conceptions echo rather archaic and partial forms. Their schema is that of varnas, not of *jati* subcastes; their paradigmatic functional relevance is to government, not to production; their imagery is one of worship, deference, and participation in various aspects of divinity, not primarily one of purity and pollution.

The only explicit and systematic comparison of Indian and Balinese concepts of caste in the literature, apart from Boon's brief remarks (1977:145–49), is Howe's critical and illuminating discussion (1987) based mainly on his own ethnographic materials from a village in Gianyar in South Bali. Howe contrasts the Balinese situation to Dumont's depiction of the Indian caste system and discusses the relative positions of kings and priests, the issue of the ritual duties of kings, the absence of subcastes and *jajmani* (reciprocal caste service) relations in Bali, and the relative restriction of the social contexts where hierarchy is made relevant in Bali. He places salutary emphasis on the extent of variation and the multiplicity of perspective that can be brought to bear on the phenomena of hierarchy in Bali.

The substantive interpretations of caste that I have suggested above are largely compatible with Howe's and Boon's accounts, apart from the specific link I see to the negara. This link, however, seems to be confirmed by the most recent interpretations of the historical evidence from the south (Vickers 1989:38). Altogether, such an account seems to make the best possible sense of the historical materials from Buleleng. Nonetheless, they must be taken as highly tentative. The court of Buleleng was reduced by the Dutch in 1850, and the last king was banished from the regency in 1872 (Worsley 1972:83). Thus little living tradition supplements the Babad Buleleng, and there is good reason to be restrained in imposing South Balinese models on our understanding of the situation in the north — for one thing, because of the dearth of collateral lines produced by the historically recent Buleleng dynasty, entailing a very different political dynamics of power and sinking status, and thus of hierarchy, from that generated in the south (cf. Geertz 1980, esp. 26ff.).

BALI AGA

My strongest evidence for the thesis that caste and kingship are thus linked, however, comes from the negative evidence provided by contemporary ethnography: the fact of the uniform *absence* of the institution of caste in the communities that were not part of the kingdom. The brief descriptions provided in chapter 5 of the villages of Julah, Sembiran, and Sida Tapa illustrate such extrastate communities. Highly variable in a diversity of features of their social organization, they share the categorical absence, or only recent and partial introduction, of caste identities and of pedanda Brahmana priests, absences also shared by other Bali Aga/Bali Mula villages in other parts of Bali. Thus they can add indirect support to a thesis that caste and kingship were interdependent.

As noted, many other communities in North Bali also lack caste distinctions in the sense that they are uniformly of commoner lineage, and many are also by custom independent of the services of Brahmana priests. What distinguishes the villages classed as Bali Aga/Bali Mula is their categorical *rejection* of the rights of kings to govern them *and* of the principle of caste – they are not commoners, but free of any instituted caste identity. This uniform conjunction of the absence of kingship and caste strongly suggests that these features were intimately associated as interconnected facets of the traditional state organized through the negara.

Today we find the ideology of caste most resoundingly rejected in Julah, the lowland and seaside Bali Aga village that is most exposed and most under pressure from the expanding state. A closer account of the contemporary history of pressures on the part of the state and its agents against this community will prove instructive of the conjunctions that concern us.

The community of Julah today fully accepts its position as part of the contemporary secular state of Indonesia, subject to its laws and administration. But like most Balinese villagers, its members are also concerned to maintain and practice their traditional body of customs, both as an expression of their cherished identity and as a safeguard against divine retribution if the sacred laws of the land were broken. Members of mainstream villages also generally acknowledge and respect such a stance. On the other hand, the history of Bali Aga villages as politically deviant and recalcitrant to state rule is remembered, and perpetuated in a general attitude ascribing lawlessness and rebelliousness to them, often summarized in the stereotype that they are unreliable, violent, and "impolite" in interaction. The obverse of these attitudes is a readiness among many Bali Aga villagers to accommodate to change by adopting mainstream conventions and idioms, such as erecting the modern style of ancestor sanggah and practicing more fashionable forms of life crisis rites, and to subsume local practices under mainstream labels.

Julah evinces a more conscious and collective revivalist stance, by which it seeks as a community to resist imposed changes. As noted (chapter 5), the modern state administration has intervened on several points over the last decades, to change the land tenure system from communal to privatized ownership and to foster participation in worship at regional shrines. The Department of Religion has also acted to reform ritual practice, particularly on the issue of purifications following the birth of twins, especially twins of opposite sex. This is a troubling issue in many communities (see, for example, the conflict between Prabakula and the authorities over the same question, chapter 2). In much of Bali, the taboo on such twin births is connected with the ideal of deference for kingship and caste: such "incestuous" intimacy between siblings is appropriate and blessed among kings and high castes (e.g., Boon 1977:138–41, and Boon 1990:95–115) but forbidden for Sudras, and elaborate purifications are imposed on the latter. An early law of the independent Indonesian state banned the practice of such purificatory hardships, but many communities have illegally continued to require them.

In Julah, outside the realm of kingship and caste, the taboo is likewise present, but its rationalization is different: to produce litters instead of single births is subhuman, animal; and the pollution (sebel) is exacerbated when further associated with incestuous intrauterine relations. Mother and infants must therefore be exiled for one moon and seven days (i.e., somewhat incongruously, the Javanese-Balinese thirty-five-day month, which is not otherwise used in the ritual life of Julah) to the seaside, the same period by the pura dalem, and again on the village boundary, before a big and expensive ritual of purification can reintegrate them as members of the normal community. The Religious Council has pressured Julah to adopt more humane practices. Their klian adat answers polemically: "Is it not more humane to do the proper rites to transform the unfortunates completely back from being like animals than to leave them in a polluted state?" Indeed, at the end of one long session with the representatives of the Religious Council, the klian adat reports gleefully to have asked them, tongue in cheek: "Are we Hindus? We have no cremation, no mantras, no flower offerings, no pedandas, no caste!" To which the delegation, after long deliberation, is supposed to have answered: "Yes, you are Hindu — but you have studied the Holy Texts poorly!"

More grave was the regency administration's requirement, in the 1960s, that the previously communally held lands be permanently allocated and privatized. This privatization had two immediate implications: the village community was weakened as a corporation by the loss of its secular estate, and the amount and quality of a person's land (and thus that person's influence) became independent of seniority in the village council. Moreover, such private title to land could now be transferred by sale to outsiders, and the village thus opened to further immigration. The village, led by its desa adat officials, almost unanimously resisted this change. They feared (though some wished also to profit from) the alienation of land out of the village community. They also feared the consequences of not following their sacred law: one reference of the *cakra* wheel-shaped symbols emblazoned on their pura desa inner-temple gates is precisely to this sacred injunction to hold all village lands in communal tenure and let them circulate. When their resistance failed, the leader and spokesman of their resistance committed suicide by taking poison. As feared, the reform led quickly to a considerable alienation of formerly village lands, particularly to the then ruling bupati of the regency.

Indeed, this same bupati, originally a native of the neighboring mainstream village of Bundalem, also advanced a claim to descent from Julah. This claim emerged during a presutri temple trance session, and the bupati swiftly made a vow that he would build a shrine to his ancestor in Julah. He contacted the village headman at that time, who happened to be working as overseer of the bupati's own Bundalem and Julah lands and immediately gave his consent. A highly incongruous and intrusive ancestor shrine was thereupon constructed in the outer court of Julah's pura desa, in violation of all local custom. The bupati started holding family rituals there, bringing in as many as fifty people from neighboring Bundalem who, according to local informants, "behaved impolitely, and sat on the sacred temple walls, which is forbidden." Indeed, these strangers are informally detracted among Julah villagers as being descendants of "slaves," i.e., bonded followers of the former kings — "but now they are rich, whereas we who were brave and independent are now poor."

By the time the present awakening of Julah's cultural revival had gained momentum, the bupati had retired and moved away from Buleleng. When the klian adat of Julah contacted him on behalf of the village council and asked for documentation of his Julah descent, he was told it derived from the presutri's revelation. The klian astutely noted how one balian says one thing, while another may say something else, and suggested that in the absence of written documentation it might be better to move the shrine to the ex-bupati's kawitan, acknowledged origin temple, in view of the complaints that had been made about his family rituals. Five years later, the family shrine remained, but unattended, and the issue was still unresolved;

Julah desa adat authorities could not muster the courage to act unilaterally and tear it down, as it is, after all, a temple.

A case was also underway against the ex-bupati's rights to some of his local properties. When asked to supply the title deeds, the ex-bupati answered that as he indeed was in possession of the lands, it was for others to document their contrary claims. The klian went next day to the Lands Office, containing the records established during the Japanese occupation, and found the maps showing the land to be communal Julah lands. However, when he requested copies of these documents, the head of the office, a friend of the ex-bupati, would not supply them. Some time later, the son of the Lands Office chief started a course in Yoga, and the klian signed up. He attended every class and became very popular with pupils and teacher alike. After a month's time, at the end of a class, he broached the topic to the Yoga teacher: "One small thing — could you ask your kind father please . . ." Indeed, some fellow villagers had wondered why the klian was suddenly so enthusiastic about Yoga. But now, with the documentation in hand, the village could file a formal claim.

No doubt also when the traditional negara was in place, villages such as Julah, ideologically outside the writ of the king, yet had to follow a pragmatic line and accommodate to the realities of regional power. Relations were deeply unequal, and the village council of Julah would have been only too aware that respect had to be paid to both the power and the dignity of Singaraja. To be outside the realm of the king is to maintain a state of mind, not to exercise full independence from the influence of the military and economic center of gravity in the region. The insistence on heterodox ritual forms and practices in Bali Aga villages, asserting the separation of their construction of the world from that of the negara, seems to have been the crucial political means by which to create and maintain that state of mind.

The most explicit symbolic statement of Julah's independence takes the form of a spectacular village rite, the Pakelem, successfully revived in 1982 under the leadership of the new klian adat. At that time it cost the village fifteen million rupees (then approx. US $20,000) to perform, and had not been done for at least one hundred years — i.e., since the king in Buleleng was deposed. And in the past few years since it was done, say the villagers, Julah has indeed prospered. The ritual stretches over several days and centers on an ox with golden horns. Colored rice-cake models of earth, sky, stars, moon, sun, man, woman, tools, plow — all the material objects of the cosmos — are made and laid out on palanquins covered with white cloth. A model boat is also constructed, carrying a green coconut container, into which rubbish from the village is placed, symbolizing disease; then the boat is set afloat on the sea. After prayers, the golden-horned ox circumambulates the pura desa, stepping on a white and a yellow cloth. More prayers are offered, followed by a dance performance in which the dancers are dressed in differently colored clothes – gold, red, green, and white – and carry lances, bows, and other objects. Then, after further prayers, the most recently married krama desa couples carry the palanquins with the cosmic replica models, and palanquins with offerings, down to the seaside. The whole population reassembles on the beach and prays there, whereupon the palanquins are pushed out onto the sea like rafts and float away. By this great rite, it is claimed, the whole world is purified of war and disease – not just the village of Julah.

We see, in other words, the humble Bali Aga village of Julah asserting its total separation from kingship by matching even the climactic Ekadasa Rudra ritual (Fox 1982) of the Balinese kings at the Mother Temple of Besakih on the slopes of the Gunung Agung, by which the land is purified. Only thus can Julah's full independence from the negara be achieved.

THE PRESENT LEGACY OF CASTE

If the caste system of Bali represents the main product of the negara and what it taught, as I have argued, then how can it be that it is found, however imperfectly, in Buleleng today, 140 years after the fall of the negara in Singaraja and more than eighty years after the terminating puputan of the south? A tradition of knowledge does not reproduce itself without an appropriate social organization; and the social organization of the kingdom and its court simply cannot be claimed to have survived in the north, not even in a most vestigial form. We need to review contemporary ideas of caste in North Bali, and their identifiable organizational context, to clarify or falsify my thesis.

As noted, many aspects of contemporary caste concepts in Buleleng appear puzzling, incomplete, or enigmatic. The stronger affirmations of the relevance of caste to people's lived experience may be summarized as follows:

1. Caste identity is clearly and unequivocally embraced by members of the higher, triwangsa warnas. Both Brahmanas and Gustis honor the impediments and prerogatives their exalted caste statuses entail. They will not assume pemangku functions in general-purpose village temples or serve as temple possession mediums; nor do they operate as possession mediums in communication with the souls of the clients' deceased ancestors. They are, however, free to act as possession balians utilizing the power and information provided them through possession by their own

ancestors, and to serve a general clientele in that capacity. On the other hand, only Brahmins born of Brahmana mothers have the right to become pedandas; and only Gustis can be the (rather rare) rsi high priests (but see Eiseman 1989:68ff. for another account of rsis).

2. Popular consciousness in North Bali largely favors a democratic and egalitarian ideology; but there is also a notion that a caste system represents a proper order of society. Thus the proved excellence of the villagers of Sawan in the performing arts is explained by reference to its distinction in its district of being a "complete" village, i.e., containing representatives of all four warnas. This is seen to give them an exemplary capacity, though deference to caste rank is explicitly in abeyance during the training and performances of the gamelan and dance societies in which they excel!

3. There is a persistent tendency — quietly but widely resented in commoner circles — for members of the upper warnas to be favored for appointments to the highest civil offices.

4. Enhanced caste status is an objective for social climbing. Thus a Gusti family of my acquaintance complained that they were being pressured by another family elsewhere, who bear the same descent name, to certify that other family's Gusti status. Without known genealogical connection, however, they refused to do this, arguing that clan names may often be territorial rather than descent-based designations.

On the other hand, caste is certainly not a very salient feature of contemporary social relations. This was indeed also indicated by the explanatory comments of the abovementioned Gusti: "You see, Balinese always want to improve their level. First, they want more money, so as to become rich. Second, they want to better their position in their office, so they can become chief of department. Third, they want to better their education, so they can become graduate from secondary school, Mr., M.A., Drs. If they have all this, then also they want to become triwangsa!"

Many aspects of caste behavior are no longer observed. The appropriate levels of language have fallen into disuse, so that many Balinese speakers, in the compelling context of direct conversation with distinguished Brahmins, are unable to observe the required niceties of speech and become acutely embarrassed and tongue-tied, or switch to Bahasa Indonesia. Levels of seating and head elevation are no longer respected by the general public, even in the context of formal ritual. Endogamy is disappearing, so that even high-caste girls are increasingly marrying down. Secular influence is no longer granted in conformity with caste status; and wealth and modern education are far more significant assets than high birth.

Indeed, there is a widespread resistance in Buleleng's vast nontriwangsa majority against subjectively embracing any identity in a scheme of warnas. There is indeed no label for such an identity in common use: "Sudra" is used as an English concept, not a word of everyday use; persons will not identify themselves and their families as jaba, "outsiders"; and jero, "insider," is used indiscriminately as an honorific without reference to caste, and not indicatively for high-caste persons. The ideological resistance to a warna scheme is also indicated by the popularity, among those who wish to obtain the services of a high priest at all, of seeking out the few mpu high priests who are found, i.e., high priests of a small number of commoner descent lines who perform the same rites as do the Brahmin pedandas.

What we see, in other words, is that caste persists incompletely as a "system," while at the same time some aspects of caste identities are vigorously embraced for certain purposes. We do not have to look very far, I would argue, for the reasons. The Bali-Hindu construction of a descent group is such, as we have noted, that deceased members remain a living part of the group: they are reincarnated in their descendants and are often conceived as hovering over, or clinging to, members they particularly "love." Their descendants must furthermore honor them appropriately, both as a proper expression of their worshipful devotion to their ancestors and on penalty of falling ill, and at worst dying, if they cause the ancestors' wrath through disinterest or disrespect. In a Brahmana, Satria, or Wesia descent group there can be no doubt about the divine ancestors' exalted rank and claims to high-caste status. But since these august souls are indeed embodied in contemporary descendants, or cling to them, that means that such persons must honor caste observances, on pain of death.

Thus a friend of ours, indeed a Muslim, was chronically ill for a while in his childhood and youth. Finally a balian was able to make the right diagnosis: he was particularly loved by certain of his Bali-Hindu ancestors, who were of high caste and followed him wherever he went. The boy had the habit of carelessly dodging under clotheslines on which polluting garments were hung for drying. In doing so, he would drag his high-caste ancestor spirits along after him under these garments, which polluted them and naturally angered them. As soon as he abstained from this, and other similarly inappropriate behavior and exposure, he became well.

There is thus a conceptual framework, a field of activities and tasks, and in the case of Bali-Hindus a social organization for the solemn affirmation of unity with one's ancestors through worship, that organize the perpetuation of caste identities and caste observations in high-caste descent groups. No wonder, then, that the body of knowledge involving these aspects of caste is reproduced, generation after generation, long after the larger public institutions of the negara that brought the whole system of caste into being have disappeared. One might say that these parts of the negara's teachings have become anchored in the alternative organizational framework of descent group membership and ancestor worship and have thereby been perpetuated beyond the life of the original institution that propounded them. In the contemporary context, on the other hand, other parts of this original body of knowledge have not been reproduced; and so "caste" in North Bali today exhibits that particularly confusing and enigmatic combination of features, ranging from firm commitment to irregularity, incoherence, and disuse.

14

The Modern Sector

The past hundred years have seen the penetration of Bali by a vast flow of persons, objects, ideas, and impositions originating in the West. The impacts of these influences on life as lived in North Bali today are profound, and their ultimate wellspring in Western culture and the modern World System is undeniable. Yet as they impinge on Bali they appear far more loosely united than do the materials in the streams discussed so far; and the bodies of knowledge which they compose — to the extent that the knowledge is present in Bali at all — are transferred in a multiplicity of organizations and media, with separate links to the larger world. It is therefore better to identify this conglomerate of influences as making up a modern "sector," so as not to prejudge precisely that degree of organization and coherence I wish to explore. As in the case of Bali-Hinduism, but partly for opposite reasons, I shall focus on the sociology of the knowledge of this sector, rather than its substance, logic, or application. Much of the knowledge in the modern sector is in principle familiar to us, and it would be tiresome to represent its outlines here; on the other hand, the way it impacts on the local scene is less familiar and provides illuminating contrasts to the other traditions of knowledge I am depicting. I shall present the materials with four somewhat overlapping foci: (1) modern education, (2) production and consumption related to the world market, and, more briefly, (3) politics and administration, and (4) styles of cultural expression in crafts, art, and mass media.

THE MODERN EDUCATIONAL SYSTEM

The development of modern public education in Indonesia since independence has been spectacular, and Bali partakes fully in this expansion. The crowds of little children on their way to school, and the swarms of adolescents on bicycles, in their immaculately clean blue-and-white school uniforms, thronging the roads at the appropriate times of day, are familiar sights throughout North Bali. These educational institutions are widely accepted, and parental support and ambition on behalf of their children are generally strong.

This is all the more remarkable considering the radical break with traditional assumptions regarding knowledge that such a modern educational system represents. Compared to the Bali-Hindu tradition of knowledge, the most salient contrasts are, briefly, the change from a secret and metaphysical to a pragmatic focus; the transfer of authority from family seniors to bureaucratic strangers; and the shift from pursuing voluntary studies late in life to receiving compulsory education as a child, in preparation for life. The contrasts with traditional Muslim education are less marked in all these three respects and more located in the substance of the curriculum, from being dogmatic and limited to now being secular and diverse. The reservations I have heard articulated by Bali-Hindu parents and grandparents are mild, limited to an unease about the fact that an account of Bali-Hindu philosophical and religious principles is included in the curriculum for young children. Muslim resistance is sometimes stronger, and it rejects the syncretistic and secular threat to orthodoxy that is seen in parts of the curriculum, as well as, for the most orthodox, the social mingling with non-Muslim children that public school attendance implies. For these reasons, many Muslim communities seek to organize Muslim madrasahs for the elementary school level, and there are Muslim teacher training institutes in Jembrana and Denpasar to train teachers for these Muslim schools.

Postindependence education is based on Bahasa Indonesia, not on local languages, with English as the major foreign language. But a flexible policy is followed in the use of mother tongues for instruction in the lower grades; and literacy in Indonesian, and indeed its place in everyday life, are swiftly expanding. A striking feature, however, is the near absence of books: even standard teaching materials are extensively produced by photocopying. Indonesian in Bali is thus saliently a language of speech, writing, and typing, but not of the printed word.

A close critical study of the Indonesian educational system is needed. The impression from North Bali is that its academic curriculum has little relevance to the concerns of ordinary people, especially in the rural sector; that the body of academic knowledge the pupils learn is relatively modest; and that only the more exceptional pupils manage to integrate school-acquired knowledge into their own active thought. Even the pupils' facility in Indonesian leaves much to be desired, and the effort to teach English is pitifully ineffective.

A striking feature that may explain some of these failures is how the class situation reflects fundamental conventions regarding authority. The appropriate response to authority in Bali, as in much of Indonesia, is deference, in the literal sense of deferring to the person in authority and letting her/him define the situation, taking care to enact an interchange where the authority person's superior knowledge, judgment, and skills are affirmed. Not only is any contradiction impolite: imposing any kind of fact or information on the superior is equally inappropriate, while affirming ignorance and inability to make an independent judgment is the polite and required way to show respect. This style of respect creates considerable difficulties for the classroom pedagogy on which the modern educational paradigm is based: it proves very difficult for the teacher to test the pupil's command of fact by asking questions, and impossible to challenge a pupil to develop and support an argument. The results are poor assimilation of the curriculum by the pupils and a passive and unquestioning acceptance of its overt content.

Peer control and sensitivity to group pressure seem to be important aspects of the school and class environment. Considerable stress may arise between parents and their teenage children over the child's commitment to the peer group, especially in urban environments.

Though the volume and practical usefulness of the knowledge provided by modern schooling may be limited, a spoken fluency and a degree of literacy in Bahasa Indonesia, and the certificate of graduation from secondary school, are essentials for obtaining salaried posts and a further career in the urban sector. They give access to college and university training and to the more modest schools of practical business and administration, down to small private schools of typing, etc. The envisaged purpose of all such further training is singlemindedly career-oriented. A friend of ours who successfully obtained medical training and practices as a doctor was widely admired for these achievements but suffered considerable informal sanctions for also, on the side, cultivating interests in marine biology and in history: these fields were considered irrelevant to him as a doctor, and his interests were therefore regarded as unsuitable and in some vague sense subversive. When, on the other hand, he launched a side enterprise in the form of a small all-purpose shop, this occasioned no unfavorable comments.

The main effects of the public educational system are thus probably those of recruitment to modernity and Indonesian nation-building. Its effects in the broader fostering of technical, scientific, and humanistic knowledge, though not negligible, are probably significantly less than the stated objectives, and time and resources expended, might lead one to expect. Seen from the point of view of most pupils and their parents, the goal of schooling is to obtain certificates of graduation, which represent prizes in the competition for social status and expand career possibilities. It is thus above all as a route to social mobility and economic advancement, not for its function in transmitting a tradition of knowledge, that school is valued. Yet by being so highly valorized as the door to a position in modern, larger society, the knowledge it teaches is inevitably granted much, and for many purposes ultimate, authority and progressively invades practice and debate in many circles.

THE MONETIZED MARKET

Monetization and the world market have had a powerful impact on the lives of villagers in North Bali since Indonesian independence. This change is the result of two major forces: an increasing felt need in the population for income to obtain an expanding range of consumer goods, and a consistent government policy for development and enhanced growth in the regional product, especially by supplying infrastructure and stimulating food production. The steady growth of a modern bureaucracy on regency and district levels has also stimulated monetization by supplying an additional influx of money; tourism has also been of considerable importance in North Bali, though nothing like as much as it has been in parts of the south.

As we saw in chapters 1, 2, 3, and 8, the most pervasive response of villagers has been intensified agricultural production. This builds on the traditional knowledge of farmers, augmented by the government's agricultural extension work and a considerable amount of local entrepreneurship. General features of this whole sector in Bali are perceptively analyzed by Poffenberger and Zurbuchen (1980).

It is instructive to focus for a moment on the tradition of knowledge farmers put to use in wet-rice agriculture. This is a complex agricultural technique (Geertz 1963) with very long traditions in Bali, requiring a combination of precise knowledge and judgments in what we would consider agronomy, botany, ecology, calendrical reckoning, and economics. We have also seen that conceptions of water management, the growth phases of rice, and the phasing of agricultural operations are deeply embedded in

Bali-Hindu ritual. The question that arises is whether this Bali-Hindu tradition of knowledge comprises the salient framework for codifying traditional Balinese knowledge in the field of wet-rice cultivation.

Such does not, in fact, seem to be the case. On the one hand, the traditional Muslim farmers in Pagatepan appear to have pursued the same techniques, and thus utilized equivalent knowledge, for centuries without benefit of Bali-Hindu codifications. We also saw that Muslim and Bali-Hindu farmers in Tegallingga can function as comembers of a single subak for agricultural purposes though not for rituals, and thus must share a universe of discourse separate from the ritual context. Finally, as noted, Bali-Hindu farmers have been adopting strains of rice, agricultural techniques, and water regimes at odds with their ritual schedules, and thus clearly must divorce their agronomical judgments from the context of Bali-Hindu knowledge.

Nor does it seem probable that modern extension work should be credited with the achievement of providing the main framework of knowledge utilized in contemporary rice cultivation: its rather modest inputs can hardly have penetrated deeply enough to displace traditional ways of knowing and thinking about agriculture; nor has it been concerned to transmit the theoretical framework of knowledge on which modern agronomy builds. Sensibly enough, its main concern has been to introduce particular innovations and particular crops, relying on the experienced farmers to integrate these elements into their wider framework of understanding. The main channels of communication for extension work have thus been banjar meetings, called by the klian banjar or the perbekel, in which extension officers of relatively modest professional standing have instructed gatherings of farmers about new possibilities and opportunities. Individual innovators working on their own, as we saw in the case of the present imam of Pagatepan, have also been active in the same way.

Indeed, listening to farmers discussing among themselves both wet-rice agriculture and the cultivation of other crops, I gain the impression that the context for such knowledge is deeply embedded in the detailed practice of agriculture itself, i.e., is tied to the operations, contexts, and specifics of tasks, plants, and soils. It is likewise, in the case of wet-rice agriculture, embedded in the collectivity of farmers cooperating in the subak and thus in the shared discourse of subak groups. I cannot but think that the beautiful and vivid imagery of Bali-Hindu ritual significantly enhances the experienced value of such knowledge and practice; but we are not justified in thinking that it provides the basic framework for knowledge and understanding of agriculture. The locus, organization, and transmission of such knowledge are, as far as my knowledge of the literature goes, still to be explored.

The major drive to participate in the monetary sector is, as noted, the desire for consumer objects. These are used to broadcast the person's modernity, most ubiquitously in dress: traditional clothes in modern, fashionable fabrics — mainly for women — and items of Western-style clothing — also for women, but more predominantly for children and men. There is a great emphasis on clothes and appearance: the items, styles, colors, their tidiness and cleanness. This goes along with a high level of personal hygiene and neatness. In the situation of deep poverty in which many find themselves, even the soap required to maintain such appearances represents a not negligible monetary expense; yet even there, qualities and scents matter and are given careful attention. Nice clothes for babies and children are important, as are neat and clean school uniforms. But other kinds of items are also much prized: wristwatches, cassette players, radios, bicycles, motor scooters. I cherish the image of a villager in a quite isolated village one Sunday morning sporting white shorts but an everyday shirt, a white towel thrown over his shoulders, and a solitary badminton racket in his hand — but no court and no one to play with. Few go that far, but then only a few old people — though they may be of high rank, such as village priests — adopt the other extreme of being unconcerned and willing to be seen half-naked in public, in old-fashioned and less than clean garments.

In addition to secular dress, everyone will also have a traditional set of festive clothes, satin and gilded and heavily embroidered, some of them heirloom items, including gold jewelry. These are regarded and judged by very different standards from the modern styles. But it should be emphasized that the modern style that is cultivated does *not* emulate what is seen on tourists. Most tourists in North Bali are Westerners (the Japanese are concentrated in the south) with a greater proportion of younger and less prosperous travelers; but in any case the generally poor taste of clothing and behavior exhibited by tourists, not to speak of their unattractive physique and repulsive body language by Balinese standards, militate against their being the dominant trendsetters for the locals — though a certain number of boys and young men are drawn in and marginalized by their attraction to tourists and their life-style. The styles to which most villagers and townspeople aspire, however, follow an indigenous aesthetics and fashion, influenced by their own local elite, all-Indonesian trends, pop singers, and cinema stars.

To participate takes not only money income but also a considerable amount of trivial consumer knowledge. It would seem a characteristic of such knowledge that it is inconstant and governed by market processes rather than logical or stylistic principles. Again, as in the field of education, a major entailment of participation in this field of knowledge is the cultivation of modern Indonesian identity through (constantly evolving) standards of appearance.

The need for enhanced money income engenders not only intensified rice production for sale from North Balinese villages, but also a diversity of petty entrepreneurship, much of it in what Poffenberger and Zurbuchen (1980) refer to as "microniches." Numerically most of these niches occur in the interface between the market economy proper and the household economies. They are often very labor-intensive and give small supplements of income only, yet contribute to the viability of struggling households. High rank creates no impediment to penny capitalism: the family of a school's principal freezes flavored ices in their home fridge for sale to school pupils during recess. As we saw in Pagatepan (chapter 8), sewing, transport, miniscule shops, and marketing of fresh produce are typical of such marginal entrepreneurial activities. All of them are based on particular knowledge, and also produce knowledge: the distribution of knowledge in the population is constantly affected by these pervasive and diverse market activities.

Some slightly larger and more successful enterprises also have more ramifying social effects. The innovations of citrus fruit cultivation pioneered by four Muslim farmers in Tegallingga have been mentioned (chapter 5). In the same village, cotton mattress production has also been expanded. In 1980 a young Muslim entrepreneur organized this formerly household-based production in a factory; within five years he was employing twenty-five women and five men in the factory on a seven-hour shift, plus drivers and agents. Processing and sales outgrew local cotton production, and a further arm of the enterprise had to be developed, purchasing raw cotton from other parts of North Bali and from East Java. Again, we see enterprise based on particular knowledge, and in turn producing new knowledge.

Moreover, increasing prosperity among Tegallingga Muslims deriving from this, the citrus developments, and other smaller ventures has in turn affected the balance between the two faiths. This trend was facilitated when the Hindus for religious reasons were pressed to cremate their uncremated dead before the great Ekadasa Rudra centennial rituals of 1963, repeated in 1979 (see Forge 1980, and Fox 1982 for a beautiful Ekadasa pictorial). To finance these cremations, many families had to sell extensive tracts of inherited land, producing a flooded market favoring buyers, prominent among whom were the Muslims.

In other words, since market participation necessarily involves the allocation of the same scarce resources needed also for other activities, it tends to have ramifying consequences in all sectors of life and affect activities organized by other traditions of knowledge in numerous and specific ways. The costs of performing Hindu rites thus affect Hindu-Muslim class relations; the savings entailed in Muhammadiya rather than traditionalist ideas affects the way the reform movement is embraced by town dwellers compared to subsistence farmers; the interests of consumerism erode the collective controls of subak and congregation membership.

Finally, the processes we are reviewing involve alternative traditions of knowledge and opportunities on another level, affecting the management of capital. In the conventions of North Balinese social relations today, we see a clash of two agonistic economic regimes: the savings, capital accumulation, and investment mode of the modern sector; and the gift-giving and feasting mode prominent in the other traditions. In traditional society, a balance was struck: haggling and husbanding were complemented by gift-giving and feasting. Spectacular feasting remains an instituted part of Bali-Hinduism today, in the calendrical rituals of temples and in the elaborate life crisis rituals. The secular feasts-of-merit formerly practiced in Pagatepan, on the other hand, have been discontinued. But the life crises of marriage and death continue to require, among Muslims as well as Hindus, sumptuous feasting. Furthermore, conspicuous gift-giving persists and flows in two networks, in which both Muslims and Hindus participate. On the one hand, the services of healers and advisors — among them the Muslim gurus of Pagatepan — are not properly the objects of pricing and demands for specified recompense; the appropriate reciprocity takes the form of gifts. Balians, dukuns, gurus, and wizards will receive initial token offerings from their clients, and also voluntary monetary gifts more equivalent to payment; but occasionally, after particular healing successes or highly valued personal advice, or as expressions of devotion, they may also be given very substantial donations. Furthermore, between political patrons and their clients there are likewise flows of gifts, in that case conspicuously *from* the patron to the client as often as vice versa. At the time of costly celebrations, ordinary families will be subsidized by their patrons for part of their expenses; a patron may even foot the costs of the whole affair for a poor family of clients. Similar gifts are offered also in higher circles: a high official may suddenly say to his friend in the better urban circle of Singaraja: "Your sofa set is looking old; turn it in and get a new one, and I will pay the difference!" Presumably there is also an inverse flow of gifts in return for favors, besides a covert practice of bribery and corruption.

The trouble is, the practice of gift-giving relations sits very uneasily with a dominant, modern concern to save and to spend one's income on consumer items from the market. The resulting clash of expectations and considerations produces recurring perplexities in daily life. The net effect may have been an increasing household isolation, noted by many as an undercurrent in their changing lives. On the one hand, the pressures of consumer ambition are constantly reducing free time, which people used to spend socializing; at the same time, avoiding engagements with neighbors and acquaintances helps to reduce the obligations of gift-giving, and the drain that represents on one's resources. Thus the community scene and ambience change, in ways that make many nostalgic for former times but unable to re-create them. These seem to be only diffusely felt and understood judgments, but ones that emerge frequently whenever people reflect about contemporary society. It seems most plausible to link them as quite direct entailments of the monetization of exchanges and life-styles.

POLITICS AND ADMINISTRATION

We shall not here be concerned with the whole modern political system of Bali; I wish only to model the ways in which political processes may have an impact on the knowledge of ordinary citizens and influence their beliefs, values, and perceived options. This means looking at the "hidden curriculum" that political activities enact and affirm and at the overt content of official statements and rhetoric and their claims to legitimacy.

In all formal bureaucratic and political authority relations we meet the same features noted in the classroom scene: conventions of propriety impose strong, explicit deference and compliance as part of the expression of respect for positions of authority and their incumbents. Of course, such conventions simultaneously make it difficult for an outsider, less attuned to the style of interaction, to judge the real degree of embracement and compliance. On the one hand, affirmation may be polite role-playing, transparent even to the participants; but inversely, glimpses of private criticism or slander of persons in authority may be moments of deflected and weak resistance only, never actualized in any relevant contexts.

The Indonesian constitution lays down the ideology on which the state is based in the form of the Pancasila basic principles of monotheism, democracy, tolerance, pluralism, and collective social commitment. These five principles have a prominent place in the school curriculum; they are frequently restated in the rhetoric of political speeches; and people — particularly educated or younger persons — may occasionally refer to them in everyday conversation as the underpinnings for a moral position. I have never heard their legitimacy questioned. Yet the actual strength of the personal embracement of this particular code is not so easily judged. Bali has a complex and tortured recent political history evincing strong and crossing commitments. The struggle for independence was active, mobilizing political movements that in North Bali had their roots as far back as the 1920s; but significant factions also supported the unsuccessful Dutch compromise of a federal republic in the aftermath of the Second World War. Factional pockets of resistance continued to be active for a considerable time after the establishment of independence. During the overthrow of the Sukarno regime in 1965, events were likewise violent and protracted, indicating the intensity of divided commitments. The same capacity for passion and commitment is presumably still present, and various political ideals and agendas may be alive under a deep layer of pretended harmony and consensus. I occasionally sense a certain impatience with the present regime for being too resistant to dissent and unnecessarily stifling diversity of opinion. Older people when they meet after long separation will sometimes recall the fellowship and excitement of political activism; and some are willing to declare their continued love for the person of Sukarno. On the other hand, the present political realities and the ambience of polite deference certainly produce a persistent affirmation of support for the regime, commitment to the Indonesian nation, and the obligation of compliance with civil authority.

Commitment to an ideology of cooperation, the value of public welfare, and a modernist desire for development permeate both public discourse and informal circles. These are conceived as goods obtainable only through a public morality that places collective welfare above self-interest. Second, the ability to implement public action is seen to arise in the political center. Add to this the conventions of deference to superiors, which further devalue the opinion and action of the individual and affirm the legitimacy of authority. The resulting model of political action is one in which power flows from the center and a citizen comes to participate in it by joining — power is *not* something delegated from a constituency. A recurring illustration of this conception is seen in how even the most trivial group interest leads to a felt need to constitute itself as a formal committee, with chair, vice-chair, secretary and treasurer, and a diagram charting the flow of command in the organization; and a major part of its activity will focus on efforts to obtain formal recognition of its existence.

The expressions of these conceptions in everyday politics are twofold: a demonstrative compliance and deference that affirms the legitimacy of instituted authority; and the establishment of an informal network of relations based on friendship, patronage, and the exchange of favors. Let us explore how activities reflecting these considerations construct the field of politics and administration. Observe Nyoman, a man of very modest influence but exceptionally sociable and with a wide network. We are riding his motor scooter; a rule has recently been passed requiring the passenger, as well as the driver, of a scooter to wear a helmet, but I do not have one. As he spies a policeman in the distance, Nyoman requests me politely to get off the scooter and walk past the policeman. As I rejoin him out of sight on the other side, Nyoman explains apologetically that the policeman was his friend!

Quite apart from the fact that my status as a foreigner probably would have protected me from any police interference in so minor a matter, the fact of Nyoman's acquaintance with the policeman would in much of the world read in favor of disregarding the helmet rule. When the chips are down, such would no doubt be the case also in Bali. Therefore, I think the episode indicates the general value of showing yourself to be a law-abiding citizen and, more important, the value of acknowledging one's friend the policeman's empowerment as a person who has been delegated authority and showing appropriate respect to him. I have seen the same in visits with a powerful elite person to minor local government offices: an exemplary deference was demonstrated by the elite visitor. Whatever network trans-actions, exchanges, and patronage were to take place should properly fol-low *after* such affirmation of the bureaucrat's authority. The same elite per-son would in other contexts brag loudly about his own power and connections: he liked, for example, to tell a story about his little son who, when lost together with his smaller brother, declared confidently: "Don't be afraid; we will find a policeman and tell him who our father is. Everyone knows our father!" But the initial, redundant message should articulate respect for empowered persons as the embodiment of legitimate authority, and one's own compliance as a responsible, reliably socialized person. Thus also in the political domain, we see the enactment of Indonesian identity and the centrality of modern Indonesian institutions, and the val-ues of collectivity, social responsibility, and harmony, being expressed within a framework of hierarchy and voluntary compliance. Dissatisfaction and resistance, on the other hand, are less easily expressed and shared. Both the idioms of respect and the realities of control militate against any such expression and make dissent largely invisible, even when it is widely present, as it must have been during the latter years of Sukarno's regime.

ARTS, CRAFTS, AND MASS MEDIA

Finally, the place of the various modern media of communication needs to be commented on briefly.

As early as the 1920s, stimulated by European artists such as the painters Walter Spies, Rudolph Bonnet, and Adrien LeMayeur de Merpres, Bali saw the development of artistic styles and productions designed on the model of the Western concept of the arts. This represented a radical break with the traditional context, where art and performance are produced to please the gods, and secondarily to embellish the royal courts' and elites' own rank in the same context of divinity.

Since the 1950s there has been a vast growth in the volume of these new forms of secular expression directed at foreign tourists, other Indonesians, and an international audience. Numerous artists and performers have emerged; small academies and showrooms for painting have been created; stage settings have been constructed for the performance of music, ballet, and theatre; and a vast cottage industry of arts and crafts has developed. It is striking that all these developments have taken place in the south, whereas North Bali participates as a minor market outlet for their products, and no more. Local art and performance in Buleleng remain firmly anchored in their traditional contexts. Some shops sell the southern products, and the urban middle class in Singaraja may purchase carved furniture and a few curios and paintings; but neither the products nor their display plays a significant part in articulating North Balinese identity, whereas participation in the ritual production of art forms is paramount in the identity of Bali-Hindus.

Television, on the other hand, brings such modern performances into North Balinese homes. The Balinese television station offers several hours a day of Balinese music, dance, and opera/theatre; and these performances reach large audiences — including also Muslims — and no doubt reinforce artistic interests and sensibilities. Other music and dance traditions from other parts of Indonesia are also shown, including styles more amenable to Muslim sensibilities; and these inspire Muslim community performances mimicking Bali-Hindu village festivals, as noted for Pagatepan.

Television also brings Indonesian and international news, and it is probably the only significant source of knowledge on current affairs. But the truly powerful mass media inputs are those associated with youth culture and comprise, besides a boisterous range of Indonesian, Indian, Japanese, and Western cinema, a very active market for pop music, both Indonesian and international. The Indonesian lyrics and music are both much influenced by international fads, but at the same time they retain a regional character; and singers are the object of much attention. As a field of interest, knowledge, and peer discussion and discrimination, pop music radiates the same intensity of attraction as among Western youth.

How might these various strands in the modern sector add up, in terms of their effects on the construction and circulation of knowledge at the present moment in Buleleng? Let me try to summarize what must remain only a very provisional and tentative evaluation. First, it would seem that the modern sector does not provide any significant vehicle for articulating separate identity and ethnicity: modern idioms and interests link persons to a pan-Indonesian identity and are conducive to nation-building, not to the articulation of regional distinctions. However, the construction of leadership and authority in the modern fields of education, administration, and public life in general shows strong continuity with the past, especially in the forms of deference and polite respect that are practiced and in the emphasis on compliance rather than participation. All other fields of modern knowledge present mainly an aspect of fragmentation and flux. The vast apparatus of modern education furthers the embracement of modernity and a sense of self-worth, but it does not foster an integrated scientific view of the material world, induce a strong historical consciousness, or firmly anchor human values or morality through familiarity with any subtle and reflective literature. It thus leaves these domains of consciousness largely open to the other, coexisting traditions of knowledge. Nor is it able to instill a knowledge of natural science of sufficient strength to integrate people's technical skills and orientations; technical knowledge seems mainly to take the form of consumer knowledge governed by a changing market and by the needs for maintenance and repair skills, and is thus characterized by a basic impermanence in the level of knowledge achieved. Perhaps the strength and vitality of the several local traditions of knowledge both reflect, and in part explain, this relatively weak integration of the modern sector as a tradition of knowledge in its own right.

15

A Sorcery View of
Social Relations

This chapter is an attempt to analyze yet another tradition of knowledge that is salient in Balinese lives and social relations, and the world it constructs: the world of magic, danger, power, and evil; especially the world of sorcery in the sense of social action that moves by means of magic. I wish to explore the reality Balinese ideas of sorcery create and the kinds of knowledge or beliefs that are involved; the way this knowledge is transmitted and applied; the effects of the resulting reality on the behavior of persons and the systematics of interaction; and the resulting experienced quality of social relationships.

First, let me provide a brief orientation to the nature of the data and method that underlie this discussion. Sorcery became one of several foci of attention for me when I noted that it represented a field of persistent concern among people whom we knew. I proceeded to try to "follow the loops": besides asking about the meaning of ideas and concepts that kept recurring, I gave close attention to the social situations in which they were embedded and the reactions or consequences to which they led. From such accumulated familiarity, I then attempted to identify the main structure of premises that these views seemed to entail and the reality that was thereby constituted, trying to control the validity of my constructions by confronting them with the detail and circumstance I could observe of those events, persons, and relations in which references to sorcery had appeared. At other times, I would engage persons with whom I had close and confident relations in open-ended, unstructured conversations on the topic. Only then did I proceed with the next phase of my analysis: to construct models of how sorcery knowledge seems to be distributed in the population, transmitted and learned, and mobilized and applied in particular life situations. Finally, using these constructions, I made interpretations of the experienced quality of sorcery events and fears in the particular situations of particular persons and tried to check or falsify them against spontaneous evidence from those persons and, with those to whom I had the closest relations, by talking about it in confidence. I never attempted any structured interviewing exploring sorcery as a "domain," nor did I apprentice myself to any expert or give the impression that I wished to acquire the skills involved. Rather, I tried — albeit somewhat more consciously and purposefully — to accumulate lay knowledge in the way that most Balinese would have come to know it.

We are used to applying our concept of "knowledge" in a somewhat more restrictive sense than I do in my present discussion — prototypically to branches of scholarship such as mechanics, physiology, history, or law — and to focusing on the way knowledge provides us with the basis for action. A moment's reflection is sufficient to make us realize that knowledge also provides the only possible basis for our *understanding* of events, and thus indeed that knowledge is what people must use to interpret the meaning of the behavior of others. In Bali, knowledge of sorcery is constantly invoked to interpret the (possible) meaning of behavior, the hidden causes of events and conditions, and the realities of social situations. Might it then be possible, and illuminating, to analyze sorcery not only as a branch of knowledge but as a separate tradition of knowledge in its own right, in the sense of searching for the connected set of relations between its substantive assertions, general principles, history of ideas, and social organization of practice and transmission?

The traditions of knowledge explored so far have been rather differently constituted, and special in certain respects. Each of them — Islam; Bali-Hinduism; the negara; modernity — could be traced to a distant, exogenous area of origin and is thus, in its impact on the Balinese scene, associated with a distinctive body of exotic cultural materials. Each of them is furthermore associated with large and formalized institutions and organizations for its reproduction and/or expression. Not so in the case of sorcery: it seems deeply embedded in local life and conceptions and distributed in the population at large; its practice is associated with no special centers and only a modest level of specialization; it is discreetly pervasive. As a tradition it may, in some sense, compose a substratum produced by the island's culture history, but knowing this neither helps us identify its parts or configuration nor provides suggestions as to its processes of reproduction.

Rangda the witch, queen of the sorcerers.

SORCERY CONCERNS IN EVERYDAY CONTEXTS

Wikan (1990:86ff. and nn. 19–35) provides an overview of some forms of sorcery and gives richly embedded materials on sorcery concerns as we constantly met them during our residences in Bali: a young woman who acts immature before a man she fears, "so he will not be angry with me. . . . You know, the black magic of that man!" (ibid.:32); another girl, who had combed her hair while on a visit, carefully collects all loose hair in her handbag to bring it safely home, from fear she might have the moral disapproval of her hostess, who could use her hair for sorcery (ibid.:42f.); people face the ubiquitous dilemma of not wishing to eat or drink during a visit, because the food might be bewitched, yet not daring to refuse it, which could offend the hosts (ibid:8); a man tells of the battle of confronting wills during a relative's magical attack on him (ibid.:56f.); a woman wakes up from the effects of temporary love magic to find herself stranded in a bad marriage in a poor village (ibid.:206f.); tell-tale lights and bird-calls signal a house besieged by sorcery (ibid.:202); an extended personal and marital crisis is conceived and pursued as a problem of sorcery con-

251

trolling the apparently rational judgments and acts of the spouses (ibid.:222ff.).

A persistent problem in representing this field of knowledge arises in that we rarely meet it forthrightly enacted. Everyone denies using black magic: it pervades life by being something that has been done *to* someone; or more pervasively, something one *fears* will be done; or almost ubiquitously, something that *might* happen any moment, and against which one needs to take precautions. It is thus not simply, for the anthropologist, a branch of knowledge that can be learned in the context of its use in action: it is above all a tool people use for interpreting and understanding events. As a result, those few anthropologists who have tried to systematize their account of it (as Weck [1937] 1976, Covarrubias [1937] 1973, and Hooykaas 1980 bravely did) have ended up with partial and somewhat distorted views. Unless every part of the account is properly embedded in the social context, among all those who interpret the presence of sorcery rather than those few who enact it, both the form of these ideas and their social significance may be lost.

Let a simple typology of contexts where sorcery is socially relevant therefore provide the first step of my discussion. We can distinguish (a) the ubiquitous awareness and the general behavioral consequences of the fact that sorcery is believed to exist and be pervasive in everyday life; (b) the relevance of sorcery knowledge and fear to one's interpretations and maneuvers during particularly critical social conflicts; and (c) the implications of sorcery for the universe of moral judgment and responsibility.

(a) Balinese seem to see themselves as existing precariously in a world full of spirits and spirit agencies, evil magic, and covertly passionate and easily offended others. Such an awareness compels a person to show vigilance: it sets a perpetual task of carefulness and watchfulness, and preparedness for metaphysical defense. Particularly, it requires a sharp ability to notice and interpret the small warning signs whereby this covert reality may reveal itself on the overt surface, and it encourages a sensitivity to the possible discomfiture, offense, and anger of others. Wikan (1987, 1990) has shown compellingly how such an awareness permeates interaction in North Bali and, together with a concern to maintain inner tranquility in the service of health and vitality, motivates the ubiquitous grace and gaiety of social encounters so characteristic of life among Balinese.

(b) In the stressing situation of bad relations, or active social conflicts with particular others, such vigilance is all the more required. In such a case, a great number of the events that happen in the life of a circle of people will become integrated into the particular conflict by being interpreted as parts of the ongoing battle and being assigned meaning as moves performed by the other party in this battle. This will, in turn, deeply affect their own acts and concerns, in that they will seek to avoid dangerous exposure and intensify their vigilance and defenses, and — to the extent that they have the required knowledge or can obtain the services of experts — it will also induce a number of magical moves on their part. Knowledge and fear of sorcery thus have the remarkable power to penetrate everyday life with its meanings, linking a great range of otherwise unconnected events as signs, threats, and covert maneuvers in a unified and complex epic of move and countermove, and thus taking over as the dominant model of reality, transforming life into what from the outside may appear a pervasive charade, but from the inside can become a terrifying and desperate battle for survival.

(c) Finally, we need to acknowledge how the reality of sorcery transforms the field of moral judgments. On the one hand, it introduces a pervasive evil into a field of social others who, but for that knowledge, present such innocuous appearances. This certainly must serve to relativize other faults and shortcomings. Second, it introduces a possible separation between actor and act: sorcery will sometimes compel persons to act in conflict with their own will and interests, and even make them the agency of other and greater powers. The ascription of responsibility in such a world becomes a far more thorny issue than in a world of free will.

To identify correctly the direct effect of sorcery knowledge in inducing and shaping the behavior of a person, we need to be discriminating in the data we use; we need to observe closely the actual events as they unfold, by being party to the one side or the other as their interpretations, decisions, and acts are made. To obtain a sense of how experience of the sorcery reality accumulates and how sorcery knowledge is reproduced and reinforced, on the other hand, we can use the much more accessible retrospective accounts, in which the significant events have been selected and woven together in an understood epic, one in which plots and dangers emerge clearly from the confusions of the passing events.

Let me illustrate with a slightly more contextualized case. I wish to depict the subjective significance of events and the knowledge of sorcery that underwrites this construction of reality, not to attend to the narrative structure of sorcery accounts. To make my case material accessible in a limited format, I can therefore give a compressed account:

> Nyoman is a Bali-Hindu in his forties. His local descent group of commoners had since the early seventies been discussing the need for a general refurbishing of their local dadia temple, including the construction of an altar to his kumpi (great-grandfather). One group

253

of collaterals, led by Wayan, kept complicating these negotiations by invoking various ritual and moral principles as well as astrological constraints, and never agreeing to pay their share.

"The background is like this: My kumpi and Wayan's grandfather were cousins, and they were both very famous balians. For many years Wayan's grandfather was married but had no children. Then his wife had a lover, and she became pregnant. The son she bore was not her husband's, but the lover's. Everyone knew, but the husband did not wish to do anything about it. The son grew up; his father was rich and left him six hectares of good land when he died. The son sold it all and lived extravagantly off the money, entertaining prostitutes and never working. He also married and had several sons, among them Wayan. Wayan struts around, and thinks he is king of the family.

"Our family temple needed repair, but Wayan was always making objections to any plan we suggested. Finally, in 1980 we decided to go ahead with the rebuilding of the temple. We had a meeting and said to Wayan: 'Your principles may be good for you; but for us, we have made our decision. If you will go along, good; if not, that's also okay. And you can come always and pray at the temple, just not decide about it.' So we went ahead and had the work done. After all, it was a good thing to cut out those other people: we are not *really* of one purusa since their father was illegitimate.

"After it was completed and blessed, Wayan went there, without telling the pemangku, on an inauspicious day, bringing in a pemangku from Tabanan. They did some offerings and buried something in the ground there — some of the family were watching from nearby houses. After they had left, my uncles dug it up again: there were offerings and some human bones. Wayan had planted a *tumbal* [the materials of a guardian spirit] there. One can do that, for protection, but it often backfires: the spirit requires offerings, and perhaps your descendants forget what to give it to eat, and it will become angry and make trouble instead of help. We knew nothing of what this tumbal required — it would have been big trouble for us if we had not discovered it.

"Now we have very bad relations with Wayan; but we keep it hidden. Actually, he kills by magic — he wanted to kill my father. He killed my father's brother, number six in my father's sibling group — a very kind man. He also killed my cousin, the son of number four, an important person: he was a policeman in Denpasar and studied law, and died only thirty-two years old.

"When my cousin was sick in Denpasar, we went to a balian here for medicine. He told me to drive with the medicine for him at night, taking care to pass over the mountain at midnight. As I drove on my scooter, a big black bird kept flying close over me, and screaming — maybe it protected me, maybe it was attacking. After I gave him the medicine, I was very tired, and sat down to rest. A big black beetle flew straight at me; if I had been asleep, it would have killed me. Leaving the house, I was attacked by a monkey. Both of them were no doubt leaks.

"My wife's cousin has Wayan for his guru. Suddenly one night that cousin came visiting — he never comes here normally. He sat watching TV till midnight. I became drowsy and went into my room: suddenly I felt a spirit attack, the power draining from my head and body. I concentrated intensely, looking straight ahead and collecting all my will, and managed to repel it. At that very moment, I heard a deep groan from my wife's cousin in the neighboring room. So it was him that had tried to do it. He left very quickly, and never came back for a long time."

Sorcery is as much a part of the life of Balinese Muslims as it is of Bali-Hindus. Even during a Koran-recitation competition, while speaking the Holy Words, you are not safe. The people of Pagatepan tell how their favored candidate for village headman was struck down by an envious competing team at such an occasion: his tongue swelled up, and he choked. But the same unwelcome death was also suffered by a careless bemo driver who inadvertently offended a potential passenger when he refused him a ride on his overloaded vehicle and was killed within an hour by the stranger's magic. To exemplify how intrusive the fear of sorcery can be into a person's life and emotions, I would point to the terror often experienced by nubile girls of being smitten by love magic, guna-guna, and thereby being drawn into a destructive relationship or life situation (Wikan 1990, e.g., 207f.).

THE FIELD OF KNOWLEDGE OF SORCERY

What might an attempt at an objective, systematic account of the assumptions and beliefs of Balinese sorcery look like: the underlying forces, the techniques supposedly employed, the principal modes of defense?

The field does not seem to present a very consistent metaphysics. According to the beliefs of most Bali-Hindus, the magical realm reflects the occurrence of a pervasive force, sakti, which is particularly concentrated in certain objects and phenomena: in certain stones, knives, temple heirlooms, etc., as well as gods and temples generally. Being inherently both holy and dangerous, sakti is essentially an amoral force, which may be used for evil as well as for good by persons who gain control of it; also, despite its historical origin in a concept of female power in Indian philosophy, sakti seems in Bali to be conceived by most as an ungendered phenomenon. Bali-Muslim sorcery, on the other hand, derives significantly from *ilmu*, mystical knowledge based on Islamic scholarship, but applied for private and nefarious purposes. But there is also a concept of *susuk*, magical prowess, which is obtained and held by people and can be transmitted, both by inheritance and by being delegated, e.g., on the holder's deathbed, to a trusted successor. And the power of sorcery also draws directly on fear of death, evil, and the unknown. There are the jerangkong, the ghosts of evil persons who wander at night and wreak evil; and magicians can raise zombies who function for them in similar manner. There are the evil contracts with iblis or with evil magicians whereby you exchange blessing in the next life for belorong/brorong in this life (magical white mice that steal money and grain from your neighbors and give you great wealth for your lifetime). Or there are the *penunggun karang* guardians of the gardens, who prowl at night and keep thieves away. "I met it once, while I was doing security duty. We were approaching a crossroads, which is a dangerous place because thieves come that way. I was in front, the others following. Suddenly I felt fear growing in me; the hair on my neck stood on end; I had goosepimples. It grew stronger and stronger — but I had to be brave, since the others were following. It was like meeting something immensely powerful; and in a climax — "whit!" — something brushed against my shoulder, like in a crowd someone bumping into you. I made way to let him by, and so did he to me, and we passed — and all the fear passed."

Much of the imagery and many objects of supposed power are familiar from Eurasian magic, or at least fairly readily evocative to a Western person. Besides corpses, midnight, burial grounds and crossroads, there are weird cries at night, black dogs that stare at you, sudden winds, snakes. Either very dark or very white eggs can be inscribed with names or magic formulas and thrown toward the victim; love magic is blown on the desired person disguised as or mixed in cigarette smoke. Brass from gamelan instruments and facial powder from a bride are exceptionally potent substances, as are *lalang* grass (used for thatching and various ritual purposes) and *janggu* leaves (used to decorate the nuptual room).

Magic formulas and written texts are prominent. These may be written on metal *(rajun/rajja)* and buried in the ground where the victim will pass over them, or they may be written on paper and wrapped in cloth. Muslims wear Koranic citations as amulets *(jimat);* both Muslims and Hindus may use magic formulas (and, in the case of Hindus, drawings — see Hooykaas 1980) offensively, burying them under the victim's threshold or hiding them over the lintel, or they may be burned, dissolved into water, or brewed into coffee or tea. Muslim sorcerers read the Koran backwards, or sit on it facing away from Mecca and praying to King Nimrud, the persecutor of the Prophet Ibrahim. Bali-Hindus go to Siwa temples or the pura dalem (death temple) at night to obtain occult powers. There appear to exist a number of manuals of sorcery, variously in Balinese, Indonesian and Arabic, which provide formulas, procedures, and recipes for magical procedures.

Personal names give access to magical control of the person and are essential for the standard forms of lethal sorcery *(pasangan* among Bali-Hindus, *sihir* among Muslims). Animal familiars and spirit agencies are a mainstay of sorcery. Bali-Hindus obtain from Siwa the ability to transform into animal familiars ("Yes, Siwa is the God of love — but he loves mankind so much, that when you ask him for these powers in the right way, he cannot bear to refuse you!"). These are the famous leaks of Bali. A leak may appear in one of a number of alternative shapes: monkey, pig, dog, tiger; it kills by sucking blood from sleeping persons or by causing internal lesions, which only become visible when the body is washed with appropriate magic waters. Leaks are associated with fears and fantasies of cannibalism and are often referred to as "witches" in the literature, as they are always the animal doubles of actual people. However, the ability to transform into a leak is a sought and learned magical skill, and so more akin to sorcery. Other spirits *(orang alus: jinn, memedi,* and *desti)* can be controlled by magicians and used as agents or as sources of information. There are no standard accounts of how persons obtain power over such spirits; perhaps the person is sought out by the spirit, rather than vice versa. In some cases, a person will enter into marriage with a spirit of the opposite sex and have children by it. If the child grows up with the human being, it becomes human; if with the jinn/desti parent, a spirit.

EXPERTS AND LAITY

If this gives us a first sense of the substantive content of the sorcery beliefs, and of the idioms and media in which the knowledge is cast, there remains to outline its social organization of persons and tasks (Barth 1987:74ff.) to depict its construction as a tradition of knowledge.

The great divide in the field is between experts and laity: while the latter may dabble in minor magical actions for defense and even occasional attempts at offense, and often command a considerable store of knowledge, all larger tasks and the empowerment of significant equipment depend on the knowledge and actions of experts. Such practitioners are generally referred to as balian or, if they are Muslim, dukun. However, being a balian means primarily having one of a series of specialties as native healer, calendrical or ritual expert, possession medium, etc.; and dukun means being a Muslim healer. The terms thus carry no necessary implication of functioning as a magician or wizard. Yet the basic premise of Balinese sorcery theory is that all special powers derive from advanced sacred knowledge or spiritual connection with the supernatural, so that all such knowledge gives a potential for sorcery. Furthermore, to be able to cure sorcery you must know it well enough so that you could also perform it yourself. It thus becomes entirely a question of the moral and personal integrity of the person whether knowledge is used for bad purposes, or for white magic only, or is indeed never pursued and applied in the realm of magic at all. Thus sacred knowledge and sorcery knowledge become conceptually fused, and expertise in the dark, left-hand world of wizardry can only exist together with acknowledged command of sacred knowledge, or association with a supernatural familiar. Among young persons and educated persons, indeed, there is an unease about using the terms *balian* and *dukun* at all in address and in public reference to a person, because the innuendo of the sorcery potential overwhelms the terms' overt sense of referring to benign healers. In the following, I shall use the term *magician* to refer to this shadowy, covert role of being an expert in sorcery and various forms of magic as distinct from morally unexceptionable healing practices.

The services of magicians are normally sought whenever one wishes to do aggressive sorcery or needs diagnoses and powerful magic to protect oneself or family members from such aggression. The extreme scenario people envisage is one in which two implacable enemies each hires an expert magician, and the magicians fight out the conflict in a dramatic battle of wits and magic. More modestly, recognized magicians are visited by a steady stream of clients seeking advice, diagnoses, amulets, protection, the means for love magic, other personal enhancement, and, in the extreme, destruction and death of victims. Among Bali-Hindus, a trajectory is also envisioned whereby a person, moved by anger, meanness, and evil, may dedicate him/herself to learning sorcery for a private purpose, studying and seeking empowerment from the supernatural; but the normal course will be to engage the expertise rather than developing it oneself.

To seek the aid of a magician, the client must provide certain gifts and promises. The means must be provided for whatever rites will be performed: incense and flowers for Bali-Hindu spirits or gods, favorite consumption items (particular brands of cigarettes, chocolate) for spirit agencies. A common gift to the magician, as to any other balian, is composed of 2.5 kilos of rice, a coconut, tobacco, lime, betelnut and leaf; and a small sum of money. After the successful completion of the task, the client further gives a substantial gift, usually money, proportionate to the magician's means and the importance of the act that has been performed. These gifts are not negotiated in advance, but they had better be ample: the client will be acutely aware of the danger of annoying and alienating a magician by inadequate gifts. Sometimes the magician will make exorbitant demands for payments: though this is considered an abuse of the relationship, we know several clients who did not dare refuse and paid sums far beyond their means; in extreme cases this can develop into an analogue of blackmail or protection money. Some people will have a stable relationship to a magician — for instance, in the person of their guru — but there is also an open market for such services, and rising and declining reputations are spread by whispered rumors. Currently famous magicians receive numerous visitors from distant places, some even outside of Bali. Balinese, on their part, generally regard the magicians of Lombok as the most dangerous and powerful sorcerers of all. While the healing balians should be spiritually compatible with their clients to be fully effective, this is not a factor in the case of the services of a magician.

Impression management becomes a major consideration in laying claim to competence in sorcery. Love magic, guna-guna, provides a topic that can be discussed with a degree of openness, since it is arguable that "to create love between people cannot be evil"; and many magicians will brag of the effectiveness of their love magic and the size of their clientele. Dramatic and successful cures for particularly ugly attacks of insanity and death magic are likewise good promotional materials, since such a reputation both brings in desperate clients with terminal cases and also implies the capacity to cause equally gruesome complaints. Battles for supremacy between rival magicians are stories much favored by lay audiences and are encouraged and cultivated by magicians. A commonly shared item of knowledge is the belief that great magicians can rarely harm each other but that sorcery directed against them is deflected onto associates and particularly onto close family. The most widely recognized and feared magician of Pagatepan capitalizes on this belief when he emphasizes how of his thirty-six children from four wives, only four are alive today, or when he describes how his first wife became lame on one side, her flesh turned putrid, and she finally died. He also describes vividly how he is alerted to the danger of such attacks: in the transitional moment as you are falling asleep, you suddenly sense a whirl of wind around you, or you see a bed of squirming snakes, or it is as if the air around your ears and face is full of fluttering butterflies. These are sure signs of sorcery attack, and that is when you must mobilize all your knowledge and all your strength to repel it.

AN OVERVIEW OF THE SORCERY TRADITION OF KNOWLEDGE

Let us note some very distinctive and important features in the demarcation and organization of this field of knowledge of sorcery. On the one hand, it functions with a very clear division of experts and laity and with a great perceived power vested in the experts. However, these experts in their capacity as magicians are organized in an agonistic field without an institutional support or superstructure.

Second, their very expertise abuts against another field of knowledge: that of healing and curing. Sorcery becomes logically linked to healing in that only those who know how to cause it can heal it, and sorcery is recognized as a significant cause of illness together with accident, a variety of diseases, ritual fault, and high emotion (Wikan 1987, 1989a, 1989b). Moreover, this also makes the two fields of knowledge pragmatically connected: any illness incident raises the question of diagnosis, and sorcery is always one of the possibilities, indeed during phases of social conflict or crisis a particularly favored one. Yet sorcery is in no sense embedded in a problematic of healing: it stands unequivocally as an acknowledged form of antagonistic social action, and it permeates, as I have tried to indicate, the whole field of social interaction and relations even more deeply and fundamentally than does the issue of healing.

Likewise, we observe that it has a clear link to religion: there is Hindu sorcery and Muslim sorcery, and there are Hindu experts and Muslim experts. This arises, similarly, from the importance of the sacred as the ultimate source of all occult powers. Nonetheless, the clienteles of practitioners belonging to distinct religions largely overlap. For routine protection, one will naturally go to the magician who employs the powers of one's own god(s) and dogmas. For critical cases, on the other hand, or to wreak evil, one goes wherever the reputation and hopes of success are greatest. Orthodox Muslims declare solemnly that sorcery based on Brahma, Wisnu, and Siwa is harmless, since such gods do not exist, but that Bali-Hindu magicians employing leaks, spirits, ogres, and magical poisons are *very* dangerous. Both Bali-Hindus and Muslims sometimes make brave efforts to declare that sorcery can only harm you if you believe in it, and they try to live lives that deny its existence and power, except for the discreet precautions one takes for the protection of one's children. But when conflict, crises, and fears arise, such purism is quickly abandoned.

Can the summary above provide the leads we need to identify the main dynamics of the sorcery tradition of knowledge, and reveal the sources of its component ideas and where these ideas draw their power to compel belief, thought, and action?

First we should turn to the existing literature on the subject. Several scholarly and tantalizing attempts have been made to sort out the main currents of ideas and imagery in the cryptic field of Bali-Hindu sorcery, particularly P. Wirz (1928), C. Hooykaas (1980), U. Ramseyer (1977), J. A. Boon (1982, 1990), and B. Lovric (1987). Through these studies, the pervasive stimuli of Tantric ideas to Balinese thought have been identified, with links back to the Indian legacy of traditions, particularly the flowering of Tantric thought in Bengal during the period when Bali's contacts with India were at their height. The key element in Indian Tantrism (cf. Lindenbaum n.d.) may be identified with the use of the ecstasy of sexual union as indexical of the supreme power in the world, and of liberation and transcendence. This power, sakti, was thus conceived as emanating from the woman and being female. Such usage was naturally opposed to Brahminical patriarchy, prudery, constraint, and duty; and Tantrism has continued to cultivate this aura of heterodoxy, shock, and inversion. Its influences in Bali are evident not only in the gross sexual imagery of enormous penises and pendulous vulvas in Bali-Hindu sorcery drawings (Hooykaas 1980). It is conspicuous in the famous Rangda figure of the fanged, fearful widow-witch of the Barong performance (Belo 1949; Bateson and Mead 1942; Geertz [1964] 1973d:180f.) supposedly memorializing the historic Queen Mahendradatta of the eleventh century, notorious for teaching Tantric rites and being the queen of the leaks. It provides the materials for the grotesque humor of carvings and temple reliefs of the butas and kalas, the gross aspects of Godhead (see chapter 12). It is furthermore highly compatible with the Bali-Hindu ontological premise that all phenomena, in their continually changing process of being, are particularly liable when approaching their one extreme to flip to their opposite extreme or aspect (Hobart 1986e; Barth 1989:132). In this manner, it is particularly appropriate that death, decay, and the gruesome may stand for life force, grotesque humor resonates with the deeply serious, and abandon can represent the ultimate of order and control. Such might be the bases for Boon's comment that "Tantric features are dispersed across the conversation of cycles in Balinese rituals" (Boon 1990:163). But it is in the field of sorcery, in particular, that these features have provided Bali-Hindu experts with the richest opportunities for elaboration and fantasy.

Yet, as Boon perceptively emphasizes, "Tantric values are propagated through polymorphous rites, texts and tactics that are not doctrinal, seldom corporate, not coherent or even necessarily cultic, and possibly contrary to several orthodoxies" (ibid.:xiii). I read this to indicate a recognition that Tantric theory, whatever that might be, does not underwrite or define a coherent system of knowledge, even in the field of sorcery. But the materials presented in this chapter allow us to go even further. I am prepared to argue that Tantrism, and other Bali-Hindu cosmology, are not even the soil from which the tradition of sorcery knowledge grows, but merely provide some of its experts with their most vivid imagery. This view is supported by the fact that other experts draw on other cosmologies for equally current imagery. Dukuns use the rich legacy of Muslim sorcery ideas as they write their *jimat* amulets, mumble backwards prayers over water that is then served to the victim, pray to the king of evil, and make pacts with the devil. Other innovative experts draw on the tradition of modernity, manipulating a power called *strom*, Dutch for electricity; and one magician explained to me the source of his omniscience in terms of his direct connection in trance with Godhead: "I am His computer terminal!" The tradition of knowledge of sorcery which various experts marginally embellish and elaborate is, I would argue, basically carried by the laity itself and renewed by it; not only in economic but also in intellectual terms, these experts are merely parasitic on a field of knowledge and a way of knowing reproduced by the population at large.

This claim may be highlighted by a comparison and contrast with the other main traditions of knowledge we have reviewed in the preceding chapters. In the practice of the religion of Islam a deeply participating laity of believers is served by a group of experts, while the experts in turn are organized in an agonistic field of competition and debate, not unlike the magicians. But on the one hand, the Muslim debate converges toward a clearly identified, limited, and shared text; and on the other hand, the populace is not able to sustain their own religiosity, their knowledge and belief, without the experts and cannot apply Islamic knowledge to their lives without the experts' help. Truly, the Book is the source and the fountainhead of this tradition, and its knowledge is reproduced through the agency of experts who disseminate it.

In the case of Bali-Hinduism, on the other hand, we were not able to identify such a core text, and we observed the multiplicity of authorities producing and reproducing Bali-Hindu knowledge. Yet, though there is no doubt about the deep and sustaining religiosity of the population at large, there can be equally no doubt about the crucial role played by the great diversity of experts in articulating and reproducing the knowledge of that tradition. Its most distinctive feature lies rather in the social organization of those experts. They do not by and large operate in an agonistic field, and they are often created and empowered by collectivities. But there are always among them, at any one time, numerous intellectuals and artists of great capacity and knowledge, without whose resources and activities the richness and subtlety of contemporary Bali-Hinduism could never be expressed, maintained, and reproduced. We can clearly identify the wellsprings of this whole tradition of knowledge in the complex social organization of such experts, and the diversity of tasks and expressions to which they attend.

The negara, and the complex of rank and caste associated with it, I have not seen in operation and cannot adequately characterize to make a useful comparison. But the fourth complex of traditions sketched, that of modernity, provides the most categorical counterpoint to my model of the tradition of sorcery. For modernity, the population at large is completely dependent on the experts and hardly able to reproduce any part of it without their services. The magic of its technology must be delivered in working order for people to participate in its use; the flow of knowledge and information is overwhelmingly into, and not out of, North Bali; and political empowerment in the modern state can only be obtained by North Balinese through their attachment to organizations that arise outside the regency of Buleleng.

What, then, are the wellsprings of the knowledge of sorcery; from where does it draw its force and its constitutive materials? To frame such questions adequately, we must remember the pattern of *use* of such knowledge. As pointed out, sorcery is pervasively feared but incomparably more rarely performed, whether for aggressive or complex defensive purposes. Its main field of use is thus to interpret events, not to act on the world. In this ubiquitous activity of interpreting events, persons cannot be dependent on experts: they must themselves control the necessary knowledge, developing and enriching it through their own experience and through the help and guidance of close persons. It follows from this fact alone that the main body of sorcery knowledge, used to understand social others and judge danger and adequacy in social action, must be embedded in the population at large. Nor are there instituted ways to reproduce such knowledge outside the family circle: there are no schools and curricula, and it must all be learned from parents and in the school of life.

And the sensibility, the awareness that such knowledge is necessary and that such interpretations provide insight — where might that arise? In large part this becomes a hen-and-egg question, as it is for all fields of knowledge. A degree of consensus as to its importance is preestablished before a person enters a thus enchanted world; people already think and act in terms of sorcery, and so it will provide a useful key to their thoughts and acts. But there are also features of social life in Bali which no doubt enhance its power to compel, for reasons I shall model in more detail in subsequent chapters. Where persons, for a variety of reasons, struggle to maintain an aura of gaiety and friendliness; where they mute the signs and thus often even the awareness of their own impulses, particularly their aggressive ones; where a facade of gracefulness is studiously and consummately maintained by others: there persons will no doubt have a tendency, with enhanced social experience, to develop a deep unease about the covert reactions and intentions of those with whom they interact, and a fear of the consequences of imperfections in their own performance. In turn, the development of a compelling imagery and knowledge of sorcery danger will only serve to reinforce the need to simulate good feelings — and thereby increase mutual perplexity regarding each others' hidden thoughts. And as case after case of sorcery-caused tragedy and death accumulate through each person's interpreted experience, the value of such perpetual vigilance is fully vindicated. Among Bali-Hindus, as noted, it is necessary to inquire of every dead ascendant through a trance medium whether the deceased died a "bad death," so as to perform the postmortuary ceremonies appropriately; and in the fortuitous sample of confidential cases we were able to collect, this frequency of reported sorcery death reached nearly 50 percent.

If the concrete materials contained in the sorcery tradition of knowledge are not the work of the sorcery experts, where then do they originate? Mainly, I would suggest, in the homely imagery of danger and fear in the ordinary person's world and experience. Indeed, that these materials resonate so directly in a Western audience indicates that they do not draw heavily on esoteric Tantrism or occult Muslim traditions for their force but spring from more shared human experiences. Mead has attempted, with considerable intuitive perceptiveness, to show that they arise largely from parent-child relations and from some ubiquitous features of Balinese folk practices (Bateson and Mead 1942). Only to the extent that they resonate with such a stratum of experience will they be embraced and be compelling to people. There can be little doubt that the body of sorcery knowledge in Bali is in constant flux, or that this flux depends heavily on the creative imagination of ordinary people for its reinvention and reproduction.

If so, what are the functions of the experts, and where do they come from? Clearly, they will be enrolled in part through the normal channels of recruitment to the various categories of healers, priests, and gurus, who by virtue of their responsibility for diagnoses and advice about illness and conflict must develop a special versatility in their handling of sorcery knowledge. No doubt, also, some of them and some others may be driven to pursue skills in sorcery by a personal thirst for power, a need for revenge, or a craving for evil. Once they have the knowledge, such experts will naturally be sought by others when the need arises, and will be in a position where they can impress clients, and embellish the tradition, with esoteric borrowings and elaborations. But the mainstream of sorcery knowledge can reproduce itself without their services.

Furthermore, experts serve their clientele very helpfully as a kind of lightning rod, a defense and relief from bad thoughts and troubling concerns. Sorrow, anger, and other strong emotions are regarded as detrimental to health in North Bali (Wikan 1989b), and the best remedy is "not to care." Delegating the work of dangerous sorcery to an expert enables the clients to avoid the full weight of thought and responsibility, thus allowing them to care less.

We need to return, finally, to the view of the world as constructed from sorcery knowledge and to how it differs from the worlds constructed from the other main traditions of knowledge. It is not a world to be taken lightly; the dangers and fears it conjures forth can be most disturbing. I would particularly emphasize three qualities. It focuses on covert causes and processes: that things are not what they seem, and that any moment the surface of bland appearances may be rent and powerful dynamics with dire consequences be revealed. Second, sorcery knowledge depicts persons as violent and turbulent: easily vexed and offended, they may take strong action, and some among us are relentlessly driven by insult, envy, lust, anger, and other strong passions. These are no doubt urges that ordinary Balinese will have felt within themselves and struggled to suppress — so their existence and threat will be only too well known. Finally, it reveals the presence of evil in the world: that we are surrounded by human and inhuman agents with nefarious purposes who cause anguish, pain, and death to foes and innocent bystanders alike. It can only serve to make our life in such a world even more precarious to realize that some of the healers, priests, gurus, and gods to whom we must give our trust participate in these acts; such a realization destroys any innocent image of the foundations of society and cosmos in kindness. Finally, since sorcery can give control over the acts of others, its presence in the world also makes moral responsibility and moral judgment deeply equivocal.

This sorcery-based view of the world emerges as deeply at odds with the desirable order of things as constructed from the knowledge contained in the other, mutually contradictory, traditions we have surveyed. Bali-Hinduism constructs a world of collective orientation, compassion, and responsibility; it celebrates harmony in the world, the importance of good thought and action, and the suppression of stupidity and greed by reflection, kindness, and the worshipful love of Godhead. These are held up as goals toward which the soul should strive through repeated incarnations that will reflect the fruits of one's previous deeds. In particular, Bali-Hinduism seems inimical to the turmoil and egotism of the world of sorcery. On the other hand, it does recognize the existence of grossness, egotism, and evil in the world, even as an aspect of godhead in the form of the buta-kala; and so as a cosmology it can accommodate this reality as well.

Islam, on its part, articulates a clear message of divine command and individual responsibility, where a failure to act in accordance with unequivocal canons leads to punishment. The legacy of the negara, in contrast, constructs a society of unequally endowed people with complementary social duties and functions and dramatically different inherent value, reflected in differentials of authority and deference. Modernity, finally, composes a world of material objects that are all simply what they appear to be, fully determined by a complex and unalterable material causality equally unaffected by passion or by morality.

Such characterizations' of whole traditions of knowledge are both far too simplistic and far too definitive to do justice to them. Each is a historical conglomerate of materials, held together by the effects of a functioning social organization and not by the logical coherence of its constituent ideas. The preceding analyses have therefore focused on the different processes that reproduce each tradition, and thereby imprint its patterns on the fickle clay of human thought and life. Yet juxtaposing the separated traditions in this way highlights the startling extent to which the worlds as constructed on the bases of the knowledge provided by each are worlds in collision. The traditions do not only differ in the particular knowledge they perpetuate; they also constitute deeply contrastive ontologies, at odds in the very assertions they contain about the categories and classes of things that are found in the world, and the relative values of these things. Thus they teach quite distinctive cosmologies: there is one God/there are many gods; to give offerings to deceased ancestors is an urgent duty/is a sin/is a waste. Each of them will provide a complex paradigm for action and for the interpretation of events, in the way discussed in chapter 10; and by the use of one or another, their users will construct substantively very different worlds in which to live.

Indeed the very same events in the lives of people may be interpreted within either one or another paradigm: for example, somebody's illness can variously be seen as caused by germs/by a neighbor's magic/by an inadvertent error in the form of worship of a Bali-Hindu God. Thus people embracing the different traditions can live, as indeed they do in North Bali, in the same physical place and observe the same events, yet construct different worlds, different realities, out of these same events all according to which tradition of knowledge they apply. But how can they then engage in meaningful interaction across such differences?

What is more, their actions become even more opaque when we acknowledge that each of these different traditions, as a paradigm, is not itself internally coherent and transparent, nor are they mutually exclusive in the sense that a person cannot embrace several. On the one hand, for example, balian native healers working in a shared tradition may have difficulties arriving at a diagnosis of an illness condition, or may disagree strongly in their identifications of it. On the other hand, what I have distinguished as different traditions of knowledge are regularly embraced, albeit with variable force and elaboration, by the same person and even often in the same situation. Only Islam and Bali-Hinduism are construed as being inimical in principle; but even for them it proves to be a never-ending and never quite successful battle for people to keep them apart in their thought and action.

We thus arrive at perplexing questions: Are people out there using multiple, simultaneous paradigms for the interpretation of events, and thereby constructing an environment of discrepant and unarticulating shapes and objects, of fragments of different worlds unpredictably transmogrifying into each other as paradigms are switched? Or do they perhaps impose a degree of order by letting competitive interpretations of the same events clash, and entering into social processes of negotiation to settle relative claims to validity in each case? Or are there rules of situation and occasion channeling and giving a degree of shared order to people's constructions and interpretations?

Each of these alternatives will entail drastically different theoretical positions; but first of all, we should raise them as empirical questions, asking how social life in Buleleng unfolds and thus is indeed constituted. We should not select a position on the basis of our theoretical beliefs, nor should we jettison the grasp that we seemed to obtain on diversity in Buleleng when we identified these major traditions of knowledge, just because it leads us into such perplexities. Rather, we should try to observe and describe the processes that take place, in their particulars — and thereby obtain answers to big theoretical questions about how experience is constructed and knowledge reproduced in the lives of people in North Bali.

PART FIVE

Action, Interpretation, and Practice

16

The Romance of Panji
and Asiah

If it is so that people can construct multiple and discrepant worlds by means of the different traditions of knowledge available to them, we need to discover how such different constructions are in fact produced and distributed in their actions and interactions. I shall start this exploration with a discussion of a particular series of events: an elopement in Pagatepan, which took place only a month after we started fieldwork there. This also allows me to depict the discovery procedure I used, which led to the perspective I have adopted.

Panji was a young man of poor family, who lived in a good house in the village center with a younger sister. His parents were dead; his elder brother was married and lived approximately three kilometers away in a scattered settlement area. Suddenly one morning, we were told the news that Panji had eloped with Asiah, a young Muslim girl from the neighboring village. We could sense a palpable tension in the community, though a subdued activity of "business as usual" was maintained by most. News of the elopement was spreading, but nobody seemed to have definite information on what was happening.

My assistant supposed that the first issue for the village elders to settle would be whether the girl was a willing party to the event or not: the concept used in Buleleng — merangkat — does not differentiate elopement and abduction. After a fruitless search for Panji at his house, we went to the home of an official in charge of the marriage register in the local district. Yes, they had been there today: Panji and Panji's elder brother. The authorities require photographs and a certified document specifying the *mahar* property that will become the wife's upon marriage; if she is between sixteen and twenty years of age, they also require the father's con-

271

sent to the marriage. The girl claims she is twenty-one, the boy twenty-three; yet the registrar will seek the father's agreement. Otherwise, the authorities require a ten-day waiting period from registration to wedding, to give the parties time to think.

As we sat there, Panji's elder brother arrived. Though to me he seemed most self-possessed and respectful, the others present judged him to be in a state of "high emotion." The girl's father was now reported to be demanding fifty thousand rupees as *wang dapur* — money to equip the bride with kitchen utensils, not a customary payment in Pagatepan. If this is maintained, the brother threatens to return the girl in disgrace to her home. The registrar counsels patience and promises to mediate.

We were told Panji was in hiding in the home of Hajji Rahman, so we went there. After negotiations, Panji emerged from the back room, willing to talk: He and Asiah have known each other for five years, but a sudden crisis precipitated the elopement; he himself had intended that they would wait two more years. Her father has been very much against the relationship. Then, two days ago, Asiah suddenly demanded: marry me now, or I go off to Denpasar. So he was forced to agree, and he arranged the elopement the next day. The father is still adamant. They have been to Singaraja for passport photos; if mediators can get the father's consent they can sign the agreement and be married tomorrow. The mas kawin — the local term for the groom's dowry payment — will be a small plot of coconut land. The house Panji recently inherited after his mother's death is occupied only by himself and his little sister; it will provide him and Asiah a good home. Hajji Rahman says he will also go and talk to the father — he is the father's friend, as well as Panji's mother's cousin. The issues probably will not be cleared up in time for the wedding to take place tomorrow, as Panji would wish, but it will all be alright in the end. Merangkat is an impolite way to do marriage; it makes the girl's family angry and often creates much trouble. But it is the customary way in Pagatepan.

By next morning, Hajji Rahman can report that most of the obstacles seem to have been cleared up, and the nikah, the wedding ceremony, will be in the afternoon. What has been the difficulty? Well, Abdullah, the girl's father, is divorced from her mother and has been living alone with his daughter and young son; he needs her to look after the house. But he has other children, who are married, in Pagatepan — could he not move in with them? Yes, only he is rather sick: a chronic infection in his leg, which Hajji Rahman keeps from spreading further by applying hot irons to his heel and knee, and by means of other medicines. That is why he and Abdullah are on good terms, and he was able to arrange a compromise. It turns out that it is Asiah who is staying his house, while Panji sleeps in the house of his cousin Fatehul. The girl's mother is remarried in the neighboring village to the east of Pagatepan, but she takes no interest in her children and will not come for the wedding.

Later, during free-floating conversation in the home of a married couple we were visiting, we tried to elicit more background information. Yes, they knew of the elopement but did not wish to involve themselves. Once the young couple has settled, they will make the customary visit to their home, bringing the customary gifts of siddiqah — rice and coconut — but till then they will keep their distance. While we were talking, Wayan Kapi, a prominent faction leader, turned up. He can report that Panji had been visiting the girl before the case broke, sitting in her house and embracing her. Her younger brother observed it and ran to their father, who became very angry, seized a piece of wood, and rushed to the house. Panji got away, but the girl was beaten. So she wrote Panji a note saying he *must* abduct her *now*. Once they had eloped, Fatehul, a relative of the boy and leader of another faction, took charge and sorted out a compromise. Fatehul led a negotiating party to the girl's father; he asked Wayan Kapi to join them, but he had to excuse himself as he was indisposed. The wedding will be at 1:00 P.M., and Wayan Kapi will see to it that we are invited. After Wayan Kapi left, Fatehul appeared. He was going from house to house and having great difficulties lining up witnesses to participate in the wedding, and he pressured our host to come. Our host was reluctant, and my impression was that he refused; nonetheless, once Fatehul had left, he changed his clothes to be prepared for the occasion.

The nikah took place in one of the small mosque buildings, after much delay. Twelve senior men were present, including our recent host, Wayan Kapi, the marriage registrar, and the imam. Fatehul was in the wings, arranging matters. After a while the groom arrived, with his senior brother accompanying him; two or three well-dressed strangers turned up, presumably the girl's brother and family. The twelve witnesses to the act sat down on both sides of a table-mat with the imam at the end; Panji was called to sit among them, at the imam's right. Since the girl's father was not present, one of the villagers was named her wakil on behalf of the village community. The imam intoned a prayer, spoke earnestly to the groom giving him advice about his responsibilities as a husband, and inquired about the mas kawin; thereupon the groom signed the papers. A rice-and-meat dish was served to the imam and the witnesses; we swiftly ate a little bit and were given banana leaves to wrap the rest and take it home for barkat, blessing. The food had been made at Fatehul's house, where a big throng of women and children were now celebrating, as also in Hajji Rahman's house. In three days, we were told, the groom's family will accompany the bride on her first visit home, carrying special cakes in a ceremony of begging forgiveness for the offense they have caused.

After the event, as we sat on the porch of the marriage registrar together with the imam, a formally dressed delegation of women arrived to report another merangkat. This, it was explained, is the proper custom: for a group of women relatives of the girl to report and to apologize for the impolite behavior of the eloping couple.

Next day, we visited the young couple and asked about the present attitude of her father, Abdullah. No, he is still adamant. He says if Panji comes, he will kill him, and if Abdullah himself dies, he will not allow his daughter to see and bid farewell to the corpse, or touch him. So there is no chance that they can go to him now. Yet they are making the ngunya cakes for such a call. Panji's brother has made the list of whom they will visit: the imam's house, and the houses of all of Asiah's relatives in the village. The cakes will be delivered to the wives of these families, when the young couple visits together with *his* relatives — who have made the cakes unaided by the bride, but in her new house. They will go tonight after dark, because then people will be home, and because they are ashamed, malu, that they are unable to visit her father.

We moved on to the house where the girl from the other elopement, reported the day before, was hiding. Here, we were finally told the sensational background for Panji and Asiah's elopement: Panji is a murderer. He killed his own teacher, Guru Ali; he served three years in jail for this murder and came back to Pagatepan only six months ago. The killing was unprovoked: as Guru Ali died, his last words were "But what wrong have I done?"

Our host continues his critique. The elopement was improper. There were no women in the elopement party, as custom demands, only three young men, all of them bad characters. Panji's best friend Rakkib was the mujati, the person who returns to cry out the message that this was an elopement. The third member was one of the two killers in another recent murder case. A merangkat should be done the way we were seeing here in this second case, in the present house.

Until this point, I had understood my quest simply to be that of finding out what was happening in a still poorly known community, mapping the social networks of the principals and the routines and procedures in such a case of elopement. I had been puzzled by the sense of resistance I had been meeting in gathering such data, but decided it had to do with ambivalences about their local custom of wife abduction. Now I realized the ambiguities of attitudes to the event, and the profound effects that positioning would be having on people's reactions to what had taken place. I saw an opportunity to explore a number of moral issues, specifically different people's evaluations of Panji as a person and their, and indeed Asiah's own, view of the reasons behind her actions. I still had the conception that I was involved in merely documenting an extended case (but more on that will emerge below), albeit one that was turning out to be particularly complex and interesting. With this view, I started unraveling more of its strands. I give, in the following, abbreviated notes of conversations from the following days, taken immediately afterward, or in the evening of the same day.

I went first to a marginal, cynical villager I had come to know. Though he had not yet heard of the elopement, he could fill me in on the participants.

> "Panji is not a good person, and his choice of accomplices was also bad. It is customary that the group should consist of the boy's family, and to include a woman — to reassure the girl, and vouch for her virtue. Instead, he chose his friends, and bad friends at that. Rakkib is a thief, he has often been caught housebreaking. He also gambles at cockfights. The third boy is a killer" — and I was given a brief account of that murder. "As for the killing of Guru Ali: Panji was discovered to have stolen a ring from his son, that created bad blood. Then Panji was told by Guru Ali not to be so free with the girls. That made Panji very angry. Before his murder of Ali, many had thought that the boy was alright, and so did Asiah's father. But after such an act, no one could approve of him; and since he came back from prison people have had a low opinion of him and kept away from him."

Panji later gave me an account of how he came to choose his accomplices.

> I had been sitting with my friend, smoking. Then Rakkib arrived with Asiah's letter — so the three of us talked about what I should do. It all had to happen so swiftly, and I knew Asiah's nature; if I did not act soon enough she might even commit suicide. But it was a mistake, I should have had someone of my family along, I see that now. Asiah's sister was married [to a boy of good family] by merangkat, and her father was furious and would not accept them either — but now that the daughter has a child, he has accepted them. perhaps it will be likewise with us. But relations are bad: once when I visited Asiah at night, just to whisper to her in the darkness, her father came with

a knife and would have killed me if I had not leaped through the window."

I ask Wayan Kapi why he would have been willing to join the negotiating party for a character like Sahid, and why he chose to be a witness at the nikah.

"One must separate the issues: one is the merangkat, the other is the murder. Panji and Asiah love each other, so they should be allowed to get married: they have loved each other so long. As for the murder, he has been tried in court, and punished: no good continuing to prosecute him, better to let bygones be bygones."

What were the circumstances of the murder? "Panji was impetuous, it was not premeditated. It was like this: Guru Ali's house is beside Panji's; the house of Asiah's brother Badrul is across from it. Guru Ali was a good man, knowledgeable in Islam and a good teacher — but he tended to be too righteous and talked too much, would gossip and be party to slander. He saw Panji often visiting Badrul's house even when Badrul, who drove a bemo, was out. So he spoke to Panji about it, that he should stay away, and he spoke to others about it, telling how Panji sometimes slept in Badrul's house when Badrul was away. Panji says he went there to talk to Badrul's wife about Asiah and his love for her. But Badrul became suspicious and jealous, and Panji became afraid of Badrul and so became very angry with Guru Ali. Suddenly, one day he saw him returning home in the village street, he rushed at him and stabbed him, then gave himself up to the police. A small wrong from Ali, a big wrong from Panji. But the judge reduced the sentence because it was not premeditated and Panji had reported it himself.

"As for the merangkat, Panji was observed trespassing in the house by Asiah's younger brother, who called his father; Panji escaped, but Asiah was beaten by her father; so she wrote a note demanding that Panji take her away immediately, and he acted precipitously again." Could he be blamed for his choice of accomplices? "They are his companions; like attracts like. Anyway, Pagatepan people have been shunning him since he returned home from prison. There are not supposed to be great differences between Muslims; but there are *gulfs*! So these were the ones he could speak to — not much chance to choose differently. His elder brother lives far away; he had to act swiftly. After the act, he contacted Fatehul and also me. I had to excuse myself, so Fatehul took immediate responsibility. But had I been free, I also would have done it: you must separate one issue from the other."

Was this also Fatehul's reasoning? "Oh no, Fatehul supported him because he is close family, Fatehul's mother was the sister of Panji's father." As for the third accomplice, Said, and his part in the other killing — again, the context must be taken into account. It was a matter of inheritance. "Said's grandfather, once rich, is slowly eating up his wealth. The other party's grandmother, now dead, had been married to him, and even brought land of her own into that marriage; and her descendants have never received their share of her estate. They attacked Said with knives — in the skirmish, one of them was killed by him. Always the same problem with Pagatepan people: too much emotionality, too little rationality. They act on impulse, rather than think first and act afterwards."

Guru Ali's widow was quite willing to tell about the killing of her husband.

"Panji was a good boy, but now that he is grown up he is not good. His elder brother put him through Koran school with Guru Ali. He was a good pupil, but undisciplined. After finishing school, he stole a ring from one of my daughters; it was worth twenty thousand rupees. Ali asked him, but he denied it. Then Ali demanded that he swear to it — but Panji refused, and finally confessed. He promised to pay for the ring when he collected the money from his coffee crop. He kept his promise and paid eight thousand rupees, and Guru Ali gave him back one thousand rupees as siddiqah. But after that, Panji was always angry [benci] toward Ali. One day, right here at the corner where the lane turns down to our house, they met, and Panji pulled a knife and stabbed him. He was able to stagger down the road to the bottom of the steps to the house." *Did he speak to her?* "Only to tell me to hurry, get a bemo to take him to the hospital. When they got him there, he was still alive, but he died before they could treat him — the doctor in charge did not turn up for more than three hours. As soon as he had stabbed his guru, Panji ran to Singaraja and gave himself up to the police and reported the killing. By Indonesian law, this reduces the punishment.

"This was three years ago; since then, I have been helped by my husband's brothers. I have seven children; six are here, and one is studying Islam in Lombok. The youngest was born shortly before the father was killed and is still nursing. We had been married for eighteen years."

She does not speak to Panji when she meets him on the street, but he always greets her politely.

> "He seems good on the surface, but inside he is bad. Asiah's father is right to reject him as a son-in-law. And Asiah stopped loving Panji after he had murdered. But when Panji came back from prison, he kept going there and bothering her. And after all, he and Rakkib are close, and Rakkib is a dukun; so he has used love magic, guna-guna, on her. Panji entered her house, and Asiah was furious: it was very disrespectful, very bad toward the father."

Another of the witnesses at the wedding:

> "The nikah for Panji was not proper, because the bride's father should have been there or sent a wakil: it was his wrong. This way the imam arbitrarily had to appoint one of the witnesses as wakil. But yes, if the father's reason was that Panji is a bad person according to the law, that is acceptable. The Shariah says you cannot use a murderer as a legal witness, or as imam. Panji is outside Islam because of his act. But we are obligated according to the Shariah to be witness at nikah, it is our duty. The perbekel was not there because Guru Ali was his misan, cousin; but I was not a relative of Ali. One must separate the issues: the private problems, and one's duty when asked."
>
> *What are the reasons for Asiah's choice?* "I was surprised, and do not know. Sometimes a girl is very much in love, she gets married despite her family's pressures. And some dukuns have very strong magic."

A married couple, unconnected with any of the parties:

> "Panji's act was very bad: the murder of your own guru places you outside Islam. But Abdullah, Asiah's father, may have had other and less honorable reasons: he is very negative in his attitudes to Pagatepan. When his elder daughter did merangkat, he refused to recognize her till she bore a child. When his son wanted to marry our young cousin and he was refused, Abdullah was very, very angry."
>
> *Why does Asiah want Panji, even though he is a murderer?* "Asiah never studied religion in Pagatepan; she spent her time over in that other village. If she had come here and learned Islam, then even if she had loved him very much, she would have recognized his moral failure and rejected Panji."

Asiah's brother was a reluctant party to any discussion of the case as a whole. But during a long conversation on other matters, he made the following comments:

"Panji has great guilt because of his murder and has placed himself outside Islam. But my father is wrong in cutting off Asiah and his potential grandchildren: she is without guilt, and so will be the children. Panji's guilt is his own only. And their marriage was jodog, predestined. It was written before she was even born, was her nasib, her fate. Though I advised her against it so often, once it is done, we must accept it. In fact, her love for Panji was lost after he killed Guru Ali. But they had both given a vow, *sumpah*, that they would be true to each other and only marry each other in all of their life. The punishment for breaking such an oath is great, so Asiah did not dare to do that; it would have created a great guilt. No, our mother did not agree to the marriage either — but she does not care. I was thirteen years old when she left us: she had no pity for her children."

Rakkib, after a detailed exposition of guna-guna and the many clients who seek him, was also willing to tell his side of the story:

"I knew Panji and Asiah would be united, if after many difficulties, because their names, especially their first letters, are close. But the value of *A* is greater, so she will be the more dominant [*berani*, brave] of the two. . . . No, I have not helped Panji with guna-guna, only with motivation and advice. I have also worked on her father, Abdullah; I chose good and auspicious days to talk to him, and Abdullah's attitude had been improving. But he will never be content with the match, because by Islam a murderer is forever a blameworthy person and cannot be used as a legal witness. People in Pagatepan condemn him — but in time they will get over it. But Guru Ali's family will never forgive him. That is Islam: *qissas* for killing, an eye for an eye, cut off a hand for theft, like in Saudi Arabia.

"Asiah was cold toward Panji when he returned from prison — but she had known no other man; he was her first and only love. Since their initials were perfectly suited, I spoke to both and encouraged them. In the end, they lay together in her father's house. Perhaps by agreement between them, to create scandal: couples sometimes do that to force their parents to consent to the marriage, from shame and the fear of gossip. Or perhaps it was Panji who tried to seduce her to intercourse. Anyway, the little brother ran and told the father, who beat Asiah, and from anger and shame she demanded the merangkat.

"It had to be done very hurriedly, and Panji did not even inform his family. No, he made no attempt to have a girl in the party — which girl would have been willing to accompany us? I was mujati, I stood apart as Panji walked past the house. The father was away, it was 2:00 P.M., and Asiah had been prepared, by agreement, from noon; she stood by the door with a bundle of clothes ready, and came as soon as she saw him. When they had gone, I shouted the *pejati*, the message of merangkat, to the little brother. It is very difficult for Abdullah now, with his poor leg: Asiah was essential for him, and now he is helpless."

The cynic, who opened this series of fragments, at another occasion also noted this circumstance:

> "Perhaps Asiah simply could not face the drudgery of looking after her sick father any more. What other means of escape did she have?"

Through all of this, Abdullah remained adamant. When I finally picked up my courage to go and visit him, he turned out to be a small and slender man with great warmth and disarming directness. During several visits, he would talk expansively on most subjects and describe in detail the various theories of what was causing the chronic septic condition of his leg that was preventing his work as a carpenter: magic formulas written on metal plates buried in the ground under the footpath to his house; yellow rice served by a fellow workman at a slametan to celebrate the completion of a house; the curse of his Communist neighbours, against whom he stood up during the years of Sukarno's regime; a particularly virulent infection obtained when he fell off a scaffolding. He also gave charming, nostalgic glimpses of Asiah's childhood: how she looked after her baby brother; how he, Abdullah, scoured the countryside for milk after the children's mother had abandoned them, and little Asiah would warm the milk and feed the baby. He told elaborate stories of the intrigues that people had pursued when his elder son-in-law had been courting his daughter, which had caused misunderstandings between Abdullah and the new son-in-law at the time of that elopement. This time, Fatehul had been terribly rude, never even trying to negotiate on behalf of Panji, only arrogantly informing him what was going to happen. There is no doubt that Panji has used love magic: Asiah is not the kind of person who could love a murderer. Abdullah had claimed wang dapur from Panji because he himself had had to pay that for his son's Javanese bride. But no, he would never take Asiah back, and never lay eyes on Panji.

With these and other accounts accumulating, my conception of my task was slowly shifting. It would obviously be important to see the effects of differences in status and previous conflicts in refracting people's views and judgments, so as to describe positioning as a phenomenon in its own right *as well as* using it to critique the accounts I obtained so as to separate out what had really happened from the partisan embellishments. But I was slowly coming to recognize that there might not be a definitive version of the real events to extract. Not only would such an extract of what actually happened be always in doubt, and Panji's, Asiah's, and Abdullah's real reasons remain always elusive — there was even no reason to assume that such a "real" core would be particularly significant if it ever were established, or that such an account would not itself be a figment. I was reminded of Strindberg's "Miss Julie," with its enigmatic exploration of a similarly precipitous and calamitous event. In his introduction to this play, Strindberg wrote: "What will offend simple minds is that my plot is not simple, nor its point of view single. In real life an action — this, by the way, is a somewhat new discovery — is generally caused by a whole series of motives, more or less fundamental, but as a rule the spectator chooses just one of these — the one which his mind can most easily grasp or that does most credit to his intelligence" (Strindberg [1888] 1963:63).

My difficulties were in part caused by a similar idea that there was *one* extended case to retrieve: Truly different things had been happening in the minds of the different parties; different but parallel stories had been unfolding, because the events that composed them had been differently interpreted by participants at the very moments when they were taking place. An extended case would have to be a Rashomon story, like Kurosawa's film showing the events as seen through the eyes of each participant.

And it would also be false to decontextualize an account so that it was no longer addressed to a particular listener. Abdullah's most honest account to me, now, would never recapture his thoughts and reactions when on the morning after the daughter's elopement he woke up in an empty house, nor would his real thoughts now when speaking to me be the same as if he were now speaking to Asiah. Likewise, her reasons for choosing Panji would be honestly different when together with Panji from what they would be if she were facing her father when reflecting on them.

And finally, even such forms of ambiguity seem incomplete: a single person also appears to be capable of entertaining simultaneous, alternative interpretations of a single fact. Thus, there can be no doubt that Abdullah's septic leg condition was simultaneously nourishing his experience of the world as a dangerous place, potentially full of undiscovered sources of evil power and magic destruction; his memory of his enmity with an obnoxious fellow workman; his bad relations with his ex-Communist fellow villagers; and his knowledge of infections, antiseptics, and antibiotics. His illness also plays a key, but different, role simultaneously in his frustrating dependency on his balian friend Hajji Rahman, the hospital in Singaraja, and his

281

daughter Asiah, and in his private economic situation of chronic monetary shortage and rising expenses. Any small change in the degree of his disability will reverberate in quite distinctive ways in each of these relationships and be in a very real sense a different kind of fact in each connection.

What were Asiah's reasons? It makes little sense to review those mentioned in different accounts and then choose one as the significant reason for her decision to elope with Panji. She did not wish to discuss her situation with me — but then, I increasingly came to doubt that there could be an unambiguous answer from her, even had she wished to speak. Surely, to herself as well as to others, she instantiated all of the reasons that had been mentioned: guiltlessness and complicity; romantic love and sexual passion; disaffection with female drudgery and a rejection of too protracted sacrifice in the service of her father; the weight of an early vow and promise; the ever-present danger of love magic. No one could sort these out and "know" what one's own reasons were.

As for Panji, he had definitely committed a condemnable murder and was still paying for it. But even in his bad act, he and others could see different aspects and stress widely different circumstances: his victim was his own guru; he was provoked; he has been judged and has served his punishment; he is an outcaste; we must separate the issues; he is my good friend.

Was he now outside Islam, as many in this fiercely Muslim community branded him? I put the question to Guru Ali Akbar, the wizened, mercurial scholar and wizard who himself was being persecuted by the authorities in another connection for refusing to bow to any other than the true law of the Shariah: "Shariah is strict; *qissas*, talion, has the sanction of the Koran Sharif. Panji's guilt is great — but he is not outside Islam. Shariah says he should pay a camel in alms to the poor: slaughter it and give away all the meat to the hungry. Till then, he is guilty; and there are no camels in Bali! But God is merciful, and Panji will be forgiven. And who were we to prevent them, when their marriage was jodog?"

But how could the guru know that they were truly fated to marry? "Mankind sees only the surface; God alone knows what is inside. There is a Hadith: A murderer who had killed 99 persons went to a guru in desperation: 'Is there any forgiveness for a man who has killed 99 times?' 'No,' said the guru — and the man became so angry, he killed the guru. So he went to the angels and asked them: 'Is there any salvation for the murderer of 100?' 'Yes, there is a sacred well very far to the west; if you repent and drink its water, you can have absolution.' So the murderer set out for there; but on the way, he died. The people would not bury him, since he was an unabsolved murderer. The angels gathered to determine his fate; they said:

'He must go to Hell.' But the angel Rahmat said: 'Look where he was heading! For his intention, I will take him to Paradise.' "

In due course, time added even one more dimension of ambiguity. Two years later, when I returned for a second visit, Asiah and Panji were living with Abdullah. She had given birth to her first child, and lost it; Abdullah could provide several alternative explanations for the sudden cramps that had led to the death of the infant. She was expecting her second child; meanwhile, she prepared and sold snacks and lunches during recess in the nearby elementary school. Their economy was pressed, and Panji was supporting them by buying agricultural produce in the district and taking it to the market in Singaraja for sale. Much of the time he spent away, on his forays among outlying farmers, where he could obtain the best prices.

These circumstances now affected Abdullah's account of many of the events I have described. Though in giving these new accounts he is no doubt aware of suppressing certain aspects and events, I would judge it to be quite illusory to claim that he consistently knew better and could match the account that I can construct on the basis of my notes taken two years earlier. The relevant facts now providing the bases for his judgments and interpretations were themselves different from what they had been for him then: Asiah had never wanted to leave him and was not to blame; Fatehul had been intolerably rude and made him mad, otherwise he would have given his consent; people of Pagatepan spread slander about everybody and had always tried to make trouble for him. No doubt the same would hold for the other main parties involved and in the village at large, though memories would certainly still differ between these differently positioned persons. There is no reason to postulate a convergence of accounts — only that the past, despite its merciless consequences for the present, is itself constantly in flux.

My purpose in exploring this case was to further our understanding of how events are interpreted by the participants in them within a face-to-face community, and how experience and action are constituted in practice, given the diversity of traditions and paradigms within which they may be understood by people in this complex region of Buleleng. The story has produced some lessons and some continuing perplexities.

First, there is a level where the members of the community of Pagatepan share a set of schemas and scenarios for action: merangkat is a recognized, albeit impolite, way to get married; it requires a mujati and should include your own kinsmen and preferably also a woman in the elopement party; a mas kawin dowry is required, but wang dapur payment for the new bride's kitchen is not; to kill your own guru is a particularly bad form of murder. These particulars — both the terms and their conceptual contents — will, on the other hand, differ from community to community. This does not create insuperable problems for our description and analysis: it can be handled as a question of variable adat and awig-awig, custom and convention, which simply need to be known for each particular community. The less the anthropologist, or other stranger, knows about the people in the village, the more will the account be composed of such data, describing institutions and local expectations with regard to their practice, as did the first pages of this chapter. In fact, what passes among anthropologists as "thick description" (despite Geertz's own call for "inspecting events." Geertz 1973c:17; see also Jacobson 1991:109f.) may often be based on data mainly, or even entirely, from this level of discourse.

Such data are absolutely necessary; but they do not reveal what is happening among people. If we want to reproduce, and understand, their own interpretations of the intentions, morality, and consequences of acts, and thus the experiences that are emerging and accumulating among participants from the flow of events, we shall need other materials as well. The present case indicates two further forms of data that are necessary in the interpretation of these social facts: a considerable dossier on each interacting party, and a command of the major traditions of knowledge that are being deployed — in this particular case Islam, sorcery, and to some extent the modern sectors of law, medicine, and economy. Only with such keys in hand can we be attuned to people's real concerns and learn to handle the materials that go into their positioned interpretations of the significances and consequences of acts.

The resulting insights allow us to see that people, even within a small community, begin with different understandings and end up with different understandings; in the interval, they have constructed different experiences. Though these are far from random and their variation is not infinite, there is no clear evidence for a progressive convergence toward a broader consensus.

And genuine perplexities arise. What might be contained in that which I metaphorically called a "dossier" when we recognize that the past is also being rewritten? And what are the effects of experience as it accumulates through time? Though it may not produce a convergence as to what really happened, may it nonetheless nourish the participants' command of the shared traditions of knowledge I have identified? In my analyses in the preceding chapters, in which I constructed my account of each of these traditions, I linked the reproduction of each of them to its particular social organization, in terms of which it was being maintained and marginally refashioned. But does this imply that the other life experiences people have are without effects on the traditions they embrace, making each, as one might sometimes fear, invulnerable to falsification and modification from the events of everyday life? To answer such questions, we need to discover how whole persons, as remembering and reflecting agents, accumulate life experiences and embrace knowledge. Recognizing that most of these experiences will be socially embedded, this can only be done if we are able to depict the experiencing and reflecting person in the context of his or her social relationships.

This will be the task of the next chapter. I also refer to vivid materials portraying persons in such a fashion, though with a different theoretical agenda, given in Wikan (1990). These materials are particularly detailed in their portrayal of a young woman in a critical phase of her life. That allows me to focus my story on a slightly older man, with whom I could achieve a closer relationship of intimacy and empathy. With the limited format I have allowed myself, my treatment will privilege the theoretical argument I am developing and be illustrative only in its treatment of the empirical data. For a more comprehensive and compelling sense of the complexities and concerns of experienced life situations among people in Buleleng, I refer readers to Wikan's account. After exploring salient features in how the person I portray links his various life experiences and draws insights and lessons from them, I shall return to the vexing question of how such a person handles the coexisting and simultaneously embraced traditions of knowledge that presumably serve as competing paradigms for his interpretation of the events in his life.

17

So Many Concerns

The crucial step in any culturally informed analysis of life among North Balinese must be to obtain access to the culturally constructed reality in which they move. This means on the one hand to observe and depict the events that take place around and among people, and the actions of particular persons in these various situations; and then successfully to join them as they, through their own interpretations, endow these events with the meanings that become salient realities in their lives. Materials people use in this operation are provided by the knowledge and values they embrace. I have sought to present such materials in parts 1 through 4, with a view to exploring the degree of social and conceptual order they show.

However, a fundamental paradox arises when we recognize, as the story of Panji and Asiah has illustrated, the diversity of interpretations and judgments of the same events that differently positioned persons produce at different times. Whom should the ethnographer try to join for an insider's view of what is happening among them?

There is a sense in which one can argue for the primacy of the perspective of the actor at the time of action. A particular interpretation of the situation and the available options presumably shaped that particular act, determining its form and moment. But the consciousness of the actor at that moment cannot be definitely retrieved; nor does that consciousness determine the social meaning the act has to others, or its material and social consequences (see chapter 10). While we need the actor's perspective to model how action is generated, we also want the interpretations of participants and onlookers, so as to characterize the space in which actors move. Yet a construction by the analyst of that space on the basis of the ethnographer's primary data — for example, my analysis of "village society," "the Balinese," "knowledgeable experts," or "factions" — provides no escape from the paradox. It merely asks us to accept, in the place of any one Balinese subjectivity, one particular ethnographer's construction, more questionable and probably less representative than a fortuitously selected Balinese account. We must transcend this paradox by reconceptualizing the kind of questions we wish to ask and the answers we seek.

An inspection of the preceding materials provides some useful leads. Observe, for example, the case of Panji and Asiah: it shows a distinct convergence among participants — not in the judgments that are made and the particular interpretations that are chosen, but in the issues that are raised, in what is at stake. Should Panji be treated as inside or outside Islam? Had Asiah made a vow that bound her? Were we witnessing the unfolding of her considered acts or the consequences of love magic? Was village custom observed in the composition of the elopement party? Were others obligated to separate the issues? In the concerns of actors and audiences we recognize a particular, and significantly restricted, range of questions; participants can significantly disagree on them, but they provide parameters for the reality people are variously constructing. To interpret everyday practice along with participants, to join them in their sense of the reality in which they move, we need above all to be attuned to these concerns. And we can only become so by attending to the concerns of particular and positioned persons (see Wikan 1990: chap. 2) — not so as to elevate their judgments to authoritative statements of cultural dogma, but so as to discover what is generated of experience when the issues that arise in everyday life are shaped and handled in terms of these various Balinese concepts and concerns. And such concepts and concerns, of course, are what I have sought to locate as component elements in particular traditions of knowledge.

To reembed these traditions of knowledge where we found them, in the lives of people, and thereby to obtain a view of the experience of living in the world they inform, we thus must not shrink from looking at the particulars. On the contrary, we need to focus precisely on the fine details of the events that engage particular, positioned persons, the interpretations they give to those events, and the experience that thereby ensues. But in these particulars we should especially look for the recurring issues and concerns that arise and accompany being-in-the-world in North Bali. It is from such concerns that practice is shaped: the struggles to cope with everyday tasks and challenges, the shifts between different knowledge for different purposes, the scenarios that recur when picking one's way among others — all the existential problems of living a life in North Bali. Let us start, then, with events in the life of one person, and see how these events are understood, and thereby endowed with meaning.

Nyoman, whom we met briefly in chapter 14, is a man in his forties who so successfully personifies the Balinese ideal of gregariousness that as he drives his scooter along the road, at least one hand seems always busy waving and greeting friends and acquaintances.

> "Everybody likes me. They want to know me, and be my friends. I am a poor man, but I am rich because I have so many friends, everywhere. I am only sorry that I am poor, because then I cannot help them and be generous, as I wish to be. I don't want material things for myself; but I would like it that I could give to people.
>
> I am good at speaking with people. But I have never done as you do: speak to strangers and ask them questions. If you are pemangku, klian desa, then you have sakti, and can speak and be excused by the God; ordinary people cannot do that. We Balinese people are like that: always afraid to speak, in case we make a mistake, or say something that is not correct."

These ambiguous imperatives of sociability and respect are clearly refracted in Nyoman's attitudes to his Bali-Hindu gods:

> "You can enter the temple and pray for anything you like. Some pray for health, or success; some for a particular gift with a pledge if it is fulfilled; some pray and concentrate to obtain direct contact with God. This is not so easy: it requires deep concentration, and fearlessness. There may be a succession of guardians of the God who are gatekeepers for him: monsters, lions, and so on that threaten and attack you as you sit concentrating. You must be pure in thought, and face them and not lose confidence and run away. Finally, you may reach the God, and he will ask you what you want. In this pura segara [the sea temple where the conversation was taking place], the God appears as a very old man. But mostly, we are afraid, and only make offerings together with others at the appropriate times.
>
> "Up there in the temple, I felt like a gambler who has been lucky. We even came without an offering, and the God did not mind that either. It is not just that your intentions should be good: you must also not have made any ritual mistake — and who can be safe from that? But the God knew me, the difficulties I have had in my life, and could promise me success."

In the privacy of confidential conversations, one syndrome of concerns repeatedly surfaces as he reflects on himself as a person, on the temperament of various particular others, and on the connection between attitudes and actions.

"I like to be friends with all people, and kind to all. But I am bad, sometimes I become very angry. If people try to cheat me, I rush up; if they are fair, I like them very much.

"My wife always moves so slowly, is so soft, so patient. She is also always very good about trying to earn some extra money to help support the family. I am impatient, I move quickly and am sometimes angry. I know I am a bad person. So I decided, so that my children would not become bad like me, I must marry an exceptionally calm woman, and that is how I chose her. My eldest son is like her, very calm and patient. The daughter is a little more like me, the next son is too much like me — but better. The next daughter is like her mother, and then the next smallest daughter is most like me: she moves very quickly. But it came out as I had planned — the children are all a mixture of their parents, and do not have my bad character."

Such fragments of confidences cannot be taken to report Nyoman's interpretations at the time of action; what motivated his choice of spouse, for example, cannot be retrieved from this account. These are interpreted experiences. They may be his honest post hoc thoughts, as a reflective observer of himself; and they are of course censored by his desire to make his self-presentation not too compromising while judged to include appropriate tokens of trust and intimacy. But in any one of these stances he will be providing us with a cultural account of the events, and of concerns and values with currency among people in his circle.

Nyoman's ubiquitous concern to understand others, to take note of their temperament and idiosyncrasies and establish their unique positioning, manifests itself most explicitly in regard to his children.

"One night last year, I was visited in my dreams by my kaki [father's father] and dadong [father's mother]. Later, my wife thought she felt a baby moving inside, and went to the hospital to be tested. She was five months pregnant! She cried, and wanted an abortion; but the baby was too big, so it would be dangerous. And it was a miracle — ask Dokter X, he too said so: no child for seven years, and regular contraceptive injections every three months.

Perhaps it was a blessing from my grandparents. When our baby had her thirty-fifth-day celebration, we went to the balian to ask, 'Who is the child?' I did not tell him about my dream. The balian went into his shrine room, and came back almost immediately and said: 'The child has a birthmark on her back; it means she is your grandfather — also your grandmother, but inside she is really your grandfather, your grandmother just hovers outside, around her. It means he wanted to be reborn: never mind that you are poor, he chose it himself.' In fact, when my eldest daughter was married, she aborted after six months: that was probably my grandfather trying to be reborn already then. 'Once she has passed three months, you have no reason to be afraid for her health,' said the balian. And she is a very quiet and content baby.

"The balian has written out a whole page statement on her: who she is, what her name must be, the good birthmark on her back, that we must make an offering at Besakih when she is seven, or three, years old, with white and yellow cloth because she/her great-grandfather was pemangku. She will be very good luck for our family. Come to think of it, my daughter's abortion could not have been my grandfather wanting to be born then, because that was a different purusa [patriline]."

An immediately salient feature of these fragments is the way different traditions are applied and combined as Nyoman interprets the passing events and copes with them. In the lived context, the traditions of knowledge seem to coexist and intermesh, while yet providing identifiable and distinctive insights. Their respective theoretical frameworks are not fused, but the items of understanding they furnish are meshed in the interpreted and experienced events they illuminate. The lab test of the hospital, which he solicits, establishes the "fact" of pregnancy and the inadvisability of induced abortion; the balian whose expertise he likewise solicits establishes the "fact" of reincarnation and the precautions that follow from it. Each fact, in its consequences for further action, becomes inextricably enmeshed with facts deriving from other traditions of knowledge within each single life course.

Second, as the reader will sense increasingly through the following text, there is a complexity of vision in Nyoman's reflections, and an awareness that a single event may be seen and understood from a multiplicity of different perspectives and be relevant to a number of simultaneous concerns.

In his understanding of himself, Nyoman seems to exercise a constantly troubled moral sensibility, which he also directs at other persons in an effort to grasp and analyze their character. But in his judgment of himself, he also has access to his own unexpressed attitudes and feelings, and he is deeply concerned to harmonize them with his own acts, to compel himself to *be* moral, not just to *act* morally, as we might put it. His reflections in the aftermath of the boat race, given in chapter 10, have already brought out the importance placed on monitoring one's own feelings and being morally of one piece, *polos*. Likewise, after a chance encounter with a self-important person, he said:

> "Did you see: he spoke only to you and ignored me! He doesn't bother to show respect, for he knows I have a good heart. Another person might be offended, and make sorcery. Because he does not fear me, he can take advantage of me. But that's okay: I make myself not care."

On caring/not caring as a technique of self-control, see Wikan (1990). Nyoman's concern here has primarily to do with the important Balinese injunction of *ngabe keneh*, guiding one's feeling-thought or managing one's heart (ibid.:95–97). It articulates a constantly recurring concern to cultivate and compel one's attitudes and feelings, not just one's actions, in the direction of morality. Conflict is inimical to this deeply social conception of morality; and putting a brave face on difficult matters is a first step toward managing one's heart.

> "My mother lives with me. My father now lives with another lady, his third wife. If I have good luck, okay, if I have bad luck, okay, for I have three mothers!
>
> "I admire my wife. Sometimes, I am angry with my mother. But my wife, she is always calm.
>
> "I am just like my grandfather, they say: he had the same personality, so I must be a reincarnation of him. And also, I am like my father. But I want to take the good from him, and leave the bad. I am afraid: three wives! I must be careful! But he cares for them, each of his wives — not like some, who think only about the young wife, the new one."

His relationship to his father is a matter of recurrent concern.

> "My father's house where he lives — I do not want to think about it. It is my little [half-]brother's home. I want to come freely to the house of my father — but I do not know what will happen to it. In Bali, the father can do as he wishes with his property — but he should do it so there will not be strife among the children. Usually, only sons inherit, though if they are rich, parents may wish to make the life of

291

A medium, possessed by a deceased woman who has been called by surviving family for an extended consultation. Note the (male) medium's hairstyle and sitting position, indicating female gender of the possessing spirit, and the recorder to allow future replaying of the meeting with the beloved dead person.

their married daughters better too; or if there are only daughters, they can inherit before nephews, if they are unmarried. If they marry later, they keep the land, and the husband moves in. If the plot is small, it may go to only one heir. Better to wait with the division till after the cremation, so the dead person's soul is taken care of first.

"My father grew up with his father's elder brother, who had no children — not with his own brothers. His uncle had good land, and my father never thought of it, just took for granted that he would inherit that land. Then after uncle died, there was much disagreement between him and his brothers and cousins. Finally they went to a great balian, with a long beard [cf. p. 303]. I was brought along, though I was only a small boy. The uncle came and possessed the trance medium, and they asked him what he wanted them to do with the land. 'You know; why do you ask! My cucu [nephew] should have everything after me.' They talked and talked. My father finally said: 'We must do as you say, but please do not give this advice. It is bad advice for your descendants; there will always be trouble about this land. It is better you divide it between us.' Finally, the uncle agreed. But now, there is the same kind of trouble after my grandfather's death, and my father and his younger brother, they do not speak together. My cousins have asked me to intervene and make a settlement between our fathers. How can I, when they are our seniors? But perhaps, in time, I can try. It is always difficult. That is why many do a very expensive cremation – it is better to use the land for that, and buy new property for yourself.

"My father is a hard man, with hard ideas. But he is good when you understand him. When we were small, we were sometimes very poor, with no rice to eat, only banana and papaya. Father was in the army, and a guerrilla fighter against the Dutch, and then he became a policeman. He never took bribes or pressed money from people. Now they come and give him coffee and other products. I am proud that he was honest, a good policeman. Many are bad – and then afterwards when they retire people no longer respect them, saying, 'Be quiet, you are no longer policeman!' "

Indeed, the relations of Nyoman, his father, and his senior brother provide a theme to which he often returns, where social solidarity, moral judgment, and power and conflict of interests clash in recurring ways. The ambiguities of joint and separate interests intrude, and difficulties arise because of the simultaneous relevance of action to the pragmatics of property and management, and to the symbolics of authority, respect, and solidarity. Add to this the self-monitored concern to harmonize feeling and action, and matters may be experienced as complicated indeed.

"My brother does not trust father about why he should want to sell land now. My father, he gambles sometimes and plays Lotto for money; my brother does not approve. My father says: 'It makes me happy!' My brother says: 'You lose it, the money!' But father says he likes to use his money for that. So my brother does not trust him with this sale of land. I must convince him. I must go to him in Jakarta. It is important that I talk to him, can see his face while talking, and have plenty of time. My father says: 'Write him a letter, call him by telephone!' But I think no, I must go. My father is intelligent, but *hard*. I must be on my father's side, and support him.

"It went very well in Jakarta: my big brother agreed to sell all but two *ara* of the land. I let my father do most of the talking, but watched them both closely, and supported him. My big brother was watching *me* all the time — he does not trust my father. It was very good that I went: now it is settled. If my father had gone alone, it would never have been.

I asked my brother about buying the land I want so at Lovina. Truly he is sorry, but studies are so expensive, with his eldest daughter becoming a doctor and his son an engineer. My sister-in-law, she supported me. If you understand her, she is a good woman sometimes. I used to look after her when my brother was engaged to her but not here, and she was living in my village. That was difficult sometimes. But there are just us two full brothers; we must help each other and stay together.

"For a while I was having difficulties, and was very poor. I could not support many children; my brother with a big salary had only four. He invited my wife with our daughter, not yet six months, to Java. She stayed a few months; then when I came to fetch them, my brother said: 'I want to help you. If I send you money every month, then perhaps after a while, you will be resentful, or your wife will be resentful. Instead, I will adopt this child.' I was reluctant to give up my own baby. 'Are we not brothers?' he asked. 'Then we share everything, and she is also *my* child. You can say she is your child, and keep her, and that is okay. But then you cannot say I am your brother. If you wish to be my brother, okay, let our children be with me.' I thought about it. It was difficult, but it was my own choice. I told my wife what my brother had said. She cried, very loud, but agreed to do as I wished. Most husbands would just have told her: do this! But for family feeling, it is important that the wives of brothers agree. To my brother, I said: 'I must do as you say. I am afraid of you [i.e., must respect you]; even if father says no, I must do as you say.' Later, my son also went there, to school. I still feel it a little bit, and do not want to think about it, that they are my children. So now I usually say I have five children — the ones living with me only. The girl, she started calling us uncle and aunt, like her cousins do. That made me sad. Now that my elder son is there studying, he tells her better. She is fourteen years old now; three months ago she wrote us a letter, saying she is sorry.

"Now when we had our last baby, my brother and sister-in-law came visiting. Hugging the new child, my brother said, 'I love this child; we must have it!' But I said, 'No, definitely no — this is my toy!'

Now my brother is ashamed before me, because it is I who looks after our mother."

The relative priorities of material success and self-advancement, as compared to complying with authority and cultivating social relations and one's moral self, are unresolvable concerns that can cause constant worry. There is a general tendency to judge success by ideas deriving from the modern sector, and morality in terms of Bali-Hindu ideas.

"I had only high school; then my father told me to go into business. He made my brother enter the army — he is very successful there, whereas I am poor. I wanted the military too, and education — but my father said no, business for you.

"I went into business buying and selling rice and agricultural produce. Slowly, I saved up so I had my own working capital. Then the devaluation came; I lost it all. I should have held it in produce over the devaluation but did not know it was coming — I had just sold everything. I have tried everything: for a while I got up very early, cycled for miles to collect ducks' eggs, and sold them to dealers in the market. Then out there herding ducks all day in the wet fields with a rag on a stick! Most friends my age are rich now, besides having gotten an education. I am still poor, and my education has come from practical experience.

"I tried my hand as a real estate agent. Someone in a government job came to me about a lucky chance connected with a government purchase of land: we could be middlemen and make many million rupees. We agreed to go fifty-fifty, and even had our wives witness our agreement. After the deal, I received an envelope from him with fifty thousand only. I was very angry, went to him, and said: 'What is this?' He offered me twenty-five thousand more! My legs started shaking, I could not think, I could not see straight, I was very upset and became very confused. I had to quit that work. But I kept telling about the fraud, carefully, to many people. Finally, the man was demoted, and transferred away from Singaraja, and lost the house he had built from the profits!"

Apart from the implicit reference of just returns, karma pala, this introduces another constant concern: the effects of suppressed anger, frustration, and disappointment in producing "confusion" (Wikan 1990:182ff.), an inauspicious and ultimately life-threatening condition opposed to the ideal of "calmness." Besides the commitment to enhance the morality of your feeling-thought as well as your acts, Bali-Hindu medical knowledge also emphasizes the essential role of calmness to the welfare of the body (ibid.:181ff., 246f.). In picking his way and handling social relations, this represents another set of considerations Nyoman needs to have constantly in mind. A further example:

> "Once, I bought some hens and placed them with a friend in a village. I brought grains for them to eat: if each hen produced twenty chickens, they would fetch a very good price in a few months. I would visit sometimes to see how they were doing. The little ones grew, and I fed them from my hand. I started coming oftener and oftener, throwing grain to them, and they would come rushing up to me to greet me. The peasant wanted to sell them, but I said: 'Better to wait a little more!' After a while, difficulties started: I would count the chickens and find that some were missing, and the peasant would tell me sad stories of how this one was taken by a dog, that one was run over by a truck, his children were sick and he had slaughtered two for them, and so on. Every time, new stories of that kind. I got so upset, I had to leave them. There must be three hundred of them now if they have thrived and not been killed off. I don't care. I told him, they are all yours, just keep them! I was afraid what I might do, and then what about my family! Every time I went there, I would be so upset. Now I am in possession of my own peace of mind."

The changing emphasis on the priority of material profits and peace of mind does not reflect an indecision and vacillation on Nyoman's part, but swift action to counteract a sudden health threat. There is a need for constant vigilance to notice, and withdraw from, such dangerous and stressful experience. If the episode furthermore can be transformed, as in this case, into an amusing story that provides an occasion for laughter and gaiety among friends, this in itself will also contribute to reducing the danger (Wikan 1990.:188ff.).

The opposed obligations of many relationships create an acute problem of balancing conflicting demands, which threaten to pull you in opposed directions. Balinese social morality favors compliant solutions and friendly and socially constructive activities that aim to please all. Nyoman reflects on his experiences and the difficulties of being discriminating in accepting and fulfilling social obligations.

> "The village elected me as village headman. I was headman for eight years, while also trying to do business. I was a great success as headman, but it was very strenuous, I was so busy — that is why my eyes are still red: from too little sleep. I had five assistants to do night

security duty in the banjar. I felt so sorry for them. So I said: 'You sleep, just be ready to come when I call you.' And then *I* went around, patrolling at night. Once I caught four thieves. I fixed the wall of the pura and the roof of the assembly hall. The present headman does nothing, just lets it slide.

"But then my wife's third birth was twin boys. At first they were healthy, then at one and a half months they became sick. They spent seven days in hospital; but it was difficult having them there and the other children at home, and doing business and being headman and doing night patrols. Besides, the staff at the hospital did not look after them too nicely, and they were getting better. So I brought them home again. They seemed to continue to improve. But one evening, one of them cried and cried and had cramps. My wife tried to nurse him, but he would not take food. So she pressed the milk out, I fed it to him with a teaspoon, and he seemed to settle down. Then I rushed off on night patrol. I usually came back at 4:00 A.M. and showered; that morning, I was going to Gilimanuk before dawn to buy vegetables for resale. After showering, I looked at the twins: they were quiet. Then I discovered that one of them was dead — without even the mother having noticed it. The same evening, the other twin died.

"I decided I had to change. First you should look after your own family, then yourself, *then* everybody else. My friends have become rich, or at least somewhat prosperous, while I am still poor, from looking after everybody else. I am not vain, so that's okay; but one should work to make life better for one's family, above all. That is why I quit the village headmanship. They still wanted me to keep it.

"I was very sorry about the twins. I remembered that when my grandfather was losing his children, all dying, he made disorder with their birth-order names — and the children lived. Grandfather was a great balian and a pemangku. So when I lost my twins, who were numbers three and four, I did not want to keep the memory; so I named the *next* child number three again.

"I decided I wanted to learn more and open my mind to the world, so I took evening lessons in English for three years. The point is to be happy, to see that one's family is healthy, to be liked, to have good friends. What is the use of a lot of money if you are sick, if you are angry with other people, or if other people are angry with you? But I would *like* to have some money too. So some years ago, when I had saved a little, I bought a boat and snorkel equipment, on the advice of a friend. I hire it out to tourists at Lovina beach — now I have four boats. I have to spend some time there, finding customers for my boats; and I like meeting the people. But some tourists do bad things. When I started going there, my elder brother called me and warned me: 'You should be careful, not involve yourself in bad things.' I explained that I just went there to try and develop some business with the tourists. Later, when my brother came visiting, my father, my brother, and I were sitting around a table like this. I told my brother that the idea of Lovina had not been so bad, that I had now saved and invested and owned four boats for snorkeling.

"My brother started crying: 'Really, I misjudged you; I thought you were up to bad things. Truly, I want to help you! But I have so many expenses for our children's education. But I will help you with money, so you can buy the land you are wishing for in Lovina.' I only need a couple of ara, and a friend of mine may be willing to sell to me, in a good location. Perhaps the thing would be to make a travel bureau – there is none there. I could arrange tours with my boats, and buses to temples, and so on. But it is still only a dream."

But even in such a project, Nyoman is drawn into cross-pressures.

"I keep my boats on the beach by one of the hotels; the manager is my friend and has been helping me find customers. But now he has built a high wall against the next hotel inland, and they are quarreling. They have even written about it in the papers. It was wrong that he did not first discuss the *height* of the wall with his neighbor. And there is another big difficulty: he did not keep Nyepi, the day of silence, and now his staff has gone on strike and someone cut down the trees on the beach in front of his houses. I cannot go there for my boats; I am losing money. If two persons are enemies like that, one can be friends with both and try to reduce the conflict. Or refuse to become involved. One should help to maintain moderation, balance, and try to make harmony and unity. But it is very difficult. We Balinese are very sensitive, and you can easily make mistake. Then they remember it and become angry inside."

Besides the general dangers of conflict and turmoil, leading to "confusion," Nyoman is no doubt here concerned that he might happen to offend someone in this agitated situation and thereby evoke sorcery. This is the concern about which Nyoman will speak least freely (balians and dukuns engaged in black magic can hear what you say), but it may be a ubiquitous consideration (Wikan 1987, 1990). My sense is that a wish to step gingerly on this issue forms a significant part of Nyoman's motivation to be sociable, attentive, and analytically alert. It certainly looms as an always possible worst-case scenario of any infelicitous social encounter or ambivalent or deteriorating social relationship — and thus as a constant risk entailed in the performance of one's social roles. Nyoman's euphemism for this threat, however, is the danger of "angering" others, which often makes the reference to sorcery elusive. Moreover, if anger is expressed, and not pent up "inside," the chance of a sorcery response is reduced.

> "I introduced my cousin's daughter to a tourist. She fell madly in love with him, and started living with him. Her mother came to me, and was very angry with me for having brought them together. But the girl is adult, so I can hardly be blamed. Even so, I felt very shy [embarrassed] and have avoided any contact with them since."

At another occasion, Nyoman and I were conversing with an old friend of Nyoman's, who brought up his current dilemma:

> "The younger brother of my wife is already married twice. Now he wants me to be go-between to the parents of a third girl. I do not wish to refuse him. Yet I do not like to do it: maybe the first two wives will be angry with me; and maybe I will be held responsible when something goes wrong in the marriage. Really, I should not do it, rather counsel him to leave it."
>
> "Yes, we older persons should be wise, and not encourage plural marriage."
>
> "But I do not want to anger him by refusing to do it."
>
> "The safest is to keep postponing it, and thus avoid saying no to him."

Most of Nyoman's explicit accounts of sorcery experiences — in contrast to the majority of those I have obtained in Muslim Pagatepan, and also from Bali-Hindu persons in various other communities — involve close relatives and affines. Thus the linked stories of sorcery between collaterals recounted in chapter 15 report Nyoman's interpretations. Likewise:

> "My wife suffered for two whole months from *pusing* [headache, confusion, listlessness]. Finally we went to the balian. He made a symbol, laid in on a tray, placed me beside it, and then started drawing the sorcery out of her with his hands. When he had hold of it, he shouted 'Now!' and had me grab it and put it on the tray. Several times we repeated it; and then he took the tray and emptied it out at the crossroads. It was caused by her brother's wife, who is angry: my wife and I have good relations to my wife's mother, whereas she has

bad relations, and so she is jealous. While she was doing her magic, she kept coming to visit us. Now she never comes!"

The problems of managing social interaction successfully are thus greatly exacerbated. The mistakes you make that cause an anger that is forcefully expressed — uncomfortable and embarrassing as that may be — are less dangerous. More important is an eternal vigilance for small signs that some inadvertent offense may have caused unexpressed anger, or signs that your behavior has generated suppressed jealousy: these are the states of mind most liable to lead to sorcery action.

Let us now try to put ourselves in the position of Nyoman as he has to act, with these many simultaneous concerns, and under the cross-pressures of the social network in which he is positioned. A sense of how some of these strands come together can be obtained in one of the many recurring ceremonial situations that punctuate Bali-Hindu life: a particular odalan (calendrical festival) in Nyoman's descent group temple where I happened to be present. The festival was the first to follow after the group had evicted their collaterals, as recounted in chapter 15, and obviated that faction's attempted magic. A pedanda high priest was brought in to sanctify the newly refurbished temple. Nyoman and his family dressed in their very finest and joined the cooperative rituals in their various capacities. As Nyoman had anticipated, his father did not come, because of the acute conflict with his junior brother over inheritance. ("He should have come . . . But it is not necessary: I am married and have children, so I represent the family — he is senior generation only . . . But he is the pemangku, he should have been here.") In his place, his junior brother served as pemangku priest, leading the rites and blessing the congregation. (After the ceremony: "My father is hard, but my uncle is hard as stone. He keeps changing, saying one thing in front of you, something else behind your back.")

Family members greeted each other graciously and respectfully, smiling and acknowledging each one particularly, including children and affines. A procession with parasols, lights, and incense was sent out to fetch the gods into the temple. Once they were present, the congregation prayed in concert for blessing, prosperity, and health.

"We must honor them and act correctly in every way. They are our ancestors, and we must help them to come closer to God, become dewas. How can they do that if they are held back by worrying for their children, distracted by our concerns? There must be no strife, no anger. Yet it is opposite with angry people: they do not manage to make themselves calm when the ancestors are close — rather, they

Priests and family on the beach, bidding farewell to the ashes after cremation.

seem to *have to* fight and quarrel. Instead, we should *help* our ancestors. It is not the size of the offering, or the size of the ceremony, that makes it successful. It is the *heart*, the intention, that matters."

A special sacrificial meal had been laid out along the central passage of the temple. At each stage of the ritual, it was purified and blessed with mantras, incense, and holy water libations of various kinds. "Afterwards, the whole descent group will share it, celebrating unity by eating together," Nyoman explained with an apologetic and ironic smile.

My main argument should by now be well prepared. To ascertain the meaning of acts in a Balinese context, i.e., the experiential realities of living in the socially and culturally constructed space that Nyoman and others occupy, it is not enough to comprehend the semiotics of ritual elements, and the moral and eschatological axioms on which person and cosmos are constructed. We must place events in their lived context to be able to judge their significance, their interpreted meaning. Nyoman's father's absence from the odalan should not be dismissed as a mere imperfection of the ritual's instantiation, a wrinkle to be smoothed out and ignored in our in-

301

terpretation of what the rite is about. On the contrary, it was a key fact of Nyoman's experience, and of many others', a fact that will necessarily color what they learned or had confirmed from the occasion. It would be only a banal and incomplete insight to say that the odalan festival and its commensality celebrates the unity of the descent group, and truly misleading if it were left at that. Yes, there is an affirmation that unity should prevail. But *no* member of the congregation meets without the knowledge that the descent group is *not* united. So what is affirmed is that unity should have prevailed, that our responsibilities toward our ancestors — who are powerful and affect our lives — demand that we should make efforts to compose our differences. Participants also have demonstrated to them that the descent group *is* divided; that the world is full of evil, sorcery, and deceit; that humanity is never perfect. Yet the ritual must go on, for important matters are at stake, and the ancestors will only bless you if no ritual errors are made and the rite is accepted by the gods and pleases them. So one must struggle simultaneously on many fronts: be moral and graceful in one's performed acts, *and* try to compel one's heart, *and* comply willingly with the demands and compromises of convention, sociability, and morality.

> "But we must always struggle with this, to counteract the faults that are inevitable for humans, but that must be reduced, minimized. We must strive for *'asah, asih, asuh.'* Asah, like to sharpen a knife, always try to learn and improve. Asih, to love, not to nourish hate and enmity. Asuh, to look after everyone, to have goodness for them *all*. Because of karma pala: in the short run or in the long run, all bad acts have consequences, as also the good ones. But therefore, we must constantly be afraid. Not like the Muslim, who thinks that you can pray and then be forgiven for killing a man. Karma pala means you pray and pray an *still* cannot escape the consequences of your bad act."

Nyoman, with his personality and positioning, has a particular constellation of concerns and priorities; but in this central concern, he certainly does not seem to differ from most — indeed (despite his contrary understanding) including Balinese Muslims, who also share these concerns. His social skills allow him to feel more at ease than most in his everyday social relations, but this does not mean any relaxation of the need for careful observation and evaluation of the subjectivity of all those with whom he is in contact. His modest economic position, compared to his reference group, means that concern for material wealth may be more salient for him than for most. His social adroitness means that his concerns about sorcery focus more strongly on complex and stable relations, where envy and jealousy can take root, and less on the dangers of inadvertently offending others, which he can generally avoid. But most fundamental: the eternal project of turning conventional demands in on yourself, of making your heart obedient, of joining the forces that impinge on you and extract compliance, gaiety, friendliness, and conformity, seems to dominate the experience of partaking in life in North Bali for Nyoman, as for most others.

Bateson captures this ambience vividly in a little-noticed and underexploited insight in which he notes how "the individual Balinese is forever picking his way, like a tightrope walker, afraid at any moment lest he make some misstep" (Bateson [1949] 1972a: 120). Elsewhere he has taken this idea in a slightly different and less felicitous direction, suggesting that "they see the world as dangerous, and themselves as avoiding, by the endless rote behaviour of ritual and courtesy, the ever-present risk of *faux pas*. Their life is built upon fear, albeit that in general they enjoy fear. The positive value with which they endow their immediate acts, not looking for a goal, is somehow associated with this enjoyment of fear. It is the acrobat's enjoyment both of the thrill and of his own virtuosity in avoiding disaster" (Bateson [1942] 1972c:174).

We need not follow Bateson into this rather extreme position. My own evidence from North Bali is quite clearly that the ever-present dangers, and the eternal demands for alertness and virtuosity, are mostly experienced as troubling and stressful. "For us Balinese, there are so many concerns, so much to think about." We can best guard against misinterpretations, such as Bateson may have committed, by not abstracting a solitary actor but observing the pressures as they manifest themselves in the contexts where they occur: namely, in the relations between people, and in people's relations to an animated world and a panoply of gods, which all seem to be experienced as equally obtrusive and real.

Most immediate are the pressures of neighborhood gossip and control. Once while I was visiting with Nyoman, his cousin, accompanied by her no fewer than seven small children, burst into the room and started talking excitedly and loudly. She had fled, deciding to move temporarily out of her own spacious house, to escape the neighbors' watchfulness, jealousy, and gossiping. "We are friends and on good terms, but they want everything the same as we have. My husband is bank branch manager, they are just office workers, so they cannot afford it. But they watch us all the time, and copy everything!"

"It is better to keep some distance from the very beginning," explained

Nyoman. "I am on good terms with my neighbors; but I have built a high wall across the [very small] lot, partitioning it completely, and with the house backed up against that wall so that we are completely divided off."

Add to this invasive sociability the constant dangers of sorcery, the ubiquitous presence of potentially malevolent spirits and demons, the powerful and critical judgments of ancestors and gods, the demands of gaiety and dutifulness toward the collectivity, and the relentlessly accumulating karma ledger of all one's acts and thoughts — and one may obtain a sense of an oppressive life experience full of simultaneous concerns, in which one is constantly required to be vigilant and to navigate, please, and comply. In this situation, Bali-Hindu knowledge advises one to act on oneself rather than on one's environment, to become the agency of this aggregate faceless collectivity of pressures and train oneself in dutifulness and conformity. To a modern Western consciousness such pressures would probably be experienced as a denial of freedom ever to act in pursuance of one's own individual will and wish. I shall return in chapter 19 to key symbols that seem to articulate a Balinese experience of these issues.

18

Coherence, Hegemony, and Productivity in Knowledge

I have sought to focus the preceding chapters to highlight what I regard as two essential aspects of the materials: on the one hand, the coexistence in one region of deeply distinctive traditions of knowledge; on the other hand, the lives of people where facts variously established by means of one or another tradition of knowledge mesh in their individual activities, from moment to moment. Such facts, then, can be seen to arise in differently constructed "worlds" but to be part of one "life."

The problem I now wish to address is the relationship *between* these coexisting worlds: can we find systematic features in this condition of pluralism? That means asking questions such as these: how distinctive are these worlds in their construction; what is entailed in their meshing in everyday life; might there be patterns in practice or thought whereby they are interrelated in a more embracing system?

Human beings must use knowledge to cope in life: to interpret events, to anticipate future states of the world, to act on the world. As anthropologists we have been accustomed to employ a rather homogenizing and synthesizing concept of "culture" for the ideas the inhabitants of a region use for these purposes. But by thinking instead of these ideas as "knowledge," we are provoked to raise more detailed questions about important issues, which arise with particular force in the ethnography of Buleleng: the logical coherence or opposition of different clusters of ideas; their forms of validation; the sociology of their distribution; the specifics of their social reproduction; and the practice of their use.

I trust that my presentation, especially in chapters 11 through 15, has shown that several ontologically distinct and contradictory systems of knowledge coexist among the people of Buleleng and are employed by

305

them to interpret events. But how, so to speak, does a person know when to use which? And does the pluralism we see today show any degree of pattern and stability, or does it simply represent a stage or perhaps a moment of disorder, during the displacement of older traditions of knowledge by other and newer ones? In terms of received anthropological wisdom and a Western ethnotheory of history, one might expect such discontinuities within culture to be resolved through one or another meta-level of order:

(a) a separation of social groups, classes, and/or professions each maintaining its distinctive tradition of knowledge – i.e., a pattern of subcultures; (b) a set of conventions governing social situations which define distinctive contexts in which each tradition may be invoked – i.e., a functional order; (c) an inequality in the embracement and authority of different knowledge – i.e., a hierarchical ordering of traditions; (d) an open competitive field, where alternative paradigms are tested and in due course will be retained or discarded according to how adequately their representations can be ascertained to correspond to the real world.

The materials presented in the last two chapters should be sufficient to show that the first three of these schemata are too simple, though questions deriving from each are still left to be explored, as I shall do in a moment. But first, a short discussion of the fourth alternative may be needed. Briefly, it raises the question of whether there is – for Balinese as for us outside observers – any way to compare the validity of facts established by means of the use of different traditions of knowledge.

I am in danger of blundering into very murky philosophical waters, but I should not simply sidestep the issues. Do we wish to argue that any and every belief held by a group be regarded as "knowledge"? Are there no cross-culturally valid criteria for establishing truth, or for its invalidation? Might we perhaps need to distinguish some fundamentally different ways (rational, magical, poetic, religious) in which persons at different times view the world?

For most of our purposes, such questions miss the point. We should acknowledge that knowledge is always involved when people engage the world, whether by magic, worship, or whatever. But as for judging the truth and rationality of such knowledge, I should wish to join Putnam (1981) in his search for some middle ground between a total relativism and a "copy" theory of truth – the view that a statement is true only insofar as it "corresponds to the (mind independent) facts" (ibid.:ix). Putnam assumes a very close connection, but not identity, between the notions of *truth* and *rationality* and makes constructive use of the distinction between the two. He holds that the only criterion for what is a fact is what it is rational for a person to accept — given a context of available information at a time in history. His argument develops a powerful critique of a scientistic view of truth and rationality. "That rationality is defined by an ideal computer program is a scientistic theory inspired by the exact sciences; that it is simply defined by the local cultural norms is a scientistic theory inspired by anthropology. . . . Both sorts of scientism are attempts to evade the issue of giving a sane and human description of the scope of reason" (ibid.:126).

AN EXCURSION INTO KNOWLEDGE AND THE PHILOSOPHY OF SCIENCE

We should keep in mind my purpose with this discussion. I am seeking precisely such a sane and human description when I try to understand the role of different traditions of knowledge in the interpretations Balinese make of events; I wish to explore how such knowledge shapes understanding and action in the world; and I hope to show how it is itself in turn shaped by the action, and experience, of people. For such purposes, it is essential that our concepts of rationality and human judgment are not preempted by a narrowly scientific vision of knowledge and truth. And yet even to an anthropological readership it may be necessary to confront possible objections to treating these different, and ontologically incompatible, sets of Balinese "beliefs and practices" as traditions of "knowledge." My position on this builds on the discussion by Putnam just noted, and on the empirical study of practice in a scientific laboratory made by Latour and Woolgar ([1979] 1986).

Basic to my position is the view that technical, ritual, magical, poetic, meditative, or worshipful modalities are different ways in which people — Balinese, as the rest of us — engage the world. Involving as they do elaborate interpretations of events, each of these modalities must of necessity deploy knowledge, and also rationality. And several of the modalities may be found to be salient within any one tradition of knowledge.

But I do not have to ascribe the same kind of *truth value* to every tradition of knowledge. Putnam stresses the need to consider what is known and assumed at any particular time and place when one attempts to judge the rationality of a statement. This may be closer to the relativism practiced by most anthropologists than he seems to recognize. But at the same time, he allows us to embrace a "realist intuition," which permits the view that "a statement can be rationally acceptable *at a time* but not *true*" (Putnam 1981:x). "In short I am saying . . . that *truth is not the bottom line*: truth itself gets its life from our criteria of rational acceptability, and these are what we must look at if we wish to discover the values which are really implicit in science" (ibid.:130).

I find this very helpful in handling the reflexive problem anthropologists must always somehow confront. It allows me to retain for my own analytic purposes whatever critical criteria of acceptability I cherish in our anthropological tradition, while at the same time being open to traditions of knowledge that embrace other criteria of rational acceptability. The crunch of relativism comes in the critique of these criteria: they can be compared and will no doubt prove to have different powers, different strengths and weaknesses. But such a critique is not presently my concern, and I can claim to be on firm ground when I assert that whatever they are, they mediate rationality within the tradition and produce systematic knowledge — even in those cases where my intuition and conventions may tell me that particular items of the knowledge may not be "true."

Next, let us consider practice in what we have been taught to accept as the model of a rational and systematic tradition of knowledge, namely modern science, to learn what it takes to describe the criteria of rational acceptability in a tradition of knowledge. Latour and Woolgar ([1979] 1986), in their analysis of a biochemical laboratory under the leadership of the Nobel laureate Dr. Jonas Salk, document the profoundly social construction of the findings produced in this and similar laboratories. Not only do they show empirically that the facts "discovered" in the laboratory are not reflected — in Putnam's, and Kant's original, phraseology "copied" — from a mind-independent reality but are laboriously constructed by the stepwise reformulation of unsubstantiated hunches, loose ideas, and even false syllogisms (ibid.:173). They also show that the operative criterion for distinguishing a better formulation from a less satisfactory one lies, not in the rules of methodology whereby it is produced, but actually in its power to convince the scientist's peers (ibid.:131f.). Of course, criteria of supposed replicability and measure are embedded in this power, but so are personal credibility (ibid.:125, 194ff.), prejudice (ibid.:155), etc. — if only because the field is developing swiftly and the scientist who works by a lumbering methodicalness will fall hopelessly behind. In other words, rationality even in this tradition of hard science is guided by a historically particular aggregate of social conventions, only some of which will have the methodologically universal, principled character Putnam's discussion evokes. Latour and Woolgar also argue forcefully that the laboratory's findings are likewise valid only within a strictly confined set of conventions (ibid.:144f., 236f.), i.e., it is tied to a practice, like any other form of knowledge. To explain the structure and content of a tradition of knowledge, it is thus above all its field of social conventions we need to expose: its criteria and procedures for validation, and the particular practice with which it is connected.

We need also to go one step further and embed the particular tradition of knowledge in the broader social context where it is found. Note that the conventions governing the credibility of Dr. Salk's scientists are valid only within a small circle of specialists. A few minutes' walk from the laboratory one finds other people, in other circles, who maintain a robust world view anchored in a locally based identity and who feel free to mock and reject the truths of the scientists. The statement that "Thyrotropin Releasing Factor is Pyro-Glu-His-Pro-NH$_2$" — the laboratory's most important discovery at the time it was studied (ibid.:147) — would not fare well in the local pub.

Such a situation will probably appear counterintuitive to most academic readers. Persons in the educated middle class have been systematically trained to identify vicariously with specialists of many kinds and to accept the objective truth of statements that may, on the face of it and in terms of the knowledge any one of us commands, sound frankly outrageous and absurd — so long as they appear to be underwritten by authoritative scholarship. But other people may be able to resist the hegemony that we accept and to relate in diverse and robust ways to plural traditions of knowledge. Martin (1987) reports class differences in the degree of abdication to medical authority in urban U.S. populations; and Scott (1985) has demonstrated the presence of a variety of resistance and compliance within a strongly stratified community in Malaysia. All I urge at this stage is that we retain a consciously open mind and seek to discover, in each case, how particular persons or populations actually cope in the face of ontological incompatibility between coexisting traditions.

We can derive three conclusions from this brief excursion into philosophy and science. (1) There may be deep variations in the criteria for judging the validity of the kinds of knowledge accepted in a local population, particularly as between different circles and between specialists and nonspecialists. (2) Knowledge produced within a tradition of knowledge is judged by criteria of validation that are internal to that tradition and not necessarily embraced in other contexts or by the population at large. (3) There may be relations of inequality between different traditions of knowledge, whereby some persons will grant hegemony to knowledge from one of the traditions — at times quite independently of the actual extent to which they themselves have a command of the knowledge in question.

THE QUESTION OF PATTERN IN THE PLURALITY

Bearing these conclusions in mind, we will recognize that the description of knowledge in terms of its forms of social acceptance, participation, and embracement can be a matter of considerable complexity. Yet these need to be sorted out to discover how knowledge actually shapes experience for differently positioned persons, and how this in turn acts back on the construction and reproduction of knowledge in a complex and large-scale society.

A special problematic arises for the five major traditions I have discussed from Buleleng, in that they overlap substantively in their relevance to questions of the human person, morality, and eschatology; i.e., the cosmologies they construct are all anthropocentric, or indeed markedly egocentric, and treat the self, others, and social relations as objects of knowledge. How does the coexistence of substantively overlapping, yet ontologically incompatible, traditions affect people's use of them in interpreting the events of their lives?

First, it is striking that people seem to have few problems with incompatibility. Even where, as in Islam, explicit dogma disallows constructs deriving from Bali-Hinduism — such as ancestral spirits, multiple gods, and karma — many Muslims are prepared to accept their existence; and a considerable effort from more purist experts and partisans is expended in attempts to keep syncretism at bay. The same openness was also illustrated in Nyoman's acceptance of facts deriving from different traditions, described in the preceding chapter.

Wikan (1990:210ff.) tells the story of a schoolteacher of our acquaintance, Wayan Wijaya, who took it on himself to demonstrate to his pupils the nonexistence of jerangkong, a category of ghosts or spooks. Such constructs are part of sorcery knowledge and marginally also of Bali-Hinduism and traditional Islam; but they were disallowed in his conception of modernism. He took his class to camp overnight in a Muslim graveyard to prove his point and raise their level of self-reliance and critical faculties. Not only was the effort a sorry failure, in that terrified pupils could report ghostly experiences after they had fled home to their parents; his initiative was also broadly condemned as subversiveness and lunacy, and he was dismissed, with severe consequences for his family and himself. Several reasons may have contributed to the harsh social reactions he suffered for his self-appointed mission; but one was certainly that such a meshing of facts from ontologically incompatible traditions of knowledge is a regular feature of North Balinese lives.

But how does a person resolve the enigma of when to use which of several possible schemata of interpretation? A plausible hypothesis might be that, at least to each single person, they are hierarchically ordered: if the collision between them becomes apparent, one tradition takes precedence over the others.

I have tried to scan Wikan's and my combined materials on persons whom we know well, in situations that seem to have this nature, and I fail to see any empirical order emerge. From one perspective, it might seem that sorcery serves as a court of last resort, and thus as the final authority: once it has been made salient, it appears to be difficult for people to abandon. But quite as often, events with the same potential for sorcery interpretation are stubbornly treated in the framework of the theory of emotions as health threats, or as spirit attacks caused by accidental provocation or ritual error. And the same person may for an apparently similar set of events turn to a rhetoric of morality and karma in a final appeal. What is more, as we saw in the case of Panji and Asiah, nothing is truly "final" in these matters: judgments can always be revised, and many of them seem to run through a long history of flux as they slowly lose their saliency. The idea that there must be a pattern, a settled hierarchy, is a compulsion we may share with schoolteacher Wayan, but apparently not with most Balinese.

Moreover, not only are these matters situationally predicated in Bali, they are also deeply social. A partly predictable, partly fortuitous circle of others will inevitably be involved in assessing such events, imposing their cacophony on the interpretation process of the individual and pushing it now in one, now in another direction. And to respond as a "polite" Balinese should is to listen, and to bend with the pressures, till you would have no way of ever knowing what your own hierarchy and mind might be. Only rarely does one see a person take a stubbornly individual stand, and then usually to that person's painful public detriment. Living with such pressures, the best refuge is, as so often in Bali, to work at modifying yourself rather than your surroundings, and to compel your heart to compliance with what emerges as general opinion. For me to analyze these issues as if they entailed the kind of solitary acts of moral and epistemological bravado in which a Western tradition of philosophy revels would be to distort them out of all recognition.

CULTURAL HEGEMONY WITHIN PAGATEPAN

In the community of Pagatepan, on the other hand, we do find Muslim discourse taking the dominant place, and all the evidence indicates an even more dominant place for it in the recent past. What may be the reasons for this dominance, and how has it been maintained?

It is no doubt relevant to the authority of Islam there that Pagatepan, as a Muslim community, exists self-consciously as an island of true Faith in a sea of pagans, ever present as an external threat. It is also relevant that Islam is so strongly founded on the single text of the Koran, claims to provide a blueprint for a complete human life, and is propagated as a body of knowledge by an elite of guru teachers (see also Barth 1990). But I see the key to its relative hegemony above all in the social conventions within which its practice is embedded: the particular social organization that makes knowing Islam into a winning game by a synergy of elite selection, payoffs, and peer controls.

Let me retrieve the main features of this organization (noted in chapters 3 and 11). Boys of the whole age cohort of Pagatepan are progressively screened for intellectual merit through a competitive training in Islam scholarship, which extends over a number of years and is clearly quite demanding. It requires only a modest material investment on the part of the candidate's family, but one made over many years, thus testing the youth's fortitude as well as his abilities. By the time he returns to Pagatepan from his studies in Lombok, Java, or Mecca as an accomplished scholar of Islam, Arabic, and magic, the successful student will be at least in his middle twenties. But at that point, the investments in his support from his family, and his own studies, start bearing fruit. In the words of one cynic: "He may have studied hard; but from the day such a person returns home, he never again does a day's work." His religious and moral duty is to teach Islam; and for doing so, he receives merit from God (pala). From villagers he will simultaneously receive voluntary labor (nulungin) and free gifts (siddiqah), as well as the daily attentions of his pupils. After a year or two, he will also normally be given a wife as siddiqah — if he is fortunate and promising, a daughter of one of the senior scholars of the circle to which he aspires. In that case, his father-in-law will be able to advise him and further his career in a way that his own father neither could nor would. If he handles his social relations with any degree of adroitness, he will progressively be drawn into active administration of mosque and wakaf lands, thereby increasing the number of forums where he visibly participates in shaping authoritative decisions.

The basic pattern of circulation into which he enters is one of generalized exchange: as guru he gives freely of the higher forms of value he possesses — sacred knowledge (ilmu) and blessing (barkat) — while the members of the community reciprocate with inferior forms of value — material gifts, labor for his land, and occasional grants of land. Thus there is no direct exchange whereby values in these two different spheres are made comparable: knowledge of Islam remains categorically supreme. The guru gives of this precious bounty to anyone who is in need and will listen; people give him labor and crops as he may need them, or from a thankful heart. This generalized exchange enables the scholar to concentrate entirely on his spiritual vocation, and it avoids the impression of any direct comparability on spiritual and material prestations (Barth 1990).

In addition, the person in possession of sacred knowledge may also engage in the darker aspect of its use in the role of dukun, as healer and magician. This takes the form of restricted exchange, whereby particular services are recompensed by ritual gifts, dependence, and gifts of money according to a conventional scale, without explicit requests or bargaining but adding up to an appreciable income to anyone recognized as a notable dukun.

Sacred knowledge thus not only places its possessor in the religious elite of scholars, teachers, and magicians and makes him party to symbolic exchanges that accumulate as rank and dominance; it also tends to elevate him into the economic elite through the greatly enhanced chances it gives him to accumulate wealth. His expenses are small, his sources of income significant, and he has access to free labor. It is not regarded as suitable in Pagatepan for religious scholars to engage in trade; but they are free to place their savings in land. And with access to free labor such land can only serve further to increase the scholar's material surplus. Add to this a religious ideology that discourages most daily forms of material ostentation, and thus the dissipation of wealth, and we understand why the religious elite is found almost entirely in the landowning sector of the population: not so much because they have their origins there as because they, regardless of their origins, swiftly rise to it. The traditional conversions made of excess wealth were in the form of Hajj pilgrimage, merit-giving wakaf donations, and secular feasts-of-merit redistributing food to the community at large.

Finally, as scholars of the law they are the only possible candidates to participate in the Majlis Ulama and thus gain access to that central organ of political power. With their influence over disciples and clients, their rank and merit, and the threat of their magic, they become overwhelming contenders to leadership. Briefly, all threads seem to converge in their hands.

No wonder, then, that the tradition of knowledge they propagate has been accepted as hegemonic in the community. In the mythology of past events, action by the community is represented as action by a faceless, magically empowered Ulama. Within the village precincts, Hinduism is banned, caste denied, and sorcery co-opted; as for modernity, the super-ordinate criterion for judging its validity, as for all forms of knowledge, is its perceived compatibility with Islam. On this point, many will reserve judgment with regard to the curriculum of the modern public school system; the laws of the nation are censored by the law of Islam (as in Guru Ali Akbar's stand on legal marriage), and the forms of artistry and entertainment are limited in accordance with it. I would suggest that this hegemony has not been maintained because of the epistemological force of Islam, but because of the demonstrated force of its social practice. I shall return shortly to how this conclusion is vindicated by the dynamics of the contemporary crumbling of its hegemony.

THE FORCE OF BALI-HINDUISM

In most North Balinese communities, on the other hand, Bali-Hinduism is ascendant; and a measure of its local strength and vitality is suggested by the history of its unique persistence as an embattled but tenacious survival in only Bali and parts of Lombok among all of Southeast Asia. Previous anthropological descriptions of Bali have represented Bali-Hinduism as the core, and indeed almost the whole, of Balinese culture. Should we then regard it as somehow hegemonic in most Balinese communities, and in the region as a whole?

The criterion I have suggested for cultural hegemony is that the hegemonic tradition is regarded as delivering the authoritative, final criteria for the validity of knowledge wherever possible interpretations of the events of life clash. To judge the issue, we thus need to identify the criteria of validity on which Bali-Hindu knowledge is based, and then investigate whether these criteria are also used by people to critique knowledge generated in other traditions.

We can first approach this by observing just where authoritative statements arise within the tradition. As we saw in chapter 12, this is very different in Bali-Hinduism and in Islam. While Muslim debate converges on the Koran as the only ultimate authority, Bali-Hindu authorities appear manifold. There are the sacred lontar manuscripts of various sorts—but access to each particular manuscript has traditionally been limited to ritual occasions within appropriate family lines or village congregations. As a body of literature, then, the lontars cannot provide a stable authority toward which discourse will converge.

Pedanda high priests have extremely high positions of respect and sacrality, and they are entered by the High God Siwa himself during the liturgy of creating holy water; but this very sacrality limits their impact on

314

mainstream religious thought, and in many communities they are excluded from all participation. Perhaps when the king of Buleleng was in power, their role as advisors to the king gave them more effective authority; but for the last century and more, they cannot have served as ultimate arbiters of valid knowledge in Buleleng.

The various kinds of pemangkus, temple priests in villages, subaks, and descent groups, are accepted authorities in their communities and direct the mainstream of religiosity. But considering how they are chosen, and lacking as they are in any centers of learning and systematics of training, it is far from clear what criteria of acceptability of knowledge they would sustain. Other specialists, such as healers and puppeteers, are in even less of a position to articulate a core set of criteria of acceptability.

Finally, there are the divinities themselves, whose authority certainly cannot be denied in a tradition celebrating their power and devoted to their worship. The fact that these divinities, from the most immediate ancestors to the High Gods of Cosmos, appear and speak discursively through persons in trance on a variety of topics in thousands of temples and other locales must pose a staggering challenge to the coherence and integrity of the tradition of knowledge in which they so authoritatively intervene. It is indeed difficult to identify the rational criteria of acceptability, or the limitations of social convention, that could survive such an onslaught of continuous, decentralized revelation from multiple gods through an uncoordinated and largely untrained plurality of inspired priests and trance-possessed mediums.

Yet in posing the problem in this fashion, I may have misled my readers into accepting a spurious conundrum. We accepted the argument that the criteria of rational acceptability that obtained within a circle of biochemical scientists were specific and lodged in the social conventions embraced within that circle. So it must be in any other tradition of knowledge. Since we know that Bali-Hinduism has flourished for generations under its particular pattern of organization, that must mean that such an organization does indeed assure the reproduction of the critical criteria and degree of coherence Bali-Hindu knowledge requires. Differently constituted traditions will presumably be based on different criteria, in each case embedded in their social organization and critical for their reproduction: our conundrum is dissolved when we recognize that the very criteria of coherence and rational acceptability embraced by Bali-Hindus are distinctive and allow forms of productivity those who embrace other traditions would eschew. Thus, for example, those who embrace Islam defend its integrity by categorically denying the possibility and validity of any further revelations. Not so Bali-Hinduism: in this respect, it seems more like Western science in allowing continual innovation and development in its body of knowledge. But one can hardly imagine, say, that a body of scientific chemical knowledge could be reproduced and developed, in accordance with its present internal criteria of rational acceptability, within a social organization composed like that of Bali-Hinduism. What might be the characteristic criteria of rational acceptability that Bali-Hindu organization ensures, and within which it flourishes as a tradition?

Mark Hobart addresses this issue on the basis of his superb ethnography from a South Balinese village, in a series of essays simultaneously discussing some of the thorniest philosophical problems of anthropological practice (Hobart 1983, 1985a, 1986b, 1986c, 1986e). First, we have noted his rendering of the distinction between sekala (visible, embodied) and niskala (invisible, unmanifest) (Hobart 1985a:112ff.). This distinction corresponds to neither present and absent nor true and false; and the two states are not dichotomous but overlapping. "The unmanifest may be invisible; it may be visible but not present; it may be present as an aspect of, or hidden within, what is visible" (ibid.:112). Thus Godhead, time but not space, another person's unexpressed thoughts, and the future are all in the category of unmanifest. Hobart stresses the ontological and epistemological gap between it and the manifest; yet the point is, the world as constructed by Bali-Hindu knowledge is full of specific constructs that are niskala — unknown and unknowably in the world, but at any moment capable of breaking in and acting on that which is sekala, and thereby becoming in that sense manifest and knowable. This must make all knowledge profoundly contingent, and constructs a world of very low predictability.

Second, the apparently stable objects in the world are, according to Bali-Hindu metaphysics, all continually changing: coming about, being sustained, and being dissolved — the principles of which Brahma, Wisnu, and Iswara are manifestations. In this Heraklitian world, moreover, an object that diverges too much toward one extreme is particularly liable to flip to its opposite (Hobart 1986e:3).

Finally, an object or phenomenon can often be recognized as being a manifestation of something else. This adds a network of correspondences, linking phenomena that may be overtly very different but are really manifestations of the same.

Obviously, these metaphysical principles may be understood with considerably greater, or even less, subtlety by various Balinese, in various connections, than I have been capable of indicating here. This adds the further diversity of positioning to the kinds of statements about the world that will be acceptable within a Bali-Hindu framework of criteria of validity. It seems to me that, given these criteria, hardly *any* statement that might be made by a priest ex officio, or a medium during trance possession, could possibly challenge or threaten the Bali-Hindu cosmology. This certainly does not mean that any statement is as good as any other. Bali-Hinduism by its constructs and axioms yields moving performances as well as humdrum ceremony; it enables the expression of highly perceptive and analytical statements and of superficial homilies; it can convey a wide range of insights into morality, personhood, and the human condition. Its main force, it seems to me, is its productivity, not its stringency.

If Bali-Hindu knowledge were directed as a striving toward becoming a unitary science based on a minimal set of axioms, it could neither sustain itself by its present social organization nor construct much of a world by means of its current criteria of rational acceptability. But the conundrum I introduced above does not arise: Bali-Hindu imagery is a vehicle for a differently constituted way of making sense of life, and its vitality is reproduced precisely by its intricate and decentered social organization. The spirituality of which I spoke in chapter 12 proves immensely productive precisely due to this fitness of conception and organization, and it infuses Bali-Hindu discourse and practice with compelling validity.

There is thus much power in a Bali-Hindu construction of the world. Its main areas of practice are found in the observation of sociability, community, and human decency; in personal relations and relations to one's close departed; in the interpretation of the microcosm of inner life, subjectivity, and life cycle, and the macrocosm of life processes and Godhead; not to speak of ubiquitous concerns of illness and healing. All of these are powerful fields for experiencing its validity. But when Bali-Hinduism also seems to permeate most other fields of life in many North Balinese communities, I would argue that this is not from a position of hegemony, whereby its standards of rational credibility are imposed on the knowledge of other traditions, but from the sheer poetic force of its imagery. The power of sorcery can movingly be represented as deriving from Siwa's love, because of his enigmatic fusion of life-giving with death and destruction; and Tantric fantasies can impregnate and eternally enrich the forms of expression in folk magic. Caste identity is wrought in Bali-Hindu terms because thus it is made most poetically compelling, as were kingship and the government of old. The Pancasila of modern Indonesia's constitution, the social morality of schoolroom theory and practice, and the arts conveying modern identity all benefit from the force of its prolix imagery. Indeed, even the celebration of the Prophet Mohammed's birthday in Pagatepan is largely cast in the poetics of Bali-Hindu symbolism — without thereby challenging Islamic knowledge. The point is, despite a use of Bali-Hindu imagery, each of these other fields of practice is above all sustained by

317

interpretations based on other traditions of knowledge not closely linked with Bali-Hindu authorities or criteria of validity.

CHANGE AND THE MODERN SECTOR

We can add to our insight into how the disparate traditions interrelate by also dwelling briefly on the modern sector as a candidate for hegemony among the traditions of knowledge in Buleleng. There is no doubt that the modern state of Indonesia has completely eclipsed all other political formations above the village level; that modern education shapes the ambitions and minds of the youth; that mass communication imprints its images increasingly on North Balinese consciousness; that the population is physically served and moved by modern technology; and that the world market sovereignly wreaks prosperity and disaster in their material lives. Yet this does not necessarily mean that modernity is hegemonic in the minds of people, that it delivers the ultimate criteria by which *they* judge the rational acceptability of categories, constructs, and facts. Indeed, judging this question correctly may be even more difficult when we see what we may wish to identify as compelling forces of causality, perhaps even the inevitable march of history.

Thus Nyoman, portrayed in the preceding chapter, certainly holds a modernist concern for material prosperity more saliently than most North Balinese. Yet in his practice we see that considerations deriving from other frameworks of interpretation arise and can take over — as in his attempted enterprise of chicken farming and the even more important investments he had made in his boats, which he left unattended to avoid conflict. In the latter case, he would even on occasion vent his frustration and argue that his interests in profit should be allowed to take priority: he was *not* involved in the conflicts surrounding the hotel owner, and soliciting tourists for diving trips would in no sense be to support one side in the local conflict. Yet the world of facts he constructed was not one of modernist hegemony: legitimate economic interests proved secondary to a harmony model of social forces, his concerns about emotion and confusion, and his need to comply to majority pressure.

Likewise, even modern Jakarta is interpreted by Nyoman as an enchanted place:

"My son asked for the use of a special ring, which is very sakti, because he needed it so in Jakarta. I thought no, but my father said yes, you should — so I gave it to him. My dog originally found it, one morning just outside the family temple; in fact the place had been

318

inside the temple before they built the road. I knew it must be old, powerful, and it made me feel different just to wear it. Jero Balian says it is more than two hundred years old. When my son got it, strange things started happening: at night, a very old man came twice and tried to strangle him; if he had not woken up he would have been dead. In a traffic accident, he came through unscathed. Then, one morning on his way to work, he suddenly noticed he had lost it. He stopped the bemo and went back looking for it. He found it there in the street — so many people passing by and no one had seen it: it was invisible to them and only visible to him! It had been run over by a car, too — but the stone was whole, even though the setting was broken!"

Thus hegemony should not be read simply from the observed fact that lives seem dominated by circumstances arising in the modern sector: it is a question of which frameworks of knowledge people use to establish valid facts. Scott (1985:304ff.) develops this caveat very convincingly, as when he argues that "what we should not do ... is to infer ideological support even from the most faithful compliance" (ibid.:325). Hidden behind such compliance may be a diversity of less immediately visible, but coexisting, models, commitments, and worlds. In a crude sense, this has already been demonstrated in recent Indonesian history: where social science tended to see a unified New Nation emerging under the political and cultural hegemony of Sukarno's regime, the sudden political changes in the center in 1965 made visible the pluralism and incoherencies that had been alive under the surface (see Geertz [1971] 1973e:234–54 for a discussion of this problematics). We need to be far more sensitive to the diversity within and between people's minds, the various ways they always have sustained ontologically incompatible systems of knowledge, and the multiple ways in which their acts and their practice can be interpreted, by themselves as well as by others.

What can we say, then, of how such discrepant systems coexist and how they change? First, we should be realistic about the way an outer reality imposes itself: physically, it affects human beings as myriad ad hoc events; the causality and systematics of these events is something *they* must construct by interpreting events as linked up in classes, causal chains, or syndromes. It is a miracle of human cultural construction that "the meaningless infinity of the world process" (Weber 1949:81) can appear to us with any degree of orderliness: events as they happen around us do not of themselves instantiate principles, and they impinge upon us in entirely unsystematic fashion. Yet we try to act on the world, because we are part of it and have vital interests and concerns in it. Our means to achieve intended effects, and to understand what is happening, is our cultural knowledge, which we collectively elaborate and connect, and individually learn through precept and experience. But to map the degree of systematicity of knowledge in any group of people we must recognize that the bottom line for people when attending to their interests is not principles, but pragmatics. There is nothing inherently necessary or universal in the vision of a unified science, the idea that knowledge should form a consistent body embracing everything: all we need so as to operate as human beings is knowledge in handy bits, to use to interpret events as they occur, to make sense of them and to be able to act in a way that looks after our concerns. There may be comfort in reducing the precariousness of living in such an eternally episodic swirl of events, which means that people may favor constructions that facilitate a recognition of events as belonging in larger classes and interlinked in chains, of recurrence and predictability. But the ideal of comprehensive consistency need not be an aim, and the assumption of its necessity would represent a scientistic interpolation in any comparative view of human knowledge.

So people can live with a lack of consistency in knowledge. But it may be troublesome to live with an embarrassment of riches, as North Balinese seem to do, where several incompatible paradigms seem equally applicable to particular events. Perhaps a close observation of small incidents in the current crumbling of the hegemony of Islam in Pagatepan can best teach us how people, in their humdrum lives, handle what I have elevated to an epistemological enigma: how to know when to use what knowledge.

THE CRUMBLING OF ISLAMIC HEGEMONY IN PAGATEPAN

My description of the situation in Pagatepan as one of relative Islamic hegemony is not a claim for the purity of the Islam that obtains in that community; it only asserts that people there have largely converged on an Islamic debate as the ultimate test of the validity of knowledge and facts in all aspects of life. Indeed, whatever degree of syncretism can be found in traditional customs may rather be read as an expression precisely of that acceptance of hegemony: that they tested and incorporated other ideas into their understanding of Islam.

As noted, the particular organization of this tradition is such that its local expression is closely connected with cosmopolitan discourse (see especially chapter 11). Ideas from distant Islamic centers have their constant local precipitate, and flux can only effectively be arrested by intellectual strength, in a debate converging on the text of the Koran. Presently, as we have noted, local views are under pressure from a Muhammadiya interpretation, which actually seems to construct a narrower, less rich and all-embracing cosmology than that fashioned in the more syncretic traditional interpretation. Yet this in itself does not seem to be the source of a weakening of hegemony; rather, on the contrary, it may serve to revitalize the commitment of some.

The erosion of hegemony in Pagatepan arises in daily life from practice and small life choices, not from an explicit, analytical discourse. Young persons postpone marriage and forsake subsistence production for money income so as to buy a wristwatch, or even only a new shirt, to enhance their modern identity. This only obliquely denies the primacy of Islam — but it enlarges the sector of life and involvement in which Islamic knowledge has no relevance. Some children have at best only a pro forma relationship to a guru. They attend regular elementary school and fail to turn up to both their guru's classes and his labor calls, whether through a failure of their parents' control or with their implicit connivance. Other career trajectories — vocational training and prestigious government jobs — emerge as tempting alternatives to the traditional apprenticeship to religious teachers in a succession of pesantrens, leading further into a world where the knowledge of the gurus is less relevant.

Through such acts and orientations people are, so to speak, voting with their feet rather than engaging in any ontological and theological debate; yet thereby they are all the more effectively and discreetly dismantling the hegemony of yore. I do not think we should trace this to a conjectured source in a new resistance to the traditional elite. There has probably always been resistance: the power of old, pious, and repressive gurus was certainly always resented, as seen in the brief discussion of the "minder," i.e., inferiority complex, they elicited, or the often vicious way they are popularly satirized and defamed in old anecdotes. What is new is rather the fact of visible life options that are located outside the turf of the gurus. The authority of gurus crumbles because today there are things going on out there that are visible to all and that the gurus clearly do not understand.

Some gurus bemoan their collective weakness in the face of this challenge and erosion of their position, blaming their own moral flaws: the rivalry and slander that divide them. My sense is that such slander and rivalry were probably always there, but in the old context they served as the hidden, petty motivation that propelled scholars into intellectual tournaments on the honorable arena of theological debate. Now such brilliant pyrotechnics matter less, particularly for those fringes of their constituency where the crumbling is most evident. Yet that is the arena where the gurus still concentrate their efforts.

The simplest and most obvious features of change may thus be most instructive for the question I pose. We see the gurus battle on, within the paradigm of their tradition's internal criteria, to build and reproduce the knowledge of Islam — even though its hegemony is threatened by other criteria of rationality, which they fail to address. At the same time we see a populace making facts and options from other constructed worlds increasingly relevant in their lives: without articulating any reasoned position, they are slowly becoming more pluralist, more like other North Balinese.

And here, possibly, is the perfectly obvious answer to my too narrowly posed question of how people choose between alternative systems of knowledge. There *is* no great degree of order in how they choose — and that is precisely a measure of the difference between building a tradition of knowledge and living a life. Most actions and decisions in life are made under conditions of uncertainty about what are facts. It makes perfectly good sense to go to a balian and ask him to make an interpretation, establish facts, according to *his* system of knowledge; and it makes sense for him to try to perfect his system further. But his client is not looking to perfect an overarching system of knowledge whereby one can settle for all time when one should go to the balian; the client is asking for guidance in the here and now. I have particularly stressed the collective process in handling such questions in Bali — how many persons influence you here and now as you decide to go, and in the judgment of the expert's advice, and later in the interpretation and reinterpretation of the outcome. There is reason exercised in this interaction, but it is not a case of certainty, based on knowledge, determining the act. Considerable uncertainty, multiple causation, many simultaneous concerns, and pressures from significant and insignificant others will all enter. There are times when a more principled discourse is also pursued (see Geertz [1964] 1973d:183ff. for one such episode in which Bali-Hindu constructs were critiqued); and gossip and popular criticism of actions are often cast in terms of ideals and principles, as we saw illustrated in the commentaries on Panji and Asiah. But these commentaries are embedded in particular circumstances, and above all in people's judgment of reasonable practice, which is constantly in flux.

Thus several distinct processes are at work. Some persons, especially experts, continue to build new knowledge within the existing paradigms and to reproduce knowledge in set forms, often in interaction with clients. By another set of processes, people respond to opportunities, interests, and strategic constraints through practical action. Each choice and action will be particular, emerging in a context of positioning, circumstance, and social participation. It will often involve a choice of which discrepant tradition of knowledge to mobilize, but such choices do not establish rules and principles; rather, they swiftly merge into the ever-shifting sands of practice, and rarely do they even receive explicit commentary. The prevalence and saliency of one world construction as against another, the relevance of distinct traditions of knowledge in the interpretation of life's episodes, emerges from innumerable decisions and commentaries in small and shifting social circles, and is seldom — and probably mainly retrospectively — addressed in principle. Above all, we need to recognize the continual flux in which these actions occur. I take it that every performed and interpreted act will change, slightly, the meanings that are ascribed to any following choice, act, or expression within the circle of persons in which it was visible. The result is a low degree of order and a high degree of flux — a flux that comes about through small and humble steps yet may cumulatively challenge, invade, and transform the relevance of whole constructed worlds.

19

Love, Freedom, and the Multivalency of Public Symbols

We have seen a tendency for specialists within each tradition to produce knowledge in accordance with that tradition's own internal criteria of validity, and thus for each tradition to have its own and separate trajectory. But people's everyday sensibilities and concerns can also have their impact. Not only do they choose, or not, to make use of the knowledge and interpretations that different traditions deliver; their interests and concerns can also act back on the traditions and affect the production of knowledge. I would suggest that this takes place mainly through the effects of how people experience the expressiveness of key symbols. Let me present some empirical materials that highlight these processes and lead to a clarification of the connections.

In the dry hills up from Celuk Terima, southwest of Pulaki, is a small temple of recent construction. Outside the international tourist circuit, it is sought by Balinese and Javanese alike in large numbers; and particularly on weekends and during school holidays an exceptionally large proportion of young people, as couples or in larger groups, form part of the steady stream of pilgrims climbing the sun-drenched hill to visit this rather distant site. The shrine itself does not have the normal Bali-Hindu layout and is rather tacky and modest, remarkable mainly for having a Muslim caretaker as well as the Bali-Hindu ones; the other notable feature is the informal gaiety of the crowd that passes through.

The story behind the shrine was told to me in 1986 by one of the visitors:

Long ago in the kingdom of Banjar there lived a young orphan by the name of Jayaprana. Since he had no food to eat and no home to

324

live in, he went to the king and asked for his help; and the king took pity on him and took him into his house. Jayaprana was a beautiful child, and very charming, and the king saw to it that he was well cared for and well trained; and everyone came to love him dearly. When he grew older, the king called for Jayaprana and said: "Soon you will be of an age so you may meet a girl, and come to love her, and wish to marry her. When that happens, you must tell me, and I shall help you to be married." "Thank you, my king," said Jayaprana, "but as yet I know no such person and have no such stirrings in my body." "Nonetheless," said the king, "remember my promise."

Jayaprana was responsible for the king's horse; and every day he went out and cut the grass for the horse, and groomed it and watered it. One day after work, as he was strolling with his friends in the market, Jayaprana saw a very beautiful young girl. So he spoke to her, and her name was Layon Sari, from the village of Banjar Sekar. When he went home that night, his heart continued trembling, and he could not put Layon Sari out of his mind. So he sought her again, and in due course they swore to be married. Jayaprana went to the king and told him; and the king sent his patih, I Gusti Saung Galing, to negotiate with the girl's parents. With such a distinguished spokesman, there could be no difficulties, and they quickly agreed that she should marry young Jayaprana.

The wedding was arranged, and the king did it lavishly, and the two were married. But after seeing Layon Sari at the wedding, the king could find no peace, and bad thoughts took shape in his mind, and he decided that he must have Jayaprana killed. So after three days he called the patih and told him to take Jayaprana to a far and forlorn place full of robbers and kill him there. I Gusti Saung Galing was a good patih, and faithful to his king, and immediately did as his king said. The slit gong of the pura called all the men together, and the patih announced that robbers were putting all the people of Celuk Terima in great fear, and said that they must march immediately and clear the land of the robbers. Jayaprana was very sad to leave his bride, and they cried together, and then he marched off.

When they came to Celuk Terima, Jayaprana understood what was on the king's mind, for here the people had not fear of robbers and lived happily. So he turned to the patih and asked him: "Tell me truly, why has the king ordered you to take me here?" And the patih, who loved Jayaprana, was sad and said: "Forgive me, but the king has ordered me to kill you." Jayaprana said: "Surely, it shall be as the king wishes; but give me first time to compose myself and pray." So he prayed for a long time, and then he stood up and bared his chest. The patih struck with his kris, again and again — but the kris made no mark, and its point was bent, and it could not penetrate.

Jayaprana said, "I have a small kris here in my sash, only it can kill me. Or you may take this flower, and kill me with it." So the patih took the flower, and flicked it at him, and Jayaprana fell dead to the ground.

The patih returned to the king and told him what had happened; and the king went to Layon Sari's house. But she realized what was on his mind, and defended herself and attacked him, and he drew his kris to defend himself from her, and killed her. He came out of her house, and he was *raja budoh*, crazy, and attacked Patih Saung Galing; and Saung Galing defended himself, and killed his king, and the king killed him at the very same moment.

The people buried Layon Sari with Jayaprana where he had died, and every full moon young and old, but particularly the young, come here and pray for the gift of blessing from Jayaprana. And in 1955 all the people contributed immensely, and took earth from the grave and brought it to Singaraja and made a very great cremation for Jayaprana.

The place used to be difficult to reach, up the hill through the dry brush forest, but even so people would come here and meditate, sometimes through the whole night, as I myself did once. Now the government has made a good path and steps, and a new shrine here; but it is still a place of great tranquility, and people come here to achieve peace of mind. There is a pemangku, who blesses with Holy Water, and one of his assistants is a venerable old Muslim. The story teaches us Hindu philosophy, with ideals of *ahimsa*, nonviolence, and *tattwa masi*, the teaching that you-are-me, compassion with everyone.

The love story of Jayaprana and Layon Sari is very widely known and accessible to Balinese in a number of versions (considerably more detailed than the one I was told), from traditional legend and ballad to school printouts in Bahasa Indonesia (Boon 1977:193). Boon discusses the accounts given in some of these literary renditions and enters into a brief debate with other scholars over their interpretation (ibid.:193ff.; Boon 1990:120ff.): the legitimacy of a reading that characterizes the theme as "romantic love," and the way in which aspects of caste, nationalism, and marital options are articulated.

But the story becomes truly challenging when we compare my 1986 rendering with a contemporary description of the events and concerns associated with the figure of Jayaprana during the year of 1949 — for that, *pace* my Celuk Terima informant, was when the cremation took place.

This, we should remember, was a time when freedom was clearly being achieved in Indonesia, but the population had gone through considerable hardships during Japanese occupation and the postwar liberation struggle; the place of Bali in a new Indonesia had not yet been clarified; and Dutch administration was still in place in the guise of the government of the Federal State of East Indonesia. At this critical point, a call to perform a belated cremation for Jayaprana became a rallying cause for a spontaneous mass movement; and the puzzled Dutch sensed so strong an undercurrent of revolutionary fervor in this ritual project that they found the movement highly ominous. A discussion of why the same Jayaprana story that now entices lovers and youths to make a Sunday picnic pilgrimage should have served then as an evocative symbol for political freedom may add to our insight into Balinese cultural codifications, experiences of constraint and liberty in life, and the versatility of public symbols.

The events as observed in 1949 by the Dutch missionary scholar H. J. Franken make fascinating reading, and the following summarizes his account ([1951] 1960:235–65). Apparently the village of Kalianget, which had a small temple to Jayaprana and was reputed to be the site of the romance, was experiencing a general economic depression and wished to enhance its luck and prosperity. The spirit of Jayaprana had for a long time been demanding a cremation, both through trance communications and by indicative signs and accidents. Village seniors made three visits to a then famous balian in Bakung, near Singaraja, to contact Jayaprana, and they received clear demands to perform the cremation, along with promises that the ceremony would benefit the village and not cost it much. An auspicious day for the event was set by a deaf-mute villager to avoid the possibility of influence by self-serving interests. From then on, apparently, the project took off, mainly led by Jayaprana himself through a series of spontaneous trance possessions.

Word spread of the forthcoming event, and a growing stream of visitors started arriving in the village during the following months of preparation, bringing offerings on their own behalf and money contributions to the ritual of cremation. Numerous gamelan orchestras also turned up and performed, the majority of them presenting *joged* courting dances (see below).

The main ritual took place during August 1949. More than fifty buses and trucks joined the procession to fetch soil from Jayaprana's grave at Celuk Terima. A spontaneous trance medium brought the message that the pedanda sanctifying the proceedings should be assisted by a person who was not wearing a gold ring, which unexpectedly precipitated a tukang banten (female expert offering-maker) from the royal residence in Singaraja into a position of leadership. This person, apparently, had much influence on the further developments in the unfolding ceremony.

As the procession returned with the soil from Jayaprana's grave and passed by the holy site of Pulaki, a small spring miraculously appeared on the dry rock face. A rumor took shape that Jayaprana and the great Siwaist pedanda Nirartha, the "Holy Newcomer" Dang Hyang Bau Rauh who first landed at this spot on arriving from Java (see chapter 1), were one and the same person. This of course was a way to claim prestige for Jayaprana — but with consequences for a number of features of the cremation (some of which were observed). However, by entailing Brahmana caste rank for him, it also weakened the symbolic identification between Jayaprana and the commoner villagers. Additionally, this new claim led to unease among the pedandas, whose ancestor was now being involved. In defense of their own separateness, they responded by withdrawing their support from the movement. In the end, they announced their collective conclusion that the Batara Bau Rauh of Kalianget is another person than Pedanda Nirartha, the Dang Hyang Bau Rauh who founded their lineage.

Another rumor spread that a letter from Jayaprana had turned up in Banjar, possibly a charter for how the cremation of himself and his wife should be performed, written on a silver plaque in an unknown script. The pemangku of Pura Besakih, the holiest all-Bali temple complex, arrived personally to inspect this charter; but when he was unable to verify its existence (it seems the plaque may have disappeared in a shower of rain), he declared he would have nothing more to do with the ceremony.

Franken reports a revivalist passion of public pressure on all and sundry to accept the rumors, identifications, and miracles associated with the movement, leading for one thing to demonstrative support from the Chinese community, who in the context of a blossoming nationalism may have had special reason to prove their commitment. Others emphasized the symbolic identity between Jayaprana and the *pemuda* freedom fighter heroes. But the climax for many was the unexpected appearance of the high king of Bali himself, the Dewa Agung of Klungkung, on the day of the cremation — reflecting, among other things, another rumor, that Jayaprana was a descendant of the house of Klungkung. Franken suggests strongly that the interests and commitments of the various participants were highly diverse, and he concludes that "the fact must be accepted that one's view of Jayaprana is determined by the place that one occupies in Balinese society" (ibid.:256).

Franken further observes how "the festival's aim was to celebrate an ordinary cremation. However, it developed into an event with a much wider purport, and one gains the impression that a particular psychological attitude of the population in the post-war period seized upon it as a means of expressing itself" (ibid.:235). Specifically, contemporary Dutch observers saw this popular significance to involve liberation, military resistance, and nationalistic and antifeudal positions (Swellengrebel in Bali 1960:69). Such seems indeed to have been the case. But why should the tragic lover and loyal subject Jayaprana have been chosen as a suitable symbol of liberation, military resistance, nationalism, and social revolution?

Formal methodologies for the anthropological analysis of symbols are not particularly useful for answering such a question. They incorporate assumptions about a degree of conventional consensus, and a set structure of codes and codification, which may be generally questionable and certainly inappropriate in this particular case. The confusion and divisions among priests certainly tell us that the processes involved in this symbol production were not those of "regular" knowledge production by experts within the routinized tradition of Bali-Hinduism, but rather reflected broader sensibilities and meanings, spontaneously seized upon by broad sectors of the population. Precisely for this reason, it can bring us in touch with a more experientially focused "meaning": how the symbol resonates in the minds of participants, what it says to them and for them. Such ways of posing the question are facilitated by the work of Obeyesekere (1981, 1990; see also Barth 1975, 1987) and, at a further remove, Turner (1967) and Weber (1949). They ask us to place the symbol of Jayaprana in the context of previous individual experience, and of the lived practice with which actors are familiar: here must have been the sources from which it, as a new and groping articulation, fetched its fitness for conveying and nourishing the surge of feeling and thought that was emerging among participants and public.

It is a familiar feature of Balinese orientations that love and marriage are somehow associated with being valiant; but this is popularly tied to the widespread practice of marriage by elopement and even capture (Boon 1977:121ff. and 1990:117ff.; but cf. Hobart 1986b:133ff. and fn. 22). In the contexts I am familiar with, this explicit association arises because such an act may cause anger, and even a sense of physical danger if a girl's outraged relatives find the escaped couple; perhaps it also stems from the aspect of ruthlessness in the act of enforcing one's will, either by the groom or by the young couple together. For this reason, elopement is also spoken of as an "impolite" way of marrying — though many, with a chuckle, admit to having done it themselves. But Jayaprana's marriage, on the contrary, had

329

the "polite" form of negotiation. This, together with Jayaprana's compliance with his king's authority, establishes him clearly as a faultless, polos person — a highly laudatory term (Wikan 1990:70–73) — but hardly heroic and revolutionary.

One aspect lost in the account I was given, but prominent in the folk ballad version of the Jayaprana story, is that of rank: as an orphan of unspecified caste he is low-ranking, whereas Layon Sari's father was the king's bendesa, an office giving high rank and perhaps even appropriate for a Wesia caste member. The socially radical theme of rejecting caste impediments and even caste in general was supposedly present in the 1949 context of revolution but was necessarily lost by the effort to glorify the hero by equating him with Pedanda Nirarthe.

I would argue that we must go deeper into subjective experience to identify the resonances that Jayaprana's story evokes. Consider a theme that I have stressed intermittently, how life in Bali can be experienced as one of "so many concerns." The sources of these concerns are the legitimate and illegitimate wishes, demands, pressures, and general coercion emanating from other people. Every person in Bali will have a pervasive and relentless experience of always having to live with such pressures and influences. The process, as I have indicated, is orchestrated in a shifting context of different others, who involve themselves in your every concern and decision and demand consideration of their interpretation and their interests as well as yours. Additionally, the whole weight of morality is directed at making you their accomplice; you should come to *wish* to be dutiful in this way and to mold your impulses to be truly social and compliant.

As a consequence, the experience of engaging in action, of being in the world, is constantly tangled up with the experience of showing consideration, of resisting your own impulses on behalf of others, of convention, of the common good. Your cannot feel-think, much less act, without engaging others — old parents, other family members, neighbors; or without being sensitive to appearances — making sure your acts are not misconstruable or arrogant but always polite, sociable and friendly to all; or above all, without monitoring and managing yourself — to compel your own consciousness to transform its animal egotism and learn to bend to the pressures and become pliant, respectful, considerate, and social.

The one experience in life, it seems, that does *not* have this weight of considerations smothering it is that of infatuation, falling in love. It is positively valued in art as in life; it is recognized to be so powerful that it should not be thwarted by others, lest it lead to insanity (see also Boon 1990:122); women who retrospectively consider that they were smitten by love magic rather than true love can yet describe the abandon of all other considerations it caused (Wikan 1990:206). Being in love would seem to be the prototype, or even the unique experience for most people, of being filled and propelled by your own feeling-thoughts without having the consideration for others invade you and redirect you; it entails a unique state of not having to subdue your own wishes, because for once they are culturally codified as valid and valuable. Thus many or most sexually mature persons will carry the heady recollection of, for a while, having been filled with a clear, overwhelming and uncomplicated desire, which even, if you were at all lucky, could be enacted and lived out directly in the way that it arose within you.

If this understanding is correct, then what better root metaphor, key symbol, could a restless and celebratory population seize upon to embody their new sense of freedom? What could better resonate for them with the promise of liberty than the celebration of sinless, faultless lover victims now vindicated and transformed to godhead by cremation?

Indeed, this was not the only way such a resonance found expression at the time. It is widely remembered by reflective older people in Singaraja, and confirmed in the literature, that 1949 was also a time when a joged dance craze swept the north coast of Bali. The joged is an elegant but quite explicitly flirting/courting dance (see Bateson and Mead 1942:plate 59). In it, a professional young girl dancer opens and "begins to dance, and men come out of the audience to dance with her, while she responds to them with aloof coquetry. She fends the man off with gestures of her left hand . . . or with her fan, while the man momentarily emphasizes his intense perception of her with his hand over his eyes and his fingers extended" (ibid.:99). The dance serves today as a popular episode during many-day ceremonies such as cremations, and both the young men who respond to the challenge and step up and dance, and the general audience, enjoy it and find it mildly titillating. But at the time of independence, it was a real craze; and the missionary Franken observes with perceptive disapproval: "Jayaprana sanctioned the joged in its most rude, primitive form, a form which, however, corresponds excellently with the passions which the spirit of resistance has awakened in the youth" (Franken [1951] 1960:257). Thus the new spirit of freedom found its appropriately resonant expression.

FURTHER ON THE MANY CONCERNS IN NORTH BALINESE LIFE

Jayaprana and the joged craze allow us to tap an undercurrent that, I would argue, looms large in the experience of being-in-the-world in North Bali:

the obtrusiveness of constraints of pressures from outside (*paksa*, social coercion) and anxieties within (*bimbang*, worry; or *bingung*, being upset or confused, when the anxiety reaches an acute level). It is against this condition of consciousness that being in love, and thus transcending the normal state of worries, resonates with freedom. But the anthropologist needs to use this discovery also to achieve a better understanding of other symbols, contexts, and institutions generally.

I have elsewhere (Barth 1975, 1987) pursued an analysis of symbols, concepts, and knowledge that emphasizes precisely such a duality of the wellsprings of meaning in all imagery: symbols are not in themselves the representation of ideas; their power of meaning arises in the conjunction of an image and the knowledge and experience you bring to it. This insight is now widely acknowledged in the thesis that symbols serve not to represent, so much as to evoke by resonating with/in memory and experience (Munn n.d.). It is when you bring the experience of a life full of concerns, dominated by having always to show consideration for the wishes of others, that the galvanizing passion of being in love will resonate so it evokes a prototypical sense of freedom.

But likewise, if Balinese bring such undercurrents of awareness to their interpretation of other images, these images will also resonate with meanings and be used for purposes that can only be grasped when an awareness of the appropriate experiences is in place.

Armed with this insight, we can now return to the question of factionalism in North Balinese villages. The characteristic forms of its practice were depicted mainly in chapters 7 and 9, and we saw how factionalism in Prabakula and Pagatepan converged in their basic patterns, despite the deep differences in formal organization between the two villages. Characteristic of the pattern are the apparent absence of faction formation as a means to rally support for particular tasks or causes, the shifting and diffuse alignments of persons in networks, and the divisiveness it produces in the village. Armed with a clearer appreciation of the longing for a freedom from constraints that is a ubiquitous feature of life in North Bali, I shall now try to trace the motivation for factional activity: not its aggregate effects on the communities, or its possible functions, but the purposes persons are trying to serve when they engage in it. This means identifying the interpretation people make of the situation and what they consider to be at stake that makes such factional activity a meaningful, necessary, or desirable activity from the partisan view of the actor.

If not to rally others for a desired political task, what might be the purpose of factional activity? Villagers sometimes blame envy: that the purpose (of others) is to reduce the stature, achievements, and recognition awarded to fellow villagers. I judge this view to be both too narrow and not consistent with the explicit generosity often shown by Balinese in acknowledging the achievements, beauty, and value of other persons. But if the undercurrent I have identified above is salient, if a perennial problem of life in Balinese communities is an experience of being crowded and pressured by others, then an adroit factionalism becomes a highly intelligent pattern of action. Given a formal political organization that requires a demonstrative deference to authority, and a code of morality and politeness that dictates you should ideally comply with any consensus surrounding you, and indeed work on your own consciousness so you *wish* to comply — how else can you defend yourself? The difficulties in securing social space for yourself, and in finding a moral and acceptable way to limit the effectiveness of the constraints imposed by others, are greatly reduced if the community surrounding you is divided into factions. Where "they" form a massive coalition and a monolithic public opinion, they become no less than overwhelming. By subtly broadening every division among these others, by seeing to it that "they" do not emerge in full concert but assert a multiplicity of pressures on you in different and opposed directions, you create interstices and space for yourself to occupy, and convenient counterpressures to which you can defer. In other words, nurturing factional divisions between others is a device for defending a degree of choice and autonomy for yourself.

This motivation for factionalism is not one I have heard from any Balinese, nor an explanation I have ever been given by a person for her or his own act. Indeed, factional intrigue is something no person will admit to practicing in any connection. Yet it makes sense of this prevalent and complex pattern of action, which is apparently ubiquitous in North Balinese communities (and perhaps in the south as well; e.g., Hobart 1985c), by linking it to an existential problem for which there is ample other evidence, and this lends considerable plausibility to the construction.

I have focused on motivation and meaning, in contradistinction to effects or functions. Nor is the motivation I construct a simple derivative from the consequences of the action, or a mere description of its asserted social function. Both villagers and we as observers may deplore features of its aggregate result, such as the atmosphere of subtle slander and conflict that factionalism creates, or the inability it causes for the village to act concertedly as a group for useful purposes. Its role in reducing somewhat the scope for the abuse of power may, on the other hand, be beneficial. It is also an interesting reflection that the resulting ambience may be an important factor in enhancing the remarkable social value placed on ceremonial work: such work does not invite the same degree of factionalism but is often spurred by a spirit of competition and rivalry between whole communities; and precisely its contrast to divisiveness in other collective activities may enhance the symbolic salience of a ritual affirmation of solidarity. Above all, we may see in the factionalism of North Balinese villages a result of the longing for enhanced freedom and autonomy on the part of individuals, who seek to divide and deflect a public opinion that otherwise threatens to overwhelm them.

FLUX IN THE MEANING OF SYMBOLS

A subsidiary theme of the shrine for Jayaprana, which has not been touched upon, is implied in the presence of a Muslim caretaker, and also, though less remarkably, of Buddhist officiators and supplicants. This ecumenical theme can be read as another modulation of the theme of liberation from the constraints of convention — and perhaps also an affirmation of universal love and compassion. Its presence adds to the characteristic multivalency and diversity of connotations so often found in symbols. What is more, it represents a kernel of evocation which so far seems largely unexploited or subdued, and shows the potential for flux in new directions. Not only has the figure of Jayaprana shifted in thirty-five years from serving as a symbol of national and social liberation to being an idolization of young love, but we can clearly see here that the symbol also has other potentialities, in features that now seem merely fortuitous but may be called forth in other contexts or may resonate in other persons.

This emphasis on flux may seem to fit poorly with the great emphasis in Balinese ritual on right performance, on avoiding any mistake no matter how inadvertent. Such an emphasis might be expected to have a highly conservative and stabilizing effect on the tradition. People's concern, one might even say pervasive anxiety, on this point is very marked, and misfortunes of every kind are expected to result from such error — leading to a veritable cottage industry among balians to identify such errors in the past and design appropriate remedial action. But this concern arises from deeper sources than the specific criteria of validity within the Bali-Hindu tradition of knowledge. It pervades social relations — for instance, in the polite phrase "if I have made a mistake, may I be excused" — and the forms of deference in all relations of authority; and it also invades the tradition of Islam. Thus the mortuary rite of pidiyah (see chapter 11), in which God is paid for any shortfall of daily prayers in the deceased's life by the congregation, though sanctioned by Islamic tradition, receives an attention in Pagatepan that I have not seen in any Muslim community in the Middle East. Again, I suggest we see here a broad, popular resonance to symbols that can convey an anxiety to act properly, conventionally, and suitably to one's modest and unassertive position — reflecting a configuration of compliance and potential guilt that is a ubiquitous partner to the felt constraints and longings for greater freedom explored in this chapter.

Nonetheless, one could argue that such a stance will have the effect of stabilizing tradition. Compared to the riotous divisions and changes that the decentered organization of Bali-Hinduism could be expected to generate, this may indeed be so. The wealth of imagery is such that the field anthropologist searching for insight will too readily assume the presence of a complex code and an elaborate structure of knowledge, and one's inability to grasp them serves one as a measure of their very intricacy, elaborateness, and dogmatic rigor. I have already, in chapters 12 and 18, questioned the assumption of rigorous structure in this cornucopia. Nor should we naively adopt a position where stability is assumed wherever change cannot be positively demonstrated: our data either way are far too poor. Stutterheim (1935) of the Dutch archaeological survey of Bali established the correspondence between a Balinese village ritual and a tenth-century inscription that, though it was unknown to the villagers, specified certain details of the ritual they indeed practiced (cf. Lansing 1983:148). This matches similar stories from European peasants who habitually made the sign of the cross before a whitewashed church wall — only to discover with modern restoration an overpainted fresco of the Virgin there, hidden since the Reformation. But one should pursue the search for mechanisms in all such cases, whether of reproduction or flux; and in the Balinese village case there is a chance that the appropriate temple contained a lontar charter for the festival — unbeknown to Stutterheim. The mechanisms involved in flux, as I have tried to show, are even more in evidence, and the sources on Jayaprana attest to one case of such flux.

Perhaps flux is even more prevalent, considering how much of it will become truly invisible after the event. Its potential arises with particular strength because of the enormous width of the semantic field each of the key symbols covers within the bounds of established convention and even orthodoxy. This allows very different statements to be entailed, very different concepts to be evoked, without the slightest sign of change in the overt image, only a shift in saliency within its established range of meaning, brought about by changes in what people *bring* to its reading.

For example, the tripartite rontlu shrine associated with most homes serves as the symbol of the Hindu trinity and can convey a variety of orthodoxies as such. But it is also said to represent ancestry, and father, mother, and Sun. If people increasingly choose to respond to it as a representation of male, female, and Sun, it will have remained unchanged and within its present assigned range of meaning; and yet it can come to resonate for them with an entirely different cosmological vision.

The offerings placed on the ground are part of the daily routine of every home and of every larger offering. The range of their interpretation is already very wide, from the appeasement of dreadful ogres and demons to a philosophical acceptance that also lust and grossness are the creations, and thus the emanations, of Godhead. One can well imagine a flux ranging from a dominant terror of evil forces demanding their sacrifice, to a hedonistic pleasure in our animal selves, being evoked by this symbol in the different contexts of changing times and concerns. But I also know a woman whose current thoughts, as she places the daily offerings on the ground, are those of gratitude to our sustaining earth, mediated by the ecologic vision of the multitude of little black ants who pour out of the ground, each to return a bit of our offering to its eternal source. Keesing (1987a) has exemplified a similar poetic productivity in the imagery of earth in Malaita. I suggest that these are not exceptions and aberrations, to be examined and enjoyed and then theoretically dismissed as not reflecting the valid and shared meaning, that is, significance, of the symbol in that culture. They are, on the contrary, evidence of the vital productivity of such traditions of knowledge, responding and expressing the flux of people's concerns and sensibilities under ever-changing circumstances. It is not a capacity, for example, of North Bali's well-organized, orthodox Islam to convey such shifts (though it was, at times, of the Sufi traditions elsewhere); but it may be truly a property and capacity of the Bali-Hindu tradition of knowledge to facilitate the ceaseless flux of people's concerns and consciousness.

Besides nuancing our perspective on the analysis of public symbols, this examination of the story of Jayaprana should have helped us to pin down, and establish the importance of, a tenor of North Balinese life that has been present in a number of the features we have observed. It highlights the ambivalent cross-pressures, the opposed attractions of compliance and of freedom, which seem to form so powerful an undercurrent in the consciousness of many. Without a clear awareness of this problematic of living and acting in North Bali, the anthropologist will provide consistently misleading interpretations of the purposes and concerns that govern much interaction and political action in communities and will fail to identify the resonance key symbols evoke in those who use and reproduce them.

PART SIX

The Complexity of
Civilization

20

A Surfeit of Culture

Some years ago, Marcus and Fischer set an agenda for cultural anthropology on the basis of their overview and critique of the field. They wrote: "Most local cultures worldwide are products of a history of appropriations, resistances, and accommodations. The [present] task . . . is . . . to revise ethnographic description away from the framing of the cultural unit toward a view of cultural situations as *always* in flux, in a perpetual historical sensitive state of resistance and accommodation to broader processes of influence that are as much inside as outside the local context" (1986:78). Much anthropological writing over the last fifteen years has converged on these issues; and the quote can be used to frame my ethnography of North Bali in the 1980s. I would particularly emphasize the importance of acknowledging flux and of conceptually merging the analysis of processes inside and outside the local context.

But to avoid seeing our new efforts fall into old ruts, there are more caveats to observe. For one, we need to be precise in our identification of the parties to historical events: who are the social entities that appropriate, resist, accommodate? To represent them naturalistically (chapter 10, and Barth 1966, 1981), in a way that acknowledges the fundamental subjectivity and consciousness of human beings, it is safest both to begin and to end up with people acting — if we take care to depict the ways people are embedded in the social organizations that empower them. Second, a strong focus on "culture" can lead us back to a reification of cultural patterns, although we know they are our own constructions, abstracted from particular and complex situations. The important anthropological insight with regard to culture — that all the elements of a local situation are affected by their context, that cultural facts are interrelated and interdepen-

339

dent in various ways — too readily led to the non sequitur that all is one functional and logical whole. Anthropology's blanket assertion of such integration came to mean that no *particular* relation needed to be privileged or demonstrated and that any one demonstrated connection could serve to illustrate the general axiom. I should like my analysis to avoid this trap and allow me to discover particular, and perhaps startling, connections.

A failure fully to escape this false ontology — on my part and on the part of my audience when I have presented outlines of my present analysis, especially that in part 4 — has sometimes led to the objection that I seem to be "taking apart" North Balinese culture into a few rather arbitrary major "traditions." On the contrary: I wish to start with a heuristic assumption of a *dis*ordered assembly and then, by modeling the way I see people interact, and the cumulative, formative effects of such action, to *generate* trends toward linkage and coherence — in this case corresponding to major traditions of knowledge — thereby to identify processes that build this degree of order. Such has been my agenda throughout. It is now time that I try to be fully explicit and draw together the analytic strategy I have followed.

First, a remark on the progression of the text. It might seem that I have not lived up to my dictum to both begin and end with people. The present text, on the contrary, starts mainly with impersonal formal organization and only slowly moves toward a more informed portrayal of persons and an interpretation of their understandings and concerns. But this is merely an artifact of the need to present large amounts of data; it does not reflect the analytical modeling I am pursuing. Since it is a premise of the analysis that people inhabit a culturally constructed reality, we must know a vast range of externalities of life, and the cultural conceptions and conventions by which those externalities are known and interpreted, to enable us to join people in the reality within which they act. A major part of any ethnographic investigation and description must be concerned with putting these facts into place. An entirely different matter is how the connections between these various facts are best discovered and modeled, once the facts are known. It is only at this final stage that I can hope properly to interlink persons, communities, and traditions and model their interdependencies.

With regard to the major traditions, an important discovery has been made about their internal processes. The traditions clearly differ profoundly in the kinds of coherence and structure that characterize them. Such differences between their salient features were linked to their social organization, the social processes whereby they are constructed and reproduced. For example, the multiple authorities of Bali-Hinduism could be shown to generate a very different kind of convergence from that found in Islam. And the resulting form of (relative) order found within a tradition seems generally to be better grasped by using images of focal "concerns", "debates", "enigmas", or "fears and longings" (i.e., values) than by positing an internal coherence of deductive logic. This is in line with Bakhtin's (1981) stress on the dialogic construction of culture but has been, I believe, more precise in its identification of processes. Substantively, I have tried to show that the world of sorcery is called forth by people's concerns and fears about the real attitudes of others in social relations, rather than by any coherent cultural theory about metaphysical power in the world; I have argued that between the negara and the Bali Aga one should hear a debate on the nature of inequality and authority, not simply look for the instantiation of two alternative, canonical orders of rank and caste; as for people's participation in the modern sector, it is driven by concerns about upward social mobility, material wealth, and security, not by a coherent world theory affirming science or democracy.

The forms of activity that emerge can best be represented as the results of social processes if one models actors with these respective concerns, equips them with knowledge that is current in Buleleng today, and then places them in an opportunity situation constructed so it depicts salient features of their material and social environment. If the model generates the features we observe, the analysis is strengthened. The most desirable analytical scheme would thus start by modeling people with appropriate dispositions and ideas; it would then simulate the actions and interactions in which they would engage, and the aggregate patterns that would eventuate. These patterns can then be explored to discover whether the model reproduces its own preconditions. If it does not do so perfectly, that might be taken as an indication of the flux one would expect in every human society.

But an enigma seems to arise from this form of analysis, and from the basic premise of the cultural construction of reality. Note what we can observe with regard to the connection between the forms of action enjoined in any particular cultural tradition and the experienced meanings that are entailed for people who practice these forms. For example, we may look at the formal rites that create the relationship of marriage between Bali-Hindu spouses, as against the rites performed by Muslims: they are strikingly divergent. Yet there is much evidence to suggest that the relationship actually established between spouses in marriage among Hindus and Muslims respectively is much more similar; the frequency of elopement in both populations, and their joint celebration of love at the shrine of Jayaprana, suggest that subjective meanings of marriage may also be not all that different.

Likewise, we have seen how radically villages vary in their formal organization of constituted groups, leadership positions, and — especially as between Muslims and the others — the very imagery in which the organization is cast. Yet we found striking convergences in the forms of local political activity, along with a ubiquitous divisive factionalism.

Or a third example: the knowledge enshrined in the cosmological constructions of Hinduism, Islam, sorcery beliefs, and the modern sector, as also the imagery through which each is expressed, could hardly be more contrastive. Yet when we enter into the experienced meanings of persons who embrace these respective cosmologies, we nonetheless find that a number of similar concerns are evoked with regard to human morality, social relations, personal health, and many other important matters. Must we then conclude that culture is not after all so formative of people's realities, since people can embrace such distinctive cultural syndromes and yet share similar orientations?

Hardly. To see this as an enigma, one would have to embrace a very homogenized ideal of cultural consistency (but not unlike that which often informs elementary anthropological reasoning) and expect all aspects of culture to conform to a single and coherent pattern. Such a template misdirects our attention. Instead, the lack of consequence should lead us to look for additional processes that shape people's values and experiences. Might there not rather be other factors, arising perhaps in the local setting, that produce convergence in the meanings constructed by people, despite the extent to which they embrace highly divergent conceptions and knowledge?

The preceding chapters and Wikan's (1990) analysis of our partly overlapping materials have portrayed some particular *concerns* as being relatively pervasive across the other differences that obtain between people in North Bali. To explore observed similarities in people's orientations, and the way they may arise, it would be methodologically sound to focus on such broadly shared compelling concerns, and to pursue their implications for people's understandings, modes of interaction, and social strategies. From the preceding descriptive materials, I would single out a small set of such concerns as particularly salient:

a pervasive fear of making an error or mistake and not acting correctly

a strong obligation to cooperate and submerge one's own impulses in the service of the common good a need for perpetual vigilance and attentiveness in social interaction to avoid causing offense in others

a concern to be humble and affirm the limits of one's own competence, while showing respect and submission to the authority of others

a need to protect oneself and one's health by surrounding oneself with happiness and harmony

a perennial pressure to manage one's heart and compel oneself to be good — in a world where others may be evil

This list of compelling concerns shows a very close family resemblance to features stressed in the classical anthropological accounts of Bali, especially to Bateson's, Mead's, and Geertz's accounts of the fundamental "ethos" of Balinese culture — though the emphases I place may be distinctive. But my critique of these earlier authors was never that their observations were unrecognizable in what I could see in Bali; the issue is how such features may be connected and generated, and what theoretical model gives the best account of (North) Bali and of complex civilizations in general. I look at the concerns I have listed as describing a set of orientations that tend to be salient in Balinese interaction, and I want to understand where they arise. I urge that we should not see their formulation as an end point in an effort to extract the essence of a Balinese culture. We have observed them merely as a set of worries people in North Bali seem to have learned to carry with them as they relate to each other and the world. Their mere ubiquity does not justify us in elevating them as foundational premises for an anthropological theory of Balinese culture, as if they existed out of time and place as logical axioms. Rather, we should understand them as a precipitate of the experience of living as a member of a Balinese community. In other words, we must not conceptualize them as "norms" for people to enact. Indeed few such norms seem to be notably effective in generating action and determining meaning. Instead, I suggest that they summarize recurring life experiences: they provide caveats, puzzles, and maxims to people who are trying to cope in a complex, unpredictable, and imperfectly known world; and they demand forethought, care, and suitable strategies.

If such is the precipitate of the experience of living, then what effects might that have on people's modes of interaction? Let us model the interconnection by posing a simple conundrum: if such concerns are salient for people, then how would they act; what community life would they generate; and what would be the lessons they could draw from the lives that they thereby came to lead? For example, if you feel a pervasive fear of making an error, how might you act as a participant in a social circle? So as not to

The cremation tower arriving at the cremation grounds. The family pemangku, riding his father's tower, is fainting from the excitement.

become entirely passive and tongue-tied in a social gathering under these conditions, it would be a useful strategy to reduce the overt seriousness of social encounters by transforming them through politeness and gaiety, turning them into pleasant and playful occasions — which also, if it comes off, reduces other people's option to be offended and is highly compatible with an orientation to cooperate and submerge yourself in the group. Indeed, if in your gaiety you tell amusing anecdotes of your own minor mishaps, you are also showing your humility, and you are creating an environment of happiness and harmony around yourself and others, and thereby defending yourself against their possible evil — while at the same time scoring socially by being amusing and the center of attention. The conjunction of the six simultaneous concerns noted above thus seems to generate a subtle blend of interactional forms that is in fact highly characteristic of a great number of North Balinese social encounters. What emerges is both a social arena with a characteristic set of pragmatic rules, and a highly patterned style of self-presentation.

But the same concerns will also generate some deep existential dilemmas and looming threats — likewise ubiquitous in the lives of Balinese. The need to avoid error, to be pervasively cooperative, humble, and surrounded by harmony, sums up a life saturated with an experience of the severity of social sanctions. It sets up overwhelming pressures toward conformity and compliance, which leave very little free space for yourself and your own wishes; there is, as people say, "so much to care about." I have tried to trace some consequences of this condition in the meanings people associate with the experience of falling in love; others in the uses to which they put divisive factionalism. And always, the ease with which other persons may take offense, combined with the danger of evil in others, will generate the ambience of the ever-present threat of sorcery that is such a powerful undercurrent in Balinese life.

There is thus much evidence that many people in North Bali live by a set of salient and consistent concerns, affecting the directions in which they think and act. I find it particularly helpful to be able to derive these attitudes and dispositions from people's everyday experience and keep them embedded in the enigmas, struggles, and indeterminacies of real lives, rather than reifying them as "values." Previous ethnographies have often pointed to the same features of politeness and grace — and gaiety — of much Balinese interaction and characterized it as ceremoniousness. But this only summarizes how things appear to an anthropological spectator, not how the features are generated in the behavior of actors. One further step would be to search behind this behavioral style and discover the presence of social sanctions favoring playfulness, conformity, and compliance, as well as the subtle and gross social pressures that enforce such behaviors. But this still leaves questions unanswered. Why should Balinese single out these particular practices and orientations as worthy of such strong sanctions? In fact, conformity and compliance are not so unambiguously valued: nowhere have I done fieldwork among people who are so self-consciously other-directed, yet who also resist social pressure so persistently and subtly, and who give such eloquent voice to their complaints about interferences and constraints. Our account, and our explanation, should be constructed so we simultaneously address all these complex and contradictory features. Likewise, the pervasive and highly valorized cooperation that is practiced in so many fields of activity by North Balinese takes place in a subtle tournament of self-assertion, opportunism, and mutual controls, quite apart from the more systematic factional engagements, and is thus also deeply ambivalent.

To my knowledge there is no explicit cultural paradigm by which Balinese themselves explicate such a set of focal concerns as a key to wise or good living. Why they should be so compelling is intelligible only when one considers the complex backdrop of life in Balinese communities, as I have attempted to depict it in the preceding chapters and as Wikan (1990) gives it in her accounts of other persons in precarious life situations: their force arises in the context of coping with life. It is only when the various elements of positioning, belief, experience, and dependency are in place that I would claim that the characteristic features of social roles played out in life in North Bali can be generated from people's attempts to reconcile and attend to this small set of simultaneous concerns. Surveying the descriptions I have been giving in the preceding chapters of episodes, persons, and communities, I am also struck by how inescapable these concerns become in the context of community participation in Bali — indeed, the extent to which they also invaded my own life and became my concerns while living there. They do not seem to obtain this force from the premises of the traditions of knowledge that people embrace so much as from pressures that arise in humdrum interaction.

To develop this analysis, I have chosen to reverse the logic usually constructed by anthropologists and put the life experience, and the concerns and orientations that it generates, in place first, and next derive the entailments that such concerns would have for people's practices and interpretations. But if this construction is valid, we must be able to show how people themselves conceptualize and institutionalize them as *their* concerns, no matter how pragmatic and contextual their source. To identify the cultural representations that people use, we need to turn to the knowledge and discourse that people employ to interpret and objectify their lives. That brings us back to the traditions of knowledge that people embrace. Thus we may ask: if people are indeed troubled by such concerns as I have formulated, what will they find that the major available traditions of knowledge have to offer them to articulate and support the saliency of these concerns? My assumption is that they will only embrace a tradition of knowledge — and conversely have the importance of their concerns vindicated — if they find that the tradition resonates with their concerns and that living by it produces experiences that reproduce a sense of the importance of such concerns. But we are faced with a surfeit of such traditions of knowledge and simultaneous constructed worlds. Let us therefore inspect the various traditions briefly, one by one, in regard to how they resonate with people's concerns.

1. Participation in Bali-Hinduism certainly conveys powerfully the obligations of cooperation as an explicit philosophy. But it also emphasizes the importance of ritually correct compliance through its recurring collective rituals. The dangers of wrong action are evocatively figured in the attention to ritual error and the frequency with which misfortunes of every kind are traced to this source. Authority is complexly symbolized as Godhead and ancestors and is abjectly worshiped with humble offerings and moving beauty; fears, evil, and good are represented in concrete symbols, and an explicit cosmology is constructed that rewards goodness through the concept of karma pala. The constitutive role of balance, happiness, and harmony in the world is powerfully conceptualized in the synergy of macrocosm and microcosm and is celebrated in ritual: "Be happy, be perfect, be glad in your heart!" enjoins the pedanda, as he purifies his paraphernalia before his rites (Forman, Mrazek, and Forman 1983:33). Thus Bali-Hinduism resonates with most of the concerns I have listed in richly evocative ways, while for most spiritual purposes embedding the person deeply in cooperative congregations of lineage and place. Yet it also allows for an individual search for enlightenment and blessing, as in sessions where the self confronts danger and the unknown in private vigil through lonely prayer and meditation.

2. Islam, in its very different way, can also facilitate some of the same concerns, as we have seen in its concepts and practice in Pagatepan. Authority is depersonalized and manifest in the Book among Muslims, and the very concept of Islam means submission to that authority; but the humble abasement of self before personified authority is powerfully retrieved in the lifelong honoring of one's guru, and in receiving barkat from his open hand; while ambivalence surfaces in the subjective experiences I have reported of shame and inferiority before such human authorities.

The guilt of wrong action is embodied in the recording angel, relentlessly inscribing your errors throughout life; but these errors can in Islam be balanced by accumulated merit and right (i.e., legally enjoined) action. However, the mortuary ceremony of pidiya certainly gives collective voice to a fear of the nemesis of ritual error, as do debates between traditionalists and modernists on the exact form and times of Muslim prayers.

Cooperation is generally less strongly enjoined and modeled in Muslim cult than in Bali-Hinduism, as is the imperative to manage your heart: Islam focuses more on action and less on inner thought and feeling. But local gurus enforce the concern by always stressing the need for true intent to obtain merit from good acts. Happiness, balance, and harmony are peripheral themes in Islamic cosmology but are represented in Pagatepan by the theory of health and illness, which is considered by villagers to be part of Islamic knowledge, ilmu. Thus Balinese Muslims can largely "read" their Islamic tradition of knowledge so as to find their concerns addressed by its teachings.

3. The experienced meanings of the contrastive negara/Bali Aga institutions in this regard are more elusive, partly because I lack the relevant data. Most of the former are historically defunct; and the latter are embedded in the emergent institution of the village community, an issue to which I return below. The formal organization of Julah, however, clearly evokes many of the concerns that I have listed, and dilemmas that arise from them. Its strongly corporative structure and balanced moieties are explicitly designed to secure cooperation and communal harmony. The ceremonialization of authority on the basis of strict seniority reflects an ambivalent concern both to respect it and to contain it. And Julah's revival of spectacular rites to purge the world of evil and secure cosmic harmony certainly highlights a strong commitment to these concerns. I find very striking the evidence for an experienced dilemma of status humility and resistance to authority that is revealed in the klian's tactics in his conflict with the bupati; and the desperation of the old klian's suicide on being forced to accept ritual error through the enforced privatization of land, as noted in chapter 13, bears witness to the strength of his concern on that issue.

On the negara side, the respect bordering on veneration practiced before Brahmanas is a powerful enactment of humbleness before authorities (while the prevalence of trying to do without pedandas is a measure of the ambivalence); and the (reluctantly practiced) elaborate apparatus of language levels is likewise expressive of the concerns surrounding status differences.

4. The ideas that have played a dominant role in the historical development of the modern sector are certainly not particularly compatible

with the concerns that are salient to Balinese. Yet when people bring their concerns to the activities that are organized within this sector, they generate an ambience in which the knowledge transmitted in the modern sector can be read as quite germane to those concerns, and in which practice and experience will confirm their salience. Thus in school classes, pupils can focus on the importance of avoiding error, being vigilant and attentive, and showing humility and respect; the same considerations, in the opposite order of priority, are also essential to all interactions with bureaucratic administration. Modern organizations and movements are occasions to cooperate and submerge oneself by joining, not to give voice to oneself and one's own interests – but they also facilitate the familiar strategy of defensive factionalism by providing options to join groups *different from* significant others. And consumerism and participation in the market are perhaps particularly attractive in providing allowed forms of personal choice and self-indulgence such as other arenas allow only to the powerful.

5. Finally, the ways in which sorcery knowledge caters to the dark side of most of these compelling concerns should be evident. The fear of making an error is fused with the need to avoid giving offense and thus precipitating sorcery sanctions; and humility coupled with grace and contageous gaiety, sustained by a carefully cultivated goodness in all one's feelings and thoughts, are the safest defenses against the evils of sorcery. At the same time, the practice of such vigilance serves subjectively to confirm the pervasiveness of sorcery and the importance of one's concern.

Note that what I am arguing at this stage is not that such concerns will of necessity *arise* from the various cosmological assertions, ritual representations, and religious doctrines of the major traditions; I am pointing to what people who come to these traditions with such concerns can find in and learn from the symbols each tradition provides: how the symbols will resonate for persons who bring these particular orientations to them. Nor do I wish to argue that the identified concerns are somehow *constitutive* of Balinese lives. They are not the origin point, but a point in a connected circle: when persons with c concerns use k knowledge in s situations, a social and material context is generated that can be interpreted as showing the vital importance of c concerns.

The generalizations I wish to draw from this have to do with the ways in which a diversity of concepts and knowledge from distinct traditions can be used by actors to address certain pervasive concerns, as we also saw illustrated in more personal detail in chapter 17. This is consistent with the thesis that no symbol represents a meaning in itself but only evokes one in its interaction with an actor's particular knowledge, agenda, and positioning. It follows that we cannot usefully inspect an abstracted tradition for its entailments; we must observe the uses to which real people put its concepts, in the practices of a range of actors in a range of circumstances.

Thus, in the activities of people attending to these compelling concerns, we observe a conjunction of two rather different kinds of cultural materials shaping behavior: the major traditions of knowledge, each containing ideas with a distinctive source and history and held together as a body mainly through a distinctive social organization, and, on the other hand, a range of concepts, values, and worries that more directly articulate the outcome of people's own lived experience.

Here again, it is essential that we do not encumber our analysis with inappropriate templates. There is not *a* culture out there, composed of parts. On the contrary, we are observing the confluence of a vast range of cultural materials, variously constituted and reproduced, which people bring to bear on their acts and interpretations. The very diversity of such cultural materials in North Bali may help us to recognize the breadth of variation in their sources and their dynamics. Some of the materials are reproduced and consolidated through the effects of distinct social organizations into identifiable and named traditions of knowledge, in part drawing on cultural streams of regional or global scale. Other materials are embraced, and perhaps even constructed, only in the painful practice of trials and errors in life's concerns. In my diagram connecting action and culture, as given on p. 159, the materials organized as major traditions would be found in the upper right, whereas the concerns we have discussed would arise along the bottom and the lower right side of the circle. The actual behavior that people design will draw on such materials of knowledge and experience in ways that serve multiple simultaneous purposes and compelling concerns, which might on purely logical grounds seem quite contradictory to the concepts of the embraced traditions, and also mutually incompatible. Indeed, such feats of adjustment are a regular feature of human activity, but they are nonetheless constrained by the resistance that the various cultural materials provide: concepts and knowledge are not infinitely and uniformly adaptable to all purposes. The singularities and practices found in a complex civilization will therefore show neither a blended fusion of all its ideas nor a stochastic sample of all their theoretically possible permutations; in its particular anatomy of disorder it will reflect identifiable, specific processes that can often be traced to social organization.

I have sought to unravel a number of these processes, but one more needs to be explicated to provide a last part of my model: the particular synergy of social controls, and their consequences in shaping arenas. We have noted how it is a characteristic of Balinese social life that the person is subject to numerous social pressures and designs her or his choices and activities in sensitive and elaborate ways to cope with them. But these social pressures will come to a head most powerfully in the context of a face-to-face village community. Here is an arena with high visibility and invasive mutual information, one where any reduction in the experienced intensity of cross-pressures will be invaluable to everyone.

In such a setting, the style of action I suggested above for a conversational encounter will emerge as the main, all-purpose refuge. Comfort depends on maintaining appearances. Because of the small scale of the community, it becomes feasible to freeze conventions and rules that obtain within it, so they provide parameters of predictability and legitimacy that are as assured as possible, enhancing both one's security and one's skill in avoiding error. All collective efforts to maintain cooperation and harmony will therefore be welcomed and valorized, encouraging a pervasive ambience of sociability, playfulness, gaiety, and mutual control. And a person will be only too happy to join others (thereby submerging her/himself in the service of the common good) in relentless social pressures to impose conformity to this ambience as a defense against potential evil – even though that same pressure, directed at yourself, may be felt to be painfully constraining.

There can be no question, from all the ethnographies of Bali including the present one, but that this style of socializing is a pervasive characteristic of Balinese villages. The thick description of its institutional machineries provides the substance of Geertz's most celebrated and criticized article ([1966] 1973a); and its experiential implications were perhaps most pithily captured by Bateson in his characterization of "Balinese social organization in which the smooth relations of etiquette and gaiety metaphorically cover the turbulence of passion" ([1967] 1972b:150), and his assertion that Balinese "see the world as dangerous, and themselves as avoiding, by the endless rote behaviour of ritual and courtesy, the ever-present risk of *faux pas*" ([1942] 1972c:174). I wish to accent this view that ceremonialism arises from subjective Balinese experience, as a powerfully motivated survival strategy in a dangerous world; but I also want to link it to our understanding of the processes that generate village organization. We may again ask: if the concerns we have discussed are constitutive of people's definitions of situations, and the strategies they adopt, what will be the aggregate effects?

That depends, of course, on a further set of parameters: the constraints of scale and arena within which social interaction takes place. So far, in line with most analysts of Balinese society, I have simply taken the obtrusive

351

fact of Balinese village communities as given: that the population aligns into conceptually discrete local units, which constitute corporative communities for numerous purposes. The existence of such villages was the starting point of my description of variations in social organization and has been a premise for most of the analyses that have followed, but it should also be seen as a problem requiring an explanation. People's social networks are in no sense contained within the village in North Bali; but its conceptual primacy as a focal arena of social life and identity is palpable. This salience of the village is attested in most ethnographies and frames the description of much of Balinese social life and cultural expression, from temple cult and village festivals to kinship organization and local-level politics. But in processual terms, we need to ask how the village as an obtrusive feature of Balinese social life might reproduce its own preconditions. I believe the processes whereby a village focus is reproduced are closely linked to the concerns and orientations we have been discussing. Briefly, the logic of my argument is as follows:

First, if the practice of etiquette, courtesy, and playfulness by villagers is a strategy to enhance their (mutual) safety in interaction, that practice will be more effective the more the village arena is insulated and segregated. Only in such an insulated microcosm will the conventions and rules be known to all so they can be unambiguously agreed upon and imposed; for the particular rules that frame social interaction within a community cannot successfully be enforced on the world at large. This helps us to understand the urgency for villagers of conceptually and socially segregating bounded communities within the wider social network.

Second, once such conventions have been established, there will be a strong shared interest in demanding compliance by sanctioning deviance. This will have the effect of combating all changes in such rules, freezing and fetishizing them by massive collective social controls. The practice, in other words, supports the emergence of unique, custom-bound village communities, so characteristic of Bali.

Third, I have provided various evidence (see also Wikan 1990, esp. 94ff.) for the deep-seated concern among Balinese to be virtuous, to compel the heart to *wish* to cooperate, comply, and be good. Yet, as insiders know only too well, the ambience of social constraints, factionalism, and covert suspicion and fear that tends to emerge in these small, closed arenas violates the fundamental imperatives of cooperation, respect, and harmony. In this situation the enactment of village cooperation and unity becomes a pressing priority, most attractively in a form where one may also demonstrate one's own community's distinctness and higher standards of virtue and beauty as against other cognate units. This encourages the feature that is so striking among Balinese: the widespread cultivation of vivid competitive displays between communities, in collective productions that merge co-villagers as a single social body, without regard even to the status distinctions of caste.

Thus a number of the characteristic social and cultural features of village organization are reinforced by this synergy of concerns, social controls, and small scale. It tends to make every village community a bearer of a distinctive set of cultural features and constitutes it as an arena that reproduces its own preconditions. The syndrome of concerns we have highlighted receives its experiential validation in the very kind of community arena that it tends to create. Thus powerful social processes are generated that consolidate the discrete, tradition-bound village communities that characterize social organization in Buleleng, as, I believe, elsewhere in Bali. The evidence of historically accumulated differences in custom — adat and awig-awig — between villages indicates that this must also have been the case when the kingdoms, through their negara organizations, asserted a contrary pressure. With their collapse under colonialism, the particularizing thrust of the village arenas would have become even more effective.

How then do I see the main traditions being reproduced under these circumstances? Again, the same theoretical considerations hold: one must look closely at the cultural concerns, assets, and resources of each separate actor and at the contexts in which she/he must act. Traditions are articulated by persons with some degree of special knowledge and distinctive positions in the relevant social organizations. Incumbents of these positions make investments and assume commitments in obtaining a command of special knowledge — most manifestly in the studies leading to Islamic scholarship, modern schoolteaching competence, or consecration as a pedanda, but also through successful experience as a pemangku, an economic entrepreneur, a balian, or even a humble client or follower. The point is, such a process provides the person with vested interests and special competence, as well as distinctive social networks and recognized rights and duties. A number of aspects of positioning are thus compounded, producing actors with highly distinctive options, interests, skills, and relevant standards of excellence. By virtue of these, an expert will be relentlessly enrolled in the reproduction of a tradition of knowledge of a distinctive design and become selectively committed to its paradigms and propelled to cultivate them in particular ways, at least in one sector of life. Thus there is no enigma in the fact that different persons within the population

353

become dedicated to the reproduction of quite distinctive traditions of knowledge, discongruous and at odds with ideas embraced by many others in the same population.

At the same time, all the persons who selectively embrace a tradition are also embedded in local communities, and in much of their lives they are influenced by local experience and therefore observant of locally more ubiquitous concerns, affecting their own interpretations in various ways. We have thereby uncovered a further reason why, of all the traditions, Bali-Hinduism is the one that shows most responsiveness to the greatest range of ubiquitous concerns within the population at large: its decentered social organization of multiple authorities, and its characteristic patterns of recruitment to specialized functions, embed its specialists most completely in the local region and give them the widest scope to address the experienced concerns of their followers.

In each tradition there will be a characteristic network linking its specialists together, often extending far outside the local region. Thus traditions will regularly transcend the boundaries not only of the community but also of the region, in different directions and in different ways, introducing multiple streams of ideas, influences, and pressures from distant and unconnected sources. Any one region at any one time will show a historically particular constellation of them, in conflict and concert. The boundaries of such a regional constellation are important to establish so as to be able to indicate the area for which a description claims to be valid and where a particular synergy obtains; but such wider boundaries have few significant theoretical entailments for the model and the processes it depicts.

We thus see in the region of Buleleng a true surfeit of culture, differentially vested as skills and knowledge and values in persons, and only partially interconnected and incompletely realized in the efforts and acts of people. The kaleidoscope of events such a population produces is in turn continually subject to discrepant interpretations by its various participants. Yet all is not chaos: people pursue purposes, schemes, and conscious designs stubbornly and often collectively, thereby shaping many events; and various traditions of knowledge are taught and embraced, allowing people to build and repair conceptual worlds even while these are being undermined by other teachings and other experiences. From such crossing processes is generated the vast cacophony of discordant voices, ideas, and interpretations that coexist in a complex civilization: a characteristically shaped, disordered system containing emergent events and discrepant worlds, in a flux generated by identifiable processes, which we are in part capable of modeling.

References

Austin, D. J. 1979. Symbols and culture: Some philosophical assumptions in the work of Clifford Geertz. *Social Analysis* 3:45–49.

Bakhtin, M. 1981. *The dialogic imagination: Four essays.* Austin: University of Texas Press.

Bali. 1960. *Bali: Studies in life, thought, and ritual.* The Hague: W. van Hoeve.

Bali. 1969. *Bali: Further studies in life, thought, and ritual.* The Hague: W. van Hoeve.

Barnes, R. H. 1974. *The Kedang: A study of the collective thought of an Eastern Indonesian people.* Oxford: Clarendon Press.

Barth, F. 1966. *Models of social organization.* Royal Anthropological Institute Occasional Paper no. 23.

———. 1967. On the study of social change. *American Anthropologist* 69: 661–69.

———. 1975. *Ritual and knowledge among the Baktaman of New Guinea.* New Haven: Yale University Press.

———. 1981. *Process and form in social life.* London: Routledge & Kegan Paul.

———. 1983. *Sohar: Culture and society in an Omani town.* Baltimore: Johns Hopkins University Press.

———. 1987. *Cosmologies in the making: A generative approach to cultural variation in inner New Guinea.* Cambridge: Cambridge University Press.

———. 1989. The analysis of culture in complex societies. *Ethnos* 54 (3–4): 120–42.

———. 1990. The guru and the conjurer: Transactions in knowledge and the shaping of culture in Southeast Asia and Melanesia. *Man,* n.s. 25: 640–53.

———. 1992. Towards greater naturalism in conceptualizing societies. In *Conceptualizing society,* ed. A. Kuper. London: Routledge.

———, ed. 1978. *Scale and social organization.* Oslo: Universitetsforlaget.

Bateson, Gregory. [1937] 1970. An old temple and a new myth. In *Traditional Balinese culture,* ed. J. Belo. New York: Columbia University Press.

355

———. [1949] 1972a. Bali: The value system of a steady state. In *Steps to an ecology of mind*. New York: Ballantine Books.

———. [1967] 1972b. Style, grace and information in primitive art. In *Steps to an ecology of mind*. New York: Ballantine Books.

———. [1942] 1972c. Social planning and the concept of deutero-learning. In *Steps to an ecology of mind*. New York: Ballantine Books.

Bateson, Gregory, and Margaret Mead. 1942. *Balinese character: A photographic analysis*. New York: New York Academy of Sciences.

Belo, J. 1949. *Bali: Rangda and Barong*. Monographs of the American Ethnological Society, vol. 16. Seattle: University of Washington Press.

———. [1953] 1966. *Bali: Temple festival*. Monographs of the American Ethnological Society, vol. 22. Seattle: University of Washington Press.

———. 1960. *Trance in Bali*. New York: Columbia University Press.

———. [1935] 1970. The Balinese temper. In *Traditional Balinese Culture*. New York: Columbia University Press.

Benda, H. J. 1958. *The crescent and the rising sun: Indonesian Islam under the Japanese occupation 1942–1945*. The Hague: W. van Hoeve.

Boon, James A. 1977. *The anthropological romance of Bali, 1597–1972. Dynamic perspectives in marriage and caste, politics and religion*. New York: Cambridge University Press.

———. 1982. *Other tribes, other scribes: Symbolic anthropology in the comparative study of cultures, histories, religions and texts*. New York: Cambridge University Press.

———. 1986. Symbols, sylphs and Siwa. In *The anthropology of experience*, ed. V. Turner and E. Bruner. Urbana: University of Illinois Press.

———. 1990. *Affinities and extremes: Crisscrossing the bittersweet ethnology of East Indies history, Hindu-Balinese culture, and Indo-European allure*. Chicago: University of Chicago Press.

Bourdieu, Pierre. 1977. *Outline of a theory of practice*. Cambridge: Cambridge University Press.

Clifford, James. 1986. Introduction: Partial truths. In *Writing culture: The poetics and politics of ethnography*. Berkeley and Los Angeles: University of California Press.

———. 1988. *The predicament of culture*. Cambridge: Harvard University Press.

Coleman, J. 1986. *Individual interests and collective action*. Cambridge: Cambridge University Press.

Colson, Elisabeth. 1974. *Tradition and contract: The problem of order*. Chicago: Aldine.

———. 1984. The reordering of experience. Anthropological involvement with time. *Journal of Anthropological Research* 40:1–13.

Connor, Linda. 1982a. The unbounded self: Balinese therapy in theory and practice. In *Cultural conceptions of mental health and therapy*, ed. A. J. Marsella and G. M. White. Dordrecht: Reidel.

———. 1984. Comment on Shankman, "The Thick and the Thin". *Current Anthropology* 25 (3): 271.

————. 1986. Balinese healing. In *Jero Tapakan: Balinese Healer*, ed. L. Connor, P. Asch, and T. Asch. Cambridge: Cambridge University Press.

Covarrubias, M. [1937] 1973. *Island of Bali*. New York: Knopf.

Danandjaja, James, 1978. The Trunyanese: The people who descended from the sky. In *Dynamics of Indonesian history*, ed. H. Soebadio and C. A. du Marchie Sarvas. Amsterdam: North-Holland.

————. 1980. *Kebudayaan petani desa Trunyan di Bali*. Jakarta: Pustaka Jaya.

Darmaputera, E. 1988. *Pancasila and the search for identity and modernity in Indonesian society*. Leiden: Brill.

Dhofier, Zamakhsyari. 1980. Kinship and marriage among the Javanese Kyai. *Indonesia* 29:47–58.

————. 1982. *Tradisi pesantren: Studi tentang pandangan hidup kyai*. Jakarta: Lembaga Penelitian, Pendidikan dan Penerangan Ekonomi dan Social.

Duff-Cooper, Andrew. 1984. *An essay in Balinese aesthetics*. Centre for South-East Asian Studies, Occasional Paper no. 7. Hull: University of Hull.

————. 1985. Ethnographic notes on two operations of the body among a community of Balinese on Lombok. *Anthropological Society of Oxford Journal* 16 (2): 121–42.

Dumont, L. 1972. *Homo hierarchicus*. London: Paladin.

Eiseman, F. B., Jr. 1989. *Bali: Sekala and niskala*. 2 vols. Berkeley: Periplus Editions.

Firth, R. 1954. Social organization and social change. *Journal of the Royal Anthropological Institute* 84 (1): 1–20.

Forge, A. 1980. Balinese religion and Indonesian identity. In *Indonesia: The Making of a Culture*. ed. J. J. Fox. Canberra: Research School of Pacific Studies, The Australian National University.

Forman, W., R. Mrazek, and B. Forman. 1983. *Bali: The split gate to heaven*. London: Orbis.

Fox, D. J. S. 1982. *Once a century: Pura Besakih and the Eka Dasa Rudra festival*. Jakarta: Penerbit Citra Indonesia.

Fox, J. J., ed. 1980. *Indonesia: The making of a culture*. Canberra: Research School of Pacific Studies, National University of Australia.

Franken, H. J. [1951] 1960. The festival of Jayaprana at Kalianget. In Bali 1960.

Geertz, C. 1959. Form and variation in Balinese village structure. *American Anthropologist* 61:991–1012.

————. 1960. *The religion of Java*. Glencoe, Ill.: Free Press.

————. 1963. *Agricultural involution*. Berkeley and Los Angeles: University of California Press.

————. 1972. The wet and the dry. Traditional irrigation in Bali and Morocco. *Human Ecology* 1 (1): 23–39.

————. [1966] 1973a. Person, time, and conduct in Bali. In *The interpretation of cultures*. New York: Basic Books.

————. [1966] 1973b. Religion as a cultural system. In *The interpretation of cultures*. New York: Basic Books.

————. 1973c. Thick description: Toward an interpretive theory of culture. In *The Interpretation of cultures*. New York: Basic Books.

———. [1964] 1973d. "Internal conversion" in contemporary Bali. In *The interpretation of cultures*. New York: Basic Books.

———. [1971] 1973e. After the revolution: The fate of nationalism in the new states. In *The interpretation of cultures*. New York: Basic Books.

———. [1972] 1973f. Deep play: notes on the Balinese cockfight. In *The interpretation of cultures*. New York: Basic Books.

———. 1980. *Negara: The theatre state in nineteenth-century Bali*. Princeton: Princeton University Press.

———. 1983. *Local knowledge: Further essays in interpretive anthropology*. New York: Basic Books.

———. [1974] 1984. "From the native's point of view": On the nature of anthropological understanding. In *Culture theory*, ed. R. A. Shweder and R. A. LeVine. Cambridge: Cambridge University Press.

Geertz, H. 1989. A theatre of cruelty: The context of a Topeng performance. Princeton University, manuscript.

Geertz, H., and C. Geertz. 1964. Teknonymy in Bali: Parenthood, age-grading and genealogical amnesia. *Journal of the Royal Anthropological Institute* 94 (2): 94–108.

———. 1975. *Kinship in Bali*. Chicago: University of Chicago Press.

Gerdin, I. 1981. The Balinese Sidikara: Ancestors, kinship and rank. *Bijdragen* 137 (1): 17–35.

Goff, J. Le. 1981. *The birth of purgatory*, tr. A. Goldhammer. Chicago: University of Chicago Press.

Gonda, J. 1952. *Sanskrit in Indonesia*. Sarasvati Vihari Series, no. 28. Nagpur: International Academy of Indian Culture.

Goodenough, W. H. 1957. Cultural anthropology and linguistics. In *Report of the Seventh Annual Round Table Meeting on Linguistics and Language Study*, ed. P. Garvin. Georgetown University Monograph Series in Language and Linguistics, vol. 9. Washington, D.C.

Goris, R. 1954. *Prasasti Bali: Inscripties voor Anak Wungcu*. 2 vols. Bandung: Kirtya Liefrinck-van der Tuuk.

———. [1935]. 1960a. The religious character of the village community. In Bali 1960.

———. [1937] 1960b. The temple system. In Bali 1960.

———. [1933] 1960c. Holidays and holy days. In Bali 1960.

———. [1937] 1969a. Pura Besakih, Bali's state temple. In Bali 1969.

———. [1948] 1969b. Pura Besakih through the centuries. In Bali 1969.

de Graaf, H. J. 1949. Gusti Pandji Sakti, vorst van Buleleng. *Bataviaasch Genootschap van Kunsten en Wetenschappen*, Tijdschrift 83:60–82.

Grader, C. J. [1939] 1960a. Pemayun Temple of the banjar of Tegal. In Bali 1960.

———. [1939] 1960b. The irrigation system of the region of Jembrana. In Bali 1960.

———. [1949] 1960c. The state temples of Mengwi. In Bali 1960.

———. [1940] 1969. Pura Meduwe Karang at Kubutambahan. In Bali 1969.

Grønhaug, R. 1978. Scale as a variable in analysis: Fields of social organization in

Herat, Northwest Afghanistan. In *Scale and social organizaiton*, ed. F. Barth. Oslo: Universitetsforlaget.

Hauser-Schäublin, B., M.-L. Nabholz-Kartaschoff, and U. Ramseyer. 1991. *Textiles in Bali*. Singapore: Periplus Editions.

Hobart, Angela. 1987. *Dancing shadows of Bali: Theatre and myth*. London: Kegan Paul International.

Hobart, Mark. 1975. Orators and patrons; two types of political leader in Bali. In *Political language and oratory in traditional society*, ed. M. Bloch. London: Academic Press.

———. 1978a. Padi, puns and the attribution of responsibility. In *Natural symbols in South East Asia*, ed. G. B. Milner. London: School of Oriental and African Studies, University of London.

———. 1978b. The path of the soul: The legitimacy of nature in Balinese conceptions of space. In *Natural symbols in South East Asia*, ed. G. B. Milner. London: School of Oriental and African Studies, University of London.

———. 1979. *A Balinese village and its field of social relations*. Unpublished Ph.D. thesis, School of Oriental and African Studies, University of London.

———. 1983. Through Western eyes, or how my Balinese neighbour became a duck. *Indonesian Circle* 30:33–47.

———. 1985a. Anthropos through the looking-glass, or how to teach the Balinese to bark. In *Reason and morality*, ed. Joanna Overing. London: Tavistock.

———. 1985b. Texte est un Con. In *Context and levels: Anthropological essays on hierarchy*, ed. R. N. Barnes, D. de Coppet, and R. J. Parkin. JASO Occasional Papers no. 4. Oxford.

———. 1985c. Violence and silence: Towards a politics of action. University of London, School of Oriental and African Studies, manuscript. Paper presented to the conference, Violence as a Social Institution, at St. Andrew's, January 4–6, 1985.

———. 1986a. Introduction: Context, meaning and power. In *Context, meaning and power in Southeast Asia*, ed. M. Hobart and R. H. Taylor. Ithaca: Cornell Southeast Asia Program.

———. 1986b. Thinker, thespian, soldier, slave? Assumptions about human nature in the study of Balinese society. In *Context, meaning and power in Southeast Asia*, ed. M. Hobart and R. H. Taylor. Ithaca: Cornell Southeast Asia Program.

———. 1986c. The patience of plants: A note on agency in Bali University of London, School of Oriental and African Studies, manuscript.

———. 1986d. Summer's days and salad days: The coming of age of anthropology. University of London, School of Oriental and African Studies, manuscript.

———. 1986e. A piece in the shape of a durian, or the state of the self in Bali. Royal Institute of Linguistics and Anthropology, International Workshop on Indonesian Studies no. 1: Balinese state and society (mimeo). Leiden.

Hooykaas, C. 1964a. *Agama Tirtha: Five studies in Hindu-Balinese religion*. Amsterdam: North-Holland.

———. 1964b. Weda and sisya, rsi and bhunjangga in presentday Bali. *Bijdragen* 120 (2): 231–44.

359

———. 1966. Surva-Sevana, the way to God of a Balinese Siva priest. Verhandelingen der Koninklijke Nederlandse Akademie van Wetenschappen, Afd. Letterkunde 72 (3). Amsterdam.

———. 1973a. *Religion in Bali*. Leiden: Brill.

———. 1973b. *Kama and Kala: Materials for the study of shadow theatre in Bali*. Verhandelingen der Koninlijke Nederlands Akademie van Wetenschappen, Afd. Letterkunde, n.s. 79. Amsterdam.

———. 1974. *Cosmogony and creation in Balinese tradition*. Bibliotheca Indonesica, Koninklijk Institut voor Taal-, Land-en Volkenkunde 9. The Hague: Nijhoff.

———. 1978. *The Balinese poem Basur: An introduction to magic*. The Hague: Nijhoff.

———. 1980. *Drawings of Balinese sorcery*. Leiden: Brill.

Hooykaas-van Leeuwen Boomkamp, J. H. 1961. *Ritual purification of a Balinese temple*. Verhandelingen der Koninklijke Nederlandse Akademie van Wetenschappen, Afd. Letterkunde, n.s. 72 (4). Amsterdam.

Howe, L. E. A. 1984. Gods, people, spirits and witches: The Balinese system of person definition. *Bijdragen tot de Taal-, Land- en Volkenkunde* 140:193–222.

———. 1987. Caste in Bali and India: Levels of comparison. In *Comparative anthropology*, ed. L. Holy. London: Blackwell.

———. 1989. Peace and violence in Bali: Culture and social organization. In *Societies at peace: Anthropological perspectives*, ed. Signe Howell and Roy Willis. London: Routledge.

Jacobson, D. 1991. *Reading ethnography*. Albany: State University of New York Press.

de Josselin de Jong, P. E. 1952. *Minangkabau and Negri Sembilan: Socio-political structure in Indonesia*. The Hague: Martinus Nijhoff.

De Kat Angelino, P. 1923. *Mudras auf Bali: Handhaltungen der Priester*. Hagen i. W. and Darmstadt: Folkwang-Verlag.

Keesing, R. M. 1987a. Anthropology as interpretive quest. *Current Anthropology* 28 (2):161–69.

———. 1987b. Models "folk" and "cultural": Paradigms regained? In *Cultural models in language and thought*, ed. D. Holland and N. Quinn. Cambridge: Cambridge University Press.

———. 1988. Exotic readings of cultural texts. *Current Anthropology* 30 (4):459–69.

Koentjaraningrat. 1985. *Javanese culture*. Singapore: Oxford University Press.

Korn, V. E. 1932. *Het Adatrecht van Bali*. The Hague.

———. [1928] 1960. The consecration of a priest. In Bali 1960.

———. [1933] 1960. The village republic of Tenganan Pegeringsingan. In Bali 1960.

Kroeber, A. L. 1949. *The nature of culture*. Chicago: University of Chicago Press.

van der Kroef, J. M. 1953. The Arabs in Indonesia. *Middle East Journal* 7 (3):300–23.

Lansing, J. Stephen. 1983. *The three worlds of Bali*. New York: Praeger.

———. 1987. Balinese "water temples" and the management of irrigation. *American Anthropologist* 89 (2):326–41.

————. 1991. *Priests and programmers: Technologies of power in the engineered landscape of Bali.* Princeton: Princeton University Press.

Latour, B., and S. Woolgar. [1979] 1986. *Laboratory life: The construction of scientific facts.* Princeton: Princeton University Press.

Leach, E. R. 1961. *Pul Eliya: A study of land tenure and kinship.* Cambridge: Cambridge University Press.

Liefrinck, F. A. [1882–89] 1934. *Noord-Balische desamonographieën.* Adatrechtbundels 38, no. 58, *Bali en Lombok.* The Hague: Martinus Nijhoff.

————. [1886–87] 1969. Rice cultivation in northern Bali. In Bali 1969.

Lindenbaum, S. n.d. Understanding Siva: An anthropological analysis. (mimeo)

Lovric, B. 1987. Bali: Myth, magic, and morbidity. In *Death and disease in Southeast Asia,* ed. N. Owen. Singapore: Oxford University Press.

McCauley, Ann. 1984. Healing as a sign of power and status in Bali. *Social Science and Medicine* 18 (2):167–72.

Mannheim, K. 1954. *Ideology and Utopia: An introduction to the sociology of knowledge.* New York: Harcourt.

Marcus, G., and M. Fischer. 1986. *Anthropology as cultural critique: An experimental moment in the human sciences.* Chicago: University of Chicago Press.

Marriott, McK. 1959. Changing channels of cultural transmission in Indian civilization. In *Intermediate societies, social mobility, and communication,* ed. V. F. Ray. Seattle: American Ethnological Society.

————, ed. 1955. *Village India: Studies in the little community.* American Anthropological Association Memoir no. 83.

Martin, E. 1987. *The Woman in the Body.* Boston: Beacon.

Mershon, K. E. 1970. Five great elementals: Pancha maha buta. In *Traditional Balinese culture,* ed. Jane Belo. New York: Columbia University Press.

Muninjaya, A. A. Gede. 1982. Balinese traditional healers in a changing world. In *Indonesian medical traditions.* Melbourne: Monash University, Annual Indonesian Lecture Series.

Munn, N. n.d. An essay on the cultural construction of memory: The Kaluli gisalo. Paper presented at the Society for Cultural Anthropology meetings, Boston, May 1991.

Napier, A. David. 1986. *Masks, transformation, and paradox.* Berkeley and Los Angeles: University of California Press.

Nielsen, Aage Krarup. 1925. *Mads Lange til Bali: En dansk Ostindiefarers Liv og Eventyr.* Copenhagen: H. Aschehoug.

Noer, D. 1973. *The modernist Muslim movement in Indonesia 1900–1942.* Singapore: Oxford University Press.

Obeyesekere, G. 1981. *Medusa's hair: An essay on personal symbols and religious experience.* Chicago: University of Chicago Press.

————. 1990. *The work of culture: Symbolic transformation in psychoanalysis and anthropology.* Chicago: University of Chicago Press.

Ortner, S. B. 1984. Theory in anthropology since the sixties. *Comparative Studies in Society and History* 26 (1): 126–66.

REFERENCES

————. 1989. *High religion: A cultural and political history of Sherpa Buddhism.* Princeton: Princeton University Press.

Peacock, J. L. 1978. *Purifying the faith: The Muhammadijah movement in Indonesian Islam.* Menlo Park, Calif.: Benjamin/Cummings.

Poffenberger, M., and M. S. Zurbuchen. 1980. The economics of village Bali: Three perspectives. *Economic Development and Cultural Change* 28:91–133.

Popper, K., and J. C. Eccles. 1984. *Self and its brain.* London: Routledge & Kegan Paul.

Putnam, H. 1981. *Reason, truth, and history.* Cambridge: Cambridge University Press.

Ramseyer, Urs. 1977. *The art and culture of Bali.* Oxford: Oxford University Press.

————. 1984. *Clothing, ritual, and society in Tenganan Pegeringsingan (Bali).* Verhandlungen der Naturforschenden Gesellschaft in Basel, vol. 95.

————. 1985. Desa adat Tenganan Peringsingan: Sozio-rituelle Organizationen einer altbalinesischen Kulturgemeinschaft. In *Der grosse Archipel,* ed. M. Marschall. Etnologica Helvetica 10, 251–73. Zurich: Etnologica Helvetica.

Rappaport, R. A. 1967. *Pigs for the ancestors: Ritual in the ecology of a New Guinea people.* New Haven: Yale University Press.

Redfield, R. 1956. *Peasant society and culture: An anthropological approach to civilization.* Chicago: University of Chicago Press.

Robinson, M. S. 1969. Some observations on the Kandyan Sinhalese kinship system. *Man,* n.s. 3 (3): 402–23.

Rosaldo, Michelle Z. 1980. *Knowledge and passion: Ilongot notions of self and social life.* Cambridge: Cambridge University Press.

Rosaldo, Renato. 1989. *Culture and truth: The remaking of social analysis.* Boston: Beacon.

Roseberry, W. 1982. Balinese cockfights and the seduction of anthropology. *Social Research* 49:1013–28.

Sartono, Kartodirjo. 1973. *Protest movements in rural Java.* Oxford: Oxford University Press.

Schaareman, D. 1986. *Tatulingga: Tradition and continuity.* Basler Beiträge zur Ethnologie, vol. 24. Basel: Ethnologisches Seminar der Universität und Museum für Völkerkunde.

Schieffelin, Edward L. 1976. *The sorrow of the lonely and the burning of the dancers.* New York: St. Martin's.

Scholte, Bob. 1984. Comment on "The thick and the thin": On the interpretive theoretical program of Clifford Geertz, *Current Anthropology* 25 (4):540–42.

Schwartz, T. 1978. The size and shape of a culture. In *Scale and Social Organization,* ed. F. Barth. Oslo: Universitetsforlaget.

Schweder, Robert, and Robert A. LeVine. 1984. *Culture theory: essays on mind, self, and emotion.* Cambridge: Cambridge University Press.

Scott, J. C. 1985. *Weapons of the weak: Everyday forms of resistance.* New Haven: Yale University Press.

Shankman, Paul. 1984. The thick and the thin: On the interpretive theoretical program of Clifford Geertz. *Current Anthropology* 25 (3): 261–81.

Snouck Hurgronje, C. 1931. *Mekka in the latter part of the nineteenth century*, tr. J. H. Monahan. London: Luzac.

Strindberg, A. [1888] 1933. Introduction to "Miss Julie." In *Twelve Plays by August Strindberg*, tr. Elizabeth Sprigge. London: Constable.

Stutterheim, W. F. 1935. *Indian influences on old-Balinese art*. London: India Society.

Swellengrebel, J. L. 1960. Introduction. In Bali 1960.

Tjandrasasmita, U. 1978. The introduction of Islam and the growth of Moslem coastal cities in the Indonesian archipelago. In *Dynamics of Indonesian history*, ed. H. Soebadio and C. A. du Marchie Sarvas. Amsterdam: North-Holland.

Turner, V. 1967. *The forest of symbols: Aspects of Ndembu ritual*. Ithaca: Cornell University Press.

Valeri, V. 1989. Reciprocal centers: The Siwa-Lima system in the central Moluccas. In *The attraction of opposites: Thought and society in the dualistic mode*, ed. D. Maybury-Lewis and U. Almagor. Ann Arbor: University of Michigan Press.

Vickers, A. 1987. Hinduism and Islam in Indonesia: Bali and the Pasisir world. *Indonesia* 44:31–58.

———. 1989. *Bali: A paradise created*. Berkeley: Periplus Editions.

Weber, M. 1949. *The methodology of the social sciences*, tr. and ed. E. A. Shils and H. A. Finch. Glencoe, Ill.: Free Press.

Weck, W. [1937] 1976. *Heilkunde und Volkstum auf Bali*. Jakarta: Bap Bali and Intermasa.

Wikan, Unni. 1987. Public grace and private fears: Gaiety, offense, and sorcery in North Bali. *Ethos* 15:337–65.

———. 1989a. Illness from fright or soulloss: A North Balinese culture-bound syndrome? *Culture, Medicine, and Psychiatry* 13:25–50.

———. 1989b. Managing the heart to brighten face and soul: Emotions in Balinese morality and health care. *American Ethnologist* 17:294–310.

———. 1990. *Managing turbulent hearts: A Balinese formula for living*. Chicago: University of Chicago Press.

———. 1991. Challenges to the concept of culture: Towards an experience-near anthropology. *Cultural Anthropology* 6 (3): 285–305.

Wirz, P. 1928. *Der Totenkult auf Bali*. Stuttgart: Ferdinand Enke.

Wittfogel, K. A. 1957. *Oriental despotism*. New Haven: Yale University Press.

Wojowasito, S., and T. Wasito W. 1980. *Kamus lengkap*. Bandung: Penerbit Hasta.

Wolf, E. R. 1966. *Peasants*. Englewood Cliffs, N.J.: Prentice-Hall.

Woodward, M. R. 1989. *Islam in Java: Normative piety and mysticism in the sultanate of Yogyakarta*. Tucson: University of Arizona Press.

Worsley, P. J. 1972. *Babad Buleleng: A Balinese dynastic genealogy*. The Hague: Martinus Nijhoff.

Zurbuchen, Mary Sabina. 1987. *The language of Balinese shadow theatre*. Princeton: Princeton University Press.

———. 1989. Internal translation in Balinese poetry. In *Writing on the tongue*, ed. A. L. Becker. University of Michigan Papers on South and Southeast Asia no. 33. Ann Arbor.

Index

365